# World Economic Situation and Prospects 2008

United Nations
New York, 2008

This report is a joint product of the Department of Economic and Social Affairs (DESA), the United Nations Conference on Trade and Development (UNCTAD) and the five United Nations regional commissions (Economic Commission for Africa (ECA), Economic Commission for Europe (ECE), Economic Commission for Latin America and the Caribbean (ECLAC), Economic and Social Commission for Asia and the Pacific (ESCAP), and Economic and Social Commission for Western Asia (ESCWA)). It provides an overview of recent global economic performance and short-term prospects for the world economy and of some key global economic policy and development issues. One of its purposes is to serve as a point of reference for discussions on economic, social and related issues taking place in various United Nations entities in 2008.

**For further information, please contact:**

*In New York*

Mr. Sha Zukang
Under-Secretary-General
Department of Economic
    and Social Affairs
Room DC2-2320
United Nations, New York 10017, U.S.A.
Phone: (212) 963-5958
Fax: (212) 963-1010
E-mail: sha@un.org

*In Geneva*

Mr. Supachai Panitchpakdi
Secretary-General
United Nations Conference on
    Trade and Development
Palais des Nations, Room E-9050
1211 Geneva 10, Switzerland
Phone: (41) (22) 917-5806/5634
Fax: (41) (22) 917-0465
E-mail: sgo@unctad.org

# Executive Summary

## The global outlook

### *The world economy facing uncertain times*

After several years of robust growth, the world economy is now facing some serious challenges in sustaining its brisk pace. The end of the housing bubble in the United States of America, as well as the unfolding credit crisis, the decline of the United States dollar vis-à-vis other major currencies, the persistence of large global imbalances and high oil prices will all threaten the sustainability of global economic growth in the coming years.

### *Slower, but nonetheless robust, global economic growth in 2008*

The growth of the world economy moderated somewhat from 3.9 per cent in 2006 to a nonetheless robust 3.7 per cent during 2007. The baseline forecast of the United Nations for 2008 is for growth of the world economy to slow further to 3.4 per cent, but the darkening clouds of downside risks are looming much larger than a year ago.

### *Slower growth of the United States economy the main drag for the world economy*

The major drag on the world economy is coming from a slowdown in the United States, driven by the slump in the housing sector. The ongoing housing downturn in the United States became much more serious in the third quarter of 2007 with the sub-prime mortgage meltdown, which triggered a full-scale credit crunch that reverberated throughout the global financial system. Central banks of the major economies have adopted various measures to attenuate the financial distress, but these measures did not address the more fundamental problems rooted in the unregulated workings of the global financial system and its links with the world economy.

Significant spillover effects of the financial turmoil originating in the sub-prime mortgage markets in the United States have been found in major European economies and, to a lesser extent, in Japan and other developed countries. The growth prospects of these economies in 2008 have been downgraded also, confirming that the growth of the other major developed economies is still not strong enough to replace the United States as the main engine of global growth.

### *Continued robust growth in most developing countries*

Economic growth in developing countries remained robust at 6.9 per cent in 2007. Growth accelerated among the economies in transition to 8.0 per cent as a result of buoyant commodity prices and strong domestic demand.

Most developing countries and economies in transition have felt the effects of the global financial turmoil, mainly through increased volatility in their local equity markets and a measurable widening of the yield spreads on their external debts, but neither effect appears to have been long lasting. The relative resilience of these economies is partly due to their improved macroeconomic conditions and their large accumulation of foreign

### World economic growth expected to slow down in 2008

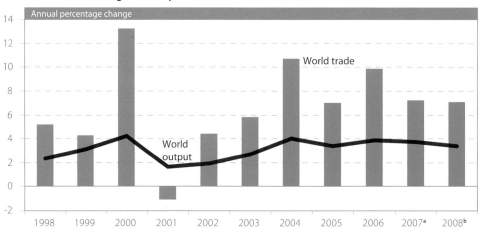

### Growth in developing countries and economies in transition weakening but still robust

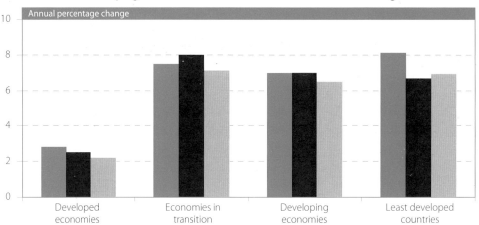

### Growth in Africa accelerating, slower growth in other developing regions

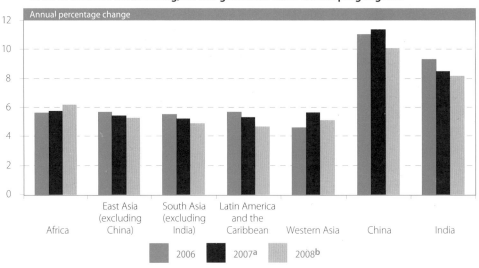

**Sources:** UN/DESA and Project LINK.

**a**   Partly estimated.

**b**   Forecast.

exchange reserves, along with vigorous growth over the past few years. Part of that strength can also be traced to their growing interdependence, driven by the sustained, rapid growth in the two most populous emerging economies, China and India. Nevertheless, the growth in most of these economies has been far from self-sustaining and remains highly dependent on the wider international economic environment, which in turn is largely determined by the economic policies and performance of the major developed countries.

Remarkably, economic growth in Africa strengthened in 2007, and that momentum is expected to be maintained in 2008 at a pace above 6 per cent. Furthermore, the performance of the least developed countries (LDCs) remained strong on average, despite slowing somewhat in 2007 compared with 2006. In 2008, the poorest countries are again expected to post an almost 7 per cent growth. This good performance of the LDCs as a group obscures important differences across countries, with several countries performing poorly as a consequence of adverse weather conditions, terms-of-trade shocks and/or continued civil strife. The countries also remain highly vulnerable to a possible downturn of the global economy.

In the outlook for 2008, economic growth in most developing countries and the economies in transition will likely moderate, albeit with considerable variance.

### *Some improvement in employment conditions, but high unemployment remaining in many developing countries*

Amidst robust economic growth, the employment situation continued to improve in 2006 and 2007 in a large number of economies. In the developed and transition economies, as well as in a number of developing countries, strong employment growth led to declining unemployment rates and has in many instances put upward pressure on wages. Many developing economies, however, witnessed only small employment gains despite robust output growth. In Africa, unemployment and underemployment rates remain especially high as labour-force increases continued to outstrip limited employment creation. In the outlook, it is expected that employment growth will retreat or remain modest in most economies in 2008 as a result of slower overall economic growth.

### *Inflation not expected to escalate*

Despite upward pressures from higher energy and food prices, worldwide inflation remains low and is expected to recede from the peak levels registered for the decade in 2006. The global trend is dominated by the deceleration of inflation in the developed countries in the second half of 2007 to an estimated 1.9 per cent for the year, with a further deceleration to 1.7 per cent expected for 2008. Inflation in the United States is expected to drop below 2 per cent in 2008 on the heels of the slowdown in the economy, and is expected to remain low in Europe, at 2 per cent. The appreciation of the European currencies is mitigating the inflationary pressures from higher world market prices for energy and food. The economies in transition are also expected to see a visible deceleration of inflation in 2008. Inflation in developing economies accelerated in 2007 to 5.6 per cent, up from 5.0 per cent in 2006. Higher energy and food prices have generally pushed the aggregate price level up, and differences in their weight in consumer baskets explain, to an important extent, the divergences in inflationary trends among developing countries. More expensive energy and food explain for a good part substantially higher inflation in the LDCs. Their impact is expected to taper off as the global economy slows and world commodity prices weaken somewhat. Consumer price inflation is expected to decelerate to 5.4 per cent on average for the developing world.

**Worldwide inflation remains low, except in the least developed countries**

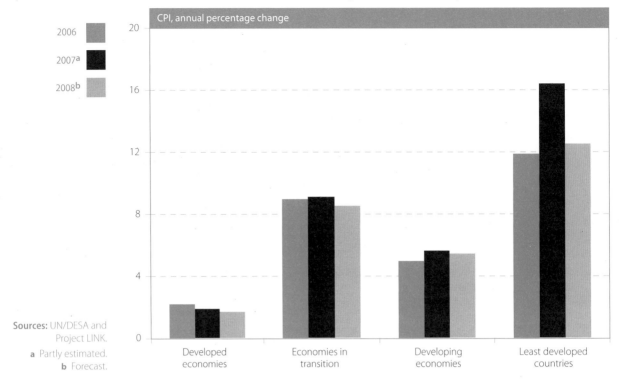

2006

2007a

2008b

**Sources:** UN/DESA and Project LINK.
**a** Partly estimated.
**b** Forecast.

CPI, annual percentage change

Developed economies | Economies in transition | Developing economies | Least developed countries

## Uncertainties and downside risks

The financial turmoil during the third quarter of 2007 has once more signalled downside risks for the global outlook. Not only did this reveal the lack of adequate supervision and regulation of domestic financial markets, it also signalled the increased threat of contagion in increasingly integrated, but also less transparent, international markets. In addition, the turmoil has again turned the spotlight on the problem of global macroeconomic imbalances. The main risks originate in the United States, where a deeper and longer slump in the housing market and a hard landing of the value of the United States dollar could trigger a worldwide recession and a disorderly adjustment of the global imbalances. These risks are not new and were anticipated in previous issues of the *World Economic Situation and Prospects*. The recent financial turmoil has heightened these risks.

### A deeper and longer housing recession in the United States

The downturn in the housing sector of the United States accelerated during the course of 2007, and the prospects for 2008 remain bleak. By the end of 2007, most housing indicators had dropped to their lowest level in a decade. In the baseline outlook, housing activity in the United States is expected to shrink further. Risks remain, however, for a much sharper correction of house prices.

The housing downturn had an impact on financial markets from mid-2007, as the debacle in the sub-prime mortgage loan sector triggered full-blown global financial turmoil. Although sub-prime mortgages are a relatively small fraction of the total mortgage market and an even smaller fraction of the total credit market, a complex financial system—with overstretched leverage, lack of transparency and inadequate regulation—served to spread and multiply the risk beyond the sub-prime market. The tightening of terms and standards in the mortgage markets, especially in the non-prime markets, is therefore likely to intensify the housing downturn in 2008. Delinquencies on these mortgages are expected to increase further, implying more stress in financial markets at large. Continued credit tightening and a sharper fall of house prices will depress consumer demand, possibly triggering a full-blown recession in the United States with worldwide repercussions.

### *Risk of a hard landing of the dollar*

In light of recent trends, the risk of a disorderly unwinding of the global imbalances has increased. Current-account imbalances across countries narrowed somewhat in 2007 and are expected to narrow further in 2008. Despite this projected narrowing of the deficit of the United States, however, the risk of a disorderly adjustment remains as the indebtedness of the United States continues to deepen. As a result of the chronic current-account deficits over the past decade, the net external liability position of the United States is estimated to be near $3 trillion in 2007, about 25 per cent of GDP.

The large current-account deficit and perceptions that the United States debt position is approaching unsustainable levels have been among the major factors underlying the depreciation of the United States dollar by about 35 per cent against other major currencies since 2002. About one quarter of this depreciation occurred between January and November 2007. This suggests that the risk of a hard landing of the dollar has heightened. Should this occur, there will likely be a disorderly unwinding of the global imbalances and much greater instability in the global financial system. This would have strong adverse effects on global economic growth. A steep fall of the dollar would immediately depress United States demand for goods from the rest of the world. In addition, since many developing countries are holding a large amount of foreign reserves in dollar-denominated assets, a sharp depreciation of the dollar would entail substantial financial losses for these countries.

**A hard landing of the dollar?**

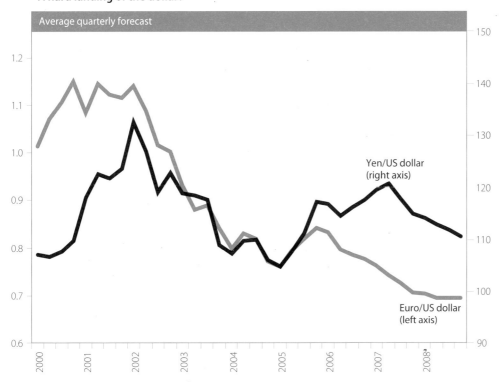

a   Forecast.

*In the pessimistic scenario, slowdown of
world economic growth to 1.6 per cent*

World economic growth would slow significantly should these risks indeed play out, and there would be a much more protracted crisis in the United States housing and mortgage markets along with a steep and accelerated fall of the dollar. A more pessimistic scenario, triggered by such a crisis, would project an outright recession in the United States and a deceleration of world economic growth to 1.6 per cent in 2008.

**Deeper housing market crisis and hard landing
of the dollar could bring the world economy down**

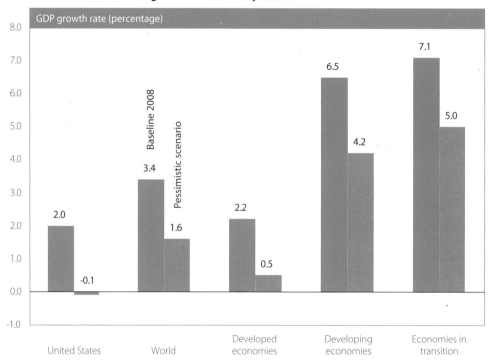

## Policy challenges

Policymakers in developed and developing countries are faced with the challenge of how to avoid a global recession and safeguard robust economic development amidst risks of continued financial turmoil and a weakening dollar. The stakes are high. For developing countries, maintaining strong economic growth, while not the only condition, is essential to supporting their endeavours and generating the necessary resources to achieve the Millennium Development Goals. For the advanced countries, too, continued expansion of economic activity is essential for tackling long-term challenges such as those posed by population ageing, and new investments are needed to address the challenge of climate change.

*Coordinated policy action to redress the global imbalances*

A global demand stimulus will be needed if the slowdown in the United States economy is not to slip into a recession and spill over to the rest of the world. The below-trend growth in the United States would justify further interest rate cuts to stimulate the economy, but this may not be sufficient in the current context if consumer and business confidence weakens sharply, and could in any event precipitate a further depreciation of the dollar. Global rebalancing would thus require stimuli from other parts of the world. In China, the appreciation of the renminbi has not prevented the growth of the external surplus. A more structural rebalancing of aggregate demand would be needed to reduce the economy's surplus, by means of stepping up public spending on social security, health and education services, especially those geared towards the rural population. In the major oil-exporting countries, there is ample room for undertaking much-needed domestic investment plans. In Europe and Japan, continued low inflationary pressures would justify putting an end to monetary tightening and preserve at least a neutral to moderately stimulatory stance.

The International Monetary Fund (IMF) has initiated multilateral consultations to deal with the global imbalances through concerted policy actions. The participants in this dialogue, which include the United States, Japan, the euro area, China and Saudi Arabia, seem to agree on the desirability of correcting the global imbalances without jeopardizing sustained growth and on the need for concerted action. They have not yet followed through with any concrete policy actions, however. It is important that the discussions be broadened to involve more parties, developing countries in particular, and that agreement be reached on multi-year policy adjustment schedules that can be monitored in order to make participants accountable and enhance the likelihood of compliance with agreed concerted action.

Parties, cognizant of the recent financial turmoil should see the urgency of addressing the problem of the global imbalances and initiate actions before the world economy moves into a recession and the dollar is forced into accelerated decline.

## Realignment of exchange rates and reform of the reserve system

A multilateral agreement to reduce global imbalances should also include a realignment of exchange rates and ensure that such realignment takes place in an orderly fashion. Thus far, the process of dollar depreciation has been orderly. Dollar depreciation by itself, however, will not resolve the global imbalances. Along with the stimulatory measures in the surplus countries, proposed above, Governments should take joint action to avoid a possible steep and abrupt decline of the dollar. The risk of a hard landing is heightened by the very nature of the global reserve system, which uses the national currency of the United States as the main reserve currency and instrument for international payments. Under this system, the only way for the rest of the world to accumulate dollar assets and reserves is for the United States to run an external deficit. However, as the net liability position of the United States continues to increase, investors will start anticipating a readjustment, and confidence in the dollar will erode.

Over time, more fundamental reforms of the current international reserve system will be needed to prevent the current constellation of imbalances from re-emerging. A more immediate reform would be to promote an officially backed multi-currency reserve system. A well-designed multilateral financial system should create equal conditions for all parties and avoid unfair competition as well as an asymmetric burden-sharing of exchange-rate adjustments. It should also help to increase stability in the international financial system by reducing the likelihood of a crisis scenario where capital flight out of the major single reserve currency causes potentially far-reaching repercussions throughout the global economy.

*Strengthening financial regulation and financial safety nets*

Some hard lessons need to be learned from the recent financial turmoil. The problems in mortgage markets have highlighted the need for greater transparency over risks in the financial sector, including off-balance-sheet exposures and risks in derivatives markets. Credit-rating mechanisms need to be closely scrutinized and stronger rulings may be required to ensure that loan originators have the right incentives to carefully assess the solvency of debtors.

Multilateral arrangements for adequate liquidity provisioning for developing countries need to be completed. While the strong build-up of reserves provides countries with a substantial degree of "self insurance" against external shocks, in the event of a hard landing of the dollar, this self insurance could quickly evaporate. The design of a new precautionary financial arrangement is under discussion at the IMF but is far from completed. If such a mechanism could emulate the lender-of-last-resort functions of central banks, it could reduce the demand for high reserve build-ups in developing countries. This would not only assist a more orderly unwinding of the global imbalances, but would also create more policy space in developing countries by easing mounting pressures towards exchange-rate appreciation.

## International trade

*Merchandise trade growing twice as fast as output*

Merchandise trade continues to be a driving force of the world economy. Both in volume and in dollar value terms, world merchandise trade has grown twice as fast as world output over the past four years. During 2007, however, world trade growth seems to have lost some of its strength, particularly for developed economies. During the upward cycle that started in 2001, merchandise trade growth has been driven by the developed countries and East Asia, led by China. The estimates and forecasts for 2007 and 2008 are below recent trend levels for both developed country and East Asian export and import growth.

Recent trends in merchandise trade growth have contributed to a slight correction of global imbalances. Strong export growth in the United States, stimulated in part by the significant depreciation of the dollar, has surpassed import demand growth, leading to a reduction in the economy's trade deficit. This is reflected in smaller surpluses elsewhere, especially in Europe, Japan and some developing country regions. The adjustments are small and are not yet contributing in any major way to the required global macroeconomic rebalancing.

*Commodity prices rising further, but a correction imminent*

Non-oil commodity prices have continued increasing on the heels of robust global demand, but they have also become more volatile. Metal prices will likely remain high in the outlook, but will be much less bullish than during 2006 and 2007. World market prices for many food crops have risen significantly during 2007. This has been the case for wheat and maize in particular, driven in part by increased biofuel demand.

Oil prices surged to nearly $100 per barrel in 2007, as strong demand, especially from developing countries, eliminated much of the slack capacity in the oil market. This, together with the weakening United States dollar, could drive further increases in oil prices. Oil prices are expected to stay high in the baseline outlook for 2008, but oil market conditions remain highly uncertain.

### *Continuing impasse in the Doha Round negotiations*

The off-again, on-again multilateral trade negotiations in the Doha Round picked up towards the end of 2007, but with less attention to the development dimension. The positions of the major negotiating parties have remained largely unchanged so far, despite intense diplomatic activities since the formal resumption of negotiations in February 2007. Discussions continue to be focused on agriculture and non-agricultural market access. The prospects for rapid conclusion of the Doha Trade Round are gloomy.

## International finance

### *Continued net financial transfers from developing to developed countries*

Developing countries continued to make significant outward transfers of financial resources to developed economies, albeit at a slower pace than in previous years. Total net financial transfers from developing countries, that is to say, net capital flows less net interest and other investment income payments, increased from $728 billion in 2006 to $760 billion in 2007. The increase in net transfers comes almost exclusively from East and South Asia, while other developing country sub-groups registered some decline in net resource outflows.

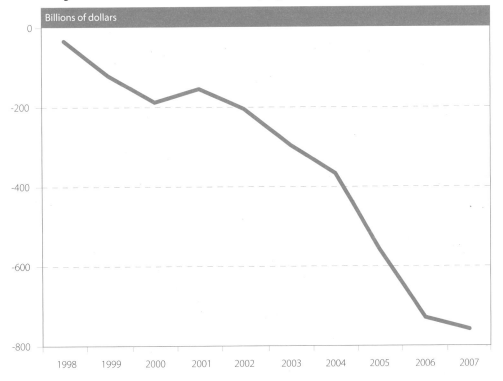

**Negative net financial transfers to developing countries continue to increase**

**Sources:** UN/DESA, based on IMF World Economic Outlook database, October 2007, and IMF Balance of Payments Statistcs.

**Note**: Net financial transfers are defined as net capital inflows less net interest and other investment income payments abroad.

## Outward net transfers taking place in a context of robust private capital flows to developing countries

These net outward transfers take place in the context of continued substantial net private capital inflows to developing and transition economies. This trend of robust private capital flows to these economies has helped to sustain growth in emerging markets and has thus far helped insulate them from the turmoil emanating from developed country financial markets. The risk of this increased exposure lies in the possibility that this form of financing could suddenly dry up if the housing-sector collapse spreads to the whole financial system, inducing a severe economic slowdown in advanced countries.

The combination of current-account surpluses and strong private capital inflows has led to an unprecedented build-up of international official reserves, part of the pattern of net outward transfers from developing countries. Most reserves are held in dollar-denominated assets. The recent sharp decline in the value of the dollar, likely to continue with the unwinding of global imbalances, adds to the pace of rebalancing, since both private and public investors must now consider further losses on their dollar investments.

## ODA below the target formulated in the Monterrey Consensus

Net real official development assistance (ODA) disbursements by Development Assistance Committee (DAC) member countries fell in 2006 for the first time since 1997 and are expected to be even lower in 2007. Moreover, ODA flows included substantial net debt-relief grants, contradictory to the commitments made by donor countries as part of the Monterrey Consensus, which provided that debt relief would be additional to conventional forms of ODA. ODA, net of debt relief, declined in 2006 to 0.25 per cent of the gross national income (GNI) of DAC members, down from 0.26 per cent in the previous year. This was well below the 0.33 per cent level that was reached in the early 1990s and the 0.7 per cent target reaffirmed at the 2002 International Conference on Financing for Development.

Since aid flows tend to be pro-cyclical, a global slowdown would have a negative impact on aid-dependent economies, as it would be accompanied by sudden changes in the size of resource commitments. When aid falls, it often leads to fiscal adjustments in the form of increased taxation and spending cuts that reinforce the cyclical impact of declining aid flows. Moreover, aid flows continue to be volatile, and such volatility is often exacerbated by the gap between commitments and disbursements. Multi-year agreements with donors on support to the medium-term expenditure frameworks of recipient countries could help mitigate the problems in aid delivery.

## Progress in providing debt relief

As part of the Heavily Indebted Poor Countries (HIPC) Initiative, debt reduction packages have so far been approved for 32 out of 41 eligible countries. The debt service paid by the beneficiary countries has declined on average by almost 2 per cent of their GDP between 1999 and 2006. In parallel with this, government expenditures on health, education and other services in the beneficiary countries increased to a level equal to about five times the amount of debt-service payments. Before the HIPC Initiative, debt servicing exceeded such social spending by eligible countries. Despite this progress, the aim of the Initiative, to bring external debt of poor countries to sustainable levels, has not yet been realized in most beneficiary countries, and a significant number of these countries continue to face moderate-to-high risk of severe debt distress.

*Insufficient progress towards governance
reform of international financial institutions*

The reform of governance at the Bretton Woods institutions continues to be high on the agenda, not least because of the recognition of the fundamental changes that have occurred in the structure of the global economy. Furthermore, for the multilateral consultations on policy coordination to work, the legitimacy of the mediator (that is to say, the IMF) needs to be enhanced. This requires a reform of the voting power and governance structure of the IMF to ensure a better representation of developing countries. Given the imminent risks of a disorderly adjustment of the global imbalances and of a hard landing of the dollar, governance reform is urgently needed. At the 2006 Annual Meetings in Singapore, the IMF Board of Governors approved an agenda and time frame for quota and voice reform to bolster the legitimacy and relevance of the institution. Yet, these reform proposals are still under discussion among member States, and reaching agreement has, thus far, proven to be challenging. Without the reform, concerted action to address the problem of the imbalances in the world will likely remain far removed from what is needed and enhance the risk of a much deeper slowdown in world economic growth.

# Contents

## Statistical annex

## Boxes

# Figures

## Tables

# Explanatory Notes

**The following symbols have been used in the tables throughout the report:**

| | |
|---|---|
| .. | **Two dots** indicate that data are not available or are not separately reported. |
| – | **A dash** indicates that the amount is nil or negligible. |
| - | **A hyphen (-)** indicates that the item is not applicable. |
| - | **A minus sign (-)** indicates deficit or decrease, except as indicated. |
| . | **A full stop (.)** is used to indicate decimals. |
| / | **A slash (/)** between years indicates a crop year or financial year, for example, 2007/08. |
| - | **Use of a hyphen (-)** between years, for example, 2007-2008, signifies the full period involved, including the beginning and end years. |

**Reference to "dollars" ($)** indicates United States dollars, unless otherwise stated.

**Reference to "billions"** indicates one thousand million.

**Reference to "tons"** indicates metric tons, unless otherwise stated.

**Annual rates** of growth or change, unless otherwise stated, refer to annual compound rates.

Details and percentages in tables do not necessarily add to totals, because of rounding.

**Project LINK** is an international collaborative research group for econometric modelling, coordinated jointly by the Development Policy and Analysis Division of the United Nations Secretariat and the University of Toronto.

**The following abbreviations have been used:**

| | |
|---|---|
| **ABCPs** | asset-backed commercial papers |
| **ACP** | African, Caribbean and Pacific partnership agreement |
| **AGOA** | African Growth Opportunity Act |
| **AMC** | Advanced Market Commitment |
| **ARMs** | adjustable-rate mortgages |
| **ASEAN** | Association of Southeast Asian Nations |
| **BIS** | Bank for International Settlements |
| **bps** | basis points |
| **CDOs** | collateralized debt obligations |
| **CEFTA** | Central European Free Trade Agreement |
| **CIS** | Commonwealth of Independent States |
| **CLOs** | collateralized loan obligations |
| **CPI** | consumer price index |
| **DAC** | Development Assistance Committee (of OECD) |
| **EBRD** | European Bank for Reconstruction and Development |
| **ECA** | Economic Commission for Africa |
| **ECB** | European Central Bank |
| **ECE** | Economic Commission for Europe |
| **ECLAC** | Economic Commission for Latin America and the Caribbean |
| **EMBI** | Emerging Markets Bond Index |
| **EMBIG** | Emerging Markets Bond Index Global |
| **EMU** | Economic and Monetary Union (of the European Union) |
| **ESCAP** | Economic and Social Commission for Asia and the Pacific |
| **ESCWA** | Economic and Social Commission for Western Asia |
| **EU** | European Union |
| **FDI** | foreign direct investment |

| | |
|---|---|
| **Fed** | United States Federal Reserve Bank |
| **FSF** | Financial Stability Forum |
| **GATS** | General Agreement on Trade in Services |
| **GCC** | Gulf Cooperation Council |
| **GDP** | gross domestic product |
| **GNI** | gross national income |
| **GNP** | gross national product |
| **HIPC** | heavily indebted poor countries |
| **ICT** | information and communication technologies |
| **IDA** | International Development Association (of the World Bank) |
| **IFIs** | international financial institutions |
| **IFS** | International Financial Statistics |
| **IGC** | International Grains Council |
| **IIF** | Institute of International Finance |
| **IMF** | International Monetary Fund |
| **IMFC** | International Monetary and Financial Committee (of the IMF) |
| **LDCs** | least developed countries |
| **LME** | London Metal Exchange |
| **M&As** | mergers and acquisitions |
| **mbd** | million barrels per day |
| **MDRI** | Multilateral Debt Relief Initiative |
| **MERCOSUR** | Mercado Común del Sur (Southern Common Market) |
| **Mtoe** | million tons of oil equivalent |
| **NAMA** | non-agriculture market access |
| **NBER** | National Bureau of Economic Research |
| **NGLs** | natural gas liquids |
| **NPV** | net present value |
| **ODA** | official development assistance |
| **OECD** | Organization for Economic Cooperation and Development |
| **OPEC** | Organization of Petroleum Exporting Countries |
| **pb** | per barrel |
| **PCE** | personal consumption expenditure |
| **PPP** | purchasing power parity |
| **PRGF** | Poverty Reduction and Growth Facility |
| **PSAs** | production-sharing agreements |
| **R&D** | research and development |
| **RTAs** | regional trade agreements |
| **SACU** | Southern African Customs Union |
| **SDR** | Special Drawing Rights |
| **SGP** | Stability and Growth Pact |
| **SIV** | special investment vehicle |
| **SWFs** | sovereign wealth funds |
| **TNCs** | transnational corporations |
| **UNCTAD** | United Nations Conference on Trade and Development |
| **UN/DESA** | United Nations Department of Economic and Social Affairs |
| **UNDP** | United Nations Development Programme |
| **UNFCCC** | United Nations Framework Convention on Climate Change |
| **VAT** | value-added tax |
| **WTO** | World Trade Organization |

The designations employed and the presentation of the material in this publication do not imply the expression of any opinion whatsoever on the part of the United Nations Secretariat concerning the legal status of any country, territory, city or area or of its authorities, or concerning the delimitation of its frontiers or boundaries.

The term "country" as used in the text of this report also refers, as appropriate, to territories or areas.

**Data presented in this publication incorporate information available as of 30 November 2007.**

**For analytical purposes, the following country groupings and subgroupings have been used:**[a]

*Developed economies (developed market economies):*
Australia, Canada, European Union, Iceland, Japan, New Zealand, Norway, Switzerland, United States of America.

*Major developed economies (the Group of Seven):*
Canada, France, Germany, Italy, Japan, United Kingdom of Great Britain and Northern Ireland, United States of America.

*European Union:*
Austria, Belgium, Bulgaria, Cyprus, Czech Republic, Denmark, Estonia, Finland, France, Germany, Greece, Hungary, Ireland, Italy, Latvia, Lithuania, Luxembourg, Malta, Netherlands, Poland, Portugal, Romania, Slovakia, Slovenia, Spain, Sweden, United Kingdom of Great Britain and Northern Ireland.

**EU-15:**
Austria, Belgium, Denmark, Finland, France, Greece, Germany, Ireland, Italy, Luxembourg, Netherlands, Portugal, Spain, Sweden, United Kingdom of Great Britain and Northern Ireland.

**New EU member States:**
Bulgaria, Cyprus, Czech Republic, Estonia, Hungary, Latvia, Lithuania, Malta, Poland, Romania, Slovakia, Slovenia.

*Economies in transition:*

**South-eastern Europe:**
Albania, Bosnia and Herzegovina, Croatia, Montenegro, Serbia, the former Yugoslav Republic of Macedonia.

**Commonwealth of Independent States (CIS):**
Armenia, Azerbaijan, Belarus, Georgia, Kazakhstan, Kyrgyzstan, Moldova, Russian Federation, Tajikistan, Turkmenistan, Ukraine, Uzbekistan.

*Net fuel exporters:*
Azerbaijan, Kazakhstan, Russian Federation, Turkmenistan, Uzbekistan.

*Net fuel importers:*
All other CIS countries.

*Developing economies:*
Africa, Asia and the Pacific (excluding Australia, Japan, New Zealand and the member States of CIS in Asia), Latin America and the Caribbean.

**Subgroupings of Africa:**

*North Africa:*
Algeria, Egypt, Libyan Arab Jamahiriya, Morocco, Tunisia.

*Sub-Saharan Africa, excluding Nigeria and South Africa (commonly contracted to "sub-Saharan Africa"):*
All other African countries except Nigeria and South Africa.

**Subgroupings of Asia and the Pacific:**

*Western Asia:*
Bahrain, Iraq, Israel, Jordan, Kuwait, Lebanon, Occupied Palestinian Territory, Oman, Qatar, Saudi Arabia, Syrian Arab Republic, Turkey, United Arab Emirates, Yemen.

*East and South Asia:*
All other developing economies in Asia and the Pacific (including China, unless stated otherwise). This group is further subdivided into:

*South Asia:*
Bangladesh, Bhutan, India, Iran (Islamic Republic of), Maldives, Nepal, Pakistan, Sri Lanka.

*East Asia:*
All other developing economies in Asia and the Pacific.

**Subgroupings of Latin America and the Caribbean:**

*South America:*
Argentina, Brazil, Chile, Colombia, Ecuador, Paraguay, Peru, Uruguay, Venezuela (Bolivarian Republic of).

*Mexico and Central America:*
Costa Rica, El Salvador, Guatemala, Honduras, Nicaragua, Panama, Mexico.

*Caribbean:*
Barbados, Cuba, Dominican Republic, Guyana, Haiti, Jamaica, Trinidad and Tobago.

**For particular analyses, developing countries have been subdivided into the following groups:**

*Oil-exporting countries:*
Algeria, Angola, Bahrain, Bolivia, Brunei Darussalam, Cameroon, Colombia, Congo, Ecuador, Egypt, Gabon, Iran (Islamic Republic of), Iraq, Kuwait, Libyan Arab Jamahiriya, Mexico, Nigeria, Oman, Qatar, Saudi Arabia, Syrian Arab Republic, Trinidad and Tobago, United Arab Emirates, Venezuela (Bolivarian Republic of), Viet Nam.

*Oil-importing countries:*
All other developing countries.

*Least developed countries:*
Afghanistan, Angola, Bangladesh, Benin, Bhutan, Burkina Faso, Burundi, Cambodia, Cape Verde, Central African Republic, Chad, Comoros, Democratic Republic of the Congo, Djibouti, Equatorial Guinea, Eritrea, Ethiopia, Gambia, Guinea, Guinea-Bissau, Haiti, Kiribati, Lao People's Democratic Republic, Lesotho, Liberia, Madagascar, Malawi, Maldives, Mali, Mauritania, Mozambique, Myanmar, Nepal, Niger, Rwanda, Samoa, Sao Tome and Principe, Senegal, Sierra Leone, Solomon Islands, Somalia, Sudan, Timor-Leste, Togo, Tuvalu, Uganda, United Republic of Tanzania, Vanuatu, Yemen, Zambia.

*Landlocked developing countries:*
Afghanistan, Armenia, Azerbaijan, Bhutan, Bolivia, Botswana, Burkina Faso, Burundi, Central African Republic, Chad, Ethiopia, Kazakhstan, Kyrgyzstan, Lao's People's Democratic Republic, Lesotho, Malawi, Mali, Moldova, Mongolia, Nepal, Niger, Paraguay, Rwanda, Swaziland, Tajikistan, the former Yugoslav Republic of Macedonia, Turkmenistan, Uganda, Uzbekistan, Zambia, Zimbabwe.

*Small island developing States:*
American Samoa, Anguilla, Antigua and Barbuda, Aruba, Bahamas, Barbados, Belize, British Virgin Islands, Cape Verde, Commonwealth of Northern Marianas, Comoros, Cook Islands, Cuba, Dominica, Dominican Republic, Fiji, French Polynesia, Grenada, Guam, Guinea-Bissau, Guyana, Haiti, Jamaica, Kiribati, Maldives, Marshall Islands, Mauritius, Micronesia (Federated States of), Montserrat, Nauru, Netherlands Antilles, New Caledonia, Niue, Palau, Papua New Guinea, Puerto Rico, Samoa, Sao Tome and Principe, Seychelles, Singapore, Solomon Islands, St. Kitts and Nevis, St. Lucia, St. Vincent and the Grenadines, Suriname, Timor-Leste, Tonga, Trinidad and Tobago, Tuvalu, U.S. Virgin Islands, Vanuatu.

*Heavily Indebted Poor Countries (countries that have reached their Completion Points or Decision Points):*
Benin, Bolivia, Burkina Faso, Burundi, Cameroon, Chad, Democratic Republic of the Congo, Ethiopia, Gambia, Ghana, Guinea, Guinea-Bissau, Guyana, Honduras, Madagascar, Malawi, Mali, Mauritania, Mozambique, Nicaragua, Niger, Rwanda, Sao Tome and Principe, Senegal, Sierra Leone, Uganda, United Republic of Tanzania, Zambia.

The designation of country groups in the text and the tables is intended solely for statistical or analytical convenience and does not necessarily express a judgement about the stage reached by a particular country or area in the development process.

---

a   For definitions of country groupings and methodology, see *World Economic and Social Survey, 2004* (United Nations publication, Sales No. E.04.II.C.1, annex, introductory text).

# Chapter I
# Global outlook

## Macroeconomic prospects for the world economy

After several years of robust growth, the world economy is now facing greater challenges in sustaining its brisk pace. The end of the housing bubble in the United States of America, as well as the unfolding credit crisis, the decline of the United States dollar vis-à-vis other major currencies, the persistence of the large global imbalances and the surging oil prices will all threaten the sustainability of global economic growth in the coming years.

The world economy is facing greater challenges

The growth of the world economy moderated somewhat from 3.9 per cent in 2006 to 3.7 per cent during 2007 (see table I.1). The baseline forecast of the United Nations for 2008 is for the growth of the world economy to slow to a pace of 3.4 per cent, but the risks are slanted towards the downside, as world economic conditions are surrounded by clouds of uncertainty. The key assumptions for the baseline scenario are explained in box I.1. Figure I.1 indicates the confidence interval for the United Nations forecast for 2008 based on past forecasting errors (see appendix I) and expresses this uncertainty, showing that world economic growth could range from 2.7 to 4.1 per cent in 2008. While the baseline projection is expected to be the more likely outcome based on current information, the factors referred to above could well imply a much slower pace of growth in 2008 and beyond, and possibly even below the lower bound of the confidence interval. A more pessimistic scenario triggered by a much deeper crisis in the United States housing and mortgage markets and a hard landing of the United States dollar would project an outright recession in the United States and a deceleration of world economic growth to 1.6 per cent in 2008. See box I.2 for a description of this pessimistic scenario.

Table I.1
**Growth of world output, 2002-2008**

| Annual percentage change | | | | | | | |
|---|---|---|---|---|---|---|---|
| | 2002 | 2003 | 2004 | 2005 | 2006 | 2007a | 2008b |
| **World output**c | 1.9 | 2.7 | 4.0 | 3.4 | 3.9 | 3.7 | 3.4 |
| *of which:* | | | | | | | |
| Developed economies | 1.3 | 1.9 | 3.0 | 2.4 | 2.8 | 2.5 | 2.2 |
| Economies in transition | 5.0 | 7.2 | 7.6 | 6.6 | 7.5 | 8.0 | 7.1 |
| Developing economies | 3.9 | 5.2 | 7.0 | 6.5 | 7.0 | 6.9 | 6.5 |
| *of which:* | | | | | | | |
| Least developed countries | 6.3 | 6.6 | 7.9 | 8.4 | 8.1 | 6.7 | 6.9 |
| *Memorandum items:* | | | | | | | |
| World trade | 4.4 | 5.8 | 10.7 | 7.0 | 9.9 | 7.2 | 7.1 |
| World output growth with PPP-based weights | 3.0 | 4.0 | 5.2 | 4.8 | 5.4 | 5.3 | 4.9 |

**Source:** UN/DESA.

a   Partly estimated.
b   Forecasts, based in part on Project LINK.
c   Calculated as a weighted average of individual country growth rates of gross domestic product (GDP), where weights are based on GDP in 2000 prices and exchange rates.

Box I.1

## Major assumptions for the baseline global economic forecast for 2008

The United Nations global economic forecast is prepared with the help of the global modelling framework of Project LINK. For an evaluation of the forecasting performance since the 1970s, see appendix 1 to this chapter.

In preparing the baseline for the global outlook, a number of assumptions are made regarding the policy stance in the major economies and key international prices. The assumptions are summarized below and justified in the text.

The United States Federal Reserve is expected to maintain the federal funds rate at the level of 4.0 per cent throughout 2008; the European Central Bank is expected to maintain its current policy stance, with the minimum bid rate on refinancing operations at 4.0 per cent through 2008; and the Bank of Japan is expected to raise its main policy interest rate, the target Uncollateralized Overnight Call Rate, by 50 basis points during 2008, bringing it to a level of 1 per cent.

The assumptions regarding fiscal policy in individual countries are based mainly on official budget plans or policy statements.

The price of Brent crude oil is estimated to average $73.50 per barrel in 2007, up from $65.14 per barrel in 2006, and is expected to rise to $76.00 in 2008.

Prices of most agricultural commodities are expected to reach a plateau in 2008, while prices of metals and minerals are expected to retreat moderately after a substantial increase over the past few years.

The United States dollar is expected to depreciate against most other major currencies in 2008. The dollar/euro exchange rate is expected to average 1.44 for 2008 and the yen/dollar exchange rate is expected to average 112 for 2008, implying a yen/euro exchange rate of 161.

Figure I.1:
**World economic growth, baseline and pessimistic scenarios, 2001-2008**

Indicates confidence interval at one standard deviation of historical forecast errors.

**Source:** UN/DESA.

**Note:** See appendix 1 to the present chapter for the estimation of forecasting errors.

**a** Partly estimated.
**b** Projections, based on Project LINK.

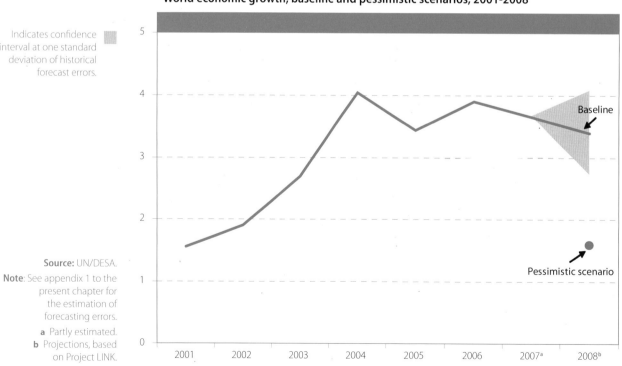

Box I.2

# The pessimistic scenario: a hard landing of the dollar

The combination of a deep housing slump in the United States and a precipitous devaluation of the United States dollar could trigger an abrupt adjustment of the global imbalances, which would not only send the economy of the United States into a recession but would also lead to a hard landing for the global economy as a whole. This box considers such a pessimistic scenario for the prospects of the world economy as an alternative to the baseline outlook discussed in the main text.

The main assumptions for this scenario include a steeper decline of the housing market prices in the United States and a much larger depreciation of the dollar than those incorporated in the baseline. Specifically, it is assumed that housing activity, as reflected in residential investment, would drop by 30 per cent in 2008, compared with a decline of about 16 per cent in the baseline, and the median prices of existing homes would fall by more than 10 per cent from baseline levels.[a] It is also assumed that the dollar would depreciate by another 20 per cent vis-à-vis a basket of other currencies, in comparison with the 5 per cent depreciation in the baseline. These assumptions, although significantly deviating from the baseline, are certainly still within the range of probability based on historical trends. It is also assumed that there is neither policy stimulus beyond what is implied in the existing policy rules in major developed economies nor extra policy stimuli in the rest of the world to counter the weaker demand in the United States.

A sharper reversal in the housing boom would significantly depress household spending in the United States through various channels: income, wealth, balance-sheets and consumer confidence. Housing and related sectors accounted for a large proportion of employment growth in the economy during the period of the housing boom. A deep housing contraction would directly reduce employment as well as income for many households. Meanwhile, given the initial conditions—a household savings rate of almost zero and the tightening terms for mortgage lending in the face of the meltdown in the sub-prime mortgages—the indirect effects of falling house prices on consumer spending via households' wealth and the balance sheet would be larger than the historical average. For example, the substantial amount of mortgage equity withdrawal registered during the housing upturn would definitely wilt amidst falling house prices and tightening scrutiny of mortgage loans. In addition, combined with a plunge in consumer confidence and the adverse income effects from the dollar devaluation, household consumption would come to a virtual standstill in this scenario, compared with a growth of 2.3 per cent in the baseline and 3 per cent on average for the past few years. Business capital spending would also be weaker. Despite most United States companies being in good financial condition owing to high profit margins over the past few years, firms would reduce capital spending in response to a pessimistic outlook. Business investment would decline in this scenario compared with a modest growth in the baseline.

As shown in the table, GDP growth in the United States would drop below zero in this scenario into an outright recession, substantially below the growth of 2 per cent in the baseline. The housing-led recession in the United States would significantly erode international confidence in the dollar, causing a recoiling of willingness in the rest of the world to hold United States financial assets. As a result, the dollar would plummet, as assumed above, and interest rates on dollar-denominated assets would be pushed up.

The weakening of household consumption and business investment would translate directly into a curtailment of import demand in the United States for foreign goods and services, and that import demand would be further aggravated by the dollar depreciation, which would switch expenditure away from foreign goods. In this scenario, real imports of the United States would decline by 7 per cent, in comparison with growth of about 3 per cent in the baseline.

The recession in the United States would be transmitted through trade linkages and other channels to the rest of the world. Imports of the United States account for about 15 per cent of total world trade, with some 44 per cent of its imports coming from other developed economies and more than 50 per cent from developing countries. The direct impact would be felt most strongly by those countries that have a large share of their exports in the United States market, for instance, Canada (82 per cent of whose exports are destined for the United States), Latin America and the Caribbean (48 per cent) and Asia (17 per cent).

a   See Global Insight, *U.S. Executive Summary*, September 2007, for more details; however, the assumptions regarding the housing slump and the dollar depreciation are more severe in this scenario than in Global Insight.

**Box I.2 (cont'd)**

In addition, other adverse impacts on the economies of the rest of the world would involve a destabilization of the financial markets in many countries due to the sharp depreciation of the dollar. Countries with a large amount of dollar-denominated foreign reserve assets would incur substantial financial losses. The prices of many commodities would fall because of a weaker global aggregate demand, particularly in real purchasing terms—though less significant in nominal dollar terms—causing income losses for many commodity-exporting countries. In an increasingly integrated global economy, the initial weakness in the United States would spread and multiply throughout the global economy via various international linkages.

As shown in the table, world economic growth would drop to about 1.6 per cent, and the growth of world trade would be lowered by nearly 4 percentage points. Across regions, the impact on Europe and Japan would range from seven to nine tenths of a percentage point, implying that no other major developed economy would replace the United States as an alternative engine of global growth. While the growth for developing countries as a whole would be lowered by more than 2.3 percentage points, the adverse effects would vary among different subregions and countries. The direct trade and financial effects of the recession in the United States would be felt predominantly in many Asian economies and in some Latin American economies—such as Mexico and Central America—while economies in Africa and Western Asia and some South American countries would suffer mostly from weaker commodity prices and lower indirect trade flows. In general, despite an increasingly robust growth over the past few years for many developing countries, developing countries as a group remain vulnerable to large adverse demand contraction and financial shocks originating from major developed countries. This also holds to a large extent for the larger fast-growing economies, such as China and India, which would also see significant dents in their growth rates.

In this scenario, the global imbalances in the current accounts across countries would visibly narrow. The current-account deficit of the United States would be reduced by $200 billion, as the recession would slow domestic and import demand and the dollar depreciation would push up exports. In this context, this scenario also highlights the possible implications of a rebalancing of the global economy at the cost of a considerable slowdown of economic activity. It strengthens the case for internationally coordinated macroeconomic policies to avert such risks.

### The pessimistic scenario

| Percentage annual growth rate | | |
|---|---|---|
| Selected indicators | Baseline | Pessimistic scenario |
| **World output growth** | 3.4 | 1.6 |
| **Developed economies** | 2.2 | 0.5 |
| United States | 2.0 | -0.1 |
| Euro area | 2.5 | 1.0 |
| Japan | 1.7 | 0.7 |
| **Developing economies** | 6.5 | 4.2 |
| Africa | 6.2 | 4.0 |
| East and South Asia | 7.5 | 4.8 |
| Western Asia | 5.2 | 3.9 |
| Latin America and the Caribbean | 4.8 | 2.6 |
| **Economies in transition** | 7.1 | 5.0 |
| World trade growth (volume) | 7.7 | 4.0 |
| US dollar exchange-rate index (annual percentage change) | -5.0 | -20.0 |
| Interest rate on 10-year US Treasury notes | 4.5 | 6.0 |
| United States current-account balance (billions of dollars) | -710 | -510 |

**Source:** UN/DESA, based on Project LINK.

Also in the baseline, the major drag on the world economy continues to be a notable slowdown in the United States, driven by the slump in the housing sector. The deteriorating housing downturn in the United States, accompanied by a meltdown of sub-prime mortgages, eventually triggered a full-scale credit crunch that reverberated throughout the global financial system during the summer of 2007. Central banks of the major economies consequently injected a large amount of liquidity into money markets and, in the case of the United States Federal Reserve Bank (Fed), lowered interest rates. These measures have largely attenuated the immediate financial stress, but they did not address the more fundamental problems rooted in the global financial system and the world economy (see below for a more detailed discussion). The housing recession in the United States will likely continue in 2008, remaining one of the major downside risks for the growth prospects of the United States and the global economy.

## World economic growth in 2007 and 2008

Except for the weakness in the United States, the growth of the world economy was broad-based in 2007. A vast majority of countries (102 out of a total of 160 countries for which recent data are available) succeeded in increasing per capita output by 3 per cent or more (see table I.2). This group of strong performers was even larger than in preceding years and includes 69 developing countries. This trend could signal further progress in poverty reduction.[1] At the same time, the number of countries that registered a decline in gross domestic product (GDP) per capita fell to only 9—less than in previous years. Nonetheless, divergence in economic performance remains across countries, particularly among the least developed countries (LDCs) (see box I.3). The divergence in economic performance among the poorest countries is also much larger than in the mainly middle-income countries of Asia and Latin America and the Caribbean (see figure I.2). Among the LDCs, per capita income growth ranged from close to zero to well over 10 per cent in 2007 at the extremes of the quartile distribution. There remain no less than 38 developing countries that did not manage to reach a growth rate of 3 per cent in GDP per capita. While Africa as a whole showed further strong performance in 2007, many of the countries with sub-par performance are in that region. In the outlook for 2008, as the world economy moderates, the number of countries that will remain above the 3 per cent benchmark is expected to decline somewhat, but on the positive side, fewer of the poorest countries are expected to suffer declining average welfare levels.

Among *developed economies*, a continued slump in the housing sector and the associated credit tightening are expected to lead the economy of the *United States* into another year of below-trend growth in the baseline scenario. GDP is expected to grow at a rate of 2.0 per cent for 2008, slightly lower than the pace estimated for 2007 (see table A.1). In the outlook, private consumption is expected to weaken as the housing downturn deteriorates further, while corporate investment spending and hiring are also likely to decelerate. Meanwhile, a slowdown in the average productivity growth over the past two years portends an additional challenge for the economy. Inflation, too, is expected to decelerate in 2008. Headline inflation in the United States had hovered above 3 per cent for two years but moderated to about 2.7 per cent during 2007. The core personal consumption expenditures (PCEs) deflator also finally dropped to the Fed's presumed 1-2 per cent

*The growth of the world economy was broad-based during 2007*

*Another year of below-trend growth for the United States*

---

1   As a rule of thumb, 3 per cent per capita income growth is sometimes seen as the minimum required growth rate for achieving significant reductions in poverty, in the absence of income redistribution.

Table I.2
**Frequency of high and low growth of per capita output, 2005-2008**

| | Number of countries monitored | Decline in GDP per capita | | | | Growth of GDP per capita exceeding 3 per cent | | | |
|---|---|---|---|---|---|---|---|---|---|
| | | 2005 | 2006 | 2007[a] | 2008[b] | 2005 | 2006 | 2007[a] | 2008[b] |
| | | **Number of countries** | | | | | | | |
| World | 160 | 14 | 12 | 9 | 4 | 87 | 95 | 102 | 95 |
| *of which:* | | | | | | | | | |
| Developed economies | 35 | 2 | 0 | 0 | 0 | 13 | 17 | 15 | 12 |
| Economies in transition | 18 | 1 | 0 | 0 | 0 | 16 | 16 | 18 | 18 |
| Developing countries | 107 | 11 | 12 | 9 | 4 | 58 | 62 | 69 | 65 |
| *of which:* | | | | | | | | | |
| Africa | 51 | 8 | 10 | 8 | 3 | 24 | 25 | 28 | 31 |
| East Asia | 13 | 1 | 0 | 1 | 0 | 10 | 11 | 12 | 10 |
| South Asia | 6 | 0 | 0 | 0 | 0 | 5 | 5 | 5 | 4 |
| Western Asia | 13 | 1 | 2 | 0 | 1 | 6 | 7 | 8 | 6 |
| Latin America | 24 | 1 | 0 | 0 | 0 | 13 | 14 | 16 | 14 |
| *Memorandum items:* | | | | | | | | | |
| Least developed countries | 39 | 5 | 8 | 7 | 2 | 18 | 16 | 18 | 18 |
| Sub-Saharan Africa[c] | 44 | 8 | 10 | 8 | 3 | 19 | 20 | 22 | 24 |
| Landlocked developing countries | 25 | 5 | 3 | 3 | 1 | 14 | 11 | 12 | 13 |
| Small island developing States | 17 | 1 | 2 | 1 | 0 | 8 | 10 | 12 | 10 |
| | Share[d] | **Percentage of world population** | | | | | | | |
| Developed economies | 15.8 | 1.1 | 0.0 | 0.0 | 0.0 | 1.8 | 2.3 | 2.3 | 1.9 |
| Economies in transition | 5.0 | 0.1 | 0.0 | 0.0 | 0.0 | 4.9 | 4.9 | 5.0 | 5.0 |
| Developing countries | 79.1 | 1.1 | 1.0 | 0.8 | 0.4 | 66.7 | 66.9 | 71.7 | 70.2 |
| *of which:* | | | | | | | | | |
| Africa | 13.5 | 1.1 | 0.9 | 0.8 | 0.4 | 9.4 | 6.9 | 10.0 | 10.8 |
| East Asia | 30.5 | 0.0 | 0.0 | 0.0 | 0.0 | 29.2 | 30.4 | 30.5 | 29.7 |
| South Asia | 23.7 | 0.0 | 0.0 | 0.0 | 0.0 | 25.3 | 25.7 | 26.1 | 25.3 |
| Western Asia | 2.8 | 0.1 | 0.1 | 0.0 | 0.0 | 1.7 | 1.7 | 1.8 | 1.6 |
| Latin America | 8.5 | 0.0 | 0.0 | 0.0 | 0.0 | 3.1 | 4.4 | 6.0 | 5.8 |
| *Memorandum items:* | | | | | | | | | |
| Least developed countries | 10.5 | 0.6 | 0.6 | 0.6 | 0.2 | 8.0 | 6.4 | 7.5 | 6.8 |
| Sub-Saharan Africa[c] | 8.4 | 1.1 | 0.9 | 0.8 | 0.4 | 5.8 | 4.4 | 5.4 | 5.7 |
| Landlocked developing countries | 4.9 | 0.6 | 0.5 | 0.5 | 0.2 | 3.4 | 2.6 | 2.7 | 2.7 |
| Small island developing States | 0.8 | 0.0 | 0.0 | 0.0 | 0.0 | 0.4 | 0.5 | 0.6 | 0.5 |

**Source:** UN/DESA, including population estimates and projections from *World Population Prospects: The 2006 Revision Population Database*, available from http://esa.un.org/unpp/.

**a**  Partly estimated.
**b**  Forecast, based on Project LINK.
**c**  Excluding Nigeria and South Africa.
**d**  Percentage of world population for 2000.

Box I.3

## Prospects for the least developed countries

GDP growth in the least developed countries (LDCs) as a whole is forecast to decelerate slightly in 2008, largely due to the pronounced slowdown in Myanmar—once one of the fastest-growing economies among the group—as well as in Mauritania. For the rest of the group, growth has been increasingly broad-based, though growth divergence among this group of countries is larger than among other groups of developing countries (see figure I.2). Eighteen countries are expected to have per capita GDP growth exceeding 3 per cent in 2008, while only two countries are likely to witness a decline in per capita GDP in 2008, as opposed to seven in 2007.

Booms in construction, manufacturing and services have contributed strongly to GDP growth in agriculture-dominated economies, including Burkina Faso, Ethiopia and the United Republic of Tanzania. Strong performance in agriculture has to some degree sustained economic recovery in mining-dependent Sierra Leone and oil-producing Angola. In addition, the small increase in aid flows and growing investment have led to a modest recovery in the Central African Republic. These factors are expected to strengthen further in 2008, thereby yielding a much stronger growth in the Central African Republic, Guinea and Togo. By contrast, GDP has contracted in Chad as a result of the strained security and social situations.

Most LDCs have used the fiscal space created by growing government domestic revenue and/or significant aid flows to scale up public spending. Additional spending has largely targeted infrastructure and social sectors, as many countries strive to relieve structural supply constraints and achieve the Millennium Development Goals. Fiscal positions remain extremely fragile in most countries, however, as government revenue remains heavily dependent on aid flows and developments in commodity prices. With rapidly growing excess liquidity and concerns over real appreciation and inflation, many central banks have tightened monetary policies by restricting money-supply growth. Mozambique is among the few exceptions where the monetary authorities have opted for an easing in the context of a positive outlook for inflation and exchange-rate stability.

Although favourable, the current economic cycle is highly vulnerable to both internal and external shocks. The main downside risks to the near-term outlook are a possible deterioration in the global environment and the potential for weather shocks, severe security problems and political uncertainty in some countries. A steep deceleration of growth in the rest of world could lead to a sharp decline in the demand for LDC exports. Inauspicious weather in the planting phases of the 2007/2008 crop cycle presents a risk for economic activity in a number of LDCs. Finally, the intensification of existing or emerging political tensions and/or civil unrest in Chad, Haiti, Mali, Nepal, Niger and the Darfur region of the Sudan will likely dampen economic activity.

tolerance band. With an anticipated slowing of economic growth, inflation is expected to remain tame for 2008, with a PCE rate of under 2 per cent.

Growth in *Western Europe* is expected to slow in 2008 after an above-trend performance in 2007. GDP is expected to grow by 2.3 per cent in 2008 for the euro area, down from the 2.7 per cent estimated for 2007, which had been the strongest growth performance since 2000. Indicators of business and consumer confidence peaked in mid-2007, but have decelerated since. Nonetheless, in most European countries, these indicators are substantially higher than they have been for most of the previous decades. Investment spending is expected to provide only modest support for 2008, with housing investment representing a substantial drag on activities. A number of European countries that have experienced rapid appreciation in housing prices, such as France, Ireland, Spain, Sweden and the United Kingdom of Great Britain and Northern Ireland, might also face a housing downturn.

Inflation, while a continuing concern for European policymakers, is expected to remain low. In the euro area, after a long period in which it was above the European

Growth is expected to slow and inflation to remain low in Europe

Figure I.2:
**Divergence in economic performance across developing countries in 2007**

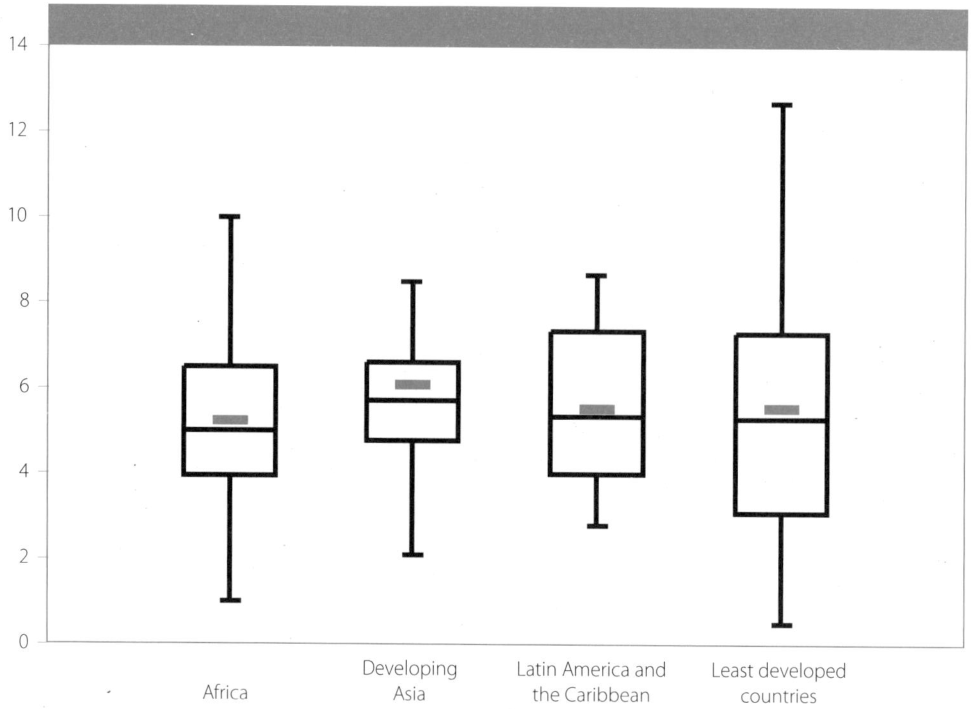

**Sources:** UN/DESA and Project LINK.

**Note:** For each region, the green bar within the box corresponds to the regional mean value of growth rates. The five black horizontal bars, from bottom to top, correspond to the smallest observation, the first quartile, the median, the third quartile and the largest observation, respectively. The outliers are excluded from the determination of the smallest and the largest observation.

Central Bank's (ECB) inflation target of less than 2 per cent, headline inflation remained below target for most of 2007. It is true, however, that core inflation rates, which do not include the prices of energy, food, alcohol and tobacco, have risen considerably since 2006, almost converging with headline inflation, and this worries policymakers. However, while impulses from rising oil and food prices remain significant, the stronger European currencies are able to mitigate some of the inflationary pressures from imported inflation.

Growth in the economies of the *new member States of the European Union* (EU) is expected to slow to about 5.4 per cent in 2008, compared with a pace of about 6 per cent in 2007. Economic activity in these countries was buoyant during 2007, the only exception being Hungary. Vibrant economic activity in the region was, however, accompanied by weakening indicators of macroeconomic stability, visible in mounting inflationary pressures, rapid expansion of domestic credit and escalating external imbalances in many countries. The worsening of the stability indicators has increased earlier concerns that some of the economies may be operating close to capacity. Aggregate demand and output growth are expected to cool down in the coming years. This might help reduce the inflationary pressures that were on the rise during 2007 as a result of credit expansion and capacity constraints related to labour shortages, as well as nominal wage pressures, increased costs of imported energy and higher regulated prices. As the cost-push factors are likely to prevail, a major drop in inflation is not expected for most economies in 2008.

*Growth in Japan is expected to moderate*

Economic growth in *Japan* is expected to reach 1.7 per cent in 2008, representing a slowdown from the 2.0 per cent expansion in 2007. Private consumption will continue to support economic growth, buttressed by improved labour-market conditions. Government consumption is expected to contract in 2008 as part of the continued process of consolidating public debt. Expansion of business investment is expected to moderate, partly related to an anticipated slowdown in the United States, which along with the expected appreciation of the yen and elevated oil prices will also reduce the trade surplus. Inflation in Japan will continue to remain close to zero. Consumer prices will remain flat in 2007 and are expected to experience a small rise, by 0.7 per cent, in 2008.

In *other developed economies*, growth in the economy of *Canada* has moderated since the second half of 2007 and is expected to remain subdued in 2008, owing to continued pressure on the Canadian dollar to appreciate, a weakening demand from the United States and a softening of the construction sector. These factors are also expected to offload inflationary pressures. Growth in *Australia* was strong during 2007, driven by robust domestic demand. A more pronounced negative effect of the global liquidity crisis on real global growth and the Australian export sector constitutes a significant downside risk for the economic outlook. Growth in 2008 is expected to moderate to 3.6 per cent from the 4.2 per cent estimate for 2007. A slight moderation is also expected for *New Zealand*, from a growth of 3.0 per cent in 2007 to 2.9 per cent in 2008. Inflation in Australia and New Zealand remains under control, but with some upside pressure in view of tight labour market conditions and high rates of capacity utilization in some sectors.

Among the *economies in transition*, growth in the *Commonwealth of Independent States* (CIS) maintained a strong pace of 8.2 per cent for 2007, but is expected to moderate to a pace of about 7.3 per cent in 2008 (see table A.2). While growth in the Russian Federation accelerated, growth in smaller economies, such as Georgia, Kyrgyzstan, Moldova and Uzbekistan, also gathered momentum. Higher international prices of primary commodities provided a favourable background, while domestic demand continued to strengthen. With the exception of Azerbaijan, fixed investment has been growing rapidly in the CIS, although the share of fixed investment in GDP is still low in comparison with other fast-growing emerging economies. The downside risks for the CIS include a steeper and more prolonged slowdown of the world economy that would lead to a sharp decline in export demand for primary commodities and a decline in commodity prices. Political uncertainty poses another risk for some countries in this group.

Furthermore, inflationary pressures have remained high throughout the CIS. The fastest inflation rate, exceeding 15 per cent, was observed in Azerbaijan, as the impact of unsterilized foreign-exchange inflows was compounded by an overtly expansionary fiscal policy and an upward adjustment in administered prices. In Ukraine, inflation reached double digits, propelled by higher food prices. There was a slight moderation in the rate of price increases in the Russian Federation in the first half of 2007, but inflation accelerated later, by far exceeding the target for the year. Upward pressure on inflation will remain strong in the short run.

Growth strengthened further in the economies of *South-eastern Europe* during 2007 to a rate of 6.0 per cent, but some moderation is expected for 2008. Robust domestic demand, particularly private consumption and fixed investment, remained the key driver. While real income continued to rise in most economies in the group, investment also rebounded, underpinned by buoyant foreign direct investment (FDI) inflows. Recent FDI inflows targeted not only privatization deals but also an increasing number of greenfield projects, although the latter still remain limited. Manufacturing and tourism are key contributors to growth, but construction activity has also surged recently. Downside risks are associated with a continued widening of the current-account deficit and high private sector indebtedness in most economies in the group. Despite strong growth in output in 2007, inflation continued to decelerate. This trend of disinflation is expected to continue in 2008, despite the growing inflationary pressures from faster real wage growth and increases in regulated prices.

Continued robust growth, albeit with some moderation, is expected for the economies in transition

Africa is expected to
maintain its strong growth
momentum

Among *developing economies*, growth in *Africa* has strengthened in 2007, and the momentum is expected to be maintained in 2008 at a pace of above 6 per cent (see table A.3). The growth in the region has been driven largely by buoyant domestic demand, booming mining and gas production and a broad-based recovery in a number of countries from a long period of economic decline. Disparities remain significant among individual countries, as indicated above. Growth in a number of economies continues to be hampered by political and social tensions, limited access to external financing and sporadic adverse climate conditions. Growth continues to be strong in the larger economies in the region, such as Algeria, Egypt, Nigeria and South Africa. Booms in construction, manufacturing and services have contributed significantly to GDP growth in some of the agriculture-dominated economies, including Burkina Faso, Ethiopia, Kenya and the United Republic of Tanzania. By contrast, GDP has contracted in Chad and Zimbabwe as a result of the strained security and social situation in the former and continued socio-political tensions and unsustainable economic policies in the latter.

Most African countries managed to lower inflation further. Only a few countries experienced episodic accelerations in consumer prices. Rising insecurity and/or transport bottlenecks caused supply shortages in Chad and Eritrea, generating significant inflationary pressures, while rapid increases in public spending in Algeria, Equatorial Guinea, Gabon, Sao Tome and Principe and the Sudan moderately pushed up consumer prices, especially those of non-traded goods. The inflation outlook appears broadly favourable, although further reductions in petroleum price subsidies and potentially lower agricultural production, instigated by the inauspicious weather in the planting phases of the 2007/2008 crop cycle, will cause some spikes in inflation in some countries.

Growth in Asia is
keeping a solid pace

Among the *Asian* economies, growth in *East Asia* maintained a solid pace of 8.4 per cent in 2007 but is expected to slow somewhat, to 7.7 per cent in 2008. Exports remain the main driver of growth for the region, but domestic demand also contributes significantly in most economies. Expanding at a pace of 11.4 per cent, *China* continues to lead growth in the region. Further tightening measures, combined with the expected deceleration in major developed economies, will likely slow the growth of the Chinese economy in 2008. Growth in Viet Nam has also been outstanding. In contrast, growth in Thailand decelerated notably in the face of political uncertainty. Among Hong Kong Special Administrative Region (SAR) of China, the Republic of Korea, Singapore and Taiwan Province of China, only Singapore experienced a higher growth in 2007 than in the previous year, but all, except the Republic of Korea, are expected to moderate in 2008. The impact of the mid-2007 global financial turmoil on the region has been limited, but most economies would be vulnerable to a significant slowdown in demand from the major developed countries.

Inflation has edged up in 2007 in most of East Asia and is expected to accelerate further in 2008. The consumer price index (CPI) in China rose at an annualized rate of above 5 per cent for several months in 2007, the highest in a decade. Inflation is mainly driven by sharp increases in food prices, particularly meat prices, but increasing upward pressures on wages and the recent large appreciations in the prices of equity and real estate have given rise to increasing inflationary concerns. Inflation also accelerated in other East Asian economies during 2007, mainly driven by higher energy and food prices.

Growth in *South Asia* decelerated during 2007, to a pace of 6.9 per cent, and is expected to moderate further in 2008 to 6.7 per cent. The growth in India slowed due to exchange-rate appreciation and capacity constraints. Rising wages led the Central Bank to tighten monetary policy, while large capital inflows also limited the degree of autonomy for monetary policy. The service sector has been a key driver of growth for many economies in the region, such as Bangladesh, India, Pakistan and Sri Lanka. Information and communication technologies (ICT) and ICT-enabled services are expected to grow rapidly in the outlook. The manufacturing sector has shown renewed dynamism, while agricultural production is lagging behind, affected by adverse weather conditions. Meanwhile, elevated oil prices coupled with fiscal expansion continue to support growth in the Islamic Republic of Iran. Political instability and insecurity pose risks for the economic outlook of a number of countries in the region.

Inflation is expected to decelerate in the region in 2008, especially following a tighter monetary policy in India. In some of the other economies, though, inflationary pressures may increase as a result of the need to further reduce subsidies on domestic fuel prices in order to curb increasing fiscal costs and expected increases in domestic and imported prices of agricultural products.

Economies in the *Western Asian* region continue to benefit from the favourable effects of higher oil prices, propelling growth to 5.7 per cent in 2007. Slower growth is expected for 2008. Growth accelerated in the Gulf Cooperation Council (GCC) economies during 2007, driven by rising oil revenues and the induced strength in consumption as well as by public and private investment. Strong growth in the oil-exporting countries has also generated positive spillover benefits, such as increased FDI, worker remittances and tourism receipts, for the more diversified economies of Jordan, the Syrian Arab Republic and, to a lesser extent, Lebanon and Yemen. Israel grew at about 5.1 per cent during 2007, driven by strong export growth, increased investment and robust domestic consumption. Several indicators also suggest that tourism is recovering from the Israeli-Lebanese conflict of 2006. Growth in Turkey rebounded in late 2007 along with monetary easing. The risks in the prospects for the region are mainly associated with a possible substantial slowdown in the United States. A further weakening of the United States dollar would aggravate the already persistent inflationary pressure in the region, because of the peg of local currencies to the dollar. Uncertainties and risks are also associated with geopolitical tensions in the region, such as the ongoing conflict between Turkey and Kurdish factions in Iraq.

Growth in *Latin America and the Caribbean* seems to have peaked after robust growth over the past four years. After growing at a rate of about 5 per cent in 2007, a moderation is expected for 2008, along with a slight weakening in macroeconomic conditions and a less favourable external economic environment (higher inflation, a smaller current-account surplus and a weaker fiscal position). From Panama to the southern tip of the continent, growth benefited greatly from favourable terms of trade, while Central America and Mexico were more sensitive to the slowdown in the United States. Much of the growth in the region can be attributed to an improved economic performance in Brazil, led by domestic demand, in particular, a strong business investment and public investment in infrastructure. Growth in the Bolivarian Republic of Venezuela was much higher than expected, mostly supported by government transfers and social programmes fuelled by oil revenues. Growth in Argentina was balanced across all sectors and strong growth was also observed in Colombia and Peru. Growth in Chile was moderate, but higher than expected, owing to higher copper prices and stimulatory macroeconomic policies. Growth in the countries of Central America decelerated in 2007. In the outlook, a further slowdown of the United States will pose risks for this region, affecting not only Mexico and Central America, but also some countries in South America. While remaining low by historical standards, greater inflationary pressures will be felt during 2008, stemming particularly from increasing costs of energy, transportation and food.

Economies in Western Asia continue to benefit from higher oil prices

Growth in Latin America and the Caribbean seems to have peaked

## Challenges facing developing countries in the international economic environment

The international economic environment for the developing economies and the economies in transition has so far withstood the global financial turmoil that originated from the sub-prime debacle in the United States in mid-2007 (see box I.4). While the trends in most indicators for international trade and finance remain favourable for these economies by historical standards, volatility has increased notably during 2007 in such indicators as international commodity prices, capital flows and yield spreads. Meanwhile, the extremely low levels of the risk premiums on lending to this group of countries might suggest a considerable degree of complacency on the part of international investors. Should the financial market conditions in major developed economies worsen and/or the large global imbalances undergo a disorderly adjustment, the international economic environment for developing economies and economies in transition would also face a significant risk of deterioration. Both policymakers in the emerging market economies and international investors stand reminded of the risky and volatile nature of these markets.

World *trade flows* grew at a slower pace during 2007 than in the previous year. The volume of world merchandise trade increased by about 7 per cent in 2007, down from 9.9 per cent in 2006 (see chapter II). World trade continues to grow twice as fast as world output. The moderation in the growth of world trade in 2007 was largely due to a weakening in import demand in the United States. Developing countries and the economies in transition continue to penetrate world markets: their share in total world trade increased from 35 per cent in 2000 to more than 40 per cent in 2007.[2] Asian economies led the dynamism in global trade, the export volumes of China and India having increased by about 20 per cent annually for several years. In addition, many developing countries in Africa and Latin America have managed to expand their export values at double-digit rates owing to the strong global demand for energy and raw materials. In parallel with this, exports of the major developed countries have also been robust, driven by global demand for capital goods as business investment in many countries continues to recover from the low levels experienced since the last downturn at the beginning of the century. In the outlook for 2008, an expected further slowdown in import demand from the United States will likely serve to keep growth of world trade at a moderate pace of about 7 per cent.

The *terms of trade* of many primary commodity-exporting developing countries continued to improve during 2007 for the fifth consecutive year. However, prices of most primary commodities are expected to moderate and become more volatile in the outlook for 2008.

The *price of oil* in terms of Brent crude hovered at over $70 per barrel (pb) for most of 2007, but surged to nearly $100 pb in November. A weakening value of the United States dollar, geopolitical tensions in the proximity of major oil-production areas, variable weather, supply restrictions by the Organization of the Petroleum Exporting Countries (OPEC) and refinery constraints have been, and will continue to be, the factors outweighing those of demand in determining price movements. Oil prices are expected to average $76 pb for 2008, compared with an estimated average of $73.50 pb for 2007.

At nearly $100 a barrel, oil prices are, after correcting for inflation, back near their peak level of the early 1980s (see chapter II, figure II.6). Thus far, increasing oil prices have not had the same impact on the world economy as in the 1970s and 1980s. At that

---

2    The share of developing countries would be even higher if intra-European trade were excluded from the world total.

Box I.4

## The hot summer of 2007:
## origins of the global financial turmoil

The United States sub-prime mortgage market formed the eye of this global financial storm. House-hold mortgage debt has traditionally been considered a low-risk instrument, being backed by the home equity of creditworthy borrowers. In recent years, however, a growing share of mortgage loans has been granted to less creditworthy (sub-prime) borrowers. More and more mortgage loans with high loan-to-value ratios were supplied based on poor information gathering about homebuyers' financial conditions and the value of houses. United States sub-prime mortgage lending increased from $120 billion in 2001 to over $600 billion in 2006. Sub-prime mortgages offered at adjustable rates represented the major risk: borrowers availing themselves of adjustable-rate mortgages (ARMs) expected rising house prices which would enable them to refinance their mortgages before the lending rate was adjusted upward as scheduled, typically after two years.

Meanwhile, financial innovations fuelled this kind of high-risk mortgage lending by se-curitizing mortgage loans and bundling these derivatives with other securities, such as traditional bonds and commercial papers, to be sold to investors worldwide. For example, collateralized debt obligations (CDOs) offered one effective instrument to banks for selling off mortgages. The repack-aged mortgages spread the risk to a broader array of investors, and the risks associated with these new financial products were typically underestimated by rating agencies and investors alike. At pres-ent, more than 50 per cent of mortgage loans in the United States are estimated to be securitized. In traditional mortgage markets, banks keep the loans they make on their own balance sheets, but under the new "originate-to-distribute" mechanisms of securitized loans, mortgage originators have much weaker incentives to underwrite prudently, as they do not see their own capital and reputation as being at risk.

Since 2006, corporate debt has also shown explosive growth in parallel with the expan-sion of mortgage lending. More than $300 billion in high-yield bonds and bank loans was scheduled to be issued in the second half of 2007, mainly to finance leveraged buyouts. In parallel with the CDOs for mortgage lenders, many private equity firms relied on similarly complicated investment pools, such as collateralized loan obligations (CLOs), to fund the buyouts. CLOs package the loans and divide them into financial instruments with different risk levels, which can then be bought by financial investors. Private equity firms bid up the prices and loosen loan terms for ever-larger lever-aged buyouts, making the transactions increasingly risky. In the three months up through July 2007, firms announced $254 billion in buyouts, as much as the combined total for 2004 and 2005.

Hedge funds further boosted the mortgage and buyout boom by investing in secu-ritized sub-prime debt and loans used to fund buyouts. With high leverage and limited disclosure, hedge funds added another layer of risk and uncertainty to the already highly leveraged markets.

Although sub-prime mortgages form a relatively small fraction of the total mortgage market and an even smaller fraction of the total credit market, this complex financial system—with its overstretched leverage, lack of transparency and inadequate regulation—spread and multiplied the risks in sub-prime lending far beyond this market segment.

Despite the large increase in credit risk, credit spreads in most markets continued to narrow into early 2007, suggesting that market agents were myopic when it came to all these risks. They found out the hard way. The delinquency rate on sub-prime mortgages reached an all-time high of 16 per cent in August 2007, and investors and lenders found themselves overleveraged with risky credits and falling asset prices. The complexity of the underlying financial mechanism led to overshooting of the price adjustment: leveraged market participants were forced to liquidate their positions, while the downgrading of the status of sub-prime debt and derivatives by rating agen-cies led to a fire sale of these instruments by those financial institutions that require holding only higher-grade debt. Furthermore, concerns that lenders and investors did not have accurate market information exacerbated the situation. As a result, liquidity dried up, prices of all securities fell and spreads widened.

**Box I.4** (cont'd)

During the financial turmoil, the pain was felt most in the market for asset-backed commercial papers (ABCPs), in which financial institutions issue commercial paper to finance a broad variety of assets, including mortgage-backed securities. The concerns about mortgage-backed securities and other structured credit products greatly reduced the willingness of investors to roll over ABCPs. The problems intensified in August 2007 as some commercial paper issuers revoked the right to extend the maturity of their paper, and a few issuers defaulted. Investors fled to the safety and liquidity of Treasury bills, sparking a plunge in T-bill rates and a sharp widening in spreads on ABCPs. Meanwhile, issuance of CLOs and CDOs fell significantly. Demand for leveraged loans slowed sharply, reducing credit access for private equity firms and other borrowers seeking to finance leveraged buyouts.

The turmoil also spread to markets in which securitization plays a much smaller role, such as corporate bond markets and equity markets. Many of the largest banks also became concerned about the possibility that they might face large withdrawals of liquidity. They recognized that they might have to provide back-up funding to programmes that were no longer able to issue ABCPs. Many large banks might be forced to hold on to the assets they had planned to sell because of the disruption in the syndication market for leveraged loans and in the securitization market for non-prime mortgages. These concerns prompted banks to become reluctant to lend, including to other banks. As a result, interbank lending rates rose notably, and the liquidity in interbank lending markets dried up.

Faced with financial turbulence and concerned with the systemic implications, central banks in major developed economies took a number of measures. Most increased daily operations to inject liquidity into money markets, but the United States Federal Reserve also cut the discount rate and reduced the federal fund interest rate by a total of 75 basis points.

The functioning of financial markets has improved somewhat since. Interest-rate spreads on ABCPs have fallen and issuance of outstanding commercial paper has edged up. Conditions in interbank term money markets have improved modestly, though spreads remain unusually wide. Some pending buyout-related loans have been brought to market with stricter terms. Risk spreads in corporate bond markets have also narrowed. However, conditions in the mortgage markets remain difficult, with little securitized sub-prime loan activity, while volatility remains high in financial markets. Moreover, the impact of the financial turbulence on the real sector of the world economy is still unfolding, heightening the downside risks for the world economic prospects.

time, the higher price of oil provided a supply shock to the major economies as they still had production-cost structures that were much more sensitive to the cost of fossil energy than is currently the case, and the oil-price shock came when global demand was in a downswing. Rising oil prices have been driven by strong global demand in recent years, especially from emerging market economies—China in particular—and energy costs weigh much less in total production costs. Even with a moderation in world economic growth, upward pressures on oil prices may remain. While moderating, growth in emerging market economies will remain fairly robust, despite the slowdown in the United States economy. A further weakening dollar will also exert upward pressure. Forecasts for the price of oil are surrounded by great uncertainty, however, with future adjustments in the quota policies of OPEC and geopolitical factors remaining somewhat unpredictable. Higher oil prices would add to inflationary pressures, but should not become a major drag on world economic growth as in the past, even if they exceed $100 pb. Should slower global demand growth affect emerging economies more significantly, it would likely become a prominent factor in downward pressure on oil prices.

*Prices of non-energy commodities* have also continued their upward trend of the past few years. While supply-side factors vary among individual commodities, a common cause for the upward movement in these prices has been a continued robust global demand growth, originating in particular from China and other fast-growing economies. Meanwhile, higher oil prices also contribute to the upward pressure on the prices of a number of non-energy commodities, either directly, in the form of higher production costs, or through an indirect substitution effect. For example, higher oil prices have induced an expansion of biofuel production and, consequently, rises in demand for and the prices of corn, soybeans and oilseeds. In the outlook, prices of most agricultural commodities are expected to reach a plateau, while prices of metals and minerals are expected to retreat moderately.

A weakening value of the United States dollar vis-à-vis other major currencies and a significant increase in the positions of investment funds in commodity markets (in search for higher returns) have also been among the factors driving up the prices of commodities in the past few years.

The *external financing costs* for emerging market economies remain low. The spreads in the Emerging Markets Bond Index (EMBI) were at all-time lows in the first half of 2007 but widened notably during the mid-year global financial turmoil (figure I.3). The spreads have since been narrowing along with the improvement in the financial market conditions of major developed economies. Meanwhile, the benchmark interest rates underlying the external financing costs for emerging market economies have been pushed downwards as a result of a "flight to safety" in the credit markets of the developed countries. There are, however, important downward risks to this scenario, particularly if the financial market conditions in the developed countries experience a relapse and the large current-account deficit of the United States undergoes an abrupt adjustment.

*Capital flows* to emerging market economies in 2007 declined slightly in net terms from the previous year, but rose significantly in gross terms, reflecting an increase in outward investment from developing countries, especially from China. As sovereign

The external financing costs for emerging market economies remain low

Figure I.3:
**Yield spreads of Emerging Market Bonds, 1998-2007**[a]

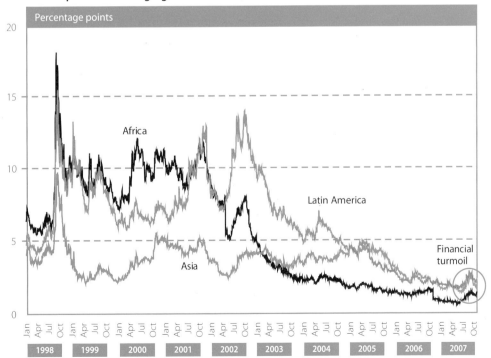

**Source:** JPMorgan Securities.
a   Until October 2007.

spreads widened and stock markets fell, capital flows to emerging markets were temporarily scaled back. This interruption was short-lived. As spreads narrowed again, equity investments reflooded emerging markets and rose to record levels. Emerging markets thus appear to serve at least as a temporary haven for portfolio funds as long as the high uncertainty and pessimistic prospects in developed country financial markets prevail. These developments add to the risk that emerging economies may be confronted with volatile external financing conditions and capital reversals in the near future.

FDI flows have continued to increase, although they are concentrated in a handful of emerging market economies. Official credit flows to this group of countries have continued to be largely negative as a result of increased net repayments to official creditors.

On balance, however, emerging market economies are net lenders to the rest of the world, financing the external deficits of the United States and a handful of other developed economies with current-account deficits. In the outlook, net private capital flows to emerging markets in 2008 will likely stay at the same level as 2007. As many of these economies have been running current-account surpluses for several consecutive years and have accumulated vast amounts of foreign reserves, they have become less dependent on international capital, at least cyclically in the short run.

*Official Development Assistance* (ODA) declined in 2006. New commitments made in 2005 were largely for debt relief and emergency assistance, and the lack of large debt-relief packages such as those approved in 2005, led to a fall in aid from the countries of the Organization for Economic Cooperation and Development (OECD) by 5.1 per cent in constant dollars in 2006. As a result, these donor countries are further from meeting their commitment to an ODA target of 0.7 per cent of their GNI by 2012. This could jeopardize the poorest countries in particular, which are in need of enhanced foreign aid to enable them to finance their efforts towards achieving the Millennium Development Goals. In addition, aid is found to be significantly more volatile than fiscal revenue and tends to be pro-cyclical on average. Multi-annual agreements between donors and recipient countries would enable aid flows to become more predictable and potentially more counter-cyclical, and would help improve the effectiveness of aid, especially for African countries (see chapter IV, box IV.3).

The massive accumulation of *official reserves* by developing countries has been continuing, totalling more than $4 trillion in 2007. The foreign exchange reserves of China alone reached $1.4 trillion in late 2007. The amassed foreign reserves have strengthened the capacity of these countries to deal with external shocks, but they also entail costs and policy challenges for these economies. One particular challenge is how to manage large foreign-exchange reserves efficiently. In the present context of a depreciating dollar, there are increasing costs in holding such large amounts of reserves, as most are held in dollar-denominated assets. This could motivate monetary authorities to diversify reserve holdings into other major currencies in order to mitigate the risk of further asset-value losses. Thus far, although there has been some currency diversification of developed and developing country reserve holdings, it has been far from massive (see box I.5). One possible reason for the rather marginal reserve diversification could be that official agents fear that a larger move away from dollar-denominated assets could precipitate an even stronger dollar depreciation and loss of value of their reserve holdings. As discussed further below, however, the accumulation of large official reserve positions by developing countries is intrinsically related to the widening global imbalances, and failure to address these imbalances soon and in a serious manner could lead to an abrupt loss of confidence in the international reserve currency. A hard landing of the dollar would, in turn, quickly erode the degree of "self-insurance" which developing countries have built up over the past decade.

Box I.5

# Diversification of international reserve holdings

Official international reserve holdings have surged from $1.6 trillion to $5.7 trillion between 1999 and the second quarter of 2007. Much of this rise has taken place in developing countries. China increased its reserve holdings from $0.1 trillion to 1.3 trillion during that period and total reserves for developing Asia now amount to about half of all holdings. Developing countries as a group have accumulated three quarters, or $4.3 trillion, of world reserves (see figure A).

The recent surge in reserve accumulation was initially driven largely by precautionary motives to provide means for crisis-insurance, especially among emerging economies in Asia in the aftermath of the financial crisis of the late 1990s. At present, however, reserve holdings probably far exceed what would be needed for self-insurance against trade shocks and sudden stops of capital flows.

An excess of reserve holdings may entail important opportunity costs, including those caused by potential inconsistencies between monetary and exchange-rate policies, as analysed in previous issues of this report.[a]

The rise in official reserve holdings, however, is intrinsically linked to the problem of the global imbalances. Export-led growth strategies and high commodity prices allow developing countries to sustain high trade surpluses, which provide the funding for, the United States current-account deficit in particular. This changes the perspective on the management of reserves. As insurance against foreign-exchange crises, reserves would typically be invested in liquid assets like treasury bills or short-term collateralized deposits. With the dollar as the dominant means of exchange and the growing external financing needs of the United States economy, most reserves are held in dollar-denominated assets. With liquidity risks more than covered, an increasing part of the foreign assets of developing countries are invested through so-called sovereign wealth funds (SWFs), which are designed for investment in less liquid and riskier assets that provide higher returns. Optimizing returns over time has become more important in reserve management. A depreciating dollar raises the question whether central banks should consider diversifying their reserves into other currencies, especially the euro or the yen, in order to avoid negative returns from asset value losses. It would be useful to know first whether central banks have already started to diversify their holdings. If they have not, what prevents them from doing so and, to the extent that they have, could a move away from dollar assets affect exchange rates and precipitate a further decline of the dollar?

### Currency diversification is more prevalent in the developing world

From 1999 through the second quarter of 2007, the currency structure of reserve holdings of all countries has diversified. This diversification is more pronounced in developing countries than in developed ones. The share of reserves of developing countries held in dollars dropped from about 70 per cent to about 60 per cent, while that of euros increased from 20 to 29 per cent (figure B). Even after discounting for the effect of the depreciation of the dollar and the appreciation of the euro, the share of the dollar in reserves has dropped about 5 percentage points, while the euro's position has strengthened by about 4 percentage points.

The dollar continues to dominate reserve holdings of developed countries. Dollar-denominated assets have remained rather stable at around 72 per cent on average, while the share of euro holdings fluctuated more during this period, between 16 and 23 per cent, the largest increases being in 2002 and 2003 when the euro began its strongest appreciation (this also coincided with lower shares of both the dollar and the Japanese yen).

If we consider the reserve holdings of both the developed and the developing countries, the shifts have been more subtle because of the consistency of the composition of reserves of the developed countries, which has partially offset the changes in the developing world. About half of the observed changes in the currency composition of official reserve holdings can be explained by exchange-rate changes.[b] After discounting for the exchange-rate effects, the share of dollar-denominated assets has decreased by about 3 percentage points since 1999, while the euro has gained around 4 percentage points in shares. In the meantime, the Japanese yen lost over two percentage points in share and the British pound gained one percentage point.

a   See *LINK Global Economic Outlook*, May 2007, available from http://www.un.org/esa/analysis/link/beijing07/linkgeomay07.pdf and *World Economic Situation and Prospects, Update as of mid-2007*, available from http://www.un.org/esa/policy/wess/wesp2007/files/wespupdate2007.pdf.

b   This analysis is based on calculations made by UN/DESA based on the International Monetary Fund's Currency Composition of Official Foreign Exchange Reserves (COFER), data available from http://www.imf.org/external/np/sta/cofer/eng/index.htm, accessed on 6 November 2007, and the International Financial Statistics. COFER includes data from 120 countries. The analysis of the shares is based on data of all allocated (or identified) reserves. A significant portion of the data, from one fourth to a third, is classified as unallocated, which is defined as the difference between total foreign exchange reserves and the allocated reserves.

## Box I.5 (cont'd)

Figure A:
**Shares of reserve holdings by major country group, 1999-2007**

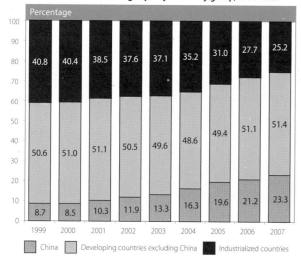

Figure B:
**Composition of reserves of developing countries, 1999-2007**

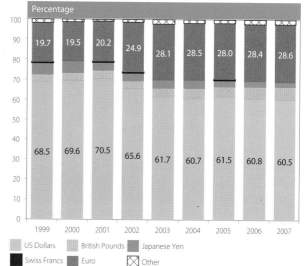

**Sources:** UN/DESA, based on data from IMF COFER and IFS.

### Reasons for diversification

Central banks manage their stock of international reserves for security, liquidity and return purposes.[c] Recently, they seem to have focused mainly on the third objective as the size of holdings has increased substantially. From the perspective of a portfolio approach, diversification of reserves in different currencies would reduce the possible negative impact of a sudden confidence crisis in one of the major currencies on the value of the stock of a country's reserves. The optimal currency composition of the reserve will have to be defined as a function of the structure of a country's trade flows and currency composition of foreign liabilities. In addition, countries with currencies pegged to the dollar may have an incentive to increasingly diversify their reserves and shift to a more flexible exchange-rate regime in order to maintain price stability by avoiding the pass-through effect that the falling dollar could have, first on the value of their currency and then on domestic prices, especially when most of their imports come from the EU.

### Reasons not to diversify

One reason why there has not been greater diversification in the face of a depreciating dollar is that central banks may be concerned that the process of diversification itself could create greater volatility in foreign-exchange markets and a move out of the dollar could precipitate further dollar depreciation and loss of the value of their reserves. Recent surveys[d] have shown that the United States dollar remains the dominant currency as a medium of exchange in payment and the foreign exchange market, as a currency of anchor, as a unit of account for invoicing in international trade and as a store of value in international bond markets. In this last category, the euro has gained ground, but mostly due to bonds issued by the Economic and Monetary Union (EMU) of the EU resident agencies and purchased by EMU financial institutions. Thus, the potential cost of a complete switch out of the dollar could be high.

The value of existing currency-reserve holdings may fall even as the central bank tries to find greater insulation from dollar depreciation. Reserve holdings in dollars by developing countries have increased threefold between 1999 and the second half of 2007. At the same time, the value of the dollar has decreased by about 17 per cent (vis-à-vis the euro). As we have seen, this depreciation was also accompanied by a drop in the share of dollars of about 10 percentage points. During the third and fourth quarter of 2007, the value of the dollar further dipped by 5 per cent.

It is not clear how much dollar depreciation could be directly caused by a more massive diversification of official reserves into other currencies. Perhaps the more important effect could come from private agents who may try to preempt the central bank's move and thereby reinforce the depreciation of the dollar. Consequently, central banks should move cautiously and gradually when implementing a broader diversification strategy.

**c** International Monetary Fund, *Guidelines for Foreign Exchange Reserve Management: Accompanying Document* (Washington, D.C.: IMF, 26 March 2003).

**d** See for example, Ewe-Ghee Lim, "The Euro's challenge to the Dollar: Different views from economists and evidence from COFER (Currency Composition of Foreign Exchange Reserves) and other data," IMF Working Paper, WP/06/153 (Washington D.C.: IMF, June 2006); and Gabriele Galati and Philip D. Wooldridge, "The euro as a reserve currency: A challenge to the pre-eminence of the US dollar?, BIS Working Papers, No. 218 (Switzerland: Bank for International Settlements, October 2006).

## Employment growth

Amidst robust economic growth, the *employment* situation continued to register marked improvements in 2006 and 2007 in a large number of economies. In the developed and transition economies, as well as in a smattering of developing economies, strong employment gains were accompanied by declining unemployment rates, leading in some instances to tight labour-market conditions and increasing wages. Many developing economies, however, witnessed only very small improvements in the employment situation, and high shares of workers continued to be without a job or underemployed (see box I.6). In the outlook, it is expected that employment growth will retreat or remain modest in most economies in 2008 as a result of slower overall economic growth.

Among the *developed economies*, the trend of improvement in the labour markets of the United States lost momentum in the second half of 2007, as the growth of payroll employment decelerated from a pace of about 2.0 per cent in 2006 to about 0.5 per cent in the second half of 2007. Unemployment also reversed course after reaching 4.5 per cent in mid-2007, the lowest level in six years, as a result of job losses primarily in housing and related sectors, as well as in manufacturing. Employment growth is expected to remain sluggish in 2008, with the unemployment rate edging up to 5 per cent (see table A.7). Canada has also been experiencing lower employment growth in 2007. Tight labour-market conditions prevail in Australia and New Zealand and were manifest in increasing wage levels. This is also the case for Japan, which is experiencing historically low unemployment rates. Employment growth remains strong in Western Europe with the rate of unemployment declining across the region, reaching 6.8 per cent on average in 2007. The labour-market situation also continued to improve in the new EU member States, partially reflecting the ongoing outward labour migration to Western Europe, but also resulting from real gains in job growth within those States. Employment should continue to expand throughout Europe in 2008, albeit at a more moderate pace, and unemployment should continue to fall.

Among the *economies in transition*, in the CIS, strong economic growth, buoyed by recent industrial dynamism led to declines in unemployment rates across the region in 2007. In the Russian Federation, the unemployment rate fell to an estimated 6.1 per cent in 2007 from 7.2 per cent in 2006 (see table A.8). Labour shortages have emerged in some countries, reflecting skill mismatches and barriers to labour mobility. In South-eastern Europe, strong output growth contributed to some improvements in the employment situation, especially in Croatia where the registered unemployment rate decreased. In general, however, unemployment is still precariously high in most of South-eastern Europe, especially in Bosnia and Herzegovina and the former Yugoslav Republic of Macedonia.

In the *developing economies*, with the exception of Latin America and the Caribbean, the employment situation witnessed only small improvements, and many economies remain plagued by high unemployment rates (see table A.9), rapid labour-force expansion and large informal economies.

In *Africa*, sustained high economic growth is believed to have triggered some employment benefits, yet high unemployment rates prevail in most countries as significant increases in the labour force continue to outstrip the limited employment gains. However, in Egypt and Morocco, robust expansion in agriculture and manufacturing has generated a significant number of jobs, and despite the growing labour force, there has been a substantial reduction in unemployment rates.

In *Western Asia*, the employment situation remains disparate despite strong economic growth, with widespread unemployment persisting among the domestic labour

Employment conditions have improved, but more job creation is needed

The employment situation in developing countries has improved only slightly despite high output growth

## Productive employment in developing economies

Recent economic trends show output growth averaging above 5 per cent in the developing econ-omies since 2003, but employment growth has not been sufficient to absorb all the new labour-market entrants in many countries. Additionally, the generation of more productive employment has been weak, leaving many workers in informal sector jobs or in conditions of underemployment. Even among those developing economies with strong GDP growth, many have not seen robust job cre-ation, and unemployment rates since 2000 have not shown significant declines.

Figure A shows the output-employment growth relationship over the period 2000-2006 in selected developing economies that have comparable data. It categorizes economies into "high-growth employment achievers" (that is to say, those with both high output and employment growth); "low-growth employment achievers" (those with low-to-moderate output growth, but with high employment growth); "high-growth employment laggards" and "low-growth employment lag-gards". The divide between high and low output growth is established at 4 per cent of GDP growth per annum and that for employment growth is set at 2.5 per cent per year, which—on average—is about the rate needed to absorb new entrants into the labour market and avoid rising unemploy-ment rates. Only half of the economies with high GDP growth witnessed sufficient job growth. Many of the high-growth employment laggards therefore continue to struggle with high, often double-digit, unemployment rates. One of the challenges for these economies is the rapid growth of the labour force, as high unemployment rates are closely associated with higher labour-force growth (see figure B).

Figure A:
**GDP and employment growth in selected developing countries, 2000-2006**

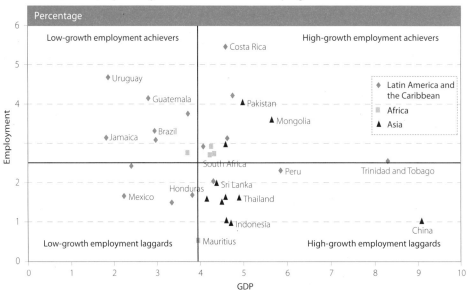

**Sources:** UN/DESA, based on International Labour Organization, *Key Indicators of the Labour Market (KILM)* 5th Edition, 2007 and World Bank, *World Development Indicators*, 2007.

An even bigger challenge for many countries is to generate sufficient productive em-ployment, as vast numbers of workers continue to rely on low-paid jobs in the informal sector. In low-income countries, the agriculture sector remains the largest employer, but with growing shares of workers engaging in urban informal services sectors. Informal service activities also tend to be the residual employers in middle-income countries, such as in Latin America and the Caribbean. Strong economic growth in recent years has been concentrated in primary export production with low labour intensity or in modern, high-productivity industry and service sectors. As a consequence, insufficient labour absorption has taken place and informal employment has remained high. Even

Box I.6 (cont'd)

China's sustained high output growth has, according to official data, only led to weak aggregate new job growth, leaving unemployment rates virtually unchanged. The strong underlying increase in labour productivity has been mainly concentrated in urban sectors and has been a factor in driving up rural-urban income inequality. Many other developing countries face similar disparities in growth across modern and informal sectors and see insufficient generation of new productive employment. These are important reasons why output growth has not led to commensurate poverty reduction.

Figure B:
**Unemployment rates, 2000 and 2006, and labour force growth, 1996-2006**

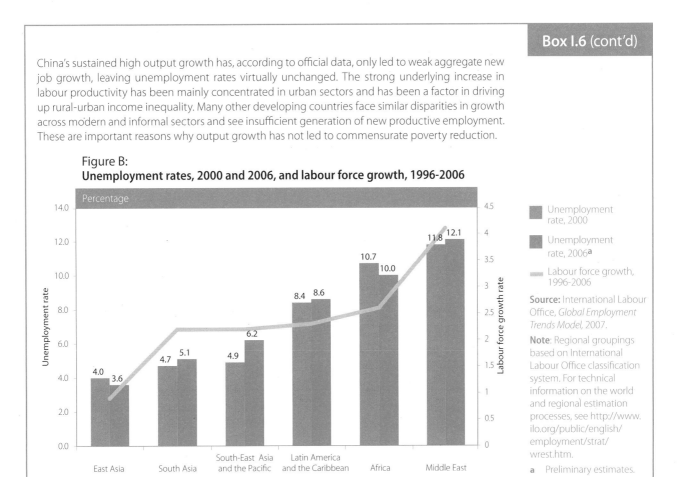

Unemployment rate, 2000

Unemployment rate, 2006[a]

Labour force growth, 1996-2006

**Source:** International Labour Office, *Global Employment Trends Model,* 2007.

**Note**: Regional groupings based on International Labour Office classification system. For technical information on the world and regional estimation processes, see http://www.ilo.org/public/english/employment/strat/wrest.htm.

**a**    Preliminary estimates.

force as the policies of "nationalization" have reached their zenith in most public sectors, which can no longer absorb new labour-market entrants. In the oil-exporting economies of Bahrain, Kuwait, Oman, Qatar, Saudi Arabia and the United Arab Emirates, the majority of the private sector—60 per cent and above—is still composed of expatriate workers.

In *East and South Asia*, only marginal declines in unemployment rates are expected for 2007 and 2008, despite strong economic growth. The unemployment rate in Indonesia will likely remain at a high level amidst the political stalemate of labour-market reform. In China, the structural transition from a State-controlled to a more market-oriented economy has kept registered urban unemployment rates stagnant at around 4 per cent; in Pakistan, unemployment rates declined from 7.7 per cent in 2005 to 6.2 per cent in 2006, and are expected to decline further in 2007. These numbers, however, do not adequately reflect the high informality and low quality of employment opportunities in the region.

Unemployment has decreased to record lows in *Latin America and the Caribbean*, supported by sustained economic growth and a strengthening of the services sector in many countries. The decline over the past four years has brought unemployment rates down to single-digit levels. Notable reductions are observed in Argentina, Chile, Peru, Venezuela (Bolivarian Republic of) and several of the Central American and Caribbean countries. Employment growth is especially strong in the formal sector, where wages have increased only modestly. In the outlook, lower output-growth prospects and structural issues may impede further substantial decreases in unemployment rates.

# Uncertainties and downside risks for the global outlook

The financial turmoil during the third quarter of 2007 has once more signalled downside risks for the global outlook. It revealed that the problems in the United States housing market are closely associated with the problem of global imbalances. It also shows the lack of adequate supervision and regulation of financial markets, which have become increasingly integrated, but also increasingly less transparent. The main risks originate in the United States, where, in particular, a deeper and longer slump in the housing market and a collapse of the value of the United States dollar could trigger a worldwide recession and a disorderly adjustment of global imbalances. These risks are not new and have been anticipated in previous issues of the *World Economic Situation and Prospects*. The recent global financial turmoil has heightened these risks and shown them to be clear and present dangers.

## A deeper and longer housing contraction in the United States

The significant downturn in the housing sector of the United States began in 2006 and accelerated in the course of 2007. The prospects for 2008 remain bleak. In the second half of 2007, new home sales plunged to their lowest level in several years (figure I.4) and existing home sales also dropped to their lowest level in eight years. Homebuilders have been aggressively curtailing construction: during 2007, starts of new houses fell by about 30 per cent from the previous year, that is to say, to their lowest level since 1993, and builder confidence dropped to a two-decade all-time low, as measured by the National Association of Home Builders index. Despite the steep fall in supply, the inventory of unsold homes now stands at a level of more than twice the average of the past few years. While the median prices of new home sales declined significantly from the previous year, those of existing home sales stagnated, putting an end to the period of booming housing prices during 1996-2005.

In the baseline outlook, housing activity in the United States is expected to shrink further, with residential investment declining by another 18 per cent in 2008. House prices are expected to register a decline of about 6 per cent, as measured by the Office of Federal Housing Enterprise Oversight (OFHEO) index. Such a continued housing downturn would likely reduce the growth rate of the United States economy by about one percentage point and have a modest impact on world economic growth. However, risks remain for a much deeper correction of house prices. Real house prices, adjusted by the CPI, rose about 90 per cent in the United States between the nadir of 1996 and the recent peak of 2006, compared with an increase of 10-20 per cent in previous housing cycles. Based on past events, some analysts argue that much steeper declines in real house prices are possible, that is to say, by more than the 15 per cent registered in the previous cycle of 1989-1996 and by as much as 50 per cent in some cities.[3]

A deeper and more protracted housing slump will likely have severe adverse effects on the United States and the global economy, as it may disrupt stability in financial

[3]   See, for example, Robert Shiller, "Understanding recent trends in house prices and home ownership", Cowles Foundation for Research in Economics, Discussion Paper, No. 1630 (New Haven, Connecticut: Yale University, September 2007), available from http://cowles.econ.yale.edu/P/cd/d16a/d1630.pdf.

Figure I.4:
**New home sales in the United States, 2002-2007**[a]

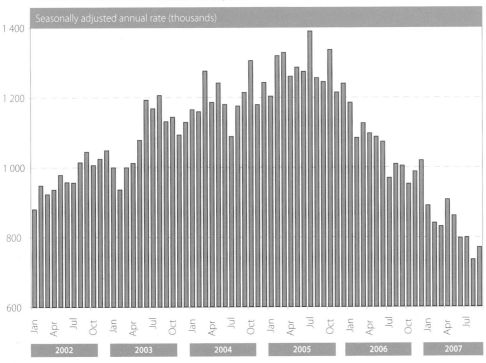

Seasonally adjusted annual rate (thousands)

**Source:** United States
Census Bureau.

a  Until September 2007.

markets and depress household consumption in the United States, which has been an important engine of global growth over the past decade. These factors may well unfold in 2008 because a further fall in housing prices in the United States will likely trigger a drop in household consumption and more defaults in mortgage markets, which could provoke a deeper credit crunch with global consequences. Even though developing countries are currently responsible for almost half of world economic growth,[4] a slowdown in the United States could significantly weaken their current good economic performance and soften prospects of their fully taking over as engines of global growth. To understand this more fully, a closer look at related transmission mechanisms may be helpful.

The impact of the housing downturn on financial markets manifested itself during the summer of 2007, as the debacle in the sub-prime mortgage loan sector triggered a full-blown global financial turmoil. The sub-prime mortgage market serves clients with poor credit histories or insufficient financial resources, who are not qualified for conventional mortgages. When house prices rose, the sub-prime mortgage market expanded rapidly. New sub-prime loans in the United States increased from $120 billion in 2001 to more than $600 billion in 2006. Financial gains on the part of lenders encouraged an excessive easing of underwriting standards. An increasing number of mortgage loans were made with high loan-to-value ratios, poor information about the borrower's financial condition and lax assessments of the value of the home to be financed.

The sub-prime adjustable-rate mortgages (ARMs), typically with an initial two-year introductory interest rate, represent the major concern. Borrowers in this cat-

Problems in United States
sub-prime mortgage
markets pose broader
financial risks

---

4    Using GDP weighted by market exchange rates, developing countries contributed 48.6 per cent of the growth of gross world product, with China alone contributing 17.3 per cent in 2007. When using PPP weights, developing countries contributed almost 70 per cent of global growth, with China accounting for half of that.

egory were counting on rising house prices to refinance their mortgages before the financing cost was reset to a higher rate after the two-year period. When house prices failed to appreciate, both delinquency rates and foreclosures increased sharply.

Although sub-prime mortgages are a relatively small fraction of the total mortgage market (about 20 per cent) and an even smaller fraction of the total credit market, a complex financial system with overstretched leverage, lack of transparency and inadequate regulation served to spread and multiply the risk beyond the sub-prime market. Financial innovations, such as collateralized debt obligations (CDOs), fuelled mortgage lending by securitizing mortgage loans and bundling them with other securities, such as traditional bonds and commercial paper, to sell to investors. The risk of these financial products was often underestimated by both the rating agencies and the investors. When the rate of delinquencies for sub-prime mortgages reached an all-time high of 16 per cent in the summer of 2007, panic among investors and lenders led to an abrupt adjustment in the prices for credit instruments. As a result, liquidity in the credit markets in the United States and a few other major developed countries dried up and spreads widened.

The responses by the central banks of the major economies have helped to calm financial markets, but conditions in mortgage markets remained difficult in late 2007. A large share of sub-prime mortgage loans provided during the period from the end of 2005 through 2006 was subject to lowered underwriting standards. These loans will experience their first interest-rate resets in late 2007 or during 2008. Tightening terms and standards in the mortgage markets, especially the non-prime markets, is therefore likely to intensify the housing downturn in 2008, while further declines in house prices will, in turn, exacerbate the financial predicament of those sub-prime borrowers expected to face a reset to much higher interest rates in 2008. Delinquencies on these mortgages are, therefore, expected to increase further, implying more stress in financial markets at large.

A protracted housing recession should significantly affect the real economy. The direct losses from the decline in housing construction and other related activities, such as mortgage banking and real estate brokerage, were estimated to be about 0.75 of a percentage point of GDP for the United States in 2007. Wealth effects from lower house prices and balance-sheet effects from tightening credit terms on household spending have not visibly affected domestic spending thus far (figure IV.1). This can probably be explained by the fact that the decline in average house prices has been only modest so far and the related loss in household wealth has been offset by the appreciation of other, albeit more volatile, assets such as equities. This has allowed household net worth to increase, but as the degree of household indebtedness has risen steeply in recent years, a plunge in United States stock markets would provoke an even more pronounced surge in the ratio of household debt to net worth and would enhance stress in financial markets (figure I.5).

Once they affect households' net worth, falling house prices should be expected to affect household consumption, even though views differ on the magnitude of the impact. One recent study finds that for each percentage point decline in net household wealth, private consumption would fall somewhere between 0.01 and 0.07 per cent for the OECD countries.[5] In the United States, consumption would fall by 0.03 per cent for each percentage point of net wealth reduction. Some analysts believe, however, that consumer demand responds more acutely to changes in housing wealth than to changes in wealth held as financial assets. One study estimates that for each percentage drop in the value of

More delinquencies on sub-prime mortgages are expected in 2008, implying more stress in financial markets at large

---

5    See Pietro Catte, Nathalie Girouard, Robert Price and Christophe André, "Housing markets, wealth, and the business cycle", OECD Economics Department Working Paper, No. 394 (Paris: Organization for Economic Co-operation and Development, June 2004).

Figure I.5:
**United States household debt and net worth relative to household disposable income, first quarter, 1970-2007**[a]

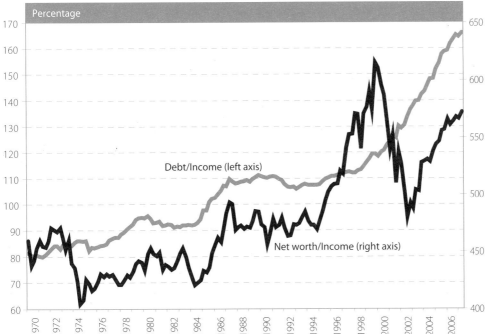

**Source:** Federal Reserve Bank, Flow of Funds, September 2007, tables D.3 and B.100.

a    Until the second quarter of 2007.

homes, consumer spending would fall by between 0.11 and 0.17 per cent, compared with only 0.02 per cent in response to a one per cent decline in financial household wealth.[6] Others, however, believe that the effects of housing prices on consumption are uncertain: higher house prices could even reduce current consumption for those planning to buy a house if they feel they would need to save more for that purpose.[7]

The prevailing view, however, is that house prices do influence consumption, as changes in home equity value influence credit constraints on households for financing consumer spending. During the last housing boom in the United States, mortgage equity withdrawals played an important role in boosting consumption spending, and estimates show they lowered the household saving rate by between 2.5 and 5.0 percentage points.[8] This effect alone was equivalent to a boost in GDP growth of about 0.3 percentage points per year on average during the most recent housing boom, which lasted a decade. The growth impulse was even larger in 2005-2006, when mortgage equity withdrawals surged.

Thus, a protracted deterioration in the United States housing markets will likely lead to a substantial fall in house prices and this could significantly affect growth worldwide. In the pessimistic scenario (see box I.2), an additional 10 per cent drop in house prices would cause a drop in GDP growth of more than 2 percentage points and

A 10 per cent drop in housing prices could bring the United States economy to a standstill

6    Karl E. Case, John M. Quigley and Robert J. Shiller, "Comparing wealth effects: the stock market versus the housing market", Cowles Foundation for Research in Economics Discussion Paper, No. 1335 (New Haven, Connecticut: Yale University, October 2001), available from http://cowles.econ.yale.edu/P/cd/d13a/d1335.pdf.

7    See, for example, Frederic S. Mishkin, "Housing and the monetary transmission mechanism", NBER Working Paper, No. 13518 (Cambridge, Massachusetts: National Bureau of Economic Research, October 2007), available from http://www.nber.org/papers/w13518.pdf.

8    Jan Hatzius, "Housing holds the key to Fed policy", Global Economics Paper, No. 137 (New York: Goldman Sachs, February 2006).

would bring the United States economy to a virtual standstill in 2008. As explained in the box, this would be due not only to negative wealth and income effects slowing United States household consumption, but also to a resultant substantial dollar depreciation which would push up interest rates on dollar-denominated assets.

Other economies are not expected to readily compensate such a slowdown in the United States economy, implying that the effects will be felt worldwide and, according to the pessimistic scenario, world economic growth would slow to 1.6 per cent in 2008, down from 3.4 per cent in the baseline scenario. As discussed, the Japanese and European economies are operating near production potential, and a recession in the United States and further dollar depreciation would significantly lower demand for their exports. Such repercussions will also be felt in developing countries. Despite robust growth and increasing importance in the generation of global welfare, growth cycles in developing countries remain closely correlated with the ups and downs of the United States economy (see appendix 2 to this chapter). Even though developing country growth has been much more solid than in the developed world and domestic growth factors have been important, it is also true that trade has gained ever-greater importance in global economic growth. The share of exports now averages nearly 40 per cent of GDP for all economies outside the United States, and global export growth over the past decade has been fed not inappreciably by excess demand in the United States. A slowdown in the United States would significantly affect Chinese, Japanese and European exports, for instance, and given the importance of demand for raw materials by these economies, would affect prices of primary commodities and, consequently, the economic growth of many primary-exporting developing countries. Stronger stimulus of domestic demand in China could compensate for slower export growth, but to the extent that this is done through a much-needed fiscal impulse addressing deficits in public infrastructure, social security, and education and health services for the rural population, it may not offset the weaker global demand for raw materials associated with manufacturing export production.

It seems premature, therefore, to speak of a decoupling of economic growth in the rest of the world from that of the United States, and the robust growth of developing countries in recent years should not be seen as a sign that they could readily avoid the occurrence of a worldwide recession.

## A hard landing of the dollar?

The housing boom and rising household indebtedness is inextricably linked to the global imbalances that have developed over the past decade: most economies that experienced a substantial appreciation of house prices also experienced widening deficits in their current account, as well as falling saving rates. This suggests that the housing boom in those countries, particularly the United States, was partially and indirectly financed by other countries running surpluses in their current accounts (figure I.6). Now that the housing cycle is on a downturn, the imbalances across countries may also start to reverse. However, the risks of a disorderly unwinding of the global imbalances may have increased due to the sharp downturn of the housing market in the United States, along with the unfolding credit crisis associated with the debacle in the sub-prime mortgage market.

Indeed, current-account imbalances across countries narrowed somewhat in 2007 and are expected to narrow further in 2008 (figure I.7). The deficit of the United States is estimated to be about $770 billion in 2007, a slight reduction from the $810 billion gap of 2006, and is expected to fall further to $720 billion in 2008. Developed

Figure I.6:
**Shift of net household lending to net household borrowing compared to the increase in the United States current-account deficit, 1990 (first quarter)-2007 (second quarter)[a]**

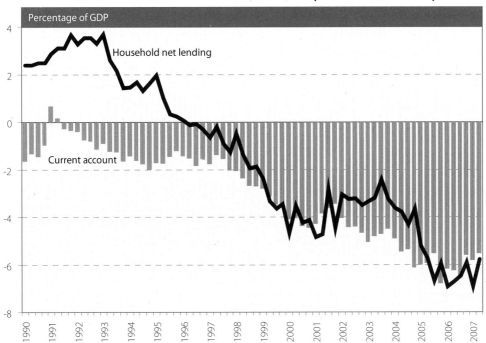

**Source:** Bureau of Economic Analysis, National Income and Production Accounts, September 2007, tables 2.1 and 5.1.

**a**   Until the second quarter of 2007.

Figure I.7:
**Current-account balances, 2003-2008**

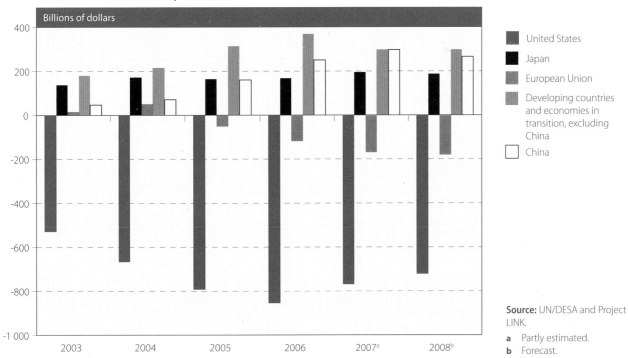

**Source:** UN/DESA and Project LINK.

**a**   Partly estimated.
**b**   Forecast.

economies as a whole registered a current-account deficit of about $600 billion in 2007. That deficit is expected to be of a similar magnitude in 2008. The euro area as a whole has moved from a surplus to a deficit position which is expected to widen further in 2008. Japan is expected to sustain its large surplus.

Most developing regions continue to run savings surpluses, to which developing Asia and oil-exporting developing countries contribute the most. China's external surplus increased further in 2007, to a level of about $300 billion, from $250 billion in 2006. The surplus in the group of oil-exporting countries reached about $500 billion. Latin America and the Caribbean have managed to run a surplus for an unprecedented five consecutive years, although it is now on the decline. Africa as a whole has a more or less balanced current account. The surplus in the CIS has surpassed $100 billion, mainly generated by the Russian Federation. This surplus outweighs the current-account deficits of the transition economies of South-eastern Europe, despite being quite substantial relative to the size of their economies.

The narrowing current-account deficit in the United States during 2007 was mirrored in a decline in the government deficit, which according to data from the Congressional Budget Office (CBO), decreased by about $80 billion during 2007 to a level of $160 billion, owing to increasing tax revenues. The household saving rate continued to be low, at close to zero per cent of disposable income. In the outlook for 2008, the anticipated further improvement in the current-account deficit will reflect a weakening of import demand combined with a comparatively stronger export performance (from the trade perspective) and a weakening in domestic investment and replenishment of household savings (from the perspective of the savings-investment balance).

...but the risks of a disorderly adjustment remain

Despite the projected narrowing of the current-account deficit in the United States, the risks of a disorderly adjustment remain as the indebtedness of the United States continues to deepen. As a result of the chronic current-account deficits over the past decade, the net international investment position of the United States reached over $2.5 trillion by the end of 2006 and is estimated to have been close to $2.8 trillion in 2007. Over several years, appreciation in the value of United States-owned assets abroad and depreciation in the value of United States-based assets have produced favourable valuation effects for the country's net debt position. For example, during 2006 (for which the latest foreign asset position data are available), a deficit in the current account of more than $800 billion was substantially offset by approximately the amount of the valuation adjustment of $350 billion from changes in the prices of assets and in the region of $220 billion from exchange-rate changes. This resulted in an increment of only about $300 billion in the net international investment position of the United States. A depreciation of the dollar seems to be an "effective" approach for the United States to write off its foreign debt position: a privilege associated with being the issuer of the international reserve currency. Nevertheless, these favourable valuation effects are not nearly large enough to outweigh the adverse trend connected with running a large current-account deficit. In the outlook for 2008, the net foreign debt position of the United States will likely exceed $3 trillion, that is to say, about 25 per cent of GDP. Despite the sizeable valuation effects in recent years, unless the current-account deficit is halved from its current level, the net debt position of the United States will continue to rise, making it less and less sustainable.

The growing current-account deficit and perceptions that the United States debt position is approaching unsustainable levels have been important factors underlying the depreciation of the United States dollar since 2002 (figure I.8). Since its peak in 2002, the dollar has depreciated vis-à-vis other major currencies by about 30 per cent, reaching

Figure I.8:
**Exchange-rate index for the United States, 1990-2007**[a]

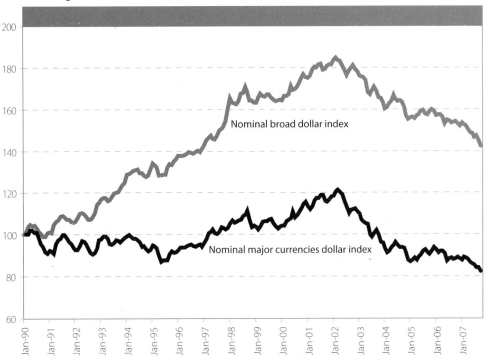

**Source:** United States Federal Reserve Board.
**Note:** The major currencies index contains currencies of most developed countries; the broad index incorporates currencies of emerging economies into the other index. A decline in the index represents a depreciation of the dollar.
**a**  Until October 2007.

the lowest point in more than two decades. The dollar depreciated most against the euro as the euro rose to an all-time high of above $1.48 in the second half of 2007, amidst the sub-prime-related financial turmoil. Among the major currencies, the only exception is the Japanese yen, which weakened against the dollar over the past year, partly because the large differential between the interest rates of the United States and Japan attracted a large amount of carry trades. The dollar also depreciated against most currencies in developing countries: the Chinese renminbi, for instance, appreciated by more than 10 per cent vis-à-vis the dollar since its de-pegging from the dollar in July 2005.

In the outlook for 2008, the dollar is expected to continue the trend of depreciation against most other currencies and to devalue further by about 5 per cent.[9] The risk of a much sharper depreciation of the dollar in association with an adjustment of its large current-account deficit has heightened, however. Since 2002, the trend of dollar depreciation has been interspersed by periodic rebounds as the differentials in the interest rates and GDP growth rates among the major economies have been in its favour, thereby offsetting the depreciation pressures stemming from the concerns surrounding the current-account deficit; but these favourable differentials for the dollar narrowed substantially in 2007 and will continue to do so in 2008.

*The dollar is expected to depreciate by a further 5 per cent in 2008, but the risk of a much sharper fall has increased*

## Policy challenges

A realignment of exchange rates is one of the ingredients needed to adjust the global imbalances. However, the question is not so much whether one should expect a further depreciation of the dollar—that trend will no doubt continue—the greater concern is that

---

9    The expected rate of depreciation compares the average dollar value for 2007 to that expected for 2008.

the adjustment may not be gradual and that the dollar could decline abruptly. A hard landing could have serious consequences. It would likely trigger a disorderly adjustment of the global imbalances and destabilize the global financial system, having strong adverse effects on global economic growth. A steep fall of the dollar would immediately depress United States demand for goods from the rest of the world. A weaker dollar would eventually be expansionary for the United States by boosting its exports, but existing estimates suggest a lag of two or more years before the full effect of depreciation is seen on the exports of the United States. In addition, since many developing countries are holding a large amount of foreign reserves in dollar-denominated assets, a sharp depreciation of the dollar would entail substantial financial losses for these countries.[10]

## Macroeconomic policy stance

The monetary policy stance has eased in several of the major developed economies

In response to the global financial turmoil in the third quarter of 2007, monetary authorities in the major developed economies altered their *monetary policy* stance somewhat. This led to monetary easing in the United States and held back the anticipated tightening in some other economies. The United States Fed reduced the federal funds rate and is expected to maintain it at 4.0 per cent during 2008. Should the financial markets deteriorate further and the growth prospects worsen, more monetary easing would be needed. The European Central Bank (ECB) raised its main policy interest rate during 2007. Policy is currently close to a neutral stance, with real short-term interest rates at about 2 per cent. The ECB is expected to maintain its current policy stance throughout 2008, while monetary policy in the United Kingdom is expected to ease slightly in the outlook. In contrast, monetary policy is expected to tighten in Japan. Inflation continues to hover around zero, but the risk of slipping back into deflation is small given the expectation of a continued recovery. However, the Bank of Japan is likely to be very cautious in implementing its desired policy of gradually bringing its policy rate to a more neutral stance. The policy rate is expected to increase to 0.75 per cent in 2008.

*Fiscal policy* is expected to be modestly stimulatory in the United States; more or less neutral to the business cycle of the European countries as a group, albeit with differences across countries; and contractionary in Japan. As mentioned, the fiscal position in the United States benefited from robust revenues during 2007. Real government expenditure grew below the pace of GDP growth for about two years, but increased during the second half of 2007 and is expected to rise further during 2008. In Western Europe, fiscal balances improved significantly across the region in 2007, stemming from both growth performance and revenue windfalls, along with expenditure cuts in some countries. In the euro area, fiscal policy was moderately contractionary in those countries with excessive deficits in line with the Stability and Growth Pact (SGP), while other countries pursued either neutral or expansionary policies. Japan, in contrast, is engaging in fiscal consolidation in order to reduce its high levels of public indebtedness.

Present macroeconomic policy stances are not conducive to an adjustment of the global imbalances

On balance, therefore, we see both monetary and fiscal easing in the main deficit economy, the United States, and a tightening in one of the major surplus economies, Japan. Europe's macroeconomic policy stance is more or less neutral to the present business cycle. As it stands, macroeconomic policies in the major developed economies are clearly not geared to reducing the global imbalances. The macroeconomic policy stimulus

---

10    For a detailed discussion on the effectiveness of currency realignment on the adjustment of external imbalances, see *World Economic Situation and Prospects 2004* (United Nations publication, Sales No. E.04.II.C.2).

in the United States may not be strong enough to avoid a visible slowing of its economy either, as can be seen in the baseline forecast.

Among the major (surplus) economies of the developing world, China tightened its monetary policy whilst mildly easing its fiscal stance. On balance, its policies are to cool the economy somewhat. India tightened monetary policies to address inflationary pressures. In addition, the Russian Federation and other surplus countries among the economies in transition have tightened their monetary policy stance to reduce inflationary pressures, leaving more flexibility for exchange-rate adjustment. Fiscal policies are slightly expansionary, however. Most major oil-exporters in Western Asia peg their currencies to the United States, and their monetary policies, which closely follow those of the Fed, remain accommodative. In Latin America, Brazil continued to cut policy interest rates during 2007, as inflation stayed below target, while Mexico tightened monetary policies under inflationary pressures. On the whole, monetary and fiscal policies vary greatly among the principal surplus economies in the developing world. They are possibly mildly expansionary on balance, but certainly not designed to provide the strong stimulus to domestic demand needed to ease global imbalances and counteract deflationary tendencies in the United States economy.

## Policies to prevent a disorderly unwinding of global imbalances

Policymakers in developed and developing countries are faced with the challenge of how to avoid a global recession and safeguard robust economic development amidst risks of further financial turmoil and a weakening dollar. For developing countries, maintaining strong economic growth, while not a sufficient condition, is essential to supporting their endeavours and generating the necessary resources to achieve the Millennium Development Goals. For the advanced countries, too, continued expansion of economic activity is essential to tackling long-term challenges such as those posed by population ageing.[11] A continued strong growth of the global economy could have a critical downside, however, as at current intensities of energy use and greenhouse gas emissions, it would enhance global warming and heighten the threat of climate change in decades to come (see table A.22).[12] This poses a different challenge, namely that of changing the growth path to substantially reduce emissions and also enable countries to adapt to the consequences of the climate changes already in progress. Achieving a sustainable development path for the global economy could, nonetheless, require continued growth in order to generate the nec-

*Policymakers face the challenge of safeguarding robust and sustainable global growth amidst risks of further financial turmoil*

---

11    See, for instance, *World Economic and Social Survey 2007: Development in an Ageing World* (United Nations publication, Sales No. E.07.II.C.1).

12    The United Nations Framework Convention on Climate Change set the goal of stabilizing greenhouse gas (GHG) concentrations to allow development to proceed in a sustainable manner. The 1997 Kyoto Protocol followed up on this goal and focused on the reduction of GHG emissions by the developed countries (the so-called Annex I Parties). The Protocol set a target for these countries to reduce their emissions by 5.2 per cent (relative to the level in 1990) over the period from 1997 to 2008-2012. Estimates in table A.22 indicate that by 2008 total emissions by the Annex I Parties will have decreased by a mere 1.2 per cent from their 1990 levels, and also that between 2000 and 2008 total GHG emissions by these countries will have increased by 3.4 per cent. The robust economic growth of recent years thus seems to have made reaching even the modest target of the Kyoto Protocol a bigger challenge. Clearly, insufficient efforts have been made to improve energy efficiency and reduce the carbon intensity of production in order to "decouple" trends in economic growth and carbon emissions and reach a stabilization of GHG concentration that indeed avoids the threat to mankind posed by climate change.

essary resources that will be needed to make substantial investments in new technologies and economic restructuring for the mitigation of and adaptation to climate change.

A disorderly unwinding of the global imbalances would almost certainly jeopardize efforts towards these longer-term goals. The present financial stress and uncertainties surrounding further dollar depreciation limit policy choices for individual Governments. These choices are likely to remain limited in the absence of multilaterally concerted collective action in a number of areas.

### *Coordinated policy action is urgently needed to redress the global imbalances*

More global demand stimulus will be needed to prevent the slowdown in the United States economy from slipping into a recession and spilling over to the rest of the world. Current and prospective policy stances in the major economies for the short run could contain, but not stop, the prospect of a slowdown of the world economy, as indicated above and as shown in the baseline forecast. Moreover, below-trend growth in the United States would justify further interest rate cuts to stimulate the economy, but in the current context these could precipitate a further depreciation of and erosion of confidence in the dollar, as impetus to domestic demand growth would induce a further widening of the current-account deficit. Global rebalancing would require that demand stimulus come from other parts of the world. In China, the appreciation of the renminbi by about 6 per cent and the flexibilization of the exchange-rate band did not prevent the widening of the country's external surplus during 2007. A more structural rebalancing of aggregate demand would be needed to reduce the economy's surplus and help the United States lower its deficit. This could be achieved through further fiscal stimulus, as indicated, by stepping up public investment efforts, expanding social security, and improving health and education services, especially those geared towards the rural population, thus creating a broader base for consumption growth.[13] In the major oil-exporting countries, there is ample room for undertaking much-needed domestic investment plans. In Europe and Japan, continued low inflationary pressures would justify putting an end to monetary tightening and would preserve at least a neutral to moderately stimulatory stance. However, since these economies currently seem to be operating near production potential, as indicated above, their contribution to global demand reflation will be limited in the immediate short run. Hence, it will be essential for these economies to accelerate implementation of their structural reform policies to raise productivity and production capacity.

In this vein, in mid-2006, the International Monetary Fund (IMF) initiated multilateral consultations to deal with the global imbalances through concerted policy actions. These consultations have thus far involved the United States, Japan, the euro area, China and Saudi Arabia, these being major stakeholders in much of the existing imbalances and representing a large share of global output. Participants in this dialogue seem to be in agreement that addressing the global imbalances without jeopardizing sustained growth requires concerted action. Consultations have led each of them to publish policy plans which are partially moving in the specified directions; the problems, however, lie in their implementation. The IMF has been following up with bilateral discussions, but these have

---

13    For a more elaborate discussion of China's role in global rebalancing, see Rob Vos and Pingfan Hong, "Towards a coordinated response to adjust the global imbalances and China's role", paper presented at the Project LINK Spring 2007 Meeting in Beijing, China, 14-17 May 2007, available from http://www.chass.utoronto.ca/link/meeting/materials/rv_ph_200705.pdf.

not led to participants' complying with the commitments made. As argued in previous issues of this report,[14] policies need to be agreed under an effective multilateral consultation process of policy coordination. To this end, it is important that there be broad participation, involving more parties, particularly developing countries, than those involved in the current consultations. For such multilateral consultations to work, the perceived legitimacy of the mediator (that is to say, the IMF) needs to be enhanced and any doubts that may exist about its impartiality in the process need to be removed. This requires a reform of the voting power and governance structure of the IMF in favour of a better representation of developing countries. Reform proposals are still under discussion among the IMF member States, but agreement is not yet within reach (see discussion in chapter III).

It will, moreover, be important to find appropriate and effective ways of monitoring the implementation efforts of the participants to enhance the probability of their compliance with agreed concerted action. One possible means, as proposed in the *World Economic Situation and Prospects 2007*, would be to have parties issue multi-year schedules for the agreed policy adjustments and targets. Announcing specific targets in the form of a schedule and subsequent failure to meet them would have costs in terms of reputation.

These conditions are currently not in place, and this reduces the likelihood of swift and effective concerted action. It must be hoped that parties, alerted by the recent financial turmoil, come to see the urgency of addressing the problem of the global imbalances, and initiate actions before the world economy moves into recession and the dollar takes a deep dive.

### *Realignment of exchange rates and reform of the reserve system*

A multilateral agreement to reduce the global imbalances should naturally also include a realignment of exchange rates but at the same time must ensure that it takes place in an orderly fashion. Thus far, the process of dollar depreciation has been strong but orderly. Dollar depreciation by itself will not resolve the global imbalances. In fact, the dollar has depreciated against other major currencies since 2002 without preventing a further widening of the United States current-account deficit. Hence, for a macroeconomic rebalancing to take place, a realignment of exchange rates will need to be aided by monetary and fiscal policies that stimulate demand in the surplus countries and limit demand in the deficit countries. This will also be needed to avoid a possible steep and abrupt decline of the dollar, which could be provoked by a further widening of global imbalances. The reason for this lies in the nature of the global reserve system, which uses the national currency of the United States as the main reserve currency and instrument for international payments. Under this system, the only way for the rest of the world to accumulate dollar assets and reserves is for the United States to run a current-account deficit. From the 1990s to date, the widening of the United States deficit has served developing countries in particular in meeting their demand for "self-insurance" against external shocks by accumulating vast amounts of dollar-denominated official reserves. In addition, the deep financial markets of the United States and the perception of United States Treasury bills as one of the safest assets in the world have provided a destination for investing the savings from export surpluses from these countries in dollar-denominated reserve assets. However, as the net liability position of the United States continues to increase, investors will start to expect a readjustment, and confidence in the dollar will erode. This will become exacerbated as the

---

14    See, in particular, *World Economic Situation and Prospects 2007* (United Nations publication, Sales No. E.07.II.C2), pp. 29-34.

perception increases that monetary easing is stimulating further dollar depreciation, which while reducing the United States external liability position, will provoke losses to those holding dollar-denominated assets. The situation gets further complicated as financial assets are no longer seen as "safe" because of financial stress and uncertainty. The recent financial turmoil and dollar depreciation could well be symptoms of being on the verge of a significant loss of confidence in the dollar as the world's reserve currency. Official agents have thus far not responded by a significant diversification out of the dollar (see box I.5), but amidst the financial turmoil, many private-sector agents have shifted interests to equity investments in emerging market economies, though much of these remain denominated in dollars. Clearly, though, a turning point may be nearing at which official agents will start to feel that the benefits of holding massive dollar-denominated reserves are outweighed by the costs. An abrupt diversification to other currencies could shock market perceptions and cause a run on the dollar, with probable strongly destabilizing consequences. A gradual adjustment in the context of a multilateral agreement on a broader set of coordinated policies to reduce the global imbalances is a much preferred option, although time to act seems to be running out.

Over time, more fundamental reforms of the current international reserve system will be needed to prevent the current constellation of imbalances from emerging again. A more immediate reform would be to promote an officially backed multi-currency reserve system. A well-designed multilateral financial system should create equal conditions for all parties and avoid unfair competition and an asymmetric burden-sharing of exchange-rate adjustments. It should also help to increase stability in the international financial system by reducing the likelihood of a crisis scenario in which capital flight out of the major single reserve currency would cause potentially far-reaching repercussions throughout the global economy.

### Strengthening financial regulation and financial safety nets

Lessons need to be learned from the recent financial turmoil to reduce vulnerabilities to future financial stress. Responses by the central banks of the major economies have focused on liquidity injections to restore financial market confidence and avoid a credit crunch. These measures have had some temporary effect, but have also raised questions regarding the quality of financial regulation and financial safety nets, both nationally and internationally.

The problems in the mortgage markets have pointed to the need for greater transparency related to risks in the financial sector, including off-balance-sheet exposures and those in derivatives markets (see also chapter III). Next to transparency in exposures, credit-rating mechanisms need to be closely scrutinized, and stronger rulings may be required to ensure that loan originators have the right incentives to carefully assess the solvency of debtors. Such a revision of prudential regulation should seek ways to eliminate incentives that lead to pro-cyclical lending behaviour based on assessments by rating agencies of both corporate and sovereign risks that tend not to adjust ratings during the build-up of risky exposures, but rather only after the risks have materialized. Some countries may also need strengthened counter-cyclical capital provisioning standards and more transparent mechanisms to resolve banks' failures to ensure that irresponsible risk-taking by financial institutions is disciplined.

Furthermore, the current effort to restore multilateral arrangements for adequate liquidity provisioning has to be completed. While the strong build-up of reserves provides countries with a substantial degree of "self-insurance" against external shocks in the event of a hard landing of the dollar, this self-insurance could quickly evaporate. The establishment in 1997 of the Supplemental Reserve Facility provides some collective insurance to countries hit by capital-account crises, but the Facility does not provide enough protection in the case of a typical sudden reversal in capital flows. The Contingent Credit Line was unused and expired in 2003, and little has been done to revitalize the Compensatory Financing Facility, which provided liquidity to developing countries to manage terms-of-trade shocks. The IMF has proposed a Reserve Augmentation Line to be established as part of the Supplemental Reserve Facility to provide emergency liquidity to members who have strong macroeconomic policies, a sustainable debt situation and proven credibility in policy implementation, but who are still faced with vulnerabilities to capital-account crises. Potential users among the emerging market economies have raised questions, however, about the criteria for eligibility, the size of the facility and whether the current design would result in additional conditionality.[15]

To overcome the potential stigma associated with the facility, there is a need to enhance the reliability of access to financial resources and reinforce positive signalling to markets. A significant number of emerging market members should qualify, based on the information available from past IMF Article IV consultation reports. Allowing automatic front-loaded drawing of up to 500 per cent of quota, based on simple and transparent guidelines, for eligible members would send a clear signal to private markets that the line is an insurance facility. If such a mechanism could emulate the lender-of-last-resort functions of central banks, it could reduce the demand for high reserve build-up in developing countries. As much as it would help to unwind the global imbalances, this in turn could create more policy space in developing countries by offloading pressures towards exchange-rate appreciation.

---

[15]   Report of the Secretary-General of United Nations on the international financial system and development, 6 July 2007 (A/62/119, p. 11).

# Appendices

## Appendix 1:
## Evaluation of the performance of the
## United Nations forecasting of the world economy

The United Nations Secretariat has published forecasts for the world economy every year since the early 1970s, based on the global model framework and expert opinions of Project LINK.[a] In order to assess the degree of accuracy of the forecasts for the growth rates of gross domestic product (GDP), these rates may be compared by main country groupings for year **t**, made at the beginning of the year (one-year-ahead forecasting) with observed economic growth based on officially released data by year **t+2**.

Forecasts, observed data and errors with regard to GDP growth of the world economy, developed economies and developing countries are shown in figures A-C below, respectively. The table below summarizes the key descriptive statistics of the forecasting errors.

**Key statistics for the forecasting errors**

|  | World | Developed economies | Developing countries |
| --- | --- | --- | --- |
| Mean | 0.02 | 0.04 | -0.36 |
| Median | 0.05 | 0.05 | -0.10 |
| Standard deviation | 0.70 | 0.76 | 1.25 |
| Fraction of positive errors | 0.52 | 0.50 | 0.42 |
| Serial correlation | -0.20 | -0.10 | 0.29 |

**Source:** UN/DESA.

After analysing the data, no systematic bias is found in the forecasts for the growth rates for any of these three country groups.[b] In other words, the forecasts have been neither too optimistic nor too pessimistic in any systematic way. Also, the forecasts are generally found to have been efficient in terms of making adequate use of the information available at the time the forecasts were produced.[c]

Furthermore, forecasting errors are not found to be significantly different across the sub-samples of each of the three decades (1972-1983, 1984-1994 and 1995-2005) as measured in terms of the means and the standard deviations of the errors. This finding suggests that the global model framework and expert opinion of Project LINK has successfully adapted to the structural changes that have taken place in the world economy over the past three decades. It should be noted, however, that for some years rather large differences between the forecast and observed GDP growth can be observed, especially for

[a] The forecasts were published in part one of the *World Economic and Social Survey* before 2000 and have since been published in the *World Economic Situation and Prospects*.

[b] It may be concluded that the means and the medians of the errors are not statistically significant from zero. For a technical discussion of the methodology, see, for example, Alberto Musso and Steven Phillips, "Comparing projections and outcomes of IMF-supported programmes", *IMF Staff Papers*, vol. 49, No. 1, April 2002.

[c] This can be concluded by the absence of any significant first-order serial correlation in the forecasting errors of GDP growth for any of the country groups.

2001 when the deceleration of world GDP growth caused by the bursting of the investment bubbles associated with information and communication technologies (ICT) stocks was not foreseen in the forecast. More generally, the timing of major financial shocks and the consequences for the real economy are difficult to predict.

The figures also make clear that the forecasting errors for GDP growth in developing countries tend to be larger than those for the group of developed countries, with the standard deviation of the errors for the former almost twice as large as that of the latter. One obvious reason for the lower degree of accuracy of the forecast for developing countries is the lower quality of available economic data for these countries. Another reason is that many developing countries generally experience greater volatility in GDP growth and that the impact of financial and other external crises tends to hit those economies harder. The forecasts for developing countries during the debt crisis in Latin America in the early 1980s and the Asian financial crisis in the late 1990s, for instance, clearly show much larger errors than in episodes where no such major international crisis took place. As indicated in figure C, the United Nations forecast for developing countries either underestimated or missed the adverse impact of these crises on GDP growth of these economies.

Forecasting errors thus tend to be larger for periods of adverse shocks and sudden downswings of the world economy. As stated, such shocks are difficult to predict in general, and the macroeconometric models used to produce the United Nations forecasts are also not well suited to predicting the timing and severity of financial and trade shocks. However, once a financial crisis has occurred, these models seem to perform relatively well in forecasting output growth in its aftermath by incorporating the observed shocks, as well as the policy responses.

Meanwhile, analysis also indicates that the conditional (model-based) United Nations forecasts are always superior to forecasts generated by a random-walk process.[d]

In addition, after considering more sophisticated evaluation techniques, it can be concluded that the United Nations forecasts are generally unbiased and fairly efficient, despite their weakness in predicting the impact of particular shocks to commodity or financial markets for developing countries.

---

[d]   This may be concluded after studying the values for the means and standard deviations of forecasting errors using the LINK global model and the random-walk estimates. The errors are consistently smaller when using the global model. For instance, the mean value of the forecasting errors for world GDP growth from the United Nations forecasts is about 0.5 in comparison with the mean of 1.3 from the random-walk forecast, and the standard deviation is about 0.7 in comparison with 1.7.

Figure A:
**Errors in United Nations forecasts of growth of world gross product, 1972-2006**

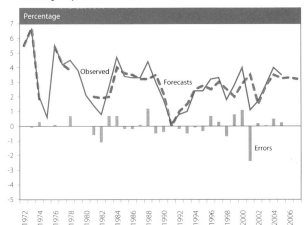

Figure B:
**Errors in United Nations forecasts of GDP growth of developed countries, 1972-2006**

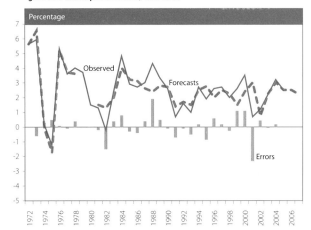

Figure C:
**Errors in United Nations forecasts of GDP growth of developing countries, 1972-2006**

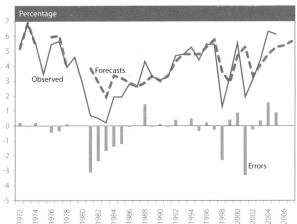

**Source**: UN/DESA.

## Appendix 2:
## Decoupling from the United States?

Will a slowdown of the United States economy equally affect economies in the rest of the world? Historically, global downward movements have occurred in tandem with recessions and slowdowns in the United States (see figure A below). Some observers have argued that in recent years the rest of the world has become less dependent on the business cycles in the United States. For a number of years now, economic growth in many developing countries and economies in transition has been higher than that of the United States and developed countries in general. This suggests the existence of strong domestic sources of growth and could be a sign of a "decoupling" of the business cycles. Further globalization has extended trade and financial networks and has added complexity to the world economy. In such a world, it would seem less likely than before that a single economy would sustain a predominant influence on business cycles in the rest of the world. For instance, more integrated financial markets would allow countries to find the necessary financing to easily absorb a trade shock emanating from a slowdown in the United States. Also, increasing South-South trade and investment flows strengthen economic ties among developing countries, reducing reliance on United States markets.

While these factors no doubt are at play, it may be too early to speak of a "decoupling" and to expect that the envisaged slowing of the United States economy will not affect developing country growth to any significant degree. Figure A shows, for instance, that although solid economic growth was recorded in the rest of the world over recent years, the fluctuations in the growth rate have continued to move hand in hand with those of the United States. As figures B.1-3 below show, in almost all instances a recession in the United States coincides with significant slowdowns in other economies, even though growth in those other economies was well above that in the United States at the onset of the slowdown.

Deeper trade and financial linkages could explain why international transmission of economic cycles in the major economies to developing regions remains strong despite strengthened domestic sources of growth. The volume of world exports has grown at an average rate of 7.6 per cent per annum since the last United States recession (2002-2006).This is more than twice the rate of global economic growth, which stood at 3.2 per cent per annum (see chapter II). Consequently, the share of exports in global GDP has increased steeply, as shown in figure C below. Indicators of trade and financial linkages further show that the United States remains the principal economic partner and is influential in the business cycle of all other major countries or regions. Such ties with the United States appear stronger at present than before, perhaps with the exception of East Asia. In the case of that subregion it holds, however, that strengthened trade and financial linkages are maintained in particular with countries and regions which in turn have strengthened ties with the United States economy.

Over the past decade, export-led growth in much of the developing world has been part of a pattern of widening global imbalances and has been fed by strong credit-driven demand in the United States. This pattern has also allowed developing countries to accumulate massive foreign reserve holdings held in dollar-denominated assets, which has helped sustain the growing external deficits in the United States. An unwinding of the global imbalances, for instance through weaker domestic demand in the United States and a strongly depreciating dollar, therefore, would have a direct impact on the growth prospects in the developing world.

Figure A:
**Growth cycles of the United States and the rest of the world, 1970-2007**[a]

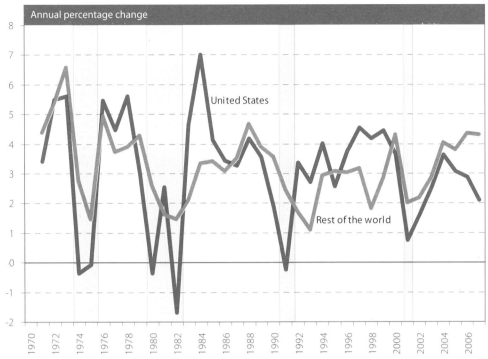

**Sources:** UN/DESA Statistics Division National Accounts data and Project LINK.
**Note**: Shaded areas represent recession periods in the United States.
**a** Partly estimated for 2007.

Figure B1:
**Growth cycle and growth differential of the United States and other developed countries, 1970-2004**

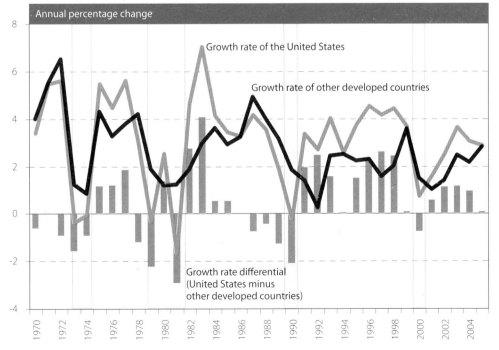

**Sources:** UN/DESA Statistics Division National Accounts data and Project LINK.
**Note**: Shaded areas represent recession periods in the United States.

Figure B2:
**Growth cycle and growth differential of the United States and East Asia, 1970-2004**

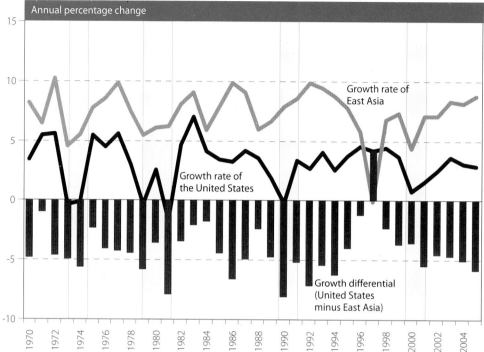

**Sources:** UN/DESA Statistics
Division National Accounts
data and Project LINK.
**Note:** Shaded areas represent
recession periods in the
United States.

Figure B3:
**Growth cycle and growth differential of the United States
and other developing regions, 1970-2004**

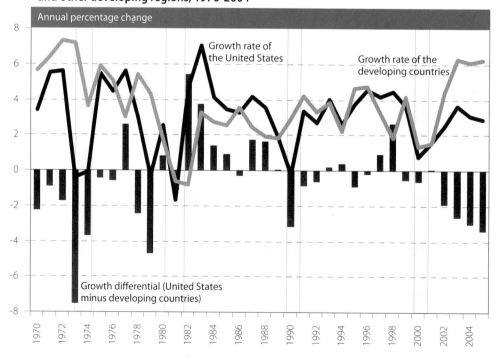

**Sources:** UN/DESA Statistics
Division National Accounts
data and Project LINK.
**Note:** Shaded areas represent
recession periods in the
United States.

Figure C:
**Growth cycles and ratio of world trade to income, 1970 - 2007**[a]

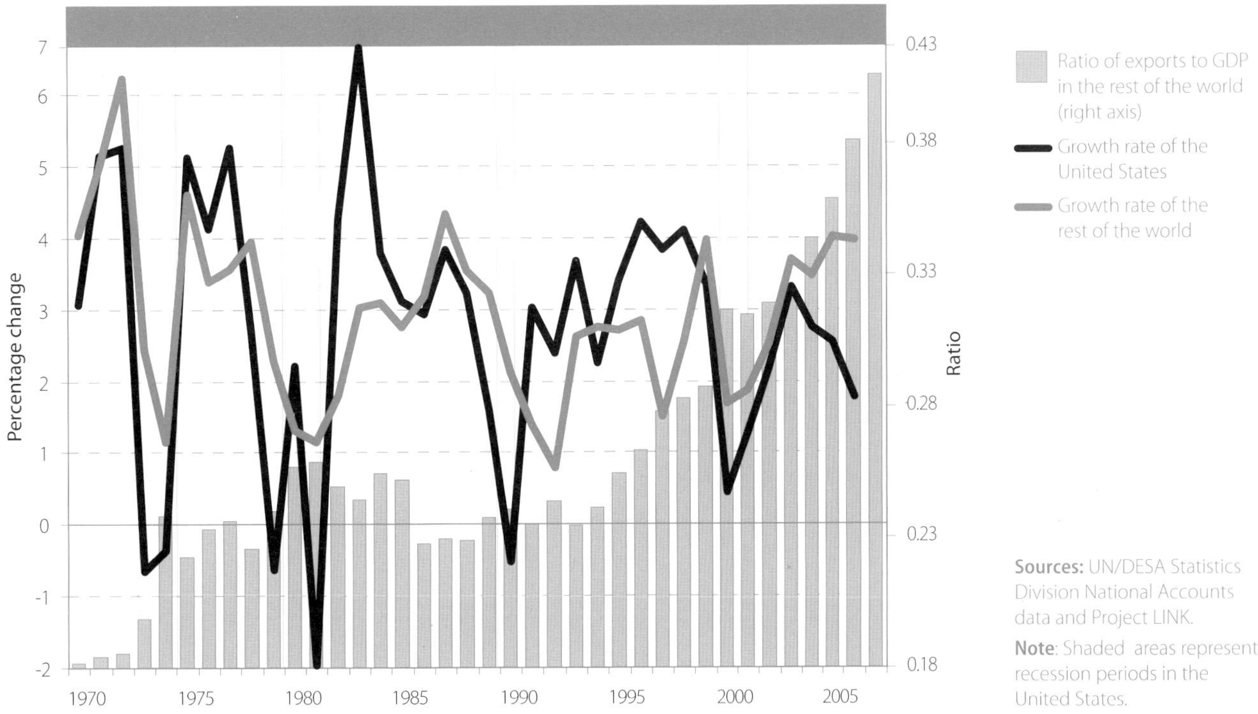

Ratio of exports to GDP in the rest of the world (right axis)

Growth rate of the United States

Growth rate of the rest of the world

**Sources:** UN/DESA Statistics Division National Accounts data and Project LINK.

**Note:** Shaded areas represent recession periods in the United States.

# Chapter II
# International trade

## Trade flows

### Merchandise trade: trade growth continues to grow twice as fast as output growth

Merchandise trade continues to be a driving force of the world economy. Both in volume and in dollar value terms, world merchandise trade has grown twice as fast as world output over the past four years. During 2007, world trade seems to have lost some of its strength, however, particularly for developed economies (see table II.1).

During the upward cycle that started in 2001, merchandise trade growth has been driven by the developed countries and East and South Asia, led by China (figure II.1). In 2007, world merchandise trade grew by 7 per cent, with developing Asia contributing about 40 per cent to the trade expansion. Developed countries have contributed about 45 per cent of the growth in 2007 and about half of the trade expansion since 2001. Other developing countries have contributed about 14–15 per cent to the growth of world merchan-

Developing Asia has been a main contributor to world trade growth…

Table II. 1:
**Selected growth rates of trade and output, 2001-2008**

| Percentage | | | | | | | | | |
|---|---|---|---|---|---|---|---|---|---|
| | | | | | | | | | Average |
| | 2001 | 2002 | 2003 | 2004 | 2005 | 2006 | 2007[a] | 2008[b] | 2004-2007 |
| **World** | | | | | | | | | |
| Export volume | -1.1 | 4.4 | 5.8 | 10.7 | 7.0 | 9.9 | 7.2 | 7.1 | 8.7 |
| Real output growth | 1.6 | 1.9 | 2.7 | 4.0 | 3.4 | 3.9 | 3.7 | .. | 3.8 |
| Export value | -3.9 | 4.8 | 16.2 | 21.2 | 14.4 | 15.7 | 15.5 | 12.4 | 16.7 |
| Value output growth | -0.2 | 3.9 | 12.3 | 12.3 | 7.8 | 6.9 | 7.2 | .. | 8.6 |
| **Developed economies** | | | | | | | | | |
| Export volume | -0.9 | 2.2 | 2.5 | 8.3 | 5.3 | 9.5 | 5.8 | 6.1 | 7.2 |
| Import volume | -0.6 | 2.5 | 4.6 | 9.3 | 6.3 | 7.8 | 4.7 | 5.7 | 7.0 |
| **Economies in transition** | | | | | | | | | |
| Export volume | 3.8 | 7.9 | 13.4 | 15.4 | 3.9 | 6.3 | 6.6 | 5.3 | 7.1 |
| Import volume | 14.0 | 11.7 | 15.9 | 19.6 | 8.2 | 20.4 | 21.9 | 15.0 | 17.5 |
| **Developing economies** | | | | | | | | | |
| Export volume | -1.9 | 8.5 | 11.3 | 14.5 | 10.3 | 10.9 | 9.4 | 8.7 | 11.3 |
| Import volume | -0.9 | 7.5 | 10.6 | 14.1 | 9.3 | 11.5 | 10.4 | 9.5 | 11.3 |
| **East and South Asia** | | | | | | | | | |
| Export volume | -3.5 | 11.8 | 14.0 | 17.6 | 12.0 | 13.0 | 12.0 | 10.5 | 13.7 |
| Import volume | -2.4 | 12.1 | 12.6 | 15 | 9.5 | 11.1 | 11.4 | 10.2 | 11.8 |

Sources: UN/DESA and Project Link.

**a** Partly estimated.
**b** Forecasts.

Figure II.1:
**Growth of world merchandise trade and contributions by region, 2001-2008**

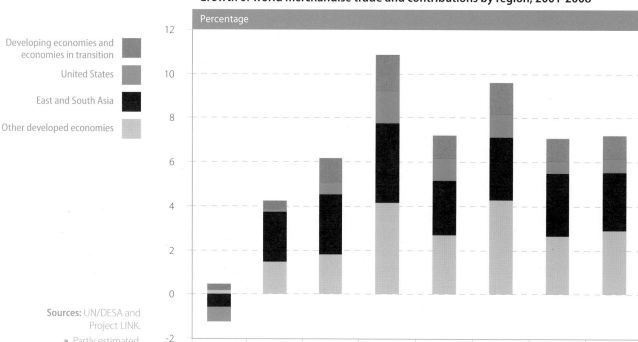

Developing economies and
economies in transition

United States

East and South Asia

Other developed economies

**Sources:** UN/DESA and
Project LINK.
**a** Partly estimated.
**b** Forecast.

... responding to the
strong pace of domestic
demand in developed
countries

Exporters of raw materials
and energy benefited also

Will trade continue its
buoyant pattern in
the coming years?

dise trade. The estimates and forecasts for 2007 and 2008 are marking the decline of the cycle, with trade growth for all regions below the recent record levels of 2004 and 2006.

World trade dynamics are strongly correlated with the evolution of domestic demand in the developed world, with consumption growth in the United States of America having been the main driver during the last decade. Figure II.2 shows that growth of domestic demand in the United States and that of other developed economies have moved in tandem with the growth of exports of manufactures from developing countries. The exception to this pattern was in 1998, which saw a steep fall in manufacturing exports from developing countries in the aftermath of the Asian crisis and the generalized decline in economic activity in many Asian countries.

Similarly, exports of energy and raw materials by developing countries have closely followed the cycles of domestic demand in the developed countries that have been supported by manufacturing exports from the developing regions (figure II.3).

Will this apparent virtuous cycle of strong demand in the developed world, industrial export-led growth in developing Asia and vigorous demand for raw materials and energy from many other developing countries be sustained in the coming years? This pattern of buoyant world trade has lasted for more than a decade now. It is also clearly part of the global imbalances that have developed over this period. Not surprisingly, therefore, the growth of world merchandise exports is closely associated with the business cycle of the major deficit economy, the United States (figure II.4). A strong slowdown in the United States economy, as in the pessimistic scenario analysed in chapter I, should therefore be expected to have a significant adverse effect on world trade. Under such circumstances, and if no stimulus to demand is given in other parts of the world as discussed in chapter I, the unravelling of the global imbalances will take place in the context of much less vibrant global trade, making the adjustment all the more painful.

Figure II.2:
**Domestic demand in the developed world and manufacturing exports from developing regions, 1990-2006**

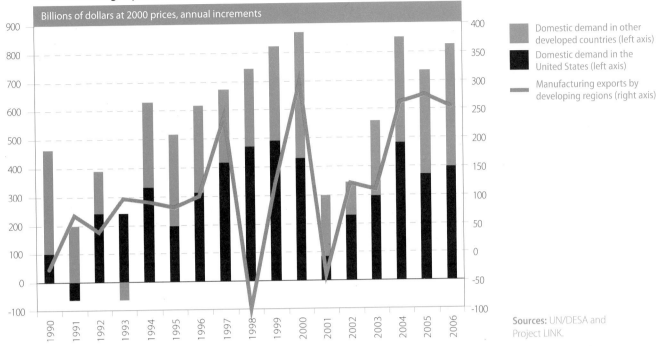

Billions of dollars at 2000 prices, annual increments

Domestic demand in other developed countries (left axis)

Domestic demand in the United States (left axis)

Manufacturing exports by developing regions (right axis)

**Sources:** UN/DESA and Project LINK.

Figure II.3:
**Export cycles in the developing world: Trade figures deflated by world price of manufactures, 1990-2006**

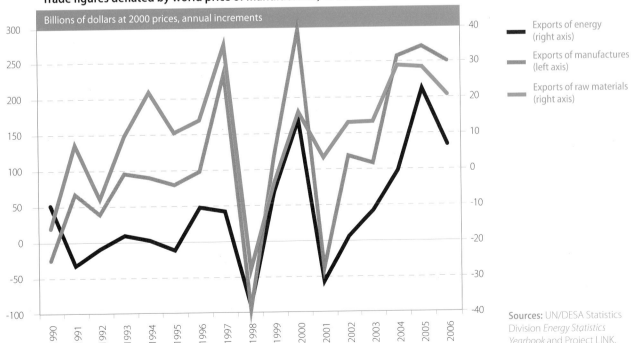

Billions of dollars at 2000 prices, annual increments

Exports of energy (right axis)

Exports of manufactures (left axis)

Exports of raw materials (right axis)

**Sources:** UN/DESA Statistics Division *Energy Statistics Yearbook* and Project LINK.

Figure II.4:
**Changes of income in the United States and world exports, 1970-2006**

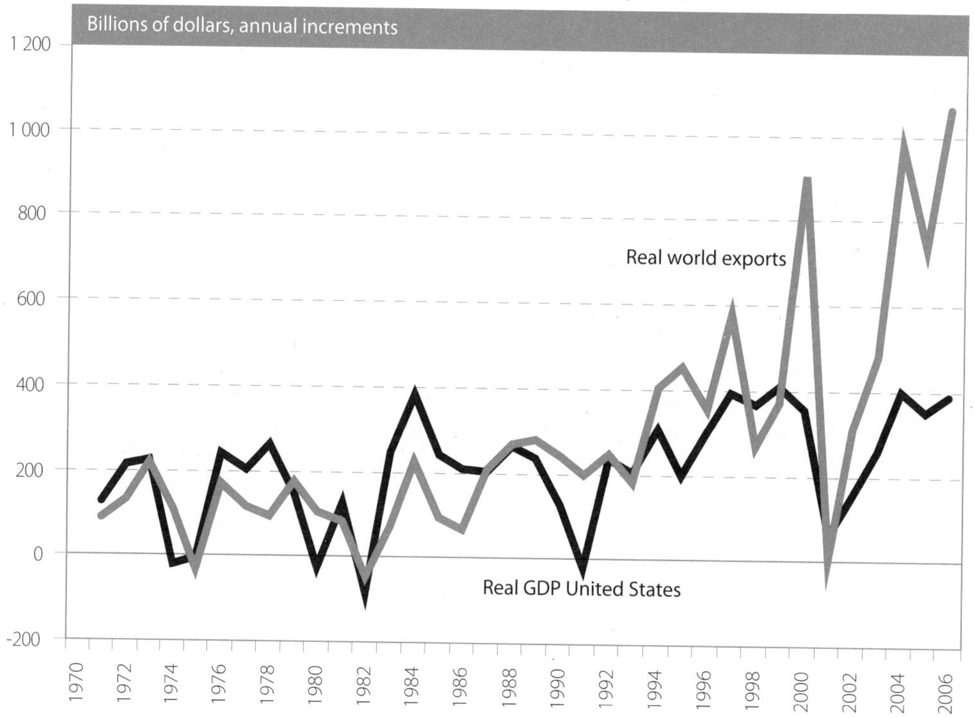

Billions of dollars, annual increments

Real world exports

Real GDP United States

Sources: UN/DESA and Project LINK.

The weakening of world trade stems from weaker demand in developed countries

Import growth moderated in regions with appreciating currencies and large-scale investment projects

In the baseline scenario, however, global demand still remains robust, but world trade is weakening on the heels of slower growth in the United States. The implications for economic growth will differ across regions.

A significant weakening of import demand from the developed world is the primary reason for the slowdown in world trade growth in 2007, and further moderation expected in 2008. In the United States, the weakening is due to more sluggish domestic demand and the depreciation of the dollar. Real import growth declined from 6 per cent in 2006 to about 2 per cent in 2007. It is expected that United States import growth will remain sluggish, at 4 per cent in 2008, under the baseline assumptions for the global outlook. Demand in Europe is also weakening and the region's import volume growth slowed from 8.6 per cent in 2006 to 4.3 per cent in 2007, although it is expected to pick up slightly in 2008 to 5.8 per cent. In Japan, meanwhile, the deceleration in the growth of import volumes is mainly due to reduced demand for investment goods.

The trends are slightly more ambiguous among the Commonwealth of Independent States (CIS), the new member States of the European Union (EU) and the economies in transition. The growth of the import volume for the CIS accelerated slightly from 22.3 per cent in 2006 to 24.1 per cent in 2007, stimulated by the strong currency appreciation which has reduced import costs, and driven by growth in investment and consumer demand. The pace of import growth will moderate in 2008 against the backdrop of the global economic slowdown. Similarly, the rapid expansion of domestic demand in the new member States of the EU has sustained a relatively fast import growth for several years, but the pace is now moderating. Import growth has moderated from 13.8 to 11.5 and 9.5 per cent in 2006, 2007 and 2008, respectively. In South-eastern Europe, import growth is still high as a result of the strong consumer demand associated with rapid domestic credit expansion and import demand linked to foreign direct investment (FDI) and large-scale infrastructure development. Nonetheless, in these countries also import growth is moderating somewhat: from 10 per cent in 2006 to 9 per cent in 2007, and is expected to slow further to 7 per cent in 2008.

In most of the developing world there is a visible deceleration of import growth. It is most pronounced in Western Asia, where merchandise import growth slowed from 12.6 per cent in 2006 to about 7 per cent in 2007. In the case of oil importers of the region, import volume growth slowed to 8.8 per cent in 2007, about half the rate of 2006.

*Import deceleration is visible in many parts of the developing world*

Import growth in Africa slowed from 13.6 to 9.0 per cent between 2006 and 2007, but is keeping a robust pace compared to the region's volatile pattern of trade growth of past decades. The recent strong import growth in Africa has been propelled by high oil and non-oil commodity prices which have strengthened foreign exchange revenues and boosted domestic demand growth. Booming equity and real estate prices in Egypt, Kenya and South Africa have further stimulated domestic demand and import growth.

In Latin America and the Caribbean, the rate of import growth also slowed somewhat during 2007, but nonetheless remained relatively strong, at 9.2 per cent, close to the record figures of 10 per cent in 2005 and 11.7 per cent in 2006.

The relatively strong import performance in the developing world is explained in part by the fact that for some of these regions, export volumes, and thus foreign revenues, remained high due to a small acceleration in demand originating in East Asia. Indeed, East Asia was the only region whose rate of import growth increased, if only slightly, from 10.5 per cent to 11 per cent 2007; however, if global patterns continue, it is likely that there will be a deceleration to about 10 per cent by 2008.

*Asia played a role in sustaining part of the trade impetus in developing regions*

In summary, global import demand remained robust by historical standards in 2007 and continued to be double that of world output growth. Compared with more recent years, merchandise trade growth has moderated, triggered by the slowdown of economic growth in the developed world.

From the export side, most regions kept their share in world merchandise exports relatively stable, with a few exceptions. The United States, for example, gained market share in 2007 for the first time in many years. Its export volume grew by 16 per cent in the third quarter of 2007, the highest in four years. Real export growth is estimated to have averaged about 7 per cent for the year in 2007, and a similar performance is expected for 2008.

*The United States may be regaining world export share …*

Exporters of energy and other primary products in some regions also gained world market shares. This is most notably the case for Africa, which saw its total merchandise export volume accelerate from 4.6 to 7.9 per cent between 2006 and 2007 in response to the continued strong global demand for energy and raw materials. African net oil-importing countries increased their export volume growth from 5.1 per cent to 7.6 per cent in 2007, and they are expected to keep up this pace in 2008 under the baseline scenario for world economic growth.

*… and exporters of energy and raw materials continued to gain a share as well*

South America's export growth also rose from 6.1 to 7.4 per cent between 2006 and 2007. The export acceleration is driven in particular by the net oil-importing countries of the region, whose export growth rose from 6.4 to 10.7 per cent over the past two years. Meanwhile, net oil exporters, including Mexico and Trinidad and Tobago lost ground as their export growth came to a near standstill.

Export performance by the economies in transition improved slightly as the result of constant growth of oil and gas activity in the resource-rich economies of the CIS as well as a surge of exports of metals and cotton elsewhere. Net oil-importing countries of the CIS, following negative export growth in 2005, experienced a slight increase in 2006 and accelerated to about a 7 per cent growth in 2007. Trade linkages between the CIS and China have strengthened (see box II.1).

---

**Box II.1**

## Increased trade linkages between the Commonwealth of Independent States and China

Trade linkages between the CIS and China have strengthened over recent decades. Merchandise trade between the CIS and China has grown much more rapidly than the GDP growth of the CIS countries, as indicated by the increased ratio of the sum of the bilateral exports and imports between the CIS and China to GDP of the CIS (see figure).

**Openness of the Commonwealth of Independent States to China**

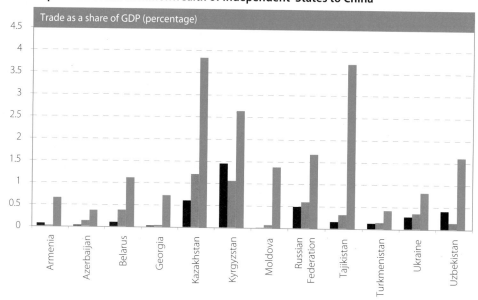

Trade as a share of GDP (percentage)

**Sources:** UN/DESA, based on the World Bank, World Development Indicators 2006 database, and UN COMTRADE database.

**a** The "gravity approach" has gained empirical success in explaining international trade since the independent studies of Jan Tinbergen, *Shaping the World Economy: Suggestions for an International Economic Policy* (New York: The Twentieth Century Fund, 1962); P. Pöyhönen, "A Tentative model for the volume of trade between countries", *Weltwirtschafliches Archiv*, vol. 90, No. 1, 1963, pp.93-100; and Hans Linnemann, *An Econometric Study of International Trade Flows*, North-Holland, 1966.

Growing trade with China has taken place in a context of reforms and the establishment of market institutions in the CIS countries. The buoyant international economic environment, as well as liberalization of exchange-rate and trade regimes and integration into the multilateral trading system through accession of some of these countries to the WTO, have largely contributed to improved trade linkages between China and the CIS countries. Armenia, China, Georgia, Kyrgyzstan and Moldova are members of the WTO, while six countries from the CIS are in the process of negotiations, with some—such as the Russian Federation and Ukraine—at an advanced phase. Moreover, the expansion of the scope of EU policy to non-EU member countries—through the implementation of the Partnership and Cooperation agreement and the European Neighbourhood Policy—has played a major role in boosting trade flows to and from the CIS. As a result, intraregional CIS trade has diminished in favour of trade with non-CIS members.

The rapid growth of the Chinese economy in recent decades is another important factor. In particular, China has increased demand for primary commodities in which the CIS specialize, such as oil, gas and cotton. Over the past five years, the value of merchandise exports from the CIS to China has increased by about 31 per cent, about 15 per cent in volume terms plus significant gains in

**Box II.1** (cont'd)

terms of trade. In addition, growing import demand driven by strong recovery in the CIS economies since 2000 pushed up Chinese exports to the CIS.

A model-based analysis using the gravity approach has been carried out to study the role of trade policies in strengthening trade links between China and the CIS countries.[a] The gravity model determines China-CIS trade openness as a function of country size of the exporters and importers (approximated by national income, population and a similarity index capturing the relative size of the trading partners) and transportation costs (measured by the distance between the capitals of the CIS and Beijing). In addition, an index of foreign and trade liberalization is introduced to account for changes in exchange-rate and trade policies, as reflected in the European Bank for Reconstruction and Development (EBRD) index of foreign exchange and trade liberalization. The WTO membership and the existence of common boundaries with China are also included as possible determinants.

The analysis leads to three main findings.[b] First, the size of the economy of the trading partners appears to be a main factor in attracting trade between the CIS countries and China, as is evident from a statistically significant and high elasticity of openness with respect to GDP. According to the model estimates, trade openness of the CIS with China increases by 0.89 per cent for each 1.0 per cent increase in GDP. In comparison, trade openness of the CIS with the EU and other regions shows similar regularity, although the magnitude of the elasticity is somewhat lower. External shocks have also affected trade, the most pronounced adverse effect having registered after the August 1998 crises. The transportation costs, including various obstacles related to geographical location, exert a strong negative effect: a one per cent increase in distance reduces openness by about 0.70 per cent. Furthermore, the similarity of the trading partners' GDPs has a strong positive effect on openness, reflecting the importance of the country's relative size on bilateral flows.[c]

Second, more liberal trade policies in the CIS, including exchange-rate policies and trade regimes, have boosted trade linkages of the CIS and both China and the EU. In the case of China, a one point increase in the trade liberalization index raises openness by 0.16 per cent. Moreover, the degree of openness between two WTO member countries, other things being equal, is higher than between non-WTO members. According to the estimates, however, participation of the CIS in the multilateral trading system does not affect their integration into the EU. This could be explained by the specific EU policy towards the CIS through various programmes.

Third, the gravity model also suggests that there is greater potential for trade between China and the CIS countries. The landlocked countries in particular face high transportation costs. Improvements in the infrastructure for transport and energy could substantially increase trade. Political tension, lack of good governance and slow institution-building in some of the CIS countries are also weakening the trade linkages of these economies.

In summary, the results of the estimations suggest that strengthened trade linkages between the CIS and China are closely associated with overall economic performance and—to a lesser extent—with advances in trade liberalization. Furthermore, participation in the WTO has helped these economies to deepen integration with the global economy. Hence, policies in support of sustainable growth—including through diversification, and improving infrastructure and governance—would further strengthen trade links and allow CIS countries to reap more of the potential benefits this may provide.

**b** For further details, see, Malinka Koparanova and Hung-Yi Li, "Openness and reforms in the CIS and China: Evidence from gravity panel data models", paper presented at the Project LINK Spring 2007 Meeting in Beijing, China, 14-17 May 2007 (available from http://www.chass.utoronto.ca/link/meeting/materials/mk200705_ppt.pdf).

**c** The factors introduced in the augmented gravity model all have the expected signs and explain over 70 per cent of the variation in openness. These empirical results are broadly consistent with similar research on transition economies (see, for example, Ian Babetskii, Oxana Babetskaia-Kukharchuk and Martin Raiser, *Transition and international integration in Eastern Europe and the former Soviet Union*, EBRD Working Paper, No. 83 (London: European Bank for Reconstruction and Development, 2003)).

Asia maintained fast and relatively stable rates of export volume growth, with a small decline in 2007 to 12 per cent, from 13 per cent in 2006. The patterns are not uniform, however. The strength of net fuel importers of East and South Asia was broadly maintained, while in Western Asia there was a pronounced deceleration from a 17 per cent growth in 2006 to 7 per cent in 2007. Similarly, net fuel exporters in Western Asia experienced negative growth to about -4 per cent in 2007, while East and South Asian net fuel exporters regained strength, from 3 to 7 per cent in 2007.

European economies have lost export shares, especially the EU-15, whose rate of growth of export volume dropped from 10.1 per cent in 2006 to 3.9 per cent in 2007.

Asia continues to gain market share

The loss of market share by Europe has been significant

Western Asia also lost market share in world trade, as the region saw a significant decline in its export volume growth, falling from a rate of 6.4 per cent in 2006 to -0.6 in 2007.

These patterns of export and import growth underpin the mild correction observed in the global imbalances (see discussion in chapter I), with the merchandise deficit in the United States narrowing slightly and surpluses in other developed countries reducing to a similar degree. Western Europe's surplus position has in fact switched to a small deficit owing to slower demand from the United States and exchange-rate appreciation of European currencies, and despite continued strong import demand from developing Asia, the Russian Federation and oil-exporting countries. Japan's trade surplus will be large but will shrink moderately into 2008, affected by demand and exchange-rate appreciation vis-à-vis the United States dollar and despite the fact that China has now become the second-ranking export-destination country for Japan and the leading country of origin for its imports. Canada will continue to run a trade surplus, albeit a smaller one, as currency appreciation is eroding the competitiveness of exporters of manufactures. Lower manufactured exports in Canada are only partially offset by rising oil exports.

Trade balances have not yet changed significantly

Trade balances in the developing world and economies in transition have remained relatively stable at the level of regional aggregates. East Asia's trade surpluses have increased in 2007 and are expected to increase further in 2008, although at a slower pace than in previous years. China's bilateral surplus with the United States remains the largest component of the region's trade surplus. South Asia's trade deficit increased slightly during 2007 and is expected to increase further in 2008. The remarkable dynamism of exports has not managed to counter greater import bills because of strong absorption and higher energy prices (with the exception of the Islamic Republic of Iran, which is an oil exporter). Africa's surpluses continue to grow, most strikingly reflecting an improved performance of exports of net fuel importers. In the Latin American and Caribbean region, the unprecedented large trade surpluses which have increased over the past five years peaked in 2006. The cycle is marked by the terms of trade experienced by commodity exporters and the continuing rise of energy prices, which negatively affect net importers of primary and energy products. Countries in South-eastern Europe continued to run large trade deficits. In Western Asia as a region, large trade surpluses may have peaked in 2006 as the import bill is accelerating owing to the rising euro value of imports for countries which for the most part have their currencies pegged to the dollar.

In conclusion, trends in merchandise trade growth have switched towards a slight correction of the global imbalances. Strong export growth, stimulated in part by the significant depreciation of the United States dollar since February 2002, has overtaken import demand growth, leading to a reduction in that economy's trade deficit. This is reflected in smaller surpluses in some of the surplus economies, especially in Europe, Japan and most developing country regions. However, the adjustments are small and do not amount to any substantial global macroeconomic rebalancing as yet.

## Trade in services: prospects for developing countries

World trade in services is growing rapidly

World trade in services nearly tripled in value terms between 1990 and 2005, reaching $2.4 trillion. This trend has been consistent with the broad trend of an increasing weight of services in production. During the same period, the share of services in GDP has grown from 65 to 72 per cent in developed countries and from 45 to 52 per cent in developing countries. Services today account for over 70 per cent of employment in developed countries and about 35 per cent in developing countries. In recent years, however, the fast growth of merchandise trade has outpaced that of services and, consequently, the share of services in total world trade in general, and that of developing countries, in particular, has fallen somewhat (see table II.2).

Table II.2:
**Exports of services: shares in economy's total trade in goods and services, 2001-2005**

| Economy | 2001 | 2002 | 2003 | 2004 | 2005 |
|---|---|---|---|---|---|
| World | 20.3 | 20.6 | 20.3 | 20.1 | 19.7 |
| Developed economies | 22.4 | 23.1 | 23.0 | 23.0 | 23.0 |
| Economies in transition | 15.3 | 16.4 | 16.1 | 15.0 | 14.1 |
| Developing economies | 15.9 | 15.4 | 14.8 | 14.5 | 14.0 |
| Africa | 19.2 | 19.8 | 19.6 | 18.4 | 16.1 |
| Latin America and the Caribbean | 14.5 | 14.3 | 14.0 | 13.1 | 12.7 |
| Asia | 15.8 | 15.2 | 14.4 | 14.3 | 14.0 |
| Oceania | 27.8 | 26.5 | 26.1 | 24.8 | 24.8 |
| *Memorandum items:* | | | | | |
| Least developed countries | 17.4 | 17.0 | 16.4 | 14.8 | 12.3 |
| Landlocked countries | 16.7 | 17.1 | 16.4 | 15.2 | 13.4 |
| Small island developing States | 45.7 | 47.2 | 44.9 | 43.7 | 39.3 |

**Source:** UNCTAD GlobStat.

Nonetheless, taken over a longer period, developing country performance in services trade has been impressive. Since 1990, services exports from developing countries have grown at an average annual rate of 8 per cent, compared with 6 per cent for developed countries. Travel and transportation continue to account for the bulk of services exports by developing countries. Business services, including information and communication technologies (ICT), as well as financial and insurance services are on the rise, however, and currently make up about one third of the services trade of developing countries (table II.3).[1]

The volume of services trade by developing countries is heavily concentrated in a few countries. No more than 20 countries accounted for 75 per cent of total developing country services trade in 2005, 6 of which accounted for 50 per cent (table II.4). An increasing number of developing countries have become successful exporters of tourism, transportation and construction services, audiovisual, computer and information technology (IT) services, and business and professional services.

For developing countries in general, trade in services is particularly important in the areas of movement of natural persons supplying services (Mode 4 of the General Agreement on Trade in Services (GATS)) and outsourcing (included in Mode 1), but is also important in commercial presence (Mode 3), mostly carried out through FDI.

FDI flows are an important driver of the increases in trade in services by developing countries. The share in world total of FDI inflows to the services sectors in developing countries climbed from 35 per cent in 1990 to nearly 50 per cent in 2004. Accumulated FDI inward stocks climbed during this period by more than 700 per cent, to about $1.2 trillion, up from $150 billion in 1990. Currently, the stock of inward FDI in developing country services sectors is now double that in manufacturing and accounts

*Developing countries' performance in services trade has been impressive*

*FDI is a main driving force of trade in services*

---

1   For further details, see UNCTAD, *Trade and development aspects of insurance services and regulatory frameworks*, UNCTAD/DITC/TNCD/2007/4 (Geneva: UNCTAD, 2007).

Table II.3:
**Exports of services by main categories in developing countries, 2001-2005**

| Main Service Category | 2001 Value (billions of dollars) | 2001 Share (percentage) | 2002 Value (billions of dollars) | 2002 Share (percentage) | 2003 Value (billions of dollars) | 2003 Share (percentage) | 2004 Value (billions of dollars) | 2004 Share (percentage) | 2005 Value (billions of dollars) | 2005 Share (percentage) |
|---|---|---|---|---|---|---|---|---|---|---|
| All sectors | 197.7 | | 207.6 | | 241.0 | | 300.0 | | 338.3 | |
| Transportation | 52.4 | 26.5 | 54.4 | 26.2 | 64.4 | 26.7 | 82.9 | 27.6 | 94.3 | 27.9 |
| Travel | 73.1 | 37.0 | 75.4 | 36.3 | 78.8 | 32.7 | 101.8 | 33.9 | 114.3 | 33.8 |
| Construction | 2.6 | 1.3 | 3.4 | 1.7 | 3.5 | 1.4 | 4.2 | 1.4 | 6.0 | 1.8 |
| Communications | 3.4 | 1.7 | 3.7 | 1.8 | 4.4 | 1.8 | 4.9 | 1.6 | 5.5 | 1.6 |
| Computer and information | 1.6 | 0.8 | 1.8 | 0.9 | 2.3 | 1.0 | 3.3 | 1.1 | 3.8 | 1.1 |
| Financial services | 3.8 | 1.9 | 4.1 | 2.0 | 5.2 | 2.1 | 6.9 | 2.3 | 9.3 | 2.7 |
| Royalties and licence fees | 2.1 | 1.0 | 1.9 | 0.9 | 2.5 | 1.0 | 3.6 | 1.2 | 3.5 | 1.0 |
| Other business services | 51.7 | 26.1 | 52.3 | 25.2 | 65.9 | 27.4 | 74.9 | 25.0 | 56.3 | 16.6 |
| Insurance | 2.3 | 1.2 | 2.6 | 1.2 | 3.3 | 1.4 | 3.7 | 1.2 | 4.1 | 1.2 |
| Personal, cultural and recreational services | 1.6 | 0.8 | 3.6 | 1.7 | 3.4 | 1.4 | 3.9 | 1.3 | 3.8 | 1.1 |
| Government services[a] | 4.9 | 2.5 | 5.7 | 2.7 | 6.8 | 2.8 | 7.1 | 2.4 | 8.6 | 2.5 |

**Source:** UNCTAD GlobStat.

**Notes:**

(1) The table contains aggregate data for a group of 35 developing countries where complete, or almost complete, statistics for a period of 2001-2005 were available.

(2) The shares of sectors may not amount to 100 per cent due to incomplete statistics of some reporting countries.

**a** Not identified elsewhere.

for 20 per cent of the worldwide stock of FDI in service sectors. Intra-developing country capital flows have become a major source of these investments. Total FDI outflows from developing countries to services sectors rose from a mere $2 billion in 1990 to nearly $30 billion in 2004. A major share of these outflows is within geographic regions, with an important share of the investments consisting of mergers and acquisitions. Developing country firms purchased over 40 per cent of all acquisitions of services firms in developing countries between 2000 and 2003.[2]

Thus far, offshore services represent only a relatively small component of the world outsourcing market. Offshore service activities mainly comprise IT services and IT-enabled business services as well as pharmaceutical and research and development (R&D) services. Current estimates indicate that the magnitude of the global offshoring market for services is slightly more than $50 billion. Developing countries have captured a sizeable and growing share of this market, however. Overall, it is a growing market providing important new export opportunities for developing countries, especially as these opportunities are seen to entail significant cost-saving benefits to (developed) countries who import these services. Key benefits for exporting countries include increased export earnings, job creation, higher wages and the upgrading of skills. FDI in offshoring can create further positive spillover effects in terms of raising the competitiveness of skill-intensive activities and improving ICT infrastructure.

---

2     UNCTAD Foreign Direct Investment database.

Table II.4:
**Top 20 exporters of services among developing countries, 2005**

| Economy | Value of exports (billions of dollars) | Share (percentage) |
|---|---|---|
| **All developing countries** | 593.4 | 100.0 |
| China | 74.4 | 12.5 |
| Hong Kong SAR[a] | 62.2 | 10.5 |
| Singapore | 51.3 | 8.6 |
| Korea, Republic of | 45.4 | 7.6 |
| Turkey | 25.9 | 4.4 |
| Taiwan Province of China | 25.8 | 4.4 |
| Thailand | 20.6 | 3.5 |
| Malaysia | 19.6 | 3.3 |
| Mexico | 16.1 | 2.7 |
| Brazil | 16.1 | 2.7 |
| Egypt | 14.6 | 2.5 |
| Indonesia | 12.9 | 2.2 |
| South Africa | 11.2 | 1.9 |
| Macao SAR[a] | 8.6 | 1.5 |
| Morocco | 8.1 | 1.4 |
| Chile | 7.2 | 1.2 |
| Iran, Islamic Republic of | 6.8 | 1.2 |
| Argentina | 6.2 | 1.1 |
| Saudi Arabia | 5.9 | 1.0 |
| Kuwait | 4.7 | 0.8 |

**Source:** UNCTAD GlobStat.

**Note:** India did not report services data for 2005.

**a** Special Administrative Region of China.

The potential of services sector development and services trade is yet to be fully realized by many developing countries, especially those in sub-Saharan Africa and the least developed countries (LDCs). The share of LDCs in world service exports is a meagre 0.8 per cent and is showing no growth.

Effective integration of developing countries into the services world economy requires more favourable terms and conditions. The international community should facilitate the realization of such conditions, including through the Doha Round. Furthermore, liberalization of trade in services, either through multilateral or regional trade agreements, needs to be pursued in areas of export interest to developing countries, especially Modes 1 and 4 of the GATS. Another challenge facing developing countries is to design and implement effective national and regional regulatory frameworks and institutions for their services economy, while at the same time carefully negotiating market access commitments that can ensure dynamic gains from a greater opening of their services markets. The private sector, as well as public-private partnerships, can contribute to the building of competitive services sectors, including in infrastructural services. International cooperation and assistance through the provision of financing, technology and investment is crucial to ensuring access to essential services and will be particularly relevant for pro-poor services development.

The services trade by LDCs remains marginal

International cooperation and assistance is needed for promoting the services trade

# World primary commodity markets and prices

## Non-oil commodities

The prices of non-oil
commodities continued
to rise …

The ascending trend in the prices of non-oil commodities that began about four years ago largely continued during 2007, albeit with increased volatility. During the year, non-oil primary commodity prices rose by nearly 15 per cent in terms of the United States dollar and by about 10 per cent in Special Drawing Rights (SDR) terms.

…driven by robust demand
for raw materials …

While moderating, the continued robust economic growth in the world economy is sustaining the upward trend of commodity prices. The demand for raw materials and food products by the rapidly growing emerging economies has remained particularly strong. For instance, China's import demand for *iron ore* increased by more than 40 per cent, for *copper* by more than 100 per cent and for *edible vegetable oils* by about 80 per cent during 2007. Meanwhile, higher oil prices as well as increasing environmental concerns relating to climate change have also redirected some demand towards alternative sources of energy, such as biofuels, and this in turn has led to further increases in the demand for maize and soybeans, driving up the prices of those commodities.

…as well as by supply
constraints

After a mild retreat at the beginning of 2007, *food* prices rose progressively over the rest of the year (figure II.5). Increases in *wheat* prices were the most dramatic, up by about 70 per cent, followed by the prices of *soybean meal*, up by about 40 per cent. The increases in wheat prices have largely been caused by adverse weather conditions in Australia and Europe, with Australian production dropping by more than 60 per cent from the previous crop level owing to the severe drought related to the El Niño phenomenon. According to the International Grains Council (IGC), production in 2006/07 is estimated to decrease by 4.6 per cent, leading to a contraction of stocks, which would reach their lowest level in 28 years.

Figure II.5:
**Monthly averages of free market price indices of
non-oil commodities, January 2000-September 2007**

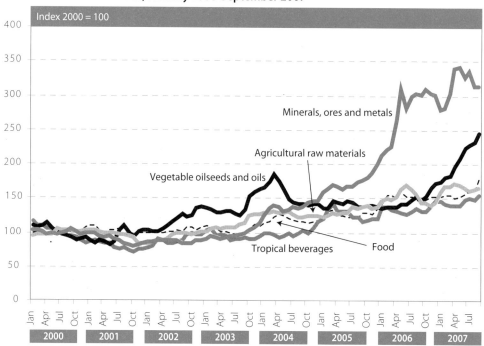

**Source:** UN/DESA, based
on UNCTAD Monthly
Commodities Prices Statistics.

*Maize* prices reached record levels during 2007, surpassing the previous record of 1996, mainly fuelled by growth in the demand for meat and, consequently, animal feed, and by the expansion of the biofuels industry. In the United States, for instance, the share of maize produced and converted into ethanol accounted for about 20 per cent in 2006/07. It is also estimated that the EU imported 8 million tons of maize in 2007, up from about 5 million in 2006. For the first time in the history of EU agricultural policy, the EU decided to set the obligatory set-aside rate at zero per cent for the autumn-2007 and spring-2008 sowings and to propose the total suspension of cereal import duties for the 2007/08 marketing year. Despite a large increase in production forecast for 2007/08, the projected rise of world consumption may lead to a further reduction in world stocks of maize.

*Sugar* prices form an exception, as they continued to decrease in 2007 owing to the substantial production surplus expected for 2006/07 and the anticipation of a similar situation for the 2007/08 crop. However, sugar prices remained about 10 per cent above their historical average.

*Tropical beverages* prices remained flat in the first half of 2007, but rose in the second half. The prices of Robusta *coffee* as well as *cocoa* increased substantially up to July 2007, by 17 per cent and 26 per cent, respectively, but have turned notably volatile since August. In the outlook, production of coffee is expected to decrease by about 10 per cent while consumption is expected to remain strong, supporting firm prices. Production of cocoa has also dropped, affected by such factors as the El Niño phenomenon in the third-largest cocoa producing country, Indonesia, and the rough harmattan for West African countries, especially Côte d'Ivoire and Ghana, the two main cocoa-producing countries.

Prices of tropical beverages remain flat

The index for prices of *vegetable oilseeds and oils* increased by about 40 per cent in the first three quarters of 2007. The prices of sunflower oil increased by about 78 per cent and the prices of palm, cotton seeds and linseed oils by more than 40 per cent. The increase in biofuels has led to higher demand for many vegetable oils that can be used in biodiesel, intensifying already tight market conditions. The major trend in the oilseeds and vegetable oils market is likely to continue due to the strong demand of the animal feed and biofuels industries.

The prices of *agricultural raw materials* rose at the beginning of 2007, but fell during the summer, increasing only modestly for the year as a whole. *Cotton* prices increased by about 20 per cent until August 2007, but the prices are 40 per cent below their 1995 level.

The *minerals, ores and metals* price index increased by more than 10 per cent during 2007, but the price movements differed notably between two sub-groups: copper, lead and tin in the first group, versus nickel and zinc in the other.

In the first group, *copper* prices rose by 35 per cent between January and September 2007, owing mainly to the contraction of stocks by about 30 per cent. With such tight market conditions, even a minor event could lead to a jump in prices: strikes in Canada or Chile, for instance. Demand from China continues to be a determining element. From November 2003 to November 2007, copper prices increased by 350 per cent. In the outlook, an anticipated increase in mine production and refinery capacity should help to reduce price pressures on copper. Like copper, *lead* prices have also been strong since mid-2003, and as of September 2007 had increased by about 90 per cent during that year. The provisional closure of the Magellan mine located in Australia, as well as the fall of Chinese metal exports since the beginning of 2007 have largely contributed to a tight market condition. *Tin* prices continued on their rising trend over the first nine months of 2007, increasing by 32 per cent, up 255 per cent since the end of 2002. The closure of a

Since mid-2003, copper prices have multiplied four and a half times

large number of illegal mines in Indonesia (the second-largest tin-producing country) may explain some of the price movement in 2007.

In the second group of metals, after reaching its record level in May 2007, *nickel* prices dropped significantly, by about 40 per cent up to September. The high prices have stimulated the substitution of nickel in the production of stainless steels by other cheaper metals. Furthermore, the fall in nickel prices was also triggered by the revelation of a speculation scheme in the London Metal Exchange (LME). The case, which led to a change in LME rules, resulted in the release of a large position of nickel contracts. Despite the drop in 2007, nickel prices remain at a historic high. *Zinc* prices fluctuated immensely during 2007, with a sharp drop of 25 per cent between May and September, but remain at more than 3 times above their level of 2004, when they started their recent upward cycle.

*Iron ore* prices are generally expected to rise again in 2008, since Chinese steel production continues to grow and mines are having difficulty in keeping up with the demand, as witnessed by very high spot prices in late 2007.

In general, metal prices will likely remain at high levels in the near future, but market fundamentals appear to be less bullish than in the past two years, so the prices may reach a plateau in 2008.

*Metal prices may reach a plateau in 2008*

## The oil market

*Oil prices surged in 2007*

The price of oil, in terms of Brent crude, exhibited a strong upward bias in 2007, surpassing previous record levels in nominal terms and also skirting record levels in terms of real prices (see figure II.6). Oil prices began their most recent upward spiral towards the end of the summer, increasing from an average of $71 per barrel (pb) in August to $92.5 pb by

Figure II.6:
**Nominal and real Brent crude oil price, 1980-2007**

**Source:** UN/DESA based on IMF International Financial Statistics CD-ROM, November 2007.

**Note:** United States consumer price inflation was used as the deflator for the nominal price of Brent oil.

November 2007, a rise of 30 per cent. Prices have been driven upwards mainly by supply-side factors, including fluctuating commercial stock levels, geopolitical tensions in the Middle East and adverse weather conditions that have impacted production. In addition, there has been a strong element of speculative investment attracted by the weakened dollar, pushing oil prices even higher than market fundamentals would suggest.

Meanwhile, strong global demand for oil, particularly from some of the rapidly growing developing economies, has eliminated much of the slack in the oil market. As a result, any supply-side disruptions, however slight, are magnified; whereas supply increases, unless they are large, leave the market relatively unaffected. Worldwide oil demand fell in the fourth quarter of 2007 owing to higher oil prices, and world oil supply showed monthly gains in production.

Nonetheless, the price of oil increased by another $10 between October and November. This is explained by a combination of factors. The dollar depreciation triggered part of the increase as investors in the oil market sought compensation for a loss in purchasing power in terms of the euro and other currencies. Geopolitical concerns aroused by the conflict between Turkey and Kurdish factions in Iraq, as well as suicide bombings in Afghanistan and an attack on an oil pipeline in Yemen, generated uncertainty and fuelled speculation that further pushed up oil prices. Uncertainty regarding the global economic outlook could continue to push prices upward. Moreover, since oil worldwide is priced in dollars, there is less incentive for oil producers to increase production substantially. The price of Brent premium is expected to rise from $73.50 on average in 2007 to $76 pb on average for the year in 2008. This expectation is based on continued tightness in the market as well as continued uncertainties.

World oil demand accelerated in 2007 by 1.2 per cent, increasing from 84.7 million barrels per day (mbd) in 2006 to 85.7 mbd in 2007. Growth is being driven almost entirely by demand in the developing economies. Weaker-than-expected fourth-quarter growth in the United States, the transition economies and Western Europe has led to depressed demand in these parts of the world. Despite the slowdown of global economic growth, world oil demand is still anticipated to increase by 2.3 per cent in 2008, raising the level of demand to 87.7 mbd.

Weaker oil demand in the developed economies is part of a longer-term trend. In the United States and Europe, the contraction is more cyclical as higher fuel prices and mild seasonal weather have constrained demand and slowed inventory build-up. Demand has particularly fallen in the area of transport fuel. Market backwardization, a situation where futures prices are lower than current prices, has also provided an economic incentive to delay any build-up of inventories and may be contributing to below-average deliveries of heating oil in Germany and France as retailers anticipate lower market prices prior to the onset of the colder winter weather. A sudden cold weather snap in Western Europe or the United States could, however, send prices spiralling as retailers scurry to rebuild inventories. Oil demand in Japan is heavily influenced by efforts to improve its energy efficiency and enhance reliance on alternative fuels.

In the developing economies, demand is expected to increase by 2.9 per cent in 2007. Healthy demand is present in all regions, but especially in the economies of China and India, and in the Middle East. China's oil demand increased by about 6.1 per cent in 2007 to average 7.6 mbd, driven by increased transport fuel consumption and energy demand to support its rapid economic growth. In spite of the reduction in some subsidies that has raised the price of oil products by about 10 per cent, demand growth is not expected to taper off. India's oil demand is also largely driven by industrial and transport

Strong global demand eliminated much of the slack in the oil market

Sustained weakness of the United States dollar is also a factor

Developing country growth explains most of the increase in world oil demand

fuel demand, as strong economic growth has expanded vehicle ownership. Likewise, oil demand in the Middle East is expected to increase by 4.6 per cent to 6.5 mbd, stimulated by the vast infrastructure-building efforts and economic expansion in that region.

In 2008, world oil demand is expected to accelerate slightly by 2.3 per cent, with economies outside of the developed region once again accounting for about 80 per cent of this growth. Although the price of oil tends to be inelastic in the short term, the impact of higher prices has led to declining demand for transport fuel in the developed economies. This could have an impact on overall demand growth, particularly if growth falters in the United States, which is the largest consumer of oil. The economies in the Middle East, along with India and China, seem less perturbed as domestic energy prices are subsidized.

In spite of the volatility in the price of oil, world supply was stable for most of 2007. Oil production even showed a slight increase in the second part of the year. World oil supply is expected to increase from 85.0 mbd at the beginning of the year to an average of 85.9 mbd in 2007. Preliminary reporting suggests some increases in the Organization of the Petroleum Exporting Countries (OPEC) oil supplies as well as recovery in non-OPEC areas. Still, demand and supply conditions have remained extremely tight for most of the year, leaving little space for disruptions on either side of the demand/supply equation.

The refinery outage issue, which plagued the market in the earlier part of the year and led to bottlenecks in the product market, has eased for now. Crude oil price increases have been rising faster than prices in the product market, suggesting that product price movements will not have a significant impact on oil prices in the near term. However, as the winter season approaches for the countries that are major consumers of oil and as refinery capacity utilization increases, any unplanned outages or scheduled maintenance would have backlash effects on the oil market and once again highlight the shortage of worldwide refinery capacity at the end of 2007 and into 2008.

More and more, increased oil production has been coming from oil fields that produce heavier, more corrosive crude oils. The lack of investment and ageing of premium grade fields has led to dwindling supplies, placing a premium on lighter crude oil, such as Brent Crude, which has a lower density and sulphur content and is more environmentally friendly. Over the past year, the spread between the price of Brent premium and OPEC basket (see figure II.7) has shown considerable volatility. In the third quarter of 2006 and the first quarter of 2007, the spread was reduced to close to one dollar, owing mainly to the decline in demand for light crude, as many refineries that handled such crude were suffering outages. After each of these incidents, however, the spread quickly widened to between 4 and 5 dollars.

Production increased in the non-OPEC economies, including Azerbaijan, Canada, China and the Russian Federation. This has helped to offset the declines in Western Europe and the Middle-Eastern economies of Oman, the Syrian Arab Republic and Yemen. Lower production in Norway and the United Kingdom of Great Britain and Northern Ireland was mainly the result of bad weather in the North Sea, while the non-OPEC Middle Eastern economies are suffering from dwindling supplies.

In spite of the decision at their extraordinary meeting in December to keep output unchanged at around 31.5 mbd "for the time being", oil production of the OPEC member States is expected to be slightly higher by January 2008. Increased production is expected from Angola and Ecuador, who were given formal production quotas of 1.9 mbd and 520,000 bd, respectively, and the United Arab Emirates, as it ends its programme of maintenance. The member States also expressed their "extreme vigilance" in keeping

Figure II.7:
**Brent oil: weekly premium over OPEC basket, January 2003-September 2007**

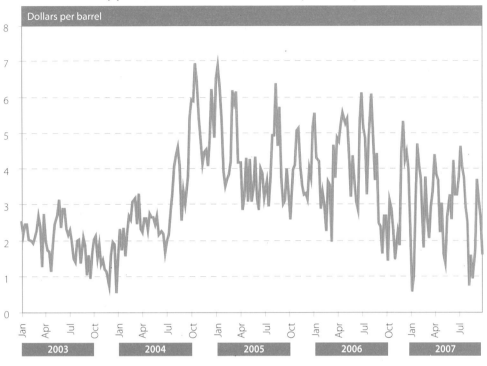

Dollars per barrel

**Source:** U.S. Energy Information Administration.

markets stable over the next few months, scheduling another extraordinary meeting in February 2008 to review the market situation.

Many of the developments in the oil price market also depend on the degree of the slowdown in the United States economy and the weakening of the dollar. In this regard, the price of oil could still remain relatively high and volatile, in spite of increased production by OPEC. A previous announcement in September of a 500,000 bd production increase was shrugged off by the market and met with a record high close in prices of oil futures. Additionally, with the prediction of colder winter weather ahead, it is likely that the price floor will increase to as high as $60 for the outlook period, as strong regional demand from Asia and other parts of the developing world continue to drive oil prices.

The outlook is subject to uncertainties on both the demand and supply sides. Significant geopolitical events as well as adverse weather conditions could trigger supply-side disruptions and lead to higher-than-expected price increases. Yet, the speculative demand that has contributed to the rapid rise in prices has left the market vulnerable to a sizeable correction that could send prices spiralling downwards at the first signs of retrenchment. Additionally, continued constrained demand brought on by higher oil prices, coupled with a stronger-than-expected global slowdown, could have a significant impact on demand growth and also push prices downwards.

Prices of oil could still remain relatively high and volatile

# Terms of trade for developing countries and economies in transition

In recent years, the terms of trade of developing countries have been strongly influenced by two basic trends: declines in the prices of manufactured goods and significant increases in the prices of primary commodities. Both trends are closely related, although not exclusively, to economic developments in Asia. Sizeable devaluations of the Asian currencies in the aftermath of the East Asian crises in 1997-1998 put a deflationary pressure on the prices of the manufactures exported by Asian countries. Prior to that, productivity growth and the information technology revolution had already set in a trend towards lowering prices of manufactures. This trend has been prolonged by the extraordinary expansion of the exports of manufactures by China and other Asian countries, produced with low labour costs. At the same time, in addition to other factors discussed in the previous section, the economic expansion of continent-sized countries, such as China and India, has spurred the demand for energy and industrial raw materials (both metals and agriculture inputs), while rising real household incomes in these countries are also adding to the global demand for food. Consequently, prices of most primary commodities have been rising significantly since 2003.

As a result of these trends, the terms of trade of developing and transition economies have shifted substantially, in particular during the past five years. Among developing countries, exporters of manufactures endured a persistent deterioration of their terms of trade, especially those who specialized in labour-intensive manufactures and are net oil importers. The unit value of their exports already declined between 1997 and 2002, but during that period this did not greatly affect their terms of trade, owing to a simultaneous reduction in the unit value of their imports. Since 2003, however, unit import costs have increased substantially, outpacing a more moderate recovery of unit export prices. On the other hand, exporters of fuels and mining products experienced the largest improvements in the terms of trade (figure II.8). The record is mixed for exporters of agricultural products. For this group of countries as a whole, the terms of trade have remained stable over the last few years. These aggregate numbers conceal diverging trends, however, with some countries benefiting from the recent increase in the price of vegetable oilseeds and oils and of some cereals, while other countries that export different agricultural products and import oil and food are experiencing a significant deterioration of their terms of trade.

The diverging trends in the terms of trade among developing and transition economies are also apparent by comparing geographical regions (figure II.9). Western Asia, which includes several of the major petroleum exporters, is the region that presents the strongest improvement in terms of trade. For economies in transition as a group, huge gains were registered also, again thanks to their exports of oil, gas and mining products, but this is driven by the major exporters in the group, the Russian Federation and Ukraine. Other economies in this group that are not oil exporters experienced a deterioration of their terms of trade. African economies also saw a rapid improvement in their terms of trade, recovering from the depressed levels of 1998-1999. The continent has benefited not only from the rise in the prices of oil and mining products, but also from the fact that in recent years a number of countries that used to be mainly exporters of agricultural products have also become net exporters of fuels and minerals. Terms-of-trade gains are not evenly distributed among the countries of the region. The relative price of exports and imports for the 24 sub-Saharan countries that do not export significant quantities of fuels or mining products has in fact deteriorated. Prices of the exports by these countries (tropi-

Figure II.8:
**Terms of trade by export structure, selected developing countries, 1995-2007**

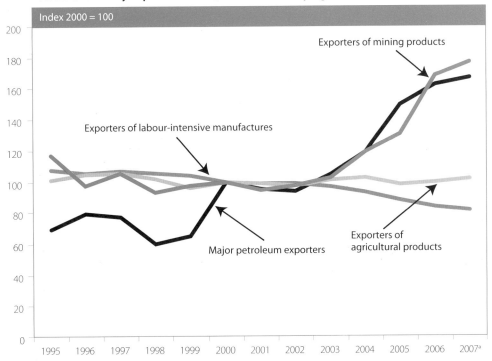

Index 2000 = 100

Exporters of mining products

Exporters of labour-intensive manufactures

Major petroleum exporters

Exporters of agricultural products

**Sources:** UNCTAD calculations, based on UN COMTRADE; United States Bureau of Labor Statistics, *Import/Export Price Indexes* database, available from www.bls.gov/mxp/home.htm; Japan Customs, Trade Statistics database, available from www.customs.go.jp; IMF, *International Financial Statistics* database; UNCTAD, *Commodity Prices Bulletin*, various issues; and ECLAC, *Balance of Payments Statistics* database.

a    Partly estimated.

Figure II.9:
**Terms of trade in developing countries and transition economies, by region, 1995-2007**

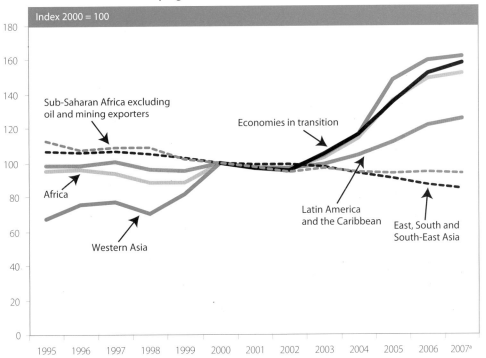

Index 2000 = 100

Sub-Saharan Africa excluding oil and mining exporters

Economies in transition

Africa

Latin America and the Caribbean

Western Asia

East, South and South-East Asia

**Sources:** UNCTAD calculations, based on UN COMTRADE; United States Bureau of Labor Statistics, *Import/Export Price Indexes* database, available from www.bls.gov/mxp/home.htm; Japan Customs, Trade Statistics database, available from www.customs.go.jp; IMF, *International Financial Statistics* database; UNCTAD, *Commodity Prices Bulletin*, various issues; and ECLAC, *Balance of Payments Statistics* database.

a    Partly estimated.

cal agricultural products or labour-intensive manufactures) have been outpaced by those of their imports (fuels, food and semi- and high-tech manufactures).

… while the picture is more mixed in Latin America and the Caribbean, and in East and South Asia

The countries in Latin America and the Caribbean also witnessed significant gains in their terms of trade, although these have been more moderate than those of the other developing country regions discussed up to this point, owing to a more diversified trade composition. Gains have been more important in the South-American subregion, while most Central American and several Caribbean countries (the majority of which depend heavily on fuel imports and export labour-intensive manufactures) have suffered losses from their terms of trade. Finally, East and South Asian countries are showing a significant deterioration of their terms of trade owing to their specialization in manufactures exports, many of which are labour-intensive, and to their dependence on the imports of energy and industrial raw materials. Only a few countries escaped that trend, namely Brunei Darussalam and the Islamic Republic of Iran, which are important oil exporters, as well as Indonesia, Malaysia, Myanmar and Viet Nam, which while predominantly exporting manufactures, are also exporters of primary commodities.

The variation in terms of trade implies a number of policy challenges

These diverging patterns in the terms of trade naturally pose different challenges for policymakers. For countries benefiting from significant terms-of-trade gains, domestic income may expand faster than the domestic product. To translate this into longer-term development gains, the challenge will be to channel the additional revenue into long-term investment in support of national development strategies. Since an important share of export production may build on FDI, the additional challenge of avoiding much of the gains leaving the country through profit remittances, for instance through taxation of foreign firms, may arise. In addition, there would be a challenge for macroeconomic policies. Terms-of-trade gains may add to pressures towards currency appreciation, which could erode export competitiveness and limit export diversification.

# Trade policy developments and trends: multilateralism at the crossroads

## Requisites for Doha to be a development Round

An ambitious "development package" is a prerequisite for a sustainable multilateral trading system

The World Trade Organization (WTO) Doha Round of multilateral trade negotiations, launched in November 2001, was originally intended to offer an opportunity to better take account of development concerns in the design of the multilateral trading system and correct inequities in the existing system. The basis for this was the recognition that a substantive, development-oriented outcome was imperative for trade's contribution to the implementation of the Millennium Development Goals, especially MDG-8 which, among others things, aims at an "open, rule-based, predictable, non-discriminatory trading and financial system". After more than six years of negotiations, the trading system still stands at a crossroad.

Five key objectives must be attained …

It was expected that following the Sixth Ministerial Conference of the WTO in Hong Kong Special Administrative Region (SAR) of China, held in December 2005,[3]

---

3    World Trade Organization, Ministerial Declaration of the Doha Work Programme adopted on 18 December 2005 at the sixth WTO Ministerial Conference held in Hong Kong, China from 13-18 December 2005 (WT/MIN(05)/DEC). For a discussion of the Hong Kong Ministerial Conference, see *World Economic Situation and Prospects 2006* (United Nations publication, Sales No. E.06.II.C.2), pp. 45-51.

the Doha Round would enter into a decisive phase. The common perception was that quick progress in the negotiations was required to find solutions on key issues, namely agricultural market access, domestic support in agriculture, industrial tariffs and services. Ambitious structural adjustment in agricultural policy and associated trade policy, which have remained "left-over" issues for so many years, is indeed crucial to enabling a balanced and development-focused outcome. In particular, five key objectives (or deliverables) for a meaningful "development package" must be attained to ensure the credibility and sustainability of the multilateral trading system.[4]

First, the Doha Round must result in significantly enhanced and additional real market access and entry for developing countries' exports of manufactured goods, commodities and services in their major markets so as to enable them to grow and prosper. This implies tariff elimination, removal of tariff escalation and peaks, and providing access in services sectors engaged in by developing countries, especially in GATS Modes 4 (movement of natural persons) and 1 (cross-border trade) of services delivery, and addressing non-tariff barriers. The provision of duty-free and quota-free treatment to all LDCs for all their products on a lasting basis, as well as the issue of addressing special concerns of African cotton-producing countries, as contemplated at the Sixth Ministerial Conference of the WTO, are important elements that remain to be implemented fully.

… enhanced and additional market access and entry for developing countries …

Second, the Doha Round should bring about improvements in multilateral rules that address and remove existing asymmetries and enhance the fairness and equity of the multilateral trading system. Substantially reducing and removing trade-distorting agricultural subsidies is indispensable for levelling the playing field for fair competition in agricultural trade. An appropriate phasing and sequencing of market opening, as well as institutional and regulatory reform, are also important, particularly in the field of services, accompanied by complementary policies in support of building domestic supply capacity.

… enhanced fairness and equity of the multilateral trading system …

Third, the development dimension signifies there is enough space for Governments to align the multilateral framework of rights and obligations under WTO with the objectives of national development strategies. This relates to measures such as the more operational special and differential treatment and less-than-full reciprocity rule; preserving tariff revenues; promoting domestic nascent industries and pre-empting de-industrialization; preserving long-standing trade preferences; safeguarding food security, livelihood security and rural development; providing for use of policies and measures to foster commodity-sector production, diversification and competitiveness; universal access to essential and infrastructure services; access to essential drugs; implementation-related issues; and other measures that address the more specific concerns of small island developing States and other vulnerable economies.

… adequate and sufficient degree of policy space …

Fourth, development solidarity is required from the international community for developing countries in undertaking adjustment and meeting implementation costs, building trade-related infrastructure and supplying capacity-building in trading and marketing. In this context, the Aid for Trade Initiative is an essential complement to the envisaged further trade liberalization under the multilateral trading system. If it provides for additional aid, it can play an important role—along with improved market access, balanced rules and sound domestic policies—in helping developing countries realize sustained gains from trade.

… Aid for Trade as an essential complement to trade liberalization in the trading system …

---

4    See, Report of the Secretary-General of UNCTAD to UNCTAD XII, Globalization for development: Opportunities and challenges, 4 July 2007 (TD/413).

Fifth, it is important to ensure greater coherence and a positive interface between regional trade agreements (RTAs) and the multilateral trading system. In respect of the apparent never-ending tide of regionalism, robust progress in and a successful conclusion to the Doha Round is the best guarantee against the continuing erosion of the multilateral system. Specifically, the WTO rules on RTAs, under negotiation in the Doha negotiations, need clarification and improvement so as to improve compliance and better take into account development aspects of RTAs.

Furthermore, the universality of WTO membership is essential for the legitimacy and governance of the trading system. Accession of about 30 developing countries and countries with economies in transition is thus a systemic priority. However, experience has shown that relatively deep liberalization and stringent reform commitments, including WTO-plus commitments, have been requested from acceding developing countries, thus affecting their balance of WTO rights and obligations in comparison with the original WTO members. It is thus crucial to ensure fair and equitable terms of accession commensurate with the individual acceding country's trade, financial and development needs, and the provision of increased support in all stages of the accession negotiations, as well as in the post-accession process.

## Prospects for the Doha Round

After the suspension of the Round in July 2006, the negotiations were formally resumed in February 2007, followed by active and intense diplomatic activities and consultations at various levels throughout 2007. In July, the centre of negotiations once again returned to Geneva to resume a "bottom-up approach", when chairpersons of the negotiating bodies on agriculture and non-agriculture market access (NAMA) submitted new texts of negotiating modalities in these two priority areas.[5]

Despite these new developments, the positions of major players have remained essentially unchanged since July 2006, when the Round was suspended. Discussions thus continue to centre on trying to find the right balance between agriculture and NAMA and setting numerical targets on various parameters in those two areas. However, unexpectedly, new and difficult issues have been added to the negotiating agenda, such as special flexibilities in NAMA requested for customs unions among developing countries (the Southern Common Market (MERCOSUR) and the Southern African Customs Union (SACU)), while China has recently emphasized that it needs more flexibility as a recently acceded WTO member.

Visible attempts have been made to intensify negotiations in other areas, including services, rules, trade facilitation and trade-related aspects of intellectual property. Most importantly, however, no significant movement was recorded on development issues of special and differential treatment, and implementation issues. Work continued on the operationalization of Aid for Trade, resulting in pledges during the WTO Global Aid for Trade Review on 20 November 2007 to increase funds for this purpose to $30 billion by 2010.[6]

[5] For more details, see Report of the Secretary-General on Trade and development, 16 August 2007 (A/62/266, section IV).

[6] For further details, see the Global Aid for Trade Review website, available from http://www.wto.org/english/tratop_e/devel_e/a4t_e/global_review_e.htm.

A number of additional and closely related political factors continue to influence directly the prospects for the Doha Round. The United States Trade Promotion Authority (the so-called Fast-Track) expired on 1 July 2007. This affects the space for United States trade negotiators to engage in concluding discussions in several key areas, especially in agriculture. Moreover, a substantial delay in passing the new United States Farm Bill (which was still being debated in Congress at the end of 2007) has also sent conflicting messages to other Doha Round participants.

It is quite clear that in order to succeed, the Round needs the firm engagement of all parties in striking final deals on core issues under negotiation. A new United States trade promotion authority, or an extension of the previous one, is thus important for the continued credible engagement of the United States in the negotiations. The recent United States debate on the approval of free-trade agreements with Panama, Peru and the Republic of Korea, revolving around new environment and labour provisions, might be indicative of prospects of a new trade promotion authority for the Doha Round. The new United States Farm Bill reform is equally important as it directly defines the terms under which the United States could offer more meaningful concessions in agricultural domestic support.

At present, no breakthrough in the negotiations is expected in the near future. New "deadlines" are being discussed for modalities aimed at an agreement in agriculture and NAMA in February or March 2008. But for some negotiators, even that seems far too optimistic. The Round's prospects are increasingly intertwined with domestic political agendas in several key participating countries, especially the United States in view of its 2008 presidential elections. Several participants are thus calling on the United States to provide a "road map" for the Round's concluding phase in conjunction with its domestic agenda.

A number of political factors continue to influence the prospects for the Doha Round

# Chapter III
# Financial flows to developing and transition economies

## Net transfers from poor to rich countries

In 2007, developing countries as a group continued to make significant outward trans-fers of financial resources to developed economies. However, compared to previous years, the rate of increase in the volume of transfers has clearly moderated. There are signs that the long-anticipated unwinding of global imbalances may have started, but this process must be viewed with anxiety because of the continuing potential for disorder. The total net financial transfers from developing countries, that is to say, net capital flows less net interest and other investment income payments, increased from $728 billion in 2006 to $760 billion in 2007 (see table III.1 and figure III.1). In relative terms, however, this 4.4 per cent increase is the smallest of the sustained increases since 1998. The increase in net transfers mainly comes from East and South Asia, where outward net transfers to developed economies continued to accelerate. All other developing country subgroupings registered some decline in net resource outflows (table III.2). The reduction of the trade surplus in the Russian Federation was also the main reason for an overall decline in net outward financial flows from countries with economies in transition, from $136 billion in 2006 to $109 billion in 2007.

The increasing net transfer of resources from developing to developed economies moderated in 2007

Table III.1:
**Net transfer of financial resources to developing economies and economies in transition, 1995-2007**

| Billions of dollars | | | | | | | | | | | | | |
|---|---|---|---|---|---|---|---|---|---|---|---|---|---|
| | 1995 | 1996 | 1997 | 1998 | 1999 | 2000 | 2001 | 2002 | 2003 | 2004 | 2005 | 2006 | 2007[a] |
| **Developing economies** | 49.5 | 24.7 | -1.3 | -33.7 | -119.5 | -185.7 | -154.8 | -204.9 | -297.9 | -368.2 | -560.0 | -728.1 | -759.8 |
| **Africa** | 5.7 | -5.8 | -5.4 | 15.6 | 2.2 | -31.6 | -16.9 | -7.5 | -22.6 | -36.2 | -68.3 | -86.2 | -59.2 |
| Sub-Saharan Africa (excluding Nigeria and South Africa) | 7.3 | 5.1 | 7.6 | 12.1 | 8.9 | 2.8 | 7.0 | 4.8 | 5.9 | 3.5 | 0.2 | -8.2 | -4.0 |
| East and South Asia | 21.3 | 19.3 | -31.1 | -127.8 | -137.2 | -119.7 | -116.4 | -144.9 | -169.9 | -178.9 | -252.4 | -369.9 | -468.1 |
| Western Asia | 23.0 | 10.9 | 12.0 | 34.9 | 6.7 | -31.4 | -24.3 | -19.6 | -43.8 | -70.4 | -132.5 | -144.7 | -132.7 |
| Latin America | -0.6 | 0.3 | 23.2 | 43.7 | 8.9 | -2.9 | 2.7 | -32.8 | -61.6 | -82.7 | -106.8 | -127.2 | -99.8 |
| **Economies in transition** | -7.6 | -11.8 | -2.9 | -6.7 | -32.1 | -58.0 | -40.3 | -38.7 | -50.5 | -78.5 | -112.3 | -135.6 | -109.2 |
| *Memorandum item:* | | | | | | | | | | | | | |
| Heavily indebted poor countries (HIPCs) | 7.0 | 7.3 | 7.9 | 9.3 | 10.6 | 8.5 | 9.1 | 11.3 | 10.6 | 11.8 | 14.7 | 13.0 | 17.9 |
| **Least developed countries** | 12.1 | 10.6 | 9.2 | 12.5 | 10.5 | 5.6 | 8.7 | 6.7 | 8.0 | 5.0 | 2.4 | -4.3 | -0.8 |

**Sources:** UN/DESA, based on IMF, World Economic Outlook database, October 2007, and IMF, Balance of Payments Statistics.
**Note:** The developing countries' category does not include economies in transition; hence, data in this table may differ from those reported for country groupings reported in the IMF sources.
**a** Partly estimated.

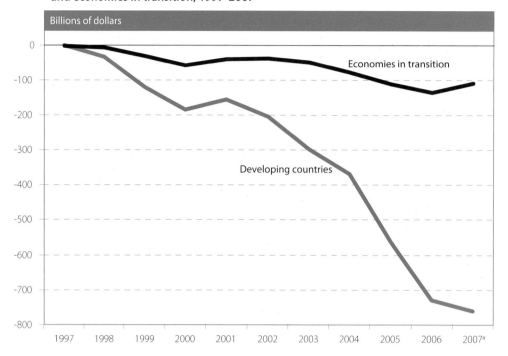

Figure III.1:
**Net financial transfers to developing countries and economies in transition, 1997-2007**

Billions of dollars

Economies in transition

Developing countries

**Source:** Table III.1.
**Note:** Net financial transfers are defined as net capital inflows less net interest and other investment income payments abroad.
**a** Partly estimated.

Table III.2:
**Net financial flows to developing countries and economies in transition, 1995-2008**

| Billions of dollars | | | | | | |
|---|---|---|---|---|---|---|
| | Average annual flow | | 2005 | 2006 | 2007a | 2008b |
| | 1995-1997 | 1998-2004 | | | | |
| **Developing countries** | | | | | | |
| Net private capital flows | 179.6 | 77.9 | 164.6 | 82.3 | 313.1 | 150.0 |
| Net direct investment | 104.7 | 143.3 | 208.4 | 187.5 | 243.4 | 212.3 |
| Net portfolio investmentc | 57.2 | -11.9 | 21.0 | -124.9 | 10.9 | -106.3 |
| Other net investmentd | 17.7 | -53.5 | -64.7 | 19.7 | 58.8 | 44.0 |
| Net official flows | 6.3 | -7.4 | -121.6 | -132.8 | -124.8 | -133.9 |
| Total net flows | 185.9 | 70.5 | 43.0 | -50.5 | 188.3 | 16.1 |
| Change in reservese | -82.0 | -180.0 | -489.0 | -608.6 | -910.5 | -779.7 |
| **Africa** | | | | | | |
| Net private capital flows | 7.1 | 9.0 | 29.4 | 14.6 | 42.3 | 53.0 |
| Net direct investment | 4.7 | 15.3 | 29.5 | 27.9 | 39.6 | 38.4 |
| Net portfolio investmentc | 5.0 | 0.5 | 4.7 | 10.8 | 9.7 | 15.0 |
| Other net investmentd | -2.6 | -6.8 | -4.8 | -24.1 | -7.0 | -0.4 |
| Net official flows | 3.6 | 2.7 | -7.2 | -12.9 | 5.1 | 4.3 |
| Total net flows | 10.7 | 11.7 | 22.3 | 1.7 | 47.5 | 57.3 |
| Change in reservese | -9.3 | -12.1 | -63.3 | -76.6 | -78.0 | -94.6 |

| Table III.2 (cont'd) | Average annual flow | | 2005 | 2006 | 2007[a] | 2008[b] |
|---|---|---|---|---|---|---|
| | 1995-1997 | 1998-2004 | 2005 | 2006 | 2007[a] | 2008[b] |
| **East and South Asia** | | | | | | |
| Net private capital flows | 88.0 | 30.8 | 83.0 | 36.5 | 153.1 | 0.2 |
| Net direct investment | 54.0 | 63.0 | 107.7 | 101.3 | 97.0 | 93.4 |
| Net portfolio investment[c] | 20.8 | -0.2 | -12.8 | -122.7 | -30.2 | -148.8 |
| Other net investment[d] | 13.2 | -32.0 | -11.9 | 57.8 | 86.3 | 55.5 |
| Net official flows | -3.1 | -2.4 | -20.8 | -22.7 | -17.8 | -18.1 |
| Total net flows | 85.0 | 28.4 | 62.2 | 13.8 | 135.3 | -18.0 |
| Change in reserves[e] | -42.2 | -148.7 | -301.9 | -387.5 | -640.1 | -535.7 |
| **Western Asia** | | | | | | |
| Net private capital flows | 19.1 | -1.6 | 16.9 | 21.3 | 33.9 | 49.4 |
| Net direct investment | 5.1 | 7.8 | 20.8 | 30.2 | 34.8 | 24.7 |
| Net portfolio investment[c] | 5.1 | -10.2 | 1.0 | 0.6 | 12.0 | 23.0 |
| Other net investment[d] | 8.9 | 0.8 | -4.8 | -9.6 | -12.9 | 1.7 |
| Net official flows | 1.0 | -14.6 | -63.1 | -78.8 | -111.7 | -120.6 |
| Total net flows | 20.1 | -16.2 | -46.3 | -57.6 | -77.8 | -71.3 |
| Change in reserves[e] | -15.3 | -12.9 | -91.4 | -95.8 | -79.5 | -98.4 |
| **Latin America and the Caribbean** | | | | | | |
| Net private capital flows | 65.3 | 39.7 | 35.3 | 9.9 | 83.7 | 47.5 |
| Net direct investment | 40.8 | 57.2 | 50.4 | 28.0 | 71.9 | 55.8 |
| Net portfolio investment[c] | 26.3 | -2.0 | 28.1 | -13.7 | 19.4 | 4.5 |
| Other net investment[d] | -1.9 | -15.5 | -43.1 | -4.4 | -7.6 | -12.7 |
| Net official flows | 4.8 | 6.9 | -30.5 | -18.4 | -0.4 | 0.6 |
| Total net flows | 70.1 | 46.6 | 4.8 | -8.5 | 83.3 | 48.1 |
| Change in reserves[e] | -15.2 | -6.3 | -32.4 | -48.6 | -113.0 | -51.1 |
| **Economies in transition** | | | | | | |
| Net private capital flows | 0.5 | 4.3 | 45.0 | 76.1 | 99.3 | 57.4 |
| Net direct investment | 5.0 | 8.0 | 15.1 | 32.0 | 18.8 | 30.8 |
| Net portfolio investment[c] | 1.7 | -0.1 | -4.3 | 12.2 | 13.3 | 6.2 |
| Other net investment[d] | -6.2 | -3.5 | 34.3 | 31.9 | 67.3 | 20.5 |
| Net official flows | -0.4 | -4.9 | -20.7 | -29.0 | -5.0 | -4.2 |
| Total net flows | 0.1 | -0.5 | 24.4 | 47.1 | 94.3 | 53.3 |
| Change in reserves[e] | -1.6 | -20.0 | -81.2 | -137.2 | -157.6 | -95.7 |

**Source:** IMF, World Economic Outlook database, October 2007.

a   Partly estimated.
b   Forecasts.
c   Including portfolio debt and equity investment.
d   Including short- and long-term bank lending, and possibly including some official flows due to data classification limitations.
e   Negative values denote increases in reserves.

These net outward transfers take place in the context of continued substantial net private capital inflows to these economies, impelled by the global liquidity glut financed by United States imbalances and buoyed by the "carry trade" owing to international differentials in interest rates. The expansive private capital flows to developing and transition economies, increasingly in domestic currency-denominated assets, has helped to sustain growth in emerging markets and so far has helped to insulate them from the turmoil emanating from developed country financial markets. The risk of this increased exposure lies in the possibility of this form of financing's suddenly drying up if the housing-sector collapse spreads to the whole financial system, thereby inducing a severe economic slowdown in advanced countries.

The combination of current-account surpluses and positive net private capital inflows has led to an unprecedented build-up of international official reserves. Most reserves are held in United States dollar-denominated assets. The recent sharp decline in the value of the dollar, which is likely to continue with the unwinding of global imbalances, adds its own impetus to the pace of rebalancing, since both private and public investors must now consider further losses on their dollar investments.

Both private and public investors must now consider potential losses on their dollar-denominated assets

Amid skyrocketing reserves, some Governments have taken steps to use part of their country's accumulated wealth for investment in long-term, diversified global assets that yield higher returns than government securities of major developed countries. In addition to foreign-exchange reserves, a growing part of foreign assets is now invested in less-liquid and riskier assets through sovereign wealth funds (SWFs). More than 20 countries have set up SWFs and more than 70 per cent of the holdings are concentrated in the top seven funds from China, Kuwait, Norway, the Russian Federation, Saudi Arabia, Singapore and the United Arab Emirates. The aggregate size of SWFs has been estimated at between $2 trillion and $3 trillion, while the total market value of private institutional investors amounts to $55 trillion, and that of hedge funds to between $1.0 trillion and $1.5 trillion. By different estimates,[1] SWF assets could reach between $8.5 trillion and $12.0 trillion by 2012.

As analysed in chapter I, a global slump will directly hurt the developing countries, especially those reliant on primary exports. Commodity prices will fall in the event of a global economic downturn, causing new growth difficulties for many of these countries. The impact of a recession on emerging economies will depend on their macroeconomic situation. Emerging economies with strong trade performance and low domestic interest rates will be affected through reduced export demand but will have the scope to grow through domestic demand. However, there are quite a few emerging economies running significant trade deficits, maintaining elevated domestic interest rates and confronting strongly appreciated currencies induced by massive portfolio inflows. These economies could suffer a severe adjustment in the event of a precipitous collapse in global finance.

## Private capital flows

### Private capital flows to developing countries

The impact of the current financial market turmoil on developing countries has, so far, been limited

The impact of the ongoing turmoil in world financial markets—sparked by the United States sub-prime mortgage difficulties—on private financial flows to developing countries has so far been limited. For a brief period in mid-2007, sovereign spreads widened, stock markets fell and capital flows decreased. However, at the time of writing, this disruption appears to have been short-lived; spreads have been tightening again (though they are still above the lows recorded earlier in 2007) (figure III.2) and emerging equity markets are

---

1    International Monetary Fund, *Global Financial Stability Report—Financial market turbulence: Causes, consequences and policies* (Washington, D.C.: IMF, September 2007), p. 45, available from http://www.imf.org/External/Pubs/FT/GFSR/2007/02/pdf/chap1.pdf; and, "Foreign reserve accumulation—some systemic implications", speech by Christian Noyer, Governor of the Bank of France, at the Salzburg Global Seminar, Salzburg, 1 October 2007, available from http://www.bis.org/review/r071024a.pdf.

Figure III.2:
**Emerging Market Bond Index spread, end February 2006-end October 2007**

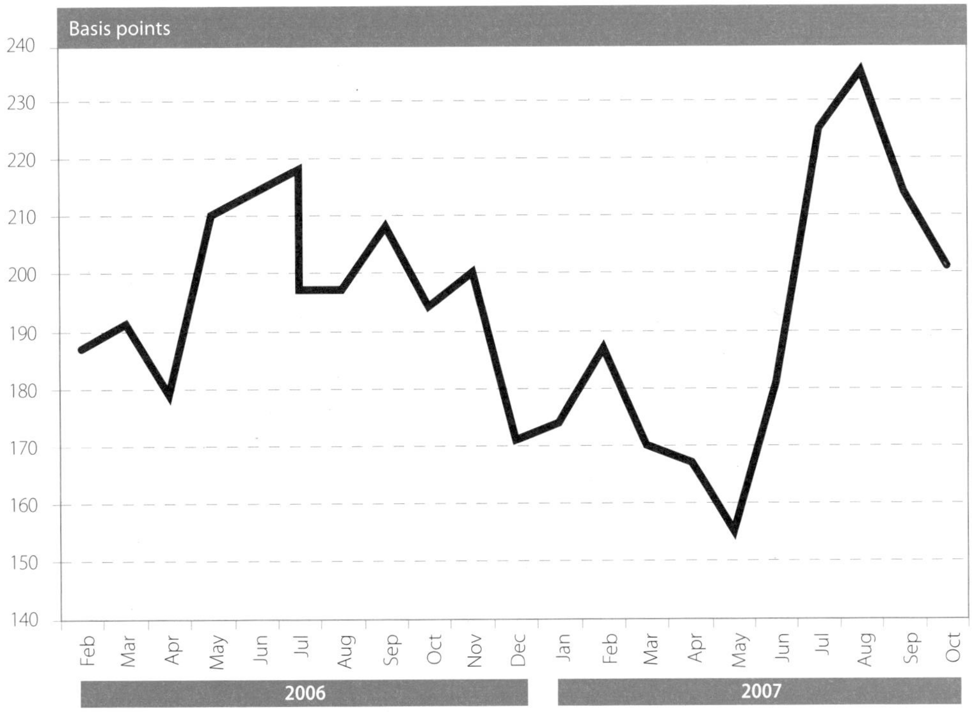

Basis points

**Source:** JPMorgan Securities.

once more rising to record levels.[2] Hence, there is a sense that emerging markets are at least a temporary haven for portfolio funds in the current situation. While they may not reach the heights registered during 2006, private capital flows to developing countries are expected to remain robust for the first few months of 2008. There are, however, important downward risks to this scenario.

The relative resilience of emerging markets to the global financial turmoil has been due to three main factors. First, the response of central banks in the major developed economies—and especially the interest rate cuts by the United States Federal Reserve Bank—has served to lift equity markets, including in emerging markets. Second, the global financial turbulence has been concentrated in innovative credit instruments that are mostly prevalent in mature financial markets, rather than in those of developing countries. Third, in recent years of robust growth, there has been a visible improvement in the macroeconomic indicators of a number of key emerging economies.

At the onset of the current turmoil, almost all the key vulnerability indicators (growth, inflation, balance of payments, levels of external debt, foreign exchange reserves) for emerging economies were looking more favourable than they had been during previous emerging market crises. For example, the Institute of International Finance (IIF) estimates that, for the economies in Asia and the Pacific, external debt as a percentage of gross domestic product (GDP) stands at about 19 per cent in comparison with 33 per cent during the crises of 1997-1998; the ratio of short-term debt to reserves for the same economies is currently estimated to be around 0.2 in comparison with 1.3 in 1997. The figures are just as striking for Latin America, where the IIF calculates external debt-to-GDP to be about

The current turbulence emanates from new financial instruments, used mainly in developed economies

---

2    International Monetary Fund, *World Economic Outlook: Globalization and Inequality* (Washington, D.C.: IMF, October 2007).

23 per cent—in comparison with 40 per cent during the emerging market crises of 2000.[3] While the improvements in these indicators have given a boost to investor confidence in a number of countries, market spreads have increased for economies with weak macroeconomic indicators.

Emerging country spreads first increased at the start of the mid-2007 financial crisis, but have declined somewhat in recent months

In line with the general repricing of risk, the spreads on emerging market bonds over United States Treasury bills widened during the summer of 2007. However, this rise was not as sharp as in industrialized countries' credit markets. From a low of 155 at the end of May 2007, the Emerging Markets Bonds Index Global (EMBIG) spread index rose to 235 basis points in mid-August and subsequently tightened to stand at 214 basis points at the end of September.[4] In any event, declining bond issuance by a number of developing country Governments would have reduced the impact of wider spreads on government finances. At the same time, emerging market corporate bond issuance has been growing to fill the void left by declining government issuance; an increased amount of international issuance has been undertaken by developing country corporate borrowers, mostly to finance acquisitions. It is possible that this will be curtailed in future months in line with the reduction in private equity activity under way in advanced markets. In particular, the widening of external-debt spreads from their mid-year lows could reduce issuance by low-grade corporate borrowers. In this respect, there are concerns that, in line with the growth in private debt, riskier borrowers may be taking a larger share of the market. According to the World Bank, unrated borrowers (both sovereign and corporate) issued 37 per cent of bonds in 2006, in comparison with 10 per cent in 2000.[5]

It is likely that international banks will curtail their mortgage exposure globally

Commercial bank lending to developing countries continued to increase over the past year. Of this, emerging Europe has attracted the largest share in new claims, followed by Asia and the Pacific, Latin America and the Caribbean, Africa and the Middle East. According to the Bank for International Settlements (BIS), emerging Europe has overtaken other emerging regions as the one to which BIS-reporting banks extend the greatest share of gross credit.[6] Some international banks, including those heavily involved in the United States mortgage market, have also played a part in financing the rapid growth in emerging market mortgage debt. This rapid growth in mortgage lending in emerging markets will not necessarily come to an end (given growing middle-class wealth and legal reforms in a number of these countries), but in the present context, it is more likely that some international banks will decide to curtail mortgage risk globally, a move that could affect the buoyancy of housing finance in some developing countries.[7] There are indications that banks have become increasingly cautious since the onset of the recent turmoil; in particular, there has been a drop in lending for acquisitions. This caution has been exacerbated by balance-sheet constraints in a number of institutions arising from mortgage-backed lending and may serve to restrict the levels of commercial bank lending to developing countries over the coming year.[8]

---

3    See Institute of International Finance, Special briefing on "The US Mortgage Crisis and Emerging Markets", 27 August 2007.

4    JPMorgan Emerging Market Analytics, online data available from www.morganmarkets.com.

5    See World Bank, *World Bank Global Development Finance 2007: The Globalization of Corporate Finance in Developing Countries* (Washington, D.C.: The World Bank, May 2007).

6    See BIS Quarterly Review, September 2007.

7    See Institute of International Finance, Special briefing, loc. cit..

8    See Institute of International Finance, Report on "Capital Flows to Emerging Market Economies", 21 October 2007.

While the global credit crunch initially led to a decline in developing country equity markets, it proved to be temporary, and emerging equity prices are rising again. According to the International Monetary Fund (IMF), consistently strong inflows into emerging equity markets over the past two years have led to their average price/earnings ratios reaching levels comparable to those in developed markets.[9] This buoyancy has been the function of perceptions of strong macroeconomic indicators for a number of emerging economies, reduced vulnerability to external shocks and strong corporate-earnings growth. Looking ahead, the main risk associated with portfolio equity flows to developing countries is the possibility of a sharp deterioration in global growth prospects, which could curtail these flows by affecting economic prospects and increasing the risk aversion of investors.

From a regional perspective, Eastern and Central Europe have experienced sharp increases in all categories of net private capital flows during the past few years. These flows have raised concerns of excessively high credit growth—from both bank and non-bank sources—which could prove unsustainable. Both domestic and foreign banks in emerging Europe (and also in Central Asia) have increasingly been borrowing from abroad to finance this high credit growth, thereby generating additional sources of vulnerability.[10] Asia has been attracting large amounts of portfolio equity inflows and, added to the trade surpluses, have enabled Governments in the region to accumulate vast foreign-exchange reserves. Of late, and despite the financial turmoil in global markets, India in particular has received a surge in equity-related inflows that have created policy dilemmas for the authorities. Private capital inflows into emerging economies in Latin America and the Caribbean, Asia and Europe have also led to currency appreciation in countries such as Brazil, Chile, Colombia, Iceland, Indonesia, Latvia, Poland and Thailand, creating similar concerns regarding competitiveness and sustainability.

An interesting recent development has been an increase in portfolio investment in sub-Saharan Africa. This has been directed mainly towards commodity-exporting countries and those with more liberalized capital markets and favourable macroeconomic indicators, such as Nigeria and Zambia. Dedicated emerging market hedge funds and other institutional investors have become increasingly active, not least in local-currency debt markets, and have been attracted by both improving economic conditions in some countries in the region and portfolio diversification, since the performance of less-prominent markets has not been correlated with that of larger emerging markets during the recent bouts of financial turbulence.[11]

There are significant downward risks associated with the continuing high levels of private capital flows to developing countries during the coming year. At the outset, it bears emphasizing that, despite monetary easing by policymakers, uncertainty regarding the total amount of losses associated with United States sub-prime mortgage securities, and where they may be located, will likely keep global investor sentiment unsettled in the near term. Against this background, there are concerns relating to investor sentiments and global growth prospects that can affect the level of private financial flows to developing countries. As mentioned earlier, the most vulnerable developing and transition economies are likely to be those running sizeable external imbalances and/or those in which credit growth has risen to unsustainable levels and is characterized by risky borrowing.

Developing country equity values were initially down at the start of the crisis, but have begun to increase again

FDI flows have increased to sub-Saharan Africa, particularly to commodity-exporting countries

---

9    International Monetary Fund, *Global Financial Stability Report—Financial Market Turbulence: Causes, Consequences and Policies* (Washington, D.C.: IMF, September 2007).

10   International Monetary Fund, *Global Financial Stability Report,* ibid.

11   International Monetary Fund, *Global Financial Stability Report: Market Developments and Issues* (Washington, D.C.: IMF, April 2007).

"Carry-trade" flows are
substantial

Over and above these broad concerns, there are additional risks facing private flows to developing countries. A possible problem could arise from the effect of carry trades, which refer to the large flows of foreign loans into emerging markets targeting local market returns. These carry trades are profitable as long as investors benefit from foreign exchange appreciation and higher domestic interest rates on local financial instruments. The huge and persistent increases in foreign exchange reserves in emerging markets suggest that the magnitudes of these carry-trade inflows may be substantial. For example, according to the IIF, the significant increase in Brazil's foreign exchange reserves during the first half of 2007 is largely a function of carry-trade inflows.[12] A key issue concerns the likelihood of reversal of some of the carry-trade flows. In addition, some developing country Governments and high-net-worth individuals, especially in Asia, have recently been making investments in higher-yielding assets and funds across the world. It is possible that some of these investments may have found their way into funds linked to sub-prime assets that have fallen in value recently. The extent to which this may have happened and the impact this may have had on net private capital flows to the country of origin are as yet unclear.

## Trends in foreign direct investment

### *Foreign direct investment flows in 2007*

FDI flows in 2007 surpassed
the record levels
achieved in 2000

At the global level, foreign direct investment (FDI) inflows reached an estimated $1.5 trillion in 2007, surpassing the record level achieved in 2000 (figure III.3). In the three major groups of economies—developed countries, developing countries, and South-eastern Eu-

Figure III.3:
**Inflows of foreign direct investment, world and by major country groups, 1980-2007**

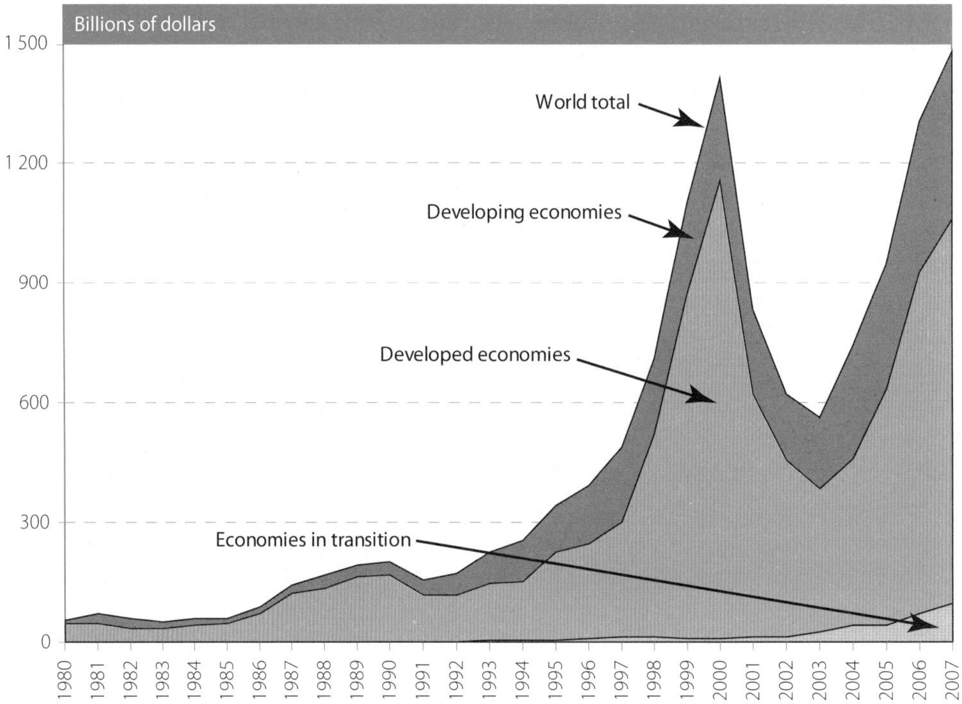

**Source:** UNCTAD, FDI/TNC
database, available from
http://www.unctad.org/fdi
statistic and own estimates

---

12        Institute of International Finance, Special briefing, loc. cit.

rope and the Commonwealth of Independent States—FDI flows rose again. The financial and credit crises that began in the latter half of 2007 have not noticeably affected FDI inflows. Transnational Corporations (TNCs) have ample liquidity to finance their own investments, including FDI, and, so far, the real economic impact of the crisis has been limited. The credit crisis in the United States has accelerated dollar depreciation, and this could actually stimulate FDI flows to the United States (the largest host country in the world), particularly from countries with appreciating currencies such as Europe and developing Asia. Thus, the expected net impact of the current financial crisis on FDI inflows into the United States might be small. Furthermore, emerging economies with a strong and growing appetite for FDI are much less exposed to the crisis. Cross-border mergers and acquisitions (M&As) in the first half of 2007 have already increased by 53 per cent compared to those in the corresponding period of 2006 (table III.3), although these flows have declined in the latter half of 2007.

Nevertheless, the ongoing financial crisis will increase the risk of negative impacts on FDI flows if it brings about drastic exchange-rate shifts, volatile oil prices, tighter financial-market conditions and increased protectionism. Private equity firms, which account for one fifth of global cross-border M&As, have become increasingly dependent on bank loans, whose volume has been declining since the start of the credit crisis.

Firms from Asian developing subregions are investing actively in other developing countries, and their investments to developed countries are also increasing. Most cross-border M&A purchases by Asian firms were in extractive industries, telecommunications, finance and other service activities. Asian firms are increasingly using cross-border M&A strategies in investing overseas and acquiring strategic assets.

The most important change in the sectoral and industrial pattern of FDI over the past quarter century was the shift towards services,[13] accompanied by a decline in the share of FDI in natural resources and manufacturing.[14] Recently, however, FDI in the extractive industries of resource-rich countries has rebounded. In 2005, FDI stock in the primary sector accounted for about 9 per cent of total world inward FDI stock (figure III.4), only slightly lower than its share in 1990, while manufacturing accounted for slightly less than a third of total FDI stock (30 per cent), a noticeable drop from its share of 41 per cent in 1990. By far the largest share of FDI in the primary industries has been in mining (grouped along with quarrying) and petroleum. Continued high commodity prices and the need for further consolidation in upstream activities have been the main drivers of the cross-border M&A surge in 2007 in the primary sectors, mainly in the mining industry.

The share of TNC investments in extractive industries flowing to developing and transition economies as destinations has more than doubled in the 1990s, and increased by another 50 per cent between 2000 and 2005. The extractive industries of some economies account for a significant share of the total inward FDI stock, and in a number of low-income, mineral-rich countries, extractive industries account for the bulk of inward FDI (figure III.5). Some developing economies are among the main producers and net exporters of various minerals, while developed countries and fast-growing emerging economies are the major consumers and importers. These imbalances sometimes create concerns among importing countries over the security of supply and concerns among exporting countries over market access.

*There is a rebound of FDI in the extractive industries*

---

13  See United Nations Conference on Trade and Development, *World Investment Report 2004: The Shift Towards Services* (United Nations publication, Sales No. E.04.II.D.33).

14  For a more elaborate analysis, see United Nations Conference on Trade and Development, *World Investment Report 2007: Transnational Corporations, Extractive Industries and Development* (United Nations publication, Sales No. E.07.II.D.9).

Table III.3:

## Inflows of foreign direct investment and cross-border mergers and acquisitions, by region and major economy, 2006-2007

| Billions of dollars | | | | Cross-border mergers and acquisitions | | | |
| --- | --- | --- | --- | --- | --- | --- | --- |
| | | | | | Sales | | |
| | Foreign direct investment inflows | | | 2006 | | 2007 | Growth rate (percentage) |
| Region/economy | 2006 | 2007[a] | Growth rate (percentage) | First half | Full year | First half | First half only |
| World | 1 305.9 | 1 479.9 | 13.3 | 377.3 | 880.5 | 580.7 | 53.9 |
| **Developed economies** | 857.5 | 962.3 | 12.2 | 298.2 | 728.0 | 496.0 | 6.3 |
| *Europe* | 566.4 | 628.2 | 10.9 | 194.7 | 451.3 | 299.8 | 54.0 |
| *European Union* | 531.0 | 580.8 | 9.4 | 190.2 | 432.1 | 281.0 | 47.7 |
| EU-15 | 492.1 | 543.6 | 10.5 | .. | .. | .. | .. |
| France | 81.1 | 116.6 | 43.8 | 19.6 | 39.9 | 39.2 | 100.0 |
| Germany | 42.9 | 28.5 | -33.6 | 24.6 | 55.3 | 37.6 | 52.7 |
| Netherlands | 4.4 | 125.6 | 2 774.0 | 5.9 | 32.0 | 23.0 | 291.6 |
| United Kingdom | 139.5 | 171.1 | 22.6 | 77.7 | 150.5 | 115.2 | 48.3 |
| *New European Union member States (10)* | 38.9 | 37.2 | -4.3 | .. | .. | .. | .. |
| Czech Republic | 6.0 | 6.4 | 8.0 | 0.7 | 1.6 | 1.4 | |
| Hungary | 6.1 | -0.2 | -103.3 | 2.0 | 2.9 | 3.7 | 84.3 |
| Poland | 13.9 | 16.7 | 20.2 | .. | .. | .. | .. |
| *United States* | 175.4 | 171.4 | -2.3 | 79.0 | 172.2 | 123.2 | 56.0 |
| *Japan* | -6.5 | 34.3 | -626.6 | 1.8 | 2.6 | 14.7 | 696.0 |
| **Developing economies** | 379.1 | 422.0 | 11.3 | 73.4 | 127.4 | 71.5 | -2.7 |
| *Africa* | 35.5 | 36.5 | 2.8 | 13.1 | 17.6 | 4.9 | -62.2 |
| Egypt | 10.0 | 9.7 | -3.9 | 1.1 | 1.2 | 1.4 | 35.0 |
| South Africa | -0.3 | 4.7 | .. | 4.3 | 5.6 | 0.2 | -94.3 |
| *Latin America and the Caribbean* | 83.8 | 105.3 | 25.8 | 16.2 | 37.6 | 16.2 | 0.3 |
| Argentina | 4.8 | 2.9 | -39.6 | 0.9 | 2.9 | 0.9 | 10.0 |
| Brazil | 18.8 | 41.9 | 123.1 | 4.0 | 10.0 | 3.7 | -7.4 |
| Chile | 8.0 | 12.7 | 59.1 | 2.7 | 3.1 | 0.2 | -92.6 |
| Colombia | 6.3 | 8.2 | 30.5 | 1.8 | 4.0 | 1.3 | -27.8 |
| Mexico | 19.0 | 26.5 | 39.1 | 0.7 | 2.0 | 3.2 | 348.0 |
| *Asia and Oceania* | 259.8 | 280.1 | 7.8 | 44.2 | 72.2 | 50.3 | 13.8 |
| *Western Asia* | 59.9 | 56.2 | -6.2 | 9.6 | 17.9 | 9.9 | 2.8 |
| Turkey | 20.1 | 20.9 | 3.7 | 7.2 | 15.3 | 5.3 | -26.0 |
| *South, East and South-East Asia* | 199.5 | 223.7 | 12.1 | 33.9 | 53.7 | 40.3 | 19.0 |
| China | 69.5 | 62.9 | -9.4 | 3.4 | 6.7 | 3.8 | 9.9 |
| Hong Kong SAR[b] | 42.9 | 54.4 | 26.9 | 9.5 | 12.8 | 3.6 | -61.7 |
| India | 16.9 | 16.3 | -3.7 | 3.7 | 6.7 | 16.0 | 328.6 |
| Singapore | 24.2 | 41.7 | 72.2 | 4.7 | 7.3 | 3.8 | -18.9 |
| Thailand | 9.8 | 10.1 | 3.2 | 4.3 | 4.3 | 0.7 | -83.1 |
| **Economies in transition** | 69.3 | 95.6 | 38.0 | 5.7 | 25.1 | 13.2 | 132.3 |
| Russian Federation | 28.7 | 55.8 | 94.2 | 0.3 | 5.4 | 0.2 | -22.1 |

**Source:** UNCTAD.

**Note:** World FDI inflows are projected on the basis of 86 economies for which data are available for part of 2007, as of 10 October 2007. Data are estimated by annualizing the available data, in most cases for the first two quarters of 2007. The proportion of inflows to these economies in total inflows to their respective region or subregion in 2006 is used to extrapolate the 2007 data.

**a**　Preliminary estimates.

**b**　Special Administrative Region of China.

Figure III.4:
**Share of extractive industries[a] in world FDI stock, 1990, 1995, 2000 and 2005**

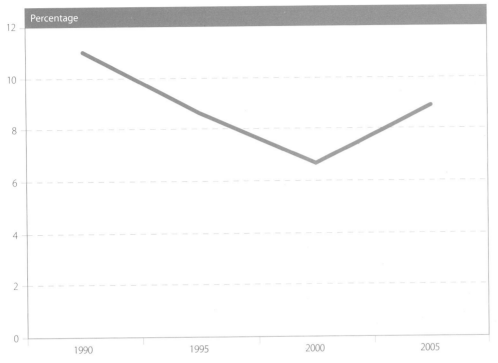

**Source:** UNCTAD, *World Investment Report 2007: Transnational Corporations, Extractive Industries and Development* (United Nations publication, Sales No. E.07.II.D.9), p. 100.

**a** Refers to mining, quarrying and petroleum in the primary sector.

Figure III.5:
**Share of extractive industries in the inward FDI stock of selected economies, 2005**

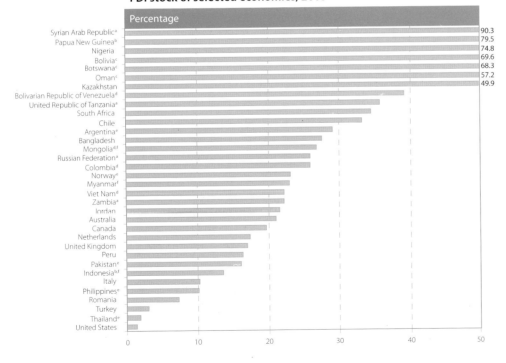

**Source:** UNCTAD estimates, based on data from the UNCTAD FDI/TNC database, available from http://www.unctad.org/fdistatistics.

**a**  2001 data.
**b**  1997 data.
**c**  2003 data.
**d**  2002 data.
**e**  2004 data.
**f**  On approval basis.

Considerable public
sector involvement is
indispensable in harnessing
FDI to development
objectives

Natural-resource endowments do not automatically translate into development gains, and considerable public-sector involvement is indispensable for overcoming the economic, environmental, social and political obstacles to harnessing foreign direct participation in extractive industries to boost development. For countries that lack the necessary indigenous capabilities for transforming their natural resources into commercial assets, TNCs can bring the needed capital, knowledge and access to markets; for home countries, they can serve as vehicles for securing access to foreign supplies. Indeed, some of the world's largest TNCs are active in extractive industries, and a number of new ones have emerged in resource extraction in the past decade, not least from developing and transition economies.

The most important economic impact of foreign investment in a country's extractive industry is increased income, including government revenue. The overall impact of revenue generated will be determined by the way in which it is shared between the foreign companies and the host country and by how the government's portion of the revenue is managed, distributed and used. Thus, even if TNC participation contributes to economic growth, in order for it to generate substantial development gains, the benefits obtained need to be wisely used and equitably distributed. Funds should be used to support development objectives and the needs of current and future generations.

In both the oil and gas and the metal mining industries, there are evolving arrangements that reflect an ongoing process through which Governments seek to find the appropriate balance between the respective rights and obligations of States and firms. As government revenue is among the most important benefits from mineral extraction, it is not surprising that policymakers devote much attention to finding a mechanism that assures the Government an appropriate share in the revenues from mineral extraction. With higher mineral prices in the past few years, a number of Governments have taken steps to increase their share of the profits generated by amending their fiscal regimes or their contractual relations. Recent regulatory changes in developed and developing, as well as transition economies, suggest that many Governments believed their previous regulations may have been overly generous vis-à-vis foreign investors.

## International financial cooperation

### Official development assistance

In 2006, ODA fell for the
first time in real terms
since 1997

The strain of meeting the set of high-minded official development assistance (ODA) pledges—which began at the 2002 United Nations International Conference on Financing for Development held in Monterrey, Mexico, and continued up to the 2005 Group of Eight (G8) Summit held at Gleneagles, Scotland—has become pronounced. Net ODA disbursement by Development Assistance Committee (DAC) member countries declined by $3 billion in 2006 and is likely to decline again in 2007. The total of $103.9 billion net ODA in 2006 represented a 5.1 per cent fall in real terms compared with the average growth of 16 per cent during the preceding three years, and amounted to 0.30 per cent of the DAC members' combined gross national product (GNP). This was the first time since 1997 that ODA actually fell in real terms (see figure III.6).

This amount included substantial net debt-relief grants as part of ODA, contradictory to the Monterrey commitment which provided that debt relief would be additional to conventional forms of ODA. ODA, net of debt relief, declined from 0.26 to 0.25

Figure III.6:
**DAC members' net ODA, 1990-2006 and**
**DAC Secretariat simulations of net ODA to 2010**

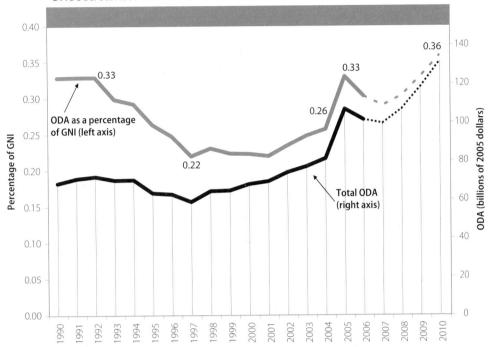

**Source:** OECD.

per cent of the GNP of DAC donor countries in 2006, well below the 0.33 per cent level of the early 1990s.[15] In terms of composition, the share of debt relief has increased to 17 per cent of total ODA from the recent historical average of 5-6 per cent. Beyond debt and humanitarian relief, traditional donor countries as a group are falling further behind the 0.7 per cent gross national income (GNI) ODA target reaffirmed at the 2002 Monterrey conference. Only 16 of the 22 DAC member countries met the 2006 targets for ODA that they set themselves at the conference.

The countries that are reaching or exceeding the United Nations target of 0.7 per cent of GNI are Denmark, Luxembourg, the Netherlands, Norway and Sweden. In contrast, as a proportion of GNI, ODA from the largest developed economies falls far short of target and indicates the enormous scope for an increase in overall ODA. For instance, net ODA by the United States fell by 20 per cent in real terms in 2006, to an ODA/GNI ratio of 0.17 per cent. The ODA of Japan fell by 9.6 per cent to 0.25 per cent of GNI, confirming its downward trend that had started in 2000.

In contrast, the combined ODA of the 15 EU-DAC members, accounting for about 57 per cent of the total, rose by 2.7 per cent in real terms in 2006. At 0.44 per cent of GNI, the 2006 performance surpasses the collective EU ODA/GNI target of 0.39 per cent. Aid provided by the European Commission also rose by 5.7 per cent, reflecting in-creased budget support and improved disbursement capacity. The EU intends to scale up its aid further to reach 0.56 per cent of its combined GNI by 2010 or a minimum target of 0.51 per cent for DAC-EU members.[16] Among DAC donors, there is a wide variation in

The EU intends to scale up its aid to reach 0.56 per cent of its combined GNI by 2010

---

15    World Bank, *World Bank Global Development Finance 2007*, op. cit., p. 56.

16    See "Development aid from OECD countries fell 5.1 per cent in 2006", Organization for Economic Cooperation and Development, news release, 3 April 2007, available from http://www.oecd.org/document/17/0,3343,en_2649_201185_38341265_1_1_1_1,00.html.

aid performance: Luxembourg gave $550 per person in ODA in 2005, while nine donor countries gave less than $100 in per capita terms.

To fulfil their existing aid commitments, donors have to at least double the annual rate of growth of their aid disbursements

Beyond the 0.7 per cent target, aid commitments have recently been stated in other forms, and these commitments are also likely to be missed. The Organization for Economic Cooperation and Development (OECD) survey of DAC members' budgetary intentions suggests that 2008 planned spending will fall short of the increases needed to attain the agreed 2010 target.[17] If donors are to fulfil their commitments to increase aid to $130 billion and double aid to Africa by 2010, they need to expand their foreign-aid disbursements faster than any other public expenditure, at a rate of about 11 per cent every year from 2008 to 2010, compared with the recent trend of 5 per cent per year.[18] For Africa alone, the pledge to increase ODA to sub-Saharan Africa to $50 billion in real terms by 2010 will require an increase in aid by an average annual rate of 16 per cent in the next 3 years.

Although the DAC member countries continue to account for roughly 95 per cent of total ODA, non-DAC countries' aid flows have increased rapidly in recent years. Because data is not available in a consolidated and comparable form, it is difficult to quantify the amount or composition of aid provided by most new donors. In order to clarify the extent of aid-related activities by emerging donors, the World Bank, in collaboration with OECD-DAC, the United Nations Development Programme (UNDP) and the Department of Economic and Social Affairs of the United Nations (UN/DESA), conducted a survey of 9 non-DAC countries; so far it has received responses from Chile, Malaysia and Thailand. The provisional results of this survey indicate that the development assistance of these countries is mostly in the form of technical assistance and is directed towards countries within their own regions.

Significantly, net ODA disbursements by the 15 donor countries that are not members of DAC but report on their aid data rose from about $1 billion before 2001 to $4.2 billion in 2005, with the share of non-Arab countries rising over time. The share in total ODA of non-DAC donors relative to that of DAC has declined from 5.5 to 4.0 per cent owing to the faster increase in DAC flows. However, this estimate does not include some of the large Asian donors, notably China, which is rapidly increasing its aid, especially to Africa.

ODA from non-DAC donors has been noticeably oriented towards stimulating productive activities

A recent UNDP report notes[19] that China, together with the IBSA Group (India, Brazil and South Africa) provides significant development assistance to other developing countries. For instance, in 2006, China disbursed $5 billion in preferential loans to encourage Chinese enterprises to invest in ASEAN countries, and is creating a $5 billion China-Africa Development Fund to stimulate Chinese investment in Africa. China also cancelled RMB 10.9 billion ($1.47 billion) of African debt and promised to double its assistance to Africa. Similarly, India has extended $1.4 billion of concessional lines of credit to other developing countries since 2004 and wrote off debts owed by African countries under the Heavily Indebted Poor Countries (HIPC) Initiative.

Given the historical experience of the OPEC countries' ODA alone reaching 30 per cent of total ODA in the late 1970s and the growing presence of large emerging donors such as China and India, the amount of non-DAC ODA is expected to rise fur-

---

17    Ibid.

18    See "Towards an inclusive development paradigm: South-South development cooperation", paper presented by Yiping Zhou at the UN/DESA panel discussion on Enhancing South-South and Triangular Cooperation, 17 October 2007.

19    Ibid.

ther from the current estimate of 5 per cent of worldwide ODA to possibly 10 per cent by 2015. This prospect raises additional issues of transparency concerning the amount and content of the aid flows and their effectiveness and impact on debt sustainability in recipient countries.

ODA from non-DAC donors has, so far, been noticeably oriented towards stimulating productive activities, suggesting a stark contrast with the framework underlying the ODA of DAC donors. Funding from DAC members are disbursed within poverty-reduction and growth facilities, with overarching macroeconomic constraints and governance conditionalities and stronger orientation towards social spending.

## Aid effectiveness

The 2005 Paris Declaration on Aid Effectiveness was a milestone in setting out the specific principles for launching a process to realize the Monterrey Consensus formulation that effective partnerships among donors and recipients should be based on the recognition of national leadership and ownership of development plans. The contrasting frameworks between DAC and non-DAC donors operating in the same countries throw light on the complexity of realizing country leadership. There is increasing recognition that the Paris Declaration process can achieve the Monterrey mandate only if recipient countries participate as full partners. It is therefore important that the effort to promote aid effectiveness expand beyond the activities of OECD-DAC, which consists only of donors. The new Development Cooperation Forum of the United Nations Economic and Social Council could play a pivotal role in accelerating progress by intensifying and regularizing the participation of developing countries in both the conceptual and operational aspects of reforming the international aid system.

In 2006, in line with the Paris process, the OECD launched a Global Forum on Development to initiate a broader discussion on aid effectiveness beyond the OECD. The first annual plenary of the Forum took place in Paris on 3 April 2007, with the participation of a large number of developing donor countries.

Although it will not be possible to establish clear trends in harmonization and alignment until the second round of monitoring of the Paris indicators in 2008, the first round of monitoring since the Paris High Level Forum, carried out in 2006, indicates some modest, practical improvements. The survey results, however, strongly suggest that increased attention is needed to further reduce the cost of delivering aid and to build stronger and more accountable country-level institutions. The 2006 survey pointed, in particular, to the need for recipient countries to deepen their ownership of the development process, for donors to make better use of partners' national budgets and for both to rely more on performance-assessment frameworks and result-oriented reporting. Demonstrating concrete achievements in practices is fundamental for a further advance in the implementation of the Paris Declaration by the next High Level Forum to be held in Ghana in September 2008.

Aid flows continue to be volatile, and such volatility is often exacerbated by the gap between commitments and disbursements. Aid is significantly more volatile than fiscal revenue. Since aid flows tend to be pro-cyclical, a global slowdown would have a negative impact on aid-dependent economies, as it would be accompanied by sudden changes in the size of resource commitments. When aid falls, it often leads to fiscal adjustments in the form of increased taxation and spending cuts that reinforce the cyclical impact of declining aid flows.

*Aid flows continue to be volatile*

## Innovative forms of development financing

Projects in innovative
financing, especially in the
field of health, have moved
from discussion to reality

A series of initiatives in so-called innovative forms of financing have moved from discussion to reality, just as arduous and deteriorating efforts to meet conventional aid pledges are becoming evident. Three initiatives, all in the field of health, are notable. The International Finance Facility for Immunisation (IFFIm), launched in January 2006, is expected to scale up spending by as much as $500 million annually up to 2015 through the issuance of $4 billion worth of floating bonds, the annual payments by donors to the Facility being recorded as part of their ODA. Air ticket levies, with 19 countries having taken at least initial steps as of September 2006, are estimated to raise about $1 billion to $1.5 billion a year, recorded as ODA upon disbursement. These funds are managed by a new mechanism known as UNITAID to fund health-related expenditures in developing countries. The Advanced Market Commitments (AMCs) programme provides incentives for the development of vaccines where market demand is not sufficient to attract investment on the part of the private sector. The AMC will not increase aid flows as such, but will stimulate research and development by drug companies for diseases prevalent in developing countries.

In the context of total ODA volume, innovative sources of financing have not yet raised significant amounts. Other, potentially significant, sources of innovative financing are currently being considered. For example, there is renewed interest in the potential for raising significant amounts globally from a minuscule currency-transaction tax in light of the fact that these transactions can be tracked in the same way that international transactions are monitored for anti-terrorism and anti-drug-money-laundering purposes. Some members of the Leading Group on Solidarity Levies to Fund Development (Brazil, Chile, France, Norway and Spain) have also expressed interest in expanding efforts to combat tax evasion and capital flight under the rubric of innovative sources of financing. Innovative financing is expected to figure more prominently in the forthcoming review of the financing for development process in Doha at the end of 2008.

## Debt relief

The amounts of freed-up
resources from debt relief
have varied widely across
countries

In 1996, the Bretton Wood institutions launched the HIPC Initiative for the provision of debt relief by bilateral and other creditors, but excluding debt owed to international financial institutions (IFIs) themselves. The aim was to release resources for development. The promise of freeing up sufficient resources proved illusory because in many countries the existence of large arrears reflected their lack of ability to pay. Thus the amount of freed-up resources for development has been at varying levels in the countries that have benefited from the HIPC Initiative.

Thus far, debt reduction packages have been approved for 32 out of 41 eligible countries, 26 of which are African. The Initiative provided $46 billion in debt-service relief in net present value terms as of October 2007.[20] Although the initial sunset clause became effective on 31 December 2006, it was decided to grandfather all countries that had been, or will be, assessed to have met the HIPC Initiative's income and indebtedness criteria based on end-2004 data. Following an agreement on its debt to the Russian

---

20    See, "Debt relief under the Heavily Indebted Poor Countries (HIPC) Initiative", International Monetary Fund factsheet, October 2007, available from http://www.imf.org/external/np/exr/facts/hipc.htm.

Federation, Afghanistan was found to have met the criteria and was added to potentially eligible countries in April 2007, reaching its decision point in July 2007.

HIPC was supplemented by the Multilateral Debt Relief Initiative (MDRI) in June 2005. The MDRI allows 100 per cent relief on eligible debts owed to the IMF, the International Development Association (IDA) of the World Bank and the African Development Bank for countries completing the HIPC Initiative. By September 2006, MDRI debt cancellation had been implemented by the three institutions. The Inter-American Development Bank joined the MDRI officially in March 2007 and decided to provide similar debt relief to the five HIPCs in Latin America and the Caribbean. It has since provided $3.9 billion in nominal terms to Bolivia, Guyana, Honduras and Nicaragua and will provide $0.5 billion to Haiti when it reaches the completion period. As of August 2007, total MDRI assistance delivered to post-completion-point HIPCs is estimated at $37.6 billion in nominal terms.

As a result of these measures, debt-service payments by the 32 beneficiary countries declined by almost 2 per cent of GDP between 1999 and 2006, and their expenditures on health, education and other services increased to about five times the amount of debt-service payments, whereas before the HIPC Initiative, debt-servicing slightly exceeded such spending by eligible countries. Ultimately, HIPC relief committed to countries that have reached their decision point should reduce their debt stock by two thirds, and the estimated MDRI assistance and additional bilateral debt relief should reduce it by more than 90 per cent. Therefore, debt-service payments for these countries are expected to decline to less than 5 per cent of exports, allowing them more space for social expenditures.

Only 22 countries have, so far, reached the completion point at which lenders provide the full debt relief committed at decision point, and their irrevocable debt relief amounts to less than half of the estimated total HIPC cost of $68 billion. The remaining interim and pre-decision-point countries face various challenges to progress under HIPC. Further implementation has been slow because of the existence of large arrears to IFIs. Speedier resolution of arrears is needed so that low-income countries can benefit from debt relief under these initiatives.

The average delay that HIPCs experience between decision and completion points has increased since 2000, and took more than six years in the case of Sao Tome and Principe. Progress has been hampered in several pre-decision countries (such as Somalia, the Sudan and Togo) by internal conflicts, difficulties in macroeconomic stabilization and poverty-reduction programmes or substantial arrears to multilateral institutions, which prevent them from accessing IMF- and IDA-supported programmes. Five interim HIPCs, all of them in Africa, have experienced interruptions in their IMF programmes, causing difficulties in meeting their completion-point triggers.[21]

Six HIPCs—Burkina Faso, Ethiopia, Malawi, Niger, Rwanda and Sao Tome and Principe—have received topped-up assistance, which is allowed at completion point in the case of a significant unanticipated deterioration in debt-burden indicators primarily due to exogenous factors. The total cost of this assistance had a net present value (NPV) of $2 billion at the end of 2006, which amounts to 3 per cent of the total HIPC Initiative cost.[22]

More significantly, the HIPC aim of reducing debt to sustainable levels has not been realized and long-term debt sustainability remains an elusive goal for most HIPCs.

*MDRI increases debt relief for countries that have reached their HIPC decision point*

*Internal conflicts and macroeconomic stabilization failures have hampered debt relief in pre-decision HIPCs*

*The goal of reducing debt to sustainable levels remains elusive for most HIPCs*

---

21    See International Development Association and International Monetary Fund, "Heavily Indebted Poor Countries (HIPC) Initiative and Multilateral Debt Relief Initiative (MDRI): Status of Implementation", report prepared by the staffs of IDA and IMF, 28 August 2007, p. 11, available from http://www.imf.org/external/np/pp/2007/eng/082807.pdf.

22    Ibid., p. 21.

Despite improved debt ratios under HIPC and the Enhanced HIPC Initiative, along with the expected $96 billion reduction in debt stock of the 31 post-decision-point HIPCs in NPV terms at the end of 2006, the risk of debt distress remains high or moderate for half of the post-completion-point HIPCs. So far, only 10 of the 22 post-completion-point HIPCs have low-range debt stress, and the threat of a rapid reaccumulation of debt by HIPCs is becoming increasingly real.[23] Besides prudent borrowing, therefore, policies to diversify exports and improve the efficiency of external-resource use are critical for longer-term debt sustainability.

There are problems on the donor side too. In financing terms, multilateral creditors account for almost 46 per cent of the estimated cost of debt relief to HIPCs, with Paris Club, non-Paris Club and commercial creditors accounting for the remaining 35, 13 and 6 per cent, respectively. However, some small multilateral institutions still do not participate in the HIPC Initiative and, not surprisingly, participation by non-Paris Club and commercial creditors remains low.

As of the end of July 2007, 25 out of 32 multilateral creditors were participating in the HIPC Initiative. Non-Paris Club creditors are believed to have delivered just over one third of their expected share. Debt relief has not yet been provided by 21 creditors, while only 6 countries have reached their full share as of August 2007. Commercial creditors now contribute less than 4 per cent, on average, to debt relief for post-decision-point HIPCs. For some individual countries, this share is higher, ranging from 10 per cent to 13 per cent in the cases of Ghana and Sierra Leone and 25 per cent for Côte d'Ivoire. The available information suggests that only a few non-bank commercial creditors have provided their share of HIPC Initiative relief directly or through market-based buy-back operations.[24]

Litigation by commercial creditors against HIPCs is a growing threat to the Initiative

Some commercial creditors have initiated litigation against HIPCs. Even though the amounts are small, these actions undermine the HIPC Initiative's objectives and represent a growing challenge to its implementation. A recent IMF staff survey reported that 11 of the 24 respondents have been targeted with lawsuits by a total of 46 creditors. More importantly, more than half of the litigation actions were won against seven HIPCs, and judgements were obtained amounting to about $1 billion on original claims of $427 million, not including out-of-court settlements. Since the 2006 survey, eight new legal actions have been reported, and the most recent litigation cases were against the Congo, Cameroon, Nicaragua and Uganda. Litigating creditors are concentrated in the United States, the United Kingdom of Great Britain and Northern Ireland and the British Virgin Islands, and their lawsuits are mainly filed in New York, Paris, and London.[25]

Lengthy court proceedings impose substantial budgetary and institutional burdens. Commercial creditors' lack of participation can also cause a delay in the release of interim debt relief. For instance, as of the end of June 2007, the IMF was not disbursing debt relief to the Congo, which reached its decision point in April 2006. Most importantly, it raises concerns regarding inequitable treatment because commercial debt is repaid on more favourable terms than that of official creditors. Inequitable treatment undermines the legitimacy of the Initiative.

---

23    Ibid., p. 17.

24    Ibid., p. 29.

25    Ibid., p. 32.

# Strengthening the international financial architecture

## Further policy challenges posed by the recent crisis in credit markets

In recent years, a number of factors have come together that have led to a significant relaxation of credit standards and to the underpricing of credit risk globally. These factors include strong global growth, relatively low interest rates (and the associated stepped-up demand for riskier, higher-yield assets) and rapid financial innovation, resulting in the increasing use of securitization via more-and-more complex and opaquely structured products and off-balance-sheet vehicles. The correction of this irregularity began in the spring of 2007 and turned, in July and August, into severe interruptions in the functioning of markets. A credit and liquidity squeeze at the core of the global financial system was triggered by rising defaults in the United States sub-prime mortgage market. This prompted massive liquidity injections by major central banks.

The turmoil in global financial markets has demonstrated that the process of globalized risk transfer via modern risk-transfer instruments and structures embodies a number of serious shortcomings, both in the markets themselves and in the regulatory and supervisory systems. The current turmoil has uncovered significant flaws in the originate-and-distribute (as opposed to the originate-and-hold) model. In the originate-and-hold model, lenders (normally, banking institutions) keep the loan assets on their balance sheets and have a stronger incentive to undertake rigorous credit analysis. In moving to the originate-and-distribute mechanism, lenders (some of whom are not banking institutions and are not subject to regulatory oversight), package the stream of earnings from these loan assets and sell them to other investors. These investors, including many pension funds, are primarily interested in comparative returns. The creation of loans for immediate securitization and sale reduced the incentives for originators to maintain high credit standards. Since the originators are immune from default risk once the loan is securitized and sold, they tend not to assess the creditworthiness of borrowers adequately. Public policy needs to be cognizant of its role in maintaining incentives for loan originators with a view to ensuring that credit quality is maintained and credit is appropriately priced.[26]

Another issue related to securitization concerns the measure and concentration of risk that the banks involved in origination activities actually take. Despite seemingly widespread sharing and dispersion of risk in the financial system, in a large number of cases, the credit risk remained in the domain of the commercial banks through their activation of back-up lines of credit for off-balance-sheet conduits or special investment vehicles (SIVs) set up by them. This has effectively put credit risk back on banks' balance sheets. Risk has proven to be considerably more concentrated than market participants and supervisory agencies had believed. This suggests that in assessing banking soundness and capital, supervisors should pay more attention to off-balance sheet exposures.

The recent market turbulence has highlighted the lack of transparency both in the new instruments themselves and in the markets more broadly. As the crisis unfolded, investors realized that they were much less informed about the nature of the assets they had bought than they originally thought.

*A number of factors have led to a significant relaxation of credit standards and the underpricing of risk*

*The originate-and-distribute credit model has reduced incentives for a careful assessment of the credit-worthiness of borrowers*

*Investors realized they were inadequately informed about the nature of the assets they had bought*

---

26   See, for instance, "Turbulence in credit markets—causes, effects, and lessons to be learned", remarks by David Dodge, Governor of the Bank of Canada, to the Vancouver Board of Trade, Vancouver, 25 September 2007, available from http://www.bis.org/review/r070928c.pdf.

The complex structures of the asset-backed instruments and the lack of transparency with regard to the underlying assets made these instruments very difficult to price, especially when market liquidity dried up under stress. In this regard, a certain degree of standardization of securitization packages and reporting may be required, as is the case in other markets.[27] Regulatory standards have to be introduced for investor protection by ensuring that financial instruments are structured in such a way that market participants can clearly see what they are buying. Public oversight of the operations of credit-rating agencies may be needed.

At the same time, concerns have increased about the lack of transparency regarding where the risks, which are widely distributed to investors all over the globe by means of securitization, reside in the financial system. Uncertainty about the location and size of potential losses has contributed significantly to elevated risk aversion, the sudden liquidity crunch and major disruptions in the money and credit markets.

Existing reporting requirements in the banking sector do not allow for a full assessment of banks' exposure to structured products or of the extent to which they have taken, on their balance-sheet, loans and liquidity commitments in the event of stress. Accordingly, there is a view that, in addition to actions to improve information and disclosure practices expected from market participants, new regulations may be needed to induce parties to reveal information they would not normally disclose.[28]

As mentioned in chapter I, the recent events have drawn attention to the value of credit ratings and the role of credit-rating agencies in the regulatory process. As the crisis has unfolded, it has become increasingly clear that their ratings for complex securities were not appropriate for determining in guiding the allocation of exposure, in contrast to their ratings for conventional bonds.[29] Complex securities incorporate refinancing and liquidity commitments which standard bond ratings do not take into account. The potential conflict of interest within the credit agencies' business model might also have hampered proper due diligence, in particular as regards structured finance instruments.[30] Investors must be discouraged from relying almost exclusively on credit ratings and urged to take more responsibility for diligent research and their own risk assessment.[31]

The crisis has also highlighted the importance of the structure of supervision, which while remaining basically national, has escalating cross-border effects. The crisis has demonstrated the importance of better coordination among supervisors, regulators, central bankers and finance ministries within individual countries, since cooperation at

*New regulations may be needed to induce parties to reveal information they would not normally disclose*

*The crisis indicates that national supervision has escalating cross-border effects*

---

27    Statement by Christine Lagarde, Minister of Economy, Finance and Employment, France, at the sixteenth meeting of the International Monetary Financial Committee, International Monetary Fund, 20 October 2007, available from http://www.imf.org/external/AM/2007/imfc/statement/eng/fra.pdf.

28    See, "Through the Looking Glass: The Links between financial globalization and systemic risk", speech by John Lipsky, First Deputy Managing Director of the IMF, at the joint IMF/Chicago Federal Reserve conference, 27 September 2007, available from http://www.imf.org/external/np/speeches/2007/092707.htm.

29    See, "Credit market turbulence and policy challenges ahead", remarks by David Dodge, Governor of the Bank of Canada, to the Institute of International Finance, Washington D.C., 21 October 2007, available from http://www.bis.org/review/r071024c.pdf.

30    See, "Recent financial market developments", speech by Yves Mersch, Governor of the Central Bank of Luxembourg, at the fiftieth anniversary of ACI Luxembourg, Luxembourg, 12 October 2007, available from http://www.bis.org/review/r071025d.pdf.

31    See, for instance, "Reflections on the global financial system", keynote speech by Jean-Claude Trichet, President of the European Central Bank, at the twenty-fifth anniversary IIF annual membership meeting, Washington D.C., 20 October 2007, available from http://www.bis.org/review/r071024b.pdf.

the international level can only be as good as cooperation at the domestic level. In some countries, there may be a need to simplify regulatory infrastructure.[32]

In response to the challenges posed by the recent market turbulence, the Financial Stability Forum (FSF), during its meeting on 25 and 26 September 2007 in New York, decided to form a working group of the relevant national authorities and chairpersons of international bodies to analyse the causes of the recent market turbulence and make proposals to enhance market and institutional resilience. The Group of Seven (G7) Finance Ministers and Central Bank Governors requested the working group to offer proposals in the areas of liquidity and risk management; accounting and valuation of financial derivatives; the role, methodologies and use of credit-agency ratings in structured finance; and basic supervisory principles of prudential oversight, including the treatment of off-balance-sheet vehicles.[33] A final report and recommendations by the FSF will be submitted to G7 Ministers and Governors at their April 2008 meeting.

There have also been calls to speed up the implementation of the New Basel Capital Accord (Basel II) rules, based on the argument that a new framework may help make the capital base more relevant to the changing risk profile of banks and may also serve to create incentives for better risk measurement and management, in particular for securitization exposures and liquidity lines for asset-backed programmes. Basel II rules require that banks disclose more information on their risk profile, including risk associated with securitization exposures, the nature of such exposures and the risks that have been retained. On the other hand, there are concerns that if Basel II, as presently designed, had been in effect during the period of easy liquidity, its emphasis on marking to market might have exacerbated the pro-cyclical relaxation of credit standards. There is a need for important revisions in the approach in the context of recent financial market developments.

Meanwhile, the Basel Committee for Banking Supervision is working on several outstanding issues, including the introduction of new standards for banks holding capital against the default risk associated with complex, less liquid credit products; approaches to supervising and regulating funding liquidity risk; and bank valuation practices.[34]

The massive liquidity injections by central banks around the world during the mid-2007 turbulence have once again raised the issue of "moral hazard". Central banks have the responsibility to ensure the continued functioning of financial markets. Under highly stressed financial conditions, this may require extraordinary measures. However, this involves a very delicate balancing act: overly aggressive interventions bail out careless operators who take on too much risk, and this is something that will be perceived as a guarantee against failure. This will increase the risk of similar or even more severe situations in the future.

---

32   See, "The world after the crisis in the credit markets: Economic outlook and challenges", speech by Rodrigo de Rato, Managing Director of the IMF, at the thirtieth anniversary of the Valencian Business Confederation, Valencia, Spain, 25 October 2007, available from http://www.imf.org/external/np/speeches/2007/102507.htm.

33   Statement of G7 Ministers and Central Bank Governors, Washington, D.C., 19 October 2007, available from http://www.g8.utoronto.ca/finance/fm071019.htm.

34   See, "Financial market developments and the work of the Basel Committee", Bank for International Settlements, press release, 9 October 2007, available from http://www.bis.org/press/p071009.htm.

## Multilateral surveillance

Surveillance is a key tool for the IMF in carrying out its assigned responsibility of preventing crises and promoting macroeconomic stability. Looming over the surveillance reform debate currently under way at the IMF is the Fund's inability to convince major economies to undertake the necessary policy adjustments to alleviate the exploding global financial imbalances as well as its rather passive image in the run-up to the mid-2007 market turbulence.

The Fund's previous exchange-rate surveillance was based on the 1977 Executive Board decision entitled "Surveillance over Exchange-rate Policies", which was drafted in the wake of the collapse of the Bretton Woods system of fixed exchange-rate parities. In June 2007, the Executive Board approved an updating of this decision, the first major revision of the surveillance framework in almost 30 years. [35] The previous approach focused on potential exchange-rate manipulation undertaken for balance-of-payments reasons and on short-term exchange-rate volatility. It did not address the current exchange-rate-related issues, such as the maintenance of overvalued or undervalued exchange-rate pegs and capital-account vulnerabilities.[36]

The main goal of the revision is to clarify the focus, scope and modalities of surveillance in the context of the changing structure of the global economy, drawing on the best practices already being used in Article IV consultations. To the three existing principles guiding members' exchange-rate policies (namely, to avoid manipulating exchange-rates in order to prevent balance-of-payments adjustment or gain an unfair competitive advantage; to intervene in the exchange market to counter disorderly conditions; and to take into account the interests of other members in intervention policies), the revised decision adds a fourth principle—to avoid exchange-rate policies that result in external instability. The decision adds seven appraisal indicators that may trigger a review by the IMF. The new decision requires the IMF to base the surveillance process on dialogue and persuasion, to treat members even-handedly and to pay due regard to countries' specific circumstances.

Under the new decision, external stability becomes the overarching principle of the surveillance framework. It is defined as a condition according to which the balance-of-payments position does not give rise to disruptive adjustments in exchange-rates. This requires that the underlying current account remain broadly in equilibrium and that the capital-account position does not create risks of abrupt shifts in capital flows. When the underlying current account is not in equilibrium, the exchange-rate is considered to be fundamentally misaligned.

The decision puts exchange-rate assessment at the centre of IMF surveillance. However, there exists wide variance in views of the concept of misalignment. Some experts even contend that estimating currency over- and undervaluation is not at all possible technically. The results of calculations are very sensitive to various assumptions.[37] The IMF

---

[35]    See, "IMF Executive Board adopts new decision on bilateral surveillance over members' policies", International Monetary Fund, Public Information Notice (PIN), No. 07/69, 21 June 2007, available from http://www.imf.org/external/np/sec/pn/2007/pn0769.htm.

[36]    See, Statement by IMF Managing Director Rodrigo de Rato on IMF Executive Board decision to approve new framework for surveillance, International Monetary Fund press release, 21 June 2007, available from http://www.imf.org/external/np/sec/pr/2007/pr07137.htm.

[37]    See, for instance, T. Ashby McCown, Patricia Pollard and John Weeks, "Equilibrium exchange-rate models and misalignments", Occasional Paper, No. 7, Department of the Treasury, Office of International Affairs, March 2007, available from http://www.treas.gov/offices/international-affairs/occasional-paper-series/docs/ExchangeRateModels.pdf.

relies on three complementary approaches to draw inferences on misalignment and makes a determination if the results are largely similar in magnitude and direction among the three approaches.[38] The problem is that even information drawn from a variety of models will not provide a definitive answer and must be supplemented with assessments based on additional considerations regarding other causes behind the exchange rates' deviations from calculated equilibrium values.[39] Hence, given the considerable uncertainties and the judgemental nature of misalignment estimates, basing the assessment of countries' policies on the current approach raises serious doubts.

Implementation of the new decision can impose undue pressure on developing and emerging economies pursuing export-led growth strategies, which in turn require maintenance of the long-run stability of competitive real-exchange rates. Because many of these countries have open capital accounts subject to volatile inflows, these countries often have to resort to policies that prevent excessive appreciation of their exchange rates. Moreover, more rigorous surveillance over systemically important countries issuing major reserve currencies is not likely, since the decision does not differentiate among countries in terms of their influence on systemic stability. This is at variance with the intended "even-handedness" of the new decision.

*Countries with open capital accounts have often resorted to interventions to prevent excessive currency appreciation*

Given the lack of consensus on many important issues, it is not surprising that there is no unified view among the IMF staff and member countries on how to implement the new decision. This creates the risk of significant differences with regard to policy assessment and policy recommendations, as well as further damage to the credibility of the IMF. The prompt adoption of clear and detailed implementation guidelines acceptable to all members practising different exchange-rate arrangements is critical.

In addition, with the new surveillance decision, the IMF Executive Board reached an agreement on a "Statement of Surveillance Priorities" in the context of the 2008 Triennial Surveillance Review (TSR). The statement defines both operational and economic priorities for surveillance over the next three years, sets out the responsibilities and accountability of all those involved in the surveillance process and provides a clearer benchmark against which the effectiveness of surveillance is assessed.

In parallel to the effort to reform the bilateral surveillance procedure, a new vehicle for multilateral consultations, involving major member countries, and regional groupings, was established to complement surveillance activities. The focus of the first multilateral consultations, involving China, the euro area, Japan, Saudi Arabia and the United States, was on narrowing global current-account imbalances while maintaining robust growth. In a report to the International Monetary and Financial Committee (IMFC) of the IMF Board of Governors in April 2007, participants in the talks made important commitments aimed at reducing global imbalances. According to the IMF, policies outlined by the countries, if implemented, could reduce global imbalances by 1.0 to 1.75 per cent of global GDP over the next four years from a baseline of about 6.0 per cent.[40]

---

[38]   See, "Challenges to the international monetary system: rebalancing currencies, institutions, and rates", presentation by Takatoshi Kato, Deputy Managing Director of the IMF, at the Salzburg Global Seminar, Salzburg, Austria, 30 September 2007, available from http://www.imf.org/external/np/speeches/2007/093007.htm.

[39]   Testimony of Treasury Deputy Assistant Secretary Mark Sobel on currency manipulation and its effect on U.S. businesses and workers, 9 May 2007, available from http://www.treas.gov/press/releases/hp394.htm.

[40]   International Monetary Fund, *IMF Survey,* vol. 36, No. 7, 23 April 2007, p. 103.

It remains to be seen whether the commitments will be implemented. Following these consultations, each participant has made some progress towards putting its policy intentions into effect. However, progress made has been insufficient and much remains to be done in terms of policy shifts. Indeed, while the United States current-account deficit has declined somewhat, the current-account surpluses in China, Japan and emerging Asian economies have continued to rise. There is continued risk of a disorderly unwinding of global imbalances and an abrupt fall in the dollar. This risk, despite some collective measures, has increased due to the recent financial turmoil. This underscores the importance of continued active policy coordination, as discussed in Chapter I, including the full implementation of the policies agreed to under the multilateral consultation process. It is also important to find appropriate and effective ways of monitoring the implementation efforts of the participants. One possible way, as proposed in the *World Economic Situation and Prospects 2007* and reiterated in chapter I of the present report, would be to have parties issue multi-year schedules for the agreed policy adjustments and targets. Announcing specific targets in the form of a schedule and subsequent failure to meet those terms would have costs in terms of reputation. Of course, in order to be credible, commitments must be attainable and readily monitored, which requires that they be explicit, measurable and public.[41]

Global imbalances are not the only issue that requires a collective approach. The recent financial-market developments have highlighted market imperfections which the current international regulatory environment has not addressed. Further work by the international community on closing monitoring and regulatory gaps in the financial system requires stronger multilateral cooperation on financial-market issues. The challenges that have been posed by the recent financial-market turbulence are global in nature and require approaches that can be applied consistently at the global level. However, it is impossible to derive effective global solutions without the participation and ownership of all countries that have to implement them. In this respect, with its global membership, comprehensive surveillance framework and growing knowledge base, the Fund, in closer collaboration with other relevant institutions, can and must play an essential part, including that of calling for a second round of multilateral consultations focused on financial-stability issues.

The Fund should be active in developing *ex ante* responses to budding financial problems. It should convene global discussions on effective countermeasures to address potential and emerging issues, rather than become actively involved only when the damage has already been done. In this regard, it has been argued that the IMF could have played a more active role in the run-up to the mid-2007 market turbulence.[42] It has also been noted that, in contrast to its role in the Asian crisis, the Fund has been excessively cautious and insufficiently specific in its recommendations concerning the present crisis, which has its epicentre in the United States economy.[43]

---

41   See, *World Economic Situation and Prospects 2007* (United Nations publication, Sales No. E.07.II.C.2), pp. 29-34.

42   Statement by the Fukushiro Nukaga, Minister of Finance of Japan at the sixteenth meeting of the International Monetary and Financial Committee, International Monetary Fund, Washington, D.C., 20 October 2007, available from http://www.imf.org/External/AM/2007/imfc/statement/eng/jpn.pdf.

43   Statement by Guido Mantega, Minister of Finance of Brazil at the sixteenth meeting of the International Monetary and Financial Committee, International Monetary Fund, Washington, D.C., 20 October 2007, available from http://www.imf.org/External/AM/2007/imfc/statement/eng/bra.pdf .

If the ongoing reform of the surveillance process is to succeed in restoring the effectiveness of surveillance by IMF, the new mechanism should enhance focus and even-handedness, and be underpinned by a legitimate process of governance. Otherwise, the IMF will be seen as a player which is partisan to specific interests and unable to play the role of an honest broker. Whatever the quality of the Fund's surveillance, its effectiveness will ultimately depend on each country's willingness to adhere to the principles of multilateral cooperation.

## Governance reform at the Bretton Woods institutions

The IMF and the World Bank, like other public institutions, were established by multilateral agreement to achieve critical public objectives. Their effectiveness and legitimacy in pursuing those assigned objectives can be attained only if their agenda and decisions better reflect the needs and concerns of the majority of countries affected by their operations, which at the present time are the developing countries. Both institutions have been undergoing what many observers, including their strong supporters, see as an "existential crisis". Net financial flows from the Bretton Woods institutions have tended to be negative over the past ten years, in some years, significantly so (table III.4). The recent build-up in international reserves by developing countries, ostensibly for reasons of "self-insurance", and their sharply reduced use of World Bank resources, particularly by middle-income countries, are another indicator of the diminished relevance of these institutions. At this point in time, significant reforms in voice and representation in these institutions are necessary for the credibility, legitimacy and institutional survival of both agencies.

*International public institutions can only be effective if their decisions better reflect the needs of the majority of their users*

Table III.4:
**Net flows of financial resources by selected multilateral institutions, 1997-2006**

| Millions of dollars | | | | | | | | | | |
|---|---|---|---|---|---|---|---|---|---|---|
| | 1997 | 1998 | 1999 | 2000 | 2001 | 2002 | 2003 | 2004 | 2005 | 2006 |
| **Net flows** | 21 227 | 28 825 | -7 450 | -10 859 | 14 931 | 2 001 | -11 655 | -20 235 | -39 609 | -25 864 |
| **Financial institutions excluding IMF** | 6 827 | 9 525 | 5 150 | -59 | 1 431 | -11 199 | -14 755 | -10 235 | 835 | 5 208 |
| Regional development banks[a] | 5 334 | 7 971 | 4 229 | 327 | 1 696 | -3 904 | -8 025 | -6 570 | -1 668 | 2 965 |
| World Bank Group | 1 493 | 1 554 | 921 | -386 | -265 | -7 295 | -6 730 | -3 665 | 2 503 | 2 243 |
| International Bank for Reconstruction and Development (IBRD) | -3 265 | -2 723 | -3 019 | -4 079 | -4 570 | -12 126 | -11 241 | -8 930 | -2 898 | -5 087 |
| International Development Association (IDA) | 4 757 | 4 276 | 3 940 | 3 693 | 4 432 | 4 831 | 4 511 | 5 265 | 5 401 | 7 330 |
| IMF (billions of dollars) | 14 | 19 | -13 | -11 | 14 | 13 | 3 | -10 | -40 | -31 |
| *Memorandum item:* (in units of 2000 purchasing power)[b] | | | | | | | | | | |
| Resource commitments | 78 696 | 87 264 | 62 446 | 63 085 | 73 650 | 97 237 | 62 586 | 47 774 | 59 760 | 54 863 |
| Net flows | 18 620 | 26 445 | -7 095 | -10 859 | 15 236 | 2 042 | -10 792 | -17 295 | -33 008 | -21 919 |

**Sources**: Annual reports, various issues of the multilateral institutions.

**a** African Development Bank (AfDB), Asian Development Bank (ADB), Caribbean Development Bank (CDB), European Bank for Reconstruction and Development (EBRD), Inter-American Development Bank (IaDB) (including Inter-American Investment Corporation (IaIC)), and the International Fund for Agricultural Development (IFAD).

**b** Totals deflated by the United Nations index of manufactured export prices (in dollars) of developed economies: 2000=100.

At the 2006 Annual Meetings in Singapore, the IMF Board of Governors approved a programme of quota and voice reform to bolster the legitimacy and relevance of the Fund and to keep members from drifting away from the institution. The Singapore resolution called for the completion of the reform programme within a two-year period.

As stated, the two main goals of the reform are to ensure that the distribution of quotas adequately reflects member countries' economic weights and roles in the global economy, and to enhance the voice of low-income countries. As a first step, the reform programme made ad hoc quota increases for a group of the most clearly under-represented countries. This was politically feasible because increased voting weight for the four countries was allocated from votes of other developing countries, not from those economies with the dominant votes on the board. The next step calls for more fundamental reforms, including an agreement on a simpler and more transparent quota formula, a second round of ad hoc quota increases based on a new formula, and an increase in basic votes. Since Singapore, a key focus of the discussions has been the new quota formula. The October 2007 Annual Meetings in Washington, D.C., provided evidence of the difficult nature of the political decision that would be required and some convergence among members on specific issues.

IMF board members agreed that voting reforms should increase the overall weight of developing countries

At the 2007 meeting, it was decided that the outcome of the second round of reforms should result in an increase in the voting share of emerging market and developing countries as a group.[44] There is, however, no agreement on the precise size of this shift. Because the total quota increase is needed to operationalize any changes in voting allocations, it is important that a reasonable increase in total quotas accompany the reallocation. On this issue, the members agreed that the total quota increase should be in the order of 10 per cent, although some countries see this as a maximum, whereas others are of the view that a larger increase is needed to achieve the objectives of the reform.[45] The issue of how to ensure the timely review and adjustment of members' quotas to reflect future changes in the global economy has not been resolved. In this regard, there is a view that the process of quota adjustment to reflect the evolution of countries' relative positions should be independent of the liquidity needs of the IMF.[46]

There is a consensus that the formula should be based on updated and modernized versions of the four variables included in the existing formulas: GDP, openness, variability and reserves, with GDP being assigned the greatest weight. It was agreed that purchasing power parity (PPP) measures of GDP should play a role, although there is still quite a wide range of views on the weight that should be given to this measurement of an economy's size. There is also substantial convergence on the need to moderate, to some degree, the influence of economic size in the formula via a compression factor.[47] As regards the other three elements, no agreement has yet been reached, either on their appropriate weights or on an acceptable definition of openness and volatility.

---

44    Communiqué of the International Monetary and Financial Committee of the Board of Governors of the International Monetary Fund, Washington, D.C., 20 October 2007, available from http://www.imf.org/external/np/cm/2007/102007a.htm.

45    See, International Monetary Fund, "Report of the Executive Board to the Board of Governors —Quota and Voice Reform—Progress since the 2006 Annual Meetings", 16 October 2007, p. 3, available from http://www.imf.org/external/np/pp/2007/eng/101607.pdf.

46    Communiqué of the Intergovernmental Group of Twenty-Four on International Monetary Affairs and Development, Washington, D.C., 19 October 2007, available from http://www.g24.org/10-07ENG.pdf.

47    A "compression factor" reduces the spread in the amounts of allocated quotas by shrinking large values and boosting small ones in a decreasing percentage as they get closer to the average.

The Singapore resolution of 2006 called for at least a doubling of basic votes that protect, at a minimum, the existing voting shares of low-income countries as a group as well as for subsequently safeguarding the proportion of basic votes in total voting power. Since then, there have been many calls for at least a tripling of the basic votes. In addition, an agreement has been reached in principle on the legal framework for an amendment to the IMF Articles of Agreement to allow for an increase in basic votes and for the future updating of voting allocations.

There are calls for a tripling of the basic votes of low-income countries

To ensure the greater representation of low-income and smaller economies, there have been suggestions to consider, in addition to an increase in basic votes, the implementation of a double-majority voting system that requires two separate majorities—based on both "one-country, one-vote" and on a weighted vote—in order for a decision to be carried. Double majority approaches have been suggested because reallocating votes based on various measures of participation in the global economy alone may not be sufficient to redress the Fund's democratic deficit.[48]

The World Bank has also launched its own process of voice and participation reform. At its October 2007 Meeting, the Development Committee welcomed the "Options Paper on Voice and Participation"[49] detailing a two-stage timetable for possible actions. The proposal reflects the Bank's specificities, needs and mandates, most notably those related to the IDA and the focus on poverty reduction. The Committee also recognized that further consultations would be necessary to reach a political consensus on a comprehensive reform package.[50]

According to the paper, the first phase would include changes in basic votes, greater representation of developing and transition country nationals in management positions, improvements in board effectiveness and composition, selected IDA questions, and special majorities. The second phase will focus on a selective capital increase, the review of the role of the IDA Board and Deputies, and the process for the selection of the President of the Bank.

It has been recognized that, although the Bank has its own mandate and needs to take into account considerations that may be different from those at the IMF, the outcome of the Fund's quota and voice reform is likely to exert profound influence on the direction of the Bank's actions. Indeed, Fund quotas have been used as a proxy for the allocation of the Bank's capital. Progress in reforms at the Fund can provide useful guidance for the general approach to governance reforms at the Bank.

---

48   See, Statement by Miguel Gustavo Peirano, Minister of Economy and Production of Argentina, at the sixteenth meeting of the International Monetary and Financial Committee, International Monetary Fund, Washington, D.C., 20 October 2007, available from http://www.imf.org/External/AM/2007/imfc/statement/eng/arg.pdf.

49   See "Voice and participation of developing and transition countries in decision making at the World Bank. Options paper", background report prepared by the staff of the World Bank for the Development Committee Meeting, 11 October 2007, available from http://siteresources.worldbank.org/DEVCOMMINT/Documentation/21510673/DC2007-0024(E)Voice.pdf.

50   Communiqué of the Development Committee, the Joint Ministerial Committee of the Board of Governors of the Bank and the Fund on the transfer of real resources to developing countries, Washington, D.C., 21 October 2007, available from http://siteresources.worldbank.org/DEVCOMMINT/NewsAndEvents/21520652/DCCommunique(E)Final.pdf .

# Chapter IV
# Regional developments and outlook

## Developed market economies

Growth decelerated in the developed market economies in 2007 and will slow further in 2008. This performance is dominated by the sharp slowdown in the United States, however, where growth slowed to well below estimates of potential, while in the other developed economies the slowdown was more muted, with rates of growth at or slightly above potential (see figure IV.1). The pattern of growth both within and across countries continues to evolve according to the rebalancing of activity, as highlighted in the *World Economic Situation and Prospects 2007*,[1] with the activity in the United States slowing more sharply and shifting away from domestic demand towards net exports, in concert with the milder slowing in Western Europe and Japan and the shifting of activity towards domestic demand, particularly consumption expenditure. However, the rebalancing has taken on a more ominous tone with the onset of the crisis in the sub-prime mortgage market—which has subsequently become a near full-blown financial crisis requiring intervention by all of the major central banks in the region—and the now heightened risks of recession in the United States.

Inflationary pressures have been another concern to central bankers as they observe headline inflation rates approaching the targets they have set (explicitly or otherwise). Inflationary pressures have surged as oil and, hence, energy prices are reaching record levels, and other commodity prices, including food, remain greatly elevated. Furthermore, in a number of countries, supply constraints are beginning to bite. Yet inflation rates remain low by historical standards and, in the outlook, inflationary pressures are expected to diminish as output growth slows. Hence, the concerns of policymakers should shift from containing inflation to guarding against recessionary forces.

### North America: a protracted slowdown in the United States

A continued slump in the housing sector is expected to lead the economy of the United States into another year of slow growth. GDP is expected to grow by 2.0 per cent for 2008, slower than the pace estimated for 2007 (see table A.1). In the outlook, private consumption is expected to weaken as the housing downturn deteriorates further, while corporate investment spending and hiring will likely decelerate also. Exports remain relatively strong, offsetting the domestic weakness to some degree. The risks for a precipitous depreciation of the United States dollar caused by an abrupt adjustment in the large global imbalances are not negligible. While this baseline forecast is based on the premise that the weakness can still be largely contained within the housing sector, downside risks will remain for a deeper and broader downturn in the economy. As analysed in chapter I, such risks were manifest in the financial turmoil of the third quarter of 2007.

---

[1]   *World Economic Situation and Prospects 2007* (United Nations publication, Sales No. E.07.II.C.2).

Figure IV.1:
**Growth and inflation in developed economies, 2001-2008**

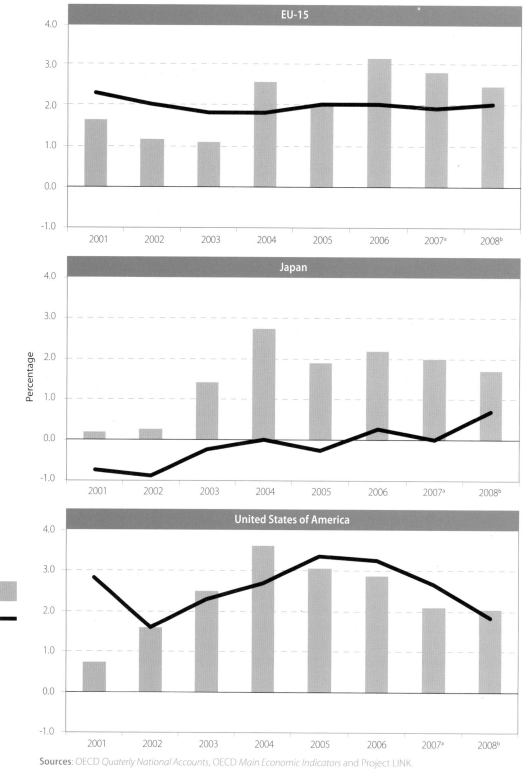

**Sources**: OECD *Quaterly National Accounts*, OECD *Main Economic Indicators* and Project LINK.
**a**  Partly estimated.
**b**  Forecasts.

The downturn in the housing sector, which began in 2006, worsened during 2007, with most indicators, such as homes sales, housing starts and the inventory of unsold homes, showing a deep contraction. For example, new home sales dropped to the lowest level in several years. Declines in house prices are also broadly dispersed over the country: the index of the national median price of homes will likely register an annual decline in 2007 for the first time since the index was set up in 1950. Delinquencies in mortgage loans have been on the rise, with the delinquency rate for sub-prime mortgages, which account for about one fifth of United States mortgages, surging to about 16 per cent in late 2007. The meltdown of the sub-prime mortgage market eventually triggered a near full-scale global financial crisis in July-August of 2007. During the crisis, issuance of short-term debt in money markets in the United States, as well as in other major developed markets, dropped abruptly, particularly for asset-backed securities. At the same time, borrowing costs increased, especially for riskier credits and for credits related to the mortgage market; investors in equity markets also sold off substantially.

*The housing sector has slowed sharply*

After the Federal Reserve Bank of the United States (Fed) adopted a number of measures, including a larger-than-expected cut in the federal funds interest rate in mid-September, stress in financial markets began to ease. Credit conditions, particularly for mortgages, remain much tighter than they were prior to the financial turmoil, and are expected to remain so in the outlook. Moreover, as many adjustable sub-prime mortgage loans are scheduled to reset interest rates in the period ahead, delinquencies on those loans will likely rise further. As a consequence, the recession in the housing sector will probably intensify, at least during the first half of 2008.

*The Fed has intervened, but credit conditions remain tight*

The housing downturn is expected to spill over increasingly to household spending, as the growth in real disposable income slows owing to lower employment growth and real wages. For the first time since 2000, the increase in consumer spending will remain below the growth of income in 2007, and the prolonged decline in the household saving rate, which had dropped to virtually zero by the end of 2006, is expected to reverse. In the outlook, as home values decline further and mortgage equity withdrawals diminish, consumers are expected to become even more cautious with regard to spending. Real consumer spending is expected to grow by 2.3 per cent in 2008, down from 3 per cent in 2007.

*Consumer spending is set to slow further*

Business spending on capital equipment decelerated notably during 2007, and the outlook for 2008 remains lacklustre, growing at a meagre 2-3 per cent per annum. Much of the weakness in the demand for equipment has been in the construction sector and in the motor vehicle industry. Demand for most other types of capital goods also softened. Spending on information equipment and software remains relatively strong, however, maintaining a pace of about 7-8 per cent. In addition, non-residential construction has been growing rapidly, at a double-digit rate for most of 2007. A significant slowdown in non-residential building spending is expected for 2008, however, along with the weakness in the housing sector.

*Investment expenditure is decelerating*

Improvements in labour-market conditions lost momentum in the second half of 2007. The growth of payroll employment decelerated from about 2.0 per cent in 2006 to 0.5 per cent in the second half of 2007. After reaching 4.5 per cent in mid-2007, the lowest level in six years, the unemployment rate is on the rise. Job losses are found mostly in housing and related sectors, as well as in manufacturing. These outweigh job growth in services, such as health care and the retail sector. In the outlook, employment growth is expected to remain sluggish in 2008, with the unemployment rate edging up to 5 per cent (see table A.7).

*Unemployment is beginning to edge up*

Inflationary pressures are
expected to diminish

After hovering above 3 per cent for two years, the headline inflation rate moderated slightly during 2007 (see table A.4). The core personal consumption expenditure (PCE) deflator has also finally dropped to the Fed's presumed 1-2 per cent tolerance band. Inflation expectations, as measured by the spread between the yield on the 10-year Treasury note and that on the Treasury Inflation-Protected Securities of the same term, also declined slightly, from about 2.5 per cent in the first half of 2007 to 2.2 per cent in late 2007. In the outlook, with the anticipated continuation of slow economic growth, inflation is expected to remain tame for 2008, with a PCE rate of under 2 per cent.

Exports are driving growth
and the trade deficit
is narrowing

The economy of the United States could have been even weaker had it not been for the robust export growth over the past two years. Driven by relatively strong foreign demand and accommodated by the depreciation of the dollar, real exports grew at a pace of about 7 per cent during 2007, continuing the pace of 2006. Exports of capital and consumer goods, as well as services, have all increased greatly. In contrast, growth in the volume of imports weakened conspicuously during 2007, dropping to only 2 per cent, from 6 per cent in 2006. As a result, the large trade deficit narrowed measurably, especially relative to GDP, for the first time since 2001. Net exports will continue to make a positive contribution to GDP growth in 2008, and both the trade deficit and the current-account deficit are expected to decline further.

Fed policy is on
hold for now

In the outlook, the Fed is expected to hold the federal funds rate at 4.0 per cent for 2008, while the fiscal stance is expected to be slightly stimulatory. Benefiting from robust revenues, the federal budget deficit continued to narrow during 2007, to about $160 billion, from $248 billion in 2006, according to data of the Congressional Budget Office. Real government expenditure has been growing below the rate of GDP growth for about two years, but is expected to rise above that rate in 2008.

Long-term supply
constraints may emerge
if the current productivity
slowdown is structural

In addition to the risks associated with the housing slump and the large external deficit, another risk has been emanating from a notable decline in the growth of productivity, which dropped to an average of about 1 per cent in 2006-2007, from an average of about 3 per cent in the past decade. The acceleration in labour productivity in the late 1990s helped reduce inflation, which contributed to a prolonged period of robust economic growth even after labour markets tightened. The current slowdown in productivity growth, if it is more structural than cyclical, will pose challenges to the macroeconomic setting (see figure IV.2).

Canada's economy is
slowing as external
demand weakens

Canada's economy had a solid growth performance in the first half of 2007, driven in particular by strong household consumption and supported by increasing government expenditure and investment demand. Economic growth is expected to slow in the second half of 2007 and in 2008, however. Exports will slow due to the appreciation of the Canadian dollar and weaker demand from the United States. Consumption will decelerate as a result of lower employment growth and the fading of one-off fiscal transfer payments. The construction sector is expected to weaken owing to moderating house prices, a large existing stock and a generally more cautious outlook in reaction to the turmoil in the United States housing market.

The expected moderation in economic performance and the associated reduction in inflationary pressure over the forecast horizon will provide sufficient justification for the Bank of Canada to leave interest rates at their current level. In addition, the appreciation of the Canadian dollar, stemming in part from the increase in the interest rate differential vis-à-vis the United States after the Fed's rate cuts, has already led to the equivalent of additional monetary tightening.

Figure IV.2:
**Productivity growth in the United States, 2000-2007**

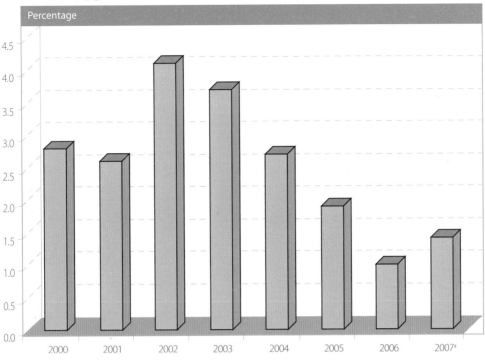

**Source**: Global Insight.
**a**   Partly estimated.

Risks in the forecast are tilted towards the downside, the major concerns being a stronger-than-expected appreciation of the Canadian dollar and a more serious slow-down in United States growth.

## Developed Asia and the Pacific:
## Japan emerging from deflation?

In Japan, real GDP growth is expected to reach 2.0 per cent in 2007, a slight downward revision from the spring forecast of 2.1 per cent. This reflects the unexpectedly weak growth performance in the second quarter owing to, among other factors, a contraction in business fixed investment. In 2008, economic growth is expected to slow to 1.7 per cent in view of increasing pressure on the external sector, with the combined effect of the appreciation of the yen against the dollar and the slowing of demand from the United States (see table A.1).

Growth is expected
to slow in Japan

On the domestic demand side, private consumption will continue to support economic growth. Consumer confidence is up as positive employment conditions prevail, with the unemployment rate at an historic low. More positive wage growth is expected to provide additional impetus to private consumption, further underpinning its emergence as the main driving force of economic growth (see figure IV.3). Government consumption will contract in 2008 for the first time in several years, holding the potential for significant progress towards consolidating public finances and, in particular, reducing the high overall level of public debt. Business investment demand is expected to moderate as firms respond to the lower growth prospects of the United States economy.

Domestic demand is
driven by consumption as
investors are cautious

Figure IV.3:
**Contributions to growth in Japan, 2000-2008**

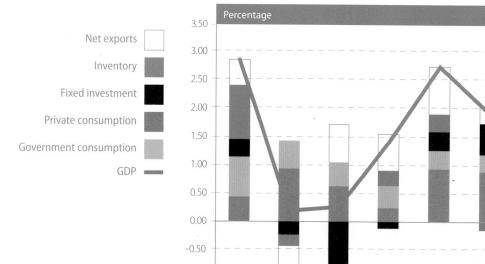

Net exports
Inventory
Fixed investment
Private consumption
Government consumption
GDP

**Sources**: OECD *Quarterly National Accounts* and Project LINK.
**a** Partly estimated.
**b** Forecast.

*Growth remains export led*

The external sector will maintain sizeable surpluses, albeit in a more challenging international environment. Continued strong demand from China and, more broadly, the Asian region will sustain a robust export performance. The impact of this intraregional export expansion on the trade balance will be mitigated by the slowdown in the United States economy, the expected appreciation of the yen and the higher level of oil prices. This drag on export growth and the rising import costs account for a significant portion of the slowdown in real GDP growth in 2008.

*Deflation finally gives way to price increases and monetary policy is expected to tighten*

While consumer prices are expected to remain flat in 2007, inflation is expected to reach 0.7 per cent in 2008, underpinned by capacity constraints, upward pressure on land prices and a continued generally positive growth performance. The weaker-than-expected inflation data for 2007 also imply a downward revision in the expected interest rate path, with the Bank of Japan now expected to increase interest rates from 0.5 to 0.75 per cent in the first quarter of 2008, down from 1.0 per cent in the previous forecast, and to 1.0 per cent by the end of 2008.

*Consumer demand leads strong growth performance in Australia*

Australia's economic growth in 2007 will reach about 4.2 per cent, driven mainly by strong domestic demand, before falling back to 3.6 per cent in 2008, owing to an envisaged weakening growth in business investment. On the domestic demand side, consumer spending continues to be stimulated by increasing disposable household incomes, supported by low unemployment, solid real wage growth and tax cuts. These favourable conditions for consumer demand, as well as prevailing capacity constraints, positively influence fixed investment. Nonetheless, fixed investment is expected to moderate as it will become increasingly difficult to find viable investment opportunities in the natural-resource based sectors, since only high-end cost projects are available and credit-market conditions are expected to tighten.

Strong domestic demand and the strong Australian dollar have fuelled import growth. Import demand is outpacing export growth and, consequently, net exports contribute negatively to output growth. This drag will diminish as the Australian dollar is expected to weaken growth in consumer-good imports, while continued strong demand for commodities from China and India is expected to keep up export growth. However, a more pronounced negative effect of the global liquidity crisis on real global growth and the Australian export sector constitutes a significant downside risk in this respect.

Inflation remains under control, but there is some upside pressure in view of tight labour-market conditions and high rates of capacity utilization in some sectors. These inflationary concerns have led to a continued tightening of monetary policy.

New Zealand's economy is estimated to have accelerated remarkably, to 3.0 per cent in 2007, up from 1.9 per cent in 2006. Aggregate demand growth has become more balanced. Household spending remains solid as disposable household incomes increased, fuelled by job growth, rising wages and tax cuts. Consumer demand is expected to moderate in 2008, however, as households' preferences are increasingly tilted towards debt reduction over consumption. In contrast, government consumption is expected to expand in view of sizeable budget surpluses. A smaller import leakage on growth is expected as private consumption growth weakens. On balance, growth is expected to remain robust at 2.9 per cent in 2008.

*Growth is accelerating in New Zealand*

As in Australia, high capacity-utilization rates and rising wages are creating upward inflationary pressures and monetary policies are expected to remain restrictive during 2008, although no further increases in interest rates are expected.

## Western Europe: moderation in 2008

Growth continued to be well above trend during 2007, boosted by the strong carry-over from the good performance in the fourth quarter of 2006 and the first quarter of 2007. Activity slowed during the year, however, and is now clearly past its cyclical peak. Indicators of business and consumer confidence peaked in mid-2007 and have fallen monotonically since, but in most cases they remain well above long-term averages and are thus consistent with continued expansion. For the European Union (EU)-15, GDP is expected to grow by 2.7 per cent in 2007, slightly down from 2.8 per cent in 2006, and is expected to slow further to 2.3 per cent in 2008 (see table A.1) This will mark the third year in a row that growth has been above potential. However, the outlook is clouded by the uncertainty stemming from the global financial crisis that hit in August, with a number of European banks directly involved, as well as by the slowdown in the United States. In addition, the euro appreciated to record levels against the dollar and the yen, which is expected to hamper export growth.

*Growth continued at a robust pace in 2007 but a slowdown is expected in 2008*

After a slow start, private consumption spending strengthened during 2007 and, with a positive labour-market outlook, overall economic growth is expected to be increasingly consumption led in 2008 (see figure IV.4 reflecting data for the euro area). The robust employment growth of 2007 is expected to continue into 2008. Real wages are also expected to pick up gradually and fuel the expected growth in consumption demand. Despite decelerating over the past few months, consumer confidence has remained well above average for the past decade. Savings rates are expected to remain stable. In Germany, consumption is expected to rebound during the year as the effects of the January 2007 increase in the value-added tax (VAT) subside, and a tax cut in France should also provide a boost to consumption spending. A weakening housing market is expected to

*Consumption demand has strengthened further*

Figure IV.4:
**Contributions to growth in the Euro area, 2001-2008**

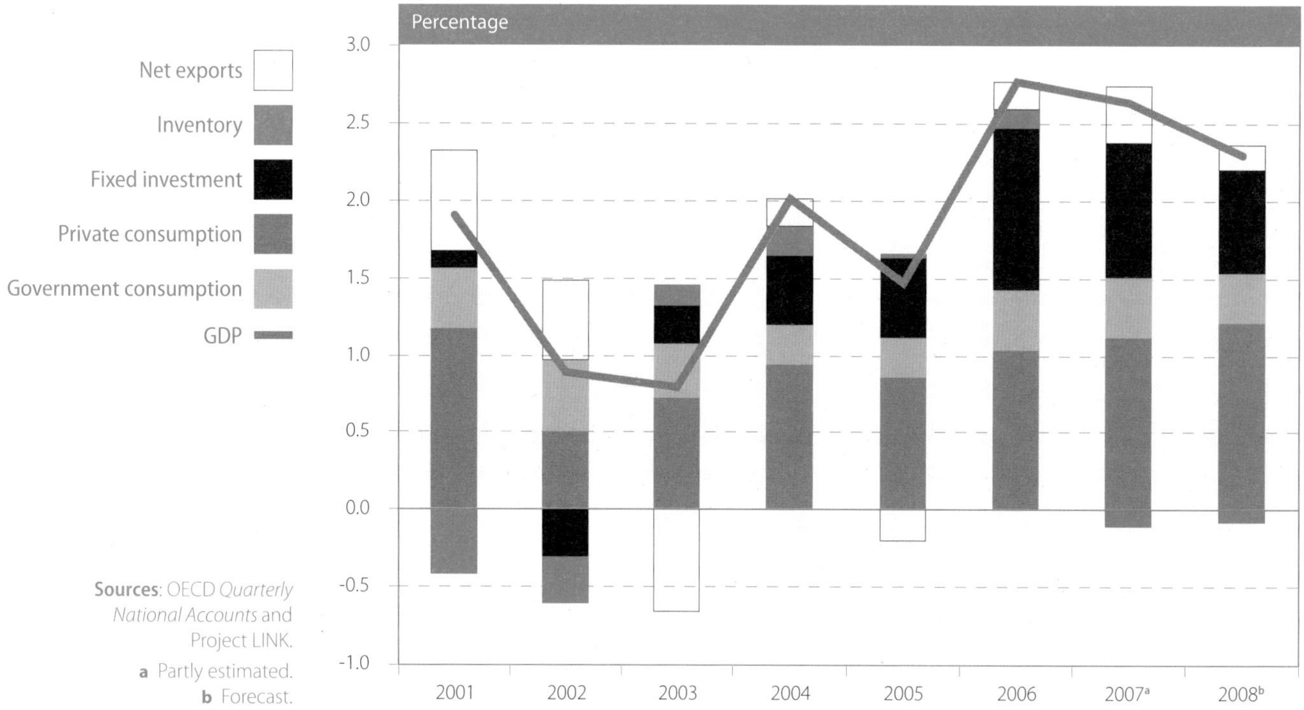

Net exports

Inventory

Fixed investment

Private consumption

Government consumption

GDP

**Sources**: OECD *Quarterly National Accounts* and Project LINK.
**a** Partly estimated.
**b** Forecast.

lead to slowing consumer demand in the United Kingdom of Great Britain and Northern Ireland, through stagnating wealth effects, and in Spain, through reduced employment in the construction sector.

*Investment is expected to slow*

Investment spending started the year as the main contributor to growth, continuing its strong performance from 2006, but it contracted in the second quarter and is expected to provide only modest support for the rest of 2007 and 2008. This profile is accentuated by a substantial decline in housing investment. High levels of capacity utilization, and a continued strong environment both in domestic and some foreign markets are positive factors. The capital goods bias of this demand should provide support for investment in equipment in some countries, but difficulties in housing markets will depress residential investment.

Investment financing conditions are uncertain. Policy rates are expected to remain close to neutral, but the full impact of past policy tightening has yet to feed fully through into activity, and market-determined interest rates have risen as spreads have widened following the repricing of risk and tensions in credit markets. However with buoyant corporate profits, it is unclear how significant tightened external financing conditions will be.

*Export growth remains strong, but is challenged by appreciating currencies*

Exports remain an important driver of growth, but have decelerated since 2006. Negative headwinds include slowing global demand, particularly from the United States, and the strengthening of the euro and other European currencies, which erode export competitiveness. These are mitigated by other factors. European exports continue to be strong in Asia, the Russian Federation and other oil-producing economies. Germany and other countries that specialize in capital goods, for which there is less price competition, are still expected to find strong demand. Countries, such as Italy, competing more directly with Asian exporters in consumer markets, will be harder hit. These factors are magnified by the relative movements in unit labour costs over the past few years, with Germany gaining and Italy and France losing competitiveness. With domestic demand holding up and its composition shifting to consumption, coupled with the appreciation of European currencies, import growth should slow less than that of exports, and the growth impulse from net exports is therefore expected to be minimal.

After a long period of remaining above the 2 per cent threshold in the euro area, headline inflation remained below that level for the twelve consecutive months up to September, after which it rose to be marginally above it. Core inflation, excluding energy, food, alcohol and tobacco, remained below 2 per cent, but has risen since 2006 to nearly converge with headline inflation. Inflationary pressures have increased. GDP growth is slightly above trend in the outlook and the output gap has essentially closed. The rate of capacity utilization is now well above its long-term average and very close to the level of its last cyclical peak. Unemployment has dropped to its lowest point in more than ten years and wages are picking up. In addition, high oil and food prices are further pushing up headline inflation. However, inflationary pressures are expected to be contained. Currency appreciation has mitigated some of the oil-price pressure as well as that of other sources of imported inflation. The growth outlook is for a slowing of activity in 2008 and is not sufficiently robust to put significant upward pressure on prices. In addition, wage negotiations have settled for modest increases, keeping labour-cost increases in check. Inflation is expected to rise slightly in 2008, but to remain close to 2 per cent (see table A.4).[2]

Inflation remains in check

Employment continues to be exceptionally strong, growing by 1.3 per cent in 2006 and an estimated 1.5 per cent in 2007 in the euro area, stemming from the robust economic activity, but also resulting from the structural reforms in labour markets undertaken by the euro countries over the past several years. Given its lagging cyclical behaviour and the expected mild slowdown, employment levels are expected to continue to expand, albeit at a more moderate pace. The rate of unemployment continued to decline across the region, averaging 6.8 per cent for the EU-15 in 2007, and is set to fall further in 2008 (see table A.7).

Employment remains robust and unemployment continues to fall

Fiscal balances generally improved in 2007 reflecting stronger-than-expected growth in revenues, but no further progress is expected in 2008. In previous years, fiscal policies were moderately restrictive, caused by the need for several countries to comply with the rules of the Stability and Growth Pact to keep budget deficits within the bound of 3 per cent of GDP. The fiscal stance for the euro area as a whole is expected to return to neutral during the forecast period, but with some variation across countries. France has scheduled significant cuts in income taxes and, as a result, its budget deficit is expected to remain close to 2.5 per cent of GDP. In the United Kingdom, planned increases in spending coupled with slower revenue growth are expected to yield a slight widening of the deficit to close to 3 per cent in 2008. Germany saw a remarkable shift in its budget position in 2007 as it moved into a slight surplus. Its government budget is expected to remain practically balanced in 2008. Italy experienced a significant reduction in its budget deficit, which fell from 4.4 per cent in 2006 to 2.3 per cent in 2007. The Italian Government is expected to maintain a similar budget position in 2008.

The fiscal policy stance is expected to be neutral on average, but is showing some variation across countries

The European Central Bank (ECB) has been in a policy-tightening mode since December 2005. Its most recent move was in June, when it raised its main policy interest

Restrictive monetary policies are expected to ease to a more neutral stance

---

2    The monthly pattern of inflation and its rise towards the end of 2007 was strongly influenced by statistical effects. In the first half of 2007, base effects from the pattern of oil prices in 2006 pushed headline inflation down, but the effects were reversed in the second half of the year. In addition, the German VAT increase in January of this year boosted the inflation rate by 0.3 percentage points in the euro area, but this will fall out of the calculation next year.

rate, the minimum bid rate, by 25 basis points (bps) bringing it to a level of 4.0 per cent, a cumulative 175 bps increase since the tightening cycle started. Currently, policy is near a neutral stance, with the real short-term policy interest rate close to 2 per cent. The inflationary pressures discussed above may concern policymakers, leading central banks to further tightening. In fact, markets have been anticipating a further interest rate increase. Other central banks in the region, such as the Bank of Sweden and the Bank of Norway have raised rates since the financial turmoil started in August. But with the progressively worsening situation in the United States and indicators of confidence in the region continuing to fall, the balance of risks is turning to the real economy rather than inflation. In addition, the appreciation of the euro as well as other regional currencies during the year, has already further tightened monetary conditions. Moreover, previous interest rate increases still need to take their full effect on economic activity, whereas the financial crisis itself has tightened conditions by raising the spread between policy and market rates. The Bank of England has already indicated that it may cut rates, and it is assumed that it will do so. The ECB is assumed to maintain its current policy stance, while other independent central banks in the region are expected to raise rates slightly.

*The euro continues to appreciate and there is upward pressure on other regional currencies as well*

As indicated, the euro continued to appreciate during 2007, reaching record highs against both the dollar and the yen. In nominal trade-weighted terms, the euro increased by 4 per cent from the beginning of 2007 through October, and by 32 per cent since the start of the prolonged dollar depreciation in mid-2000.[3] The major short-term driver of the rise in the euro has been the gradual elimination of the initially large interest rate differential that was in favour of the United States currency, coupled with the longer-term pressure stemming from the eroding confidence in the dollar as the United States net liability position increases. The recent cuts in policy interest rates by the Fed along with the maintainence of the ECB policy stance have further reduced the differential. With the outlook far less favourable for the United States than for Europe over the forecast, the risks are that the interest rate differential will reverse sign. In the outlook, it is assumed that the euro will average $1.44 in 2008, after $1.37 in 2007, a yearly appreciation of 8.5 per cent. The yen is expected to appreciate against the euro during 2008, as the Bank of Japan is assumed to raise its policy interest rate.

*Risks are slanted towards the downside*

Risks to the outlook for Western Europe are mostly on the downside, dominated by the expected slowdown in the United States, which will affect United States-European trade directly as well as indirectly through a moderation in export demand from the rest of the world. There is also a risk that the current difficulties in financial markets, which affect a large number of countries in the region, will last longer and be more severe than anticipated. Similarly, there could be contagion from the United States to European housing markets, although this would be limited to those countries which have experienced rapid house-price rises over the past few years, such as Ireland, Spain and the United Kingdom. Finally, a key risk is that the euro could appreciate even more than in the baseline forecast, as confidence in the dollar erodes further and investors start to redirect their funds from the United States to Europe.

---

3    See European Central Bank nominal effective exchange rate index against 24 major trading partners, Series No. EXR.M.Z50.EUR.EN00.A, available from http://sdw.ecb.europa.eu/browse.do?node=2018795.

# The new European Union member States: strong economic growth, increasing risks

Economic activity in the new EU member States remained buoyant in 2007 as strong GDP growth continued and even accelerated in some of the countries, including in the biggest economy of the region, Poland (see table A.1). GDP growth averaged 6.0 per cent for the group as a whole. Hungary did not share in the strong performance as its economy grew by a mere 2 per cent in response to fiscal tightening. The vibrant activity elsewhere was accompanied, however, by weakening indicators of macroeconomic stability, exacerbating earlier concerns of an overheating in some of the economies. Growth in the region is expected to slow to about 5.4 per cent in 2008 as the economies face labour-supply constraints, and aggregate demand is expected to cool in line with slowing credit expansion.

*Buoyant activity is accompanied by increasing concerns about macroeconomic stability*

In most of the economies, growth is led by robust domestic demand. Private consumption was bolstered by increasing disposable household incomes in the Baltic States and Romania. Fixed investment increased at double-digit rates and led growth in Bulgaria and Poland. The boom in both residential and business construction continued along with the expansion of infrastructure projects in all new EU member States, fuelled by sustained buoyant mortgage markets and official transfers from the EU.

*Domestic demand remains the main driver of growth*

Inflationary pressures continued to rise in 2007. Labour shortages, caused by outward migration and skill mismatches in the labour market, led to strong real wage growth's outpacing productivity gains. Ongoing credit expansion, increased energy costs, higher regulated prices and excise taxes exerted additional pressure. While remaining low in the Czech Republic, Poland and Slovakia, inflation jumped in Hungary owing to changes in regulated prices and VAT. Inflation reached double digits in Latvia.

*Inflationary pressures are increasing as labour shortages drive up wages*

No significant disinflation is expected for 2008. Inflation in some of the Baltic States may even accelerate against the backdrop of planned increases in regulated prices and indirect taxes, along with higher prices for Russian natural gas (see figure IV.5). These inflationary pressures could delay the adoption of the euro in those economies (see box IV.1).

Unemployment has decreased, most notably in Poland and the Baltic States. This partially reflects ongoing outward migration as well as significant new job creation. Strong real wage growth is reducing profit margins in private businesses and could affect economic activity in the outlook.

Monetary policy stances vary among the new EU member States. On 1 January 2007, Slovenia joined the European Economic and Monetary Union (EMU), and Cyprus and Malta are set to adopt the euro in 2008. The currency boards in the Baltic States and Bulgaria leave no room for these countries to conduct active monetary policies. Large current-account deficits and growing levels of external indebtedness of the private sector in these countries are creating concerns about the credibility of the exchange-rate fix. In Estonia and Latvia, in particular, there are pressures to devalue. The countries with flexible exchange-rate regimes have to choose between giving priority to controlling inflation or to avoiding further currency appreciation. To meet inflation targets, interest rates were raised in the Czech Republic and Poland, while monetary policy was relaxed in Hungary, Romania and Slovakia to limit exchange-rate appreciation. In the outlook, although further tightening is possible in the Czech Republic and Poland, monetary policy is expected to remain accommodative in most countries.

In Central Europe, stronger-than-anticipated economic growth and improved tax administration created an opportunity to consolidate public finances in order to meet

*Fiscal restructuring in Central Europe remains inadequate*

Figure IV.5:
**Inflation in the Baltic States, 2002-2008**

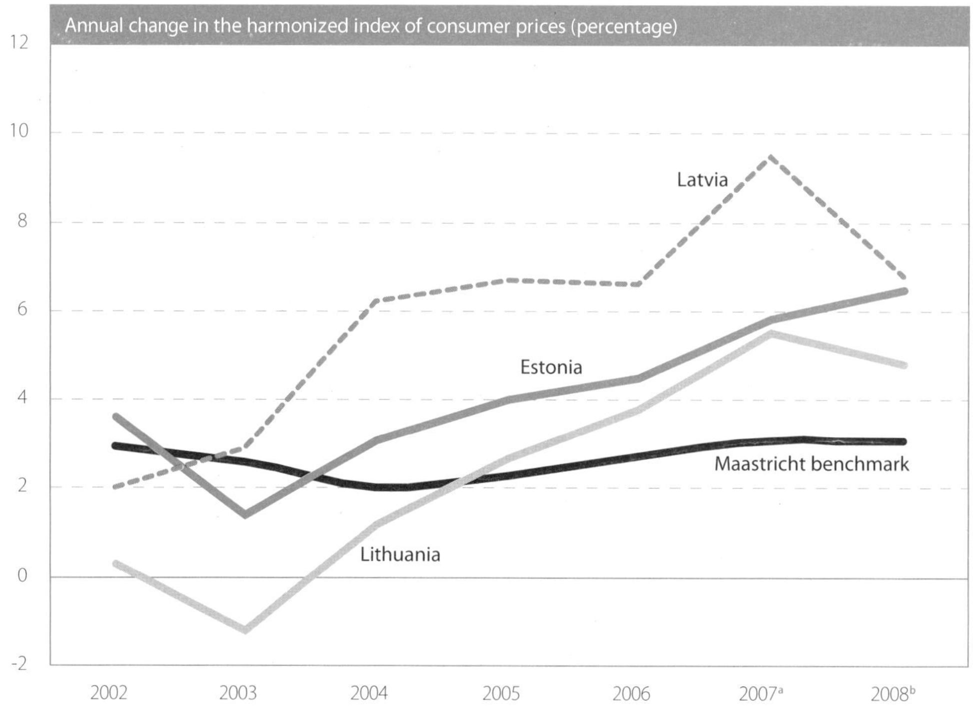

Annual change in the harmonized index of consumer prices (percentage)

**Sources**: European
Commission and
Project LINK.
**a** Partly estimated.
**b** Forecast.

---

**Box IV.1**

## The challenges facing the new member States
## of the European Union in adopting the euro

The twelve new member States (NMSs) of the European Union (EU) that have joined since 2004 (including Bulgaria and Romania, which joined in 2007) agreed as part of their accession treaties that they would adopt the euro in place of their national currencies. These countries are therefore in a position similar to that of Sweden in that they have a commitment to join the euro at some future date and do not have the right, as do the United Kingdom and Denmark, to preserve their national currencies indefinitely. The accession treaties do not fix a firm date for euro adoption; they do, however, specify five macroeconomic conditions that must be fulfilled, referred to as the Maastricht criteria, before they can adopt the euro. These stipulate that (a) inflation should not exceed by more than 1.5 per cent the average of that of the three members of the EU with the lowest rates (not only those already in the euro zone); (b) interest rates may not exceed by more than 2 per cent the average of the three members with the lowest interest rates; (c) the national Government budget deficit must be below 3 per cent of GDP; (d) public debt must be below 60 per cent of GDP; and (e) the exchange rate had to have been relatively stable for two years prior to joining. In addition to these economic performance criteria, there are several legal requirements, such as one that requires that the country's central bank be legally independent of the Government. These conditions are neither necessary nor sufficient to ensure that euro accession will be completely successful. Additional factors contributing to success include the synchronization of their business cycles, establishing relatively similar financial conditions so that euro monetary policy will have a similar effect on their economies, and more flexible labour and product markets. Large current-account deficits, a factor which could potentially pose a threat to financial stability in these economies, is not part of the Maastricht criteria.

**Box IV.1** (cont'd)

There is some debate regarding the adequate timing of euro accession. Some argue that the benefits are substantial in terms of further trade and financial integration and that every effort should be made to join as soon as possible. In addition to these benefits, adoption of the euro would considerably decrease the possibility of an economy's experiencing a currency crisis: a significant consideration given the very large economic costs associated with these events. On the other end of the spectrum are those who argue that, given these economies' much lower per capita incomes and their need for additional institutional reform—since their transition from planned economies are not fully complete—it would be optimal to remain outside the euro area until greater convergence has taken place. Remaining outside the euro area would give the Governments more flexibility with regard to macroeconomic policy and would give the economies more time to develop the labour- and product-market structures consistent with being part of a larger currency bloc. Within each country, to varying degrees, different intellectual and political factions have developed which have led to a changing policy emphasis as political power shifts. Even within Governments, the now independent central banks have often pursued one objective while the Government or Finance Ministry has pursued another. For example, in Poland, the independent Central Bank has pursued a rather tight monetary policy in support of fast-track euro accession, while successive Governments have been far less committed to early adoption and unwilling to implement the tighter fiscal regime necessary for achieving the deficit objective. Moreover, the main political parties are divided over the topic. Slovenia, being more committed to early adoption, was able to satisfy these requirements in its first two years of membership and joined the euro beginning in 2007 (although it now has the highest inflation rate in the euro zone), and Malta and Cyprus are now set to join at the beginning of 2008. The remaining economies have encountered difficulties in meeting these macroeconomic objectives, and their proposed date of entry keeps being postponed. Currently, the Baltic economies and Slovakia hope to join by 2010, while the accession date for the others is probably at least five years away. Although there are a number of situations where countries are close to exceeding several or even all five requirements, two criteria are proving to be particularly problematic: namely, the requirements for keeping inflation and budget deficits within established limits.

The degree to which the problematic requirement is either inflation or a budget deficit appears to be closely related to whether the country has either a fixed or a flexible exchange-rate regime as shown in the figure below (which shows only ten out of the twelve new EU members).

Those economies with fixed exchange rates (or currency boards) do not have control over their money supply. This leaves them with more limited macroeconomic policy space to control aggregate demand and inflation. A tight fiscal stance is the primary policy tool left for containing inflation. These countries generally have a firm objective of early euro accession since they have already given up the advantages of an independent monetary and exchange-rate policy. In addition, their economies are already characterized by high degrees of de facto euroization reflected in the sizeable percentage of banking loans, which are currently denominated in euros. These economies have therefore followed rather prudent fiscal policies, although additional tightening may be necessary if the inflation target is to be met. In addition, credit growth has been quite high in these economies on account of the rapid development of their financial markets and surging capital inflows. A more active policy in containing this credit growth may therefore also be required.

The countries with flexible exchange rates have been able to reduce inflation by allowing their currencies to appreciate. This has not only constrained aggregate demand but has also reduced inflation from the supply side by lowering import costs. Romania and Slovakia have managed to reduce inflation the most in recent years, but they are also the ones that have experienced stronger currency appreciation. However, since those countries adopting flexible exchange rates have been able to rely on monetary policy to constrain inflation, the need to tighten fiscal policy has been less pressing. In addition, these countries are generally less committed to an early adoption of the euro and therefore show less political will to push for fiscal consolidation.

In summary, although conditions vary, maintaining a tight fiscal policy or an even further tightening appears to be a basic requirement for euro accession for all the NMSs. The recent rapid economic growth of these economies has provided the potential for reducing fiscal deficits, but not all have seized this opportunity. The reasons for this are as follows: raising government revenue

**Box IV.1** (cont'd)

has been constrained by ongoing competition among the NMSs to lower taxes in order to attract business investment; it has been difficult to cut expenditures given the need for large infrastructure investments to promote competitiveness; and "reform fatigue" has made reducing transfers and other social expenditures politically difficult.

Inflation in all the NMSs is likely to remain problematic regardless of aggregate demand considerations owing to supply-side effects from real convergence, assuming that they continue to grow more rapidly than the advanced economies. The overall price levels in the NMSs are lower (in some cases by almost 50 per cent) than those in the existing member States owing to the Balassa-Samuelson effect, since they have significantly lower per capita incomes. When their real incomes converge to that of the existing member States, their price levels must converge as well.

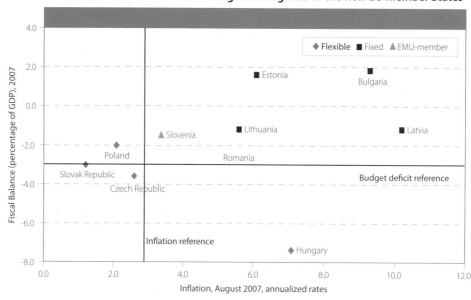

**Maastricht criteria and the exchange-rate regimes of the new EU member States**

**Sources**: UN/DESA and ECE, based on data from Eurostat.

the Maastricht criteria for joining the euro zone and to release funds necessary for cofinancing the EU-related programmes. This opportunity has not been fully exploited, as public spending has increased in line with stronger GDP growth. Most of the budgets for 2008 are based on optimistic revenue estimates, and there are doubts whether official targets will be met.

*The impact of the global financial turmoil remains limited*

The impact of the global financial turmoil in August 2007 proved to be short-lived for the new EU member States, but the economies with large current-account or fiscal deficits and a large stock of foreign currency-denominated private debt may become vulnerable to worsening external conditions. More restrictive fiscal policy will be needed to avoid a further widening of macroeconomic imbalances. The aspiration of most countries to adopt the euro in the medium run should help lock in prudent macroeconomic policies in the coming years. The main risks are associated with a possible slowdown in the EU-15, emerging labour-supply constraints, excessive domestic credit growth and persisting current-account deficits in some economies.

# Economies in transition: robust but moderating growth in 2008

In 2007, economic growth in the economies in transition accelerated and recorded its fastest rate since the start of transition. GDP growth of the group as a whole averaged 8.0 per cent in 2007, up from 7.5 per cent in 2006 (see chapter I, table I.1). Strong private consumption and investment demand will support a robust growth rate in these economies in 2008, albeit at a more modest pace of about 7 per cent.

The continued strong growth performance is broad-based and above expectations in the two sub-groups of countries, the Commonwealth of Independent States (CIS) and South-eastern Europe. In the CIS, growth maintained a rapid pace of 7 per cent or more for a fifth consecutive year. The economic expansion benefited from high prices for oil, gas, metals and cotton; growing capital inflows; and worker remittances from abroad. In South-eastern Europe, growth accelerated to 6.0 per cent in 2007.

## South-eastern Europe: vibrant growth will continue

Economic activity further strengthened in South-eastern Europe in 2007 and was broad-based. Only in the former Yugoslav Republic of Macedonia was growth well below average at 4.5 per cent (see table A.2). Manufacturing and tourism continued to make significant contributions to aggregate output growth. Recently, there has also been a surge in activity in the construction sector. Output growth weakened gradually during the year. Measures restricting credit growth are expected to contribute to the projected moderation of GDP growth.

As in previous years, robust domestic demand remained the key driver of economic growth. In 2007, most countries witnessed rising real incomes. The continuing rebound in investment activity, underpinned by buoyant foreign direct investment (FDI) inflows, should be seen in the light of greater macroeconomic stability and improvements in the overall business climate. An important change from previous years is that recent inward FDI is no longer aimed at lucrative privatization deals but is increasingly targeted towards greenfield projects. The ongoing credit boom fuelled both private consumption and fixed investment in 2007.

Strong output performance in 2007 was accompanied by further disinflation. Exchange-rate stability in Bosnia and Herzegovina, Croatia and the former Yugoslav Republic of Macedonia helped lower inflationary expectations emanating from higher energy and commodity prices. While decelerating somewhat, inflation remains high in Serbia owing to increases in regulated prices and surges in public spending. There are no obvious signs that the trend towards disinflation will be reversed in 2008. There are growing inflationary pressures from the strong real wage growth and increasing production costs. These pressures are more than offset, however, by strong labour productivity growth and appreciating currencies (owing to strong FDI inflows), with the latter helping to contain imported inflation.

The external deficits of most economies of this sub-region have widened. Despite rapid merchandise export growth, current-account deficits generally increased both in dollar terms and as a share of GDP, except in the case of the former Yugoslav Republic of Macedonia. Rapid import growth and rising deficits on the services accounts are behind this. So far, the large current-account deficits do not seem to pose an immediate threat to macroeconomic stability, as they are financed to a significant extent by large inflows of FDI (see figure IV.6). The widening external deficits are mainly driven by excess private spending rather than by fiscal deficits.

*Economic activity in South-eastern Europe accelerated in 2007, but is expected to weaken in 2008*

*Growth is led by domestic demand*

*Disinflation is continuing*

*Strong import demand is deepening external imbalances*

Figure IV.6:
**Current-account deficit and FDI in South-eastern Europe, 2006-2007**

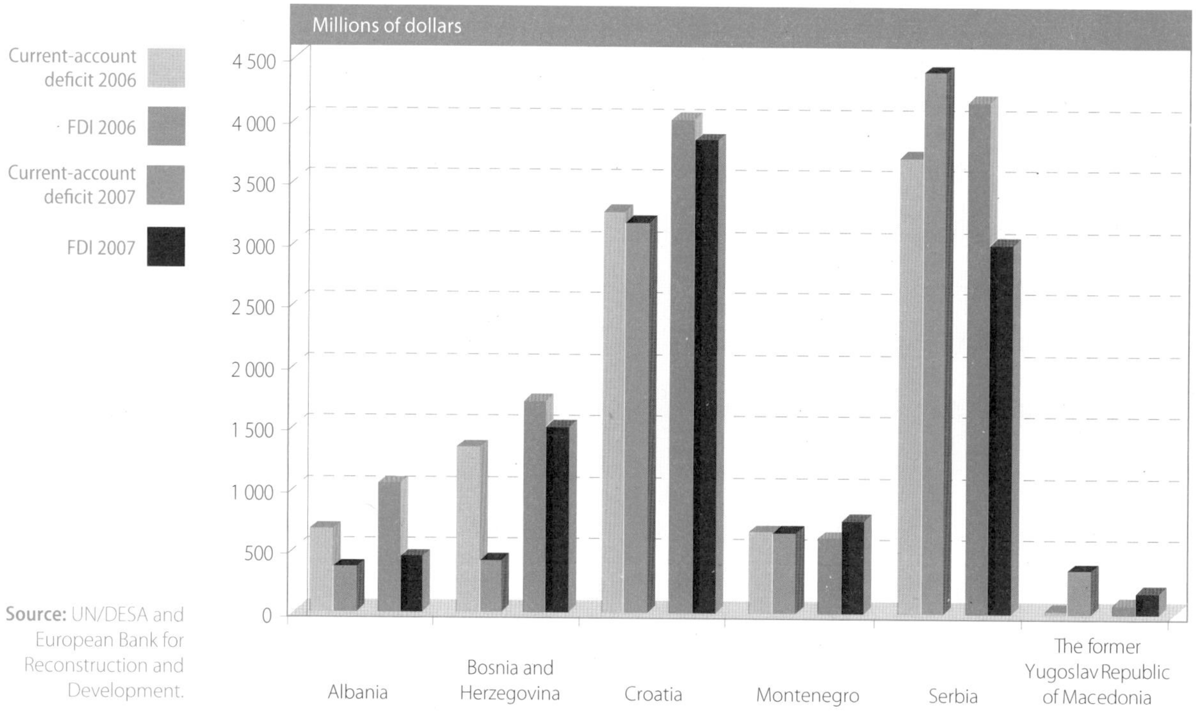

Current-account
deficit 2006

FDI 2006

Current-account
deficit 2007

FDI 2007

Millions of dollars

**Source:** UN/DESA and
European Bank for
Reconstruction and
Development.

Public finances have
been kept in check

The process of consolidation of public finances which has been under way for a number of years continued in 2007, and none of the South-eastern European economies expects to surpass the threshold for the general government fiscal deficit of 3 per cent of GDP. In the majority of countries, the deficits are even lower and may decrease further. It should be noted, however, that in some cases budget projections also include expected revenue from privatizations.

The ongoing fiscal consolidation suggests that policymakers do not have enough fiscal levers to counter the widening current-account deficits. The policy responses were mostly confined to the monetary sphere, attempting to limit private sector demand. Monetary policy was generally tightened in most countries that conduct independent monetary policy.[4] The central banks of Albania and Serbia raised intervention rates, while the Croatian National Bank increased restrictions on credit growth.

EU accession remains
the primary goal

The goal of eventual EU accession continues to dominate the economic policymaking in the countries of the region. The recent signing of the Stabilisation and Association Agreement with the EU by Montenegro is the country's first step towards the long-term goal of EU membership. The expansion of the Central European Free Trade Agreement (CEFTA), agreed in 2006 and eventually ratified by all South-eastern European countries as well as Moldova, should have a favourable impact on further intraregional trade integration. A global credit crunch may bring some risks to the countries that are running large current-account deficits and that have significant external financing needs.

---

4    Bosnia and Herzegovina adheres to a currency board arrangement, and Montenegro unilaterally introduced the euro as the currency in circulation in 2002 and, hence, has forfeited monetary policy as well.

## The Commonwealth of Independent States: robust growth, rising inflationary pressures

In 2007, economic activity accelerated in the CIS, reaching a record high of 8.2 per cent – the fastest pace since the start of transition. This expansion was mainly the result of faster growth in the Russian Federation (see box IV.2), but growth also gathered momentum in several of the smaller economies, such as Kyrgyzstan and Moldova (see table A.2). High commodity prices provided a favourable background, which is likely to continue into next year. The effects of the 2007 global liquidity squeeze were initially relatively limited in the CIS, but they signal some downside risks. In 2008, growth in the CIS will stay robust, but its pace will moderate by about one percentage point.

*Growth has accelerated to the fastest pace since the start of transition*

**Box IV.2**

### The Russian Federation: a resurgent economic power

The economy of the Russian Federation has undergone a remarkable recovery since the 1998 crisis, driven by a favourable external environment for energy exporters and radically improved macroeconomic and structural policies. It is now a trillion dollar economy, as sustained strong economic growth and real exchange-rate appreciation have resulted in a fivefold expansion of nominal GDP in current dollars since the post-crisis low of 1999. The expansion on a purchasing power parity (PPP) basis, although less spectacular, has been sufficient to increase Russia's share in total world output by about half a percentage point since 1998. It is expected that in 2007 the Russian Federation will become the eighth-largest economy in the world in PPP terms.

The growing international weight of the Russian Federation is grounded in its key role as energy producer and exporter. The reassertion of State control over the hydrocarbon sector has been somewhat controversial but has resulted in the formation of large corporations with significant global influence; it has not dented foreign interest in the energy sector either. The liberalization of share ownership of Gazprom and the resulting impact on stock-market capitalization propelled the Russian gas giant to the position of tenth-largest corporation in the world in 2006.

The efforts to establish a coherent macroeconomic policy framework after the short-lived crisis of 1998 has helped shield the economy from the destabilizing effects of massive foreign exchange inflows. More recently, the economy has maintained its dynamism despite the deceleration of growth in oil production and exports. Growth has been kept up by a strengthening domestic demand—initially mainly through private consumption growth, but more recently also through fixed investment.

Massive energy exports contribute to persistent current-account surpluses. Although in recent years it has been shrinking as a percentage of GDP, the external surplus of the Russian Federation was the fourth largest in the world in 2006 in absolute terms and roughly equal to that of Saudi Arabia. Current-account surpluses and massive net private capital inflows over the past several years have led to sizeable increases in Russia's foreign currency reserves. Official reserves became the third-largest, after those of China and Japan, reaching $416 billion (or about 32 per cent of GDP) by the end of August 2007 . At present, these holdings also include the assets accumulated in the Stabilization Fund, which is the repository of a large part of the oil earnings accruing to the State budget. Holdings in the Stabilization Fund, which reached $133 billion by the end of August 2007, have until now been invested in highly rated foreign government securities and currencies. The authorities of the Russian Federation envisage the gradual introduction of a more diversified investment strategy, with a shift towards investing in higher-yield—and riskier—assets when these resources exceed 10 per cent of GDP, a point which has now been reached. In comparison with other more established sovereign wealth funds, the size of Russian assets remains relatively modest but has grown rapidly since the creation of the Stabilization Fund at the end of 2003.

After years of stagnation, the inflow of FDI into the Russian Federation has picked up noticeably in recent years. By 2006, the Russian Federation had become the third most targeted

## Box IV.2 (cont'd)

destination among the emerging markets. The robust growth in fixed investment, underpinned by inward FDI, has helped speed up the process of active restructuring in many sectors of the Russian economy, including the manufacturing industry.

Russian companies have also been active investors abroad, and the stock of outward FDI almost doubled in the period from 2004 to 2006, reaching $210 billion. Domestic consolidation and good access to external resources to finance acquisitions have facilitated the foreign expansion of Russian firms. Resource-based groups with global ambitions dominate the FDI outflows, but Russian companies have also increased FDI to other CIS countries in sectors such as telecommunications, retail trade and finance.

The relative importance of the Russian market for the neighbouring CIS countries has generally declined, in line with the geographic reorientation of their trade resulting from economic transition and independent statehood. However, new channels of economic interdependence have emerged as Russia's robust growth has attracted large inflows of permanent and temporary workers from other CIS countries. As a result, the Russian Federation has become the fifth-largest source of remittances worldwide, reaching $11.4 billion in 2006.[a]

Despite the recent achievements, the dependence of the Russian economy on the exploitation of hydrocarbons represents a source of risk. Moreover, the current-account surplus is projected to fall in the coming years. As a consequence, the pace of accumulation of resources in the reformed Stabilization Fund is also expected to slow down. Thus, while increased global financial integration has brought benefits, including access to external finance and portfolio diversification for Russian residents, it has also created new channels for the transmission of shocks and risks that need to be adequately monitored.

Although the domestic momentum of the Russian economy and the prolongation of relatively favourable external circumstances suggest continued dynamism in the short run, sustaining high economic growth in the long run calls for an increased policy focus on economic diversification. In this regard, the Russian Federation could build on the advantages derived from its position as a key oil and gas producer, which should provide ample fiscal space to devise financially sound policies for production-sector development and diversification.

**a** For more details, see *World Economic Situation and Prospects 2007* (United Nations publication, Sales No. E.07.II.C.2), box IV.1.

---

**Domestic demand growth remains strong**

While the external environment was generally benign in 2007, the main impetus for economic expansion came from continued strong domestic demand growth. In the Russian Federation, output growth in the extractive industries remained sluggish, in contrast with the good performance in the manufacturing and construction sectors. A similar pattern was observed in Ukraine, where agriculture posted dismal results. Industrial production was relatively weak in Armenia and very weak in Moldova, where wine production was depressed by trade bans imposed by the Russian Federation. In contrast, Azerbaijan enjoyed another year of blistering (above 30 per cent) growth of industrial output. Remittances have also provided a source of financing in some of the smaller economies, notably in Armenia, Moldova and Tajikistan.

Consumer demand remained the mainstay of economic expansion (Azerbaijan being a notable exception), fuelled by rapid income growth and increased household borrowing. In addition, the volume of fixed investment accelerated significantly in most countries, increasing by around 20 per cent in the Russian Federation and 30 per cent in Ukraine. Investment growth was relatively modest in Azerbaijan, following years of exceptional investment in oil-related infrastructure.

**Employment growth has benefited from the construction boom**

Rapid economic expansion has fuelled employment growth—largely owing to a construction boom—despite large wage increases in most economies. Unemployment fell at an accelerated pace in the Russian Federation, despite a strong increase in migratory inflows. Unemployment rates also reached record lows in Kazakhstan and Ukraine. Localized labour shortages have emerged in some countries, reflecting skill mismatches and barriers to labour mobility.

Inflation pressures have remained high throughout the sub-region, fuelled by relatively loose fiscal and monetary policies, high food prices and increases in tariffs of regulated services. In most countries, consumer prices accelerated, in some cases significantly overshooting the official inflation targets. The fastest increases were observed in Azerbaijan and Tajikistan, where the rates of inflation almost doubled in 2007(see figure IV.7). There was a slight moderation of inflation in the Russian Federation at the beginning of 2007, but it accelerated subsequently, largely owing to rising food prices. Given robust demand growth and high energy prices, inflationary pressures will remain strong in most countries (though to a lesser degree in Armenia) and containing them will be a challenge to monetary policy in many of these economies.

Inflation is on the rise, pushed upwards by loose monetary policies and sky-rocketing food prices

Figure IV.7:
**Consumer price index inflation in selected Commonwealth of Independent States economies, January-September 2006 and 2007**

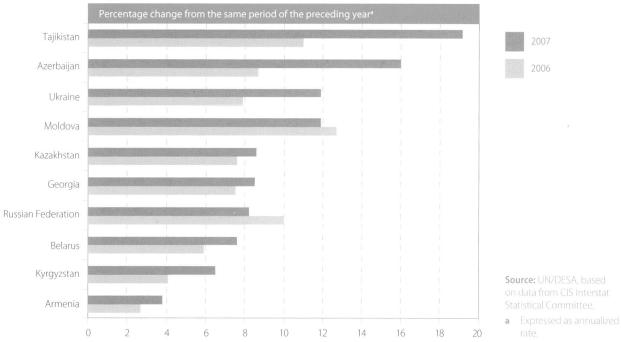

Percentage change from the same period of the preceding year[a]

2007
2006

Source: UN/DESA, based on data from CIS Interstat Statistical Committee.
a Expressed as annualized rate.

The management of large foreign inflows remains a challenge for the CIS countries. The authorities have generally been reluctant to introduce greater flexibility in exchange-rate policies, fearing that the expected currency appreciation would erode competitiveness. On the other hand, the global liquidity squeeze in 2007 (see chapter I) resulted in temporary capital outflows and downward pressures on the exchange rates in some countries. Monetary authorities—in particular in the Russian Federation and Kazakhstan—pumped liquidity into their banking systems through a variety of means. Looking ahead, many of these economies will be challenged to shift to a tighter monetary policy and return to a focus on inflation control.

Controlling inflation is the main objective of monetary policy in 2008

Economic expansion and high commodity prices boosted fiscal revenues throughout the CIS. In the Russian Federation, higher spending sharply reduced the federal surplus, despite proceeds from the sale of the Yukos company. The non-oil budget deficits increased in the other energy-exporting CIS countries, in particular Azerbaijan, with a more moderate stance observed in Kazakhstan. Some of the smaller economies,

Expansionary fiscal policies prevail

such as Armenia and Georgia, made some progress in improving tax collection, though tax intakes remain low. Ukraine managed further fiscal consolidation. In 2008, fiscal policies will remain expansionary in many CIS countries because of the rising expenditures required for infrastructure investment, increasing costs of education and health services, and rising public-sector wages and pensions.

Despite high prices for oil and gas, the current-account surplus of the Russian Federation declined owing to the rapid increase of imports and sluggish growth of export production in energy-related sectors. Other hydrocarbon exporters continued to generate large current-account surpluses relative to their GDP. The only exception is Kazakhstan, which is running a deficit. The country's external deficit is expected to decline, however, in line with the development of the hydrocarbon sector and the acceleration of export growth. In contrast, the current-account surplus of the Russian Federation is projected to shrink further. The financing of large current-account deficits in the non-energy exporting countries has not been a major problem, as these have attracted growing FDI inflows.

While economic expansion in the region is expected to remain robust, the recent turmoil in the global financial markets has highlighted the vulnerabilities that have been building in the banking sector of some countries, the negative implications of the rapid growth of private foreign debt and the importance of mobilizing domestic financial resources. Kazakhstan is a case in point: banks are particularly dependent on external funding and thus extremely vulnerable to refinancing risks. Aggressive lending strategies of commercial banks led to heavy borrowing in international markets. Foreign ownership in the Kazakh banking system is limited, so banks do not enjoy access to funding through this channel. As a result, foreign liabilities represent about half of the total liabilities of the banking sector. The credit boom in Kazakhstan has fuelled rapid growth of local real estate prices, with banks increasingly exposed to the construction sector and household mortgage lending. While banks have been passing on the foreign currency risk to borrowers, an eventual depreciation of the national currency would increase the repayment burden for their customers, resulting in a deterioration of the banks' loan portfolios. Such a business model is under question, and although banks do not seem to face immediate problems—since the term structure has generally shifted to debt of longer maturity following recent changes in regulation—they will inevitably have to slow the pace of their activities. If access to international markets remains problematic over a longer period, the slowdown will spread over construction and other economic sectors.

A possible steeper and more prolonged slowdown of the world economy poses an additional downside risk, as it would likely cause a decline in export demand of primary commodities. Heavy dependence on exports of oil, gas, metals and cotton remains a source of structural vulnerability to many CIS countries. Economic diversification remains a long-term challenge.

## Developing economies

The developing economies expanded at 7 per cent in 2007, the same rate as in 2006 and the fifth consecutive year of growth of more than 5 per cent. The strong economic performance was underpinned by the enduring primary-commodity boom that began in 2003, but it is also being supported by growth in non-primary-commodity exports and increased domestic demand in many economies. East and South Asia continue to lead developing country growth based on continued dynamics in industry and services sectors. Africa's economic performance remains remarkably strong also, owing to a large extent to buoyant commodity markets, but also to strengthened domestic sources of growth.

Recent problems in international financial markets have as yet not made a visible imprint on the growth prospects for developing countries, apart from the impact of a slowdown in the United States economy. The weakening dollar is of immediate concern, however, as it has led to the dramatic appreciation of the national currencies of many developing countries, thereby eroding export competitiveness. There are also increasing concerns about inflationary pressures emerging from the rise in fuel and oil prices. Currency appreciation has helped to contain these pressures in many of the economies for now; nonetheless, inflation rates are expected to be on the rise in 2008. The outlook for 2008 remains one of continued strong developing country growth at 6.5 per cent. The main downside risks are associated with a possible stronger global economic slowdown and a hard landing of the dollar.

## Africa: economic performance continues to improve

Africa has sustained the strong economic performance that began in 2003, achieving a 5.8 per cent growth rate in 2007, up from 5.7 per cent in 2006 (figure IV.8). This economic performance is a continuation of the growth cycle driven in part by the primary-commodity boom. Rising oil prices are an important factor for some economies. While growth performance has been fairly broad-based throughout the continent, oil-exporting countries averaged stronger growth than the oil-importing countries in 2007.

The commodity boom is driving growth….

Other factors underpinning the sustained growth momentum in Africa include improved macroeconomic management, continued structural reforms, increased private

…but other factors have also been important

Figure IV.8:
**Gross domestic product of Africa, 2002-2008**

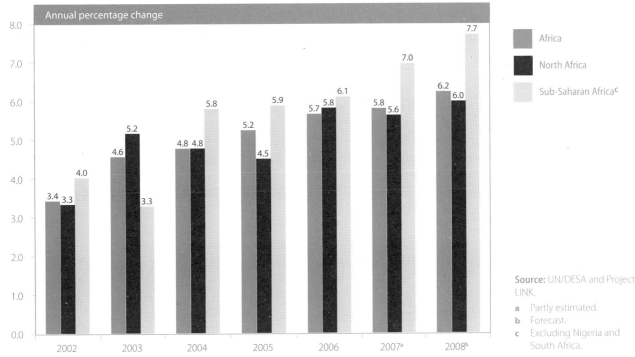

Annual percentage change

Legend:
- Africa
- North Africa
- Sub-Saharan Africa[c]

Values by year:
- 2002: 3.4, 3.3, 4.0
- 2003: 4.6, 5.2, 3.3
- 2004: 4.8, 4.8, 5.8
- 2005: 5.2, 4.5, 5.9
- 2006: 5.7, 5.8, 6.1
- 2007[a]: 5.8, 5.6, 7.0
- 2008[b]: 6.2, 6.0, 7.7

**Source:** UN/DESA and Project LINK.
a  Partly estimated.
b  Forecast.
c  Excluding Nigeria and South Africa.

capital flows, debt relief, rising domestic demand and robust non-fuel exports. Africa has also witnessed a decline in political conflicts and wars, especially in West and Central Africa, though peace remains fragile in some parts of the continent. Many African countries have also implemented macroeconomic and microeconomic reforms that have resulted in a generally improved business environment and investment climate. Along with increased aid and debt relief, this helped attract high net private capital inflows and contributed to boosting domestic spending. Such improvements in macroeconomic performance need to be widened and deepened, however, if Africa is to accelerate and sustain growth beyond the ongoing commodity boom. The continent also needs to promote diversification of its production base to ensure that growth can be shared more broadly and to stimulate more productive employment so as to accelerate poverty reduction as well as the achievement of the other Millennium Development Goals.

Despite the economic recovery in some countries, growth continues to be uneven across countries and subregions. Growth has been strong in North Africa. A noticeable rebound in the tourism sector and vibrant domestic demand, instigated by large cuts in income taxes and wealth effects from booming asset prices, have provided a strong impetus to growth in Egypt. In Algeria, GDP growth has benefited from buoyant public spending and increased FDI flows in the hydrocarbon sector. In Morocco, in contrast, economic activity has slowed markedly owing to the significant drop in agricultural output.

Economic performance in sub-Saharan Africa, excluding Nigeria and South Africa, improved in 2007, reaching 7 per cent, up from 6.1 per cent in 2006. Despite the temporary slowdown in consumer spending, South Africa maintained a relatively robust growth of 4.8 per cent in 2007 resulting from the expansion in construction and mining and increased investment in the corporate sector. GDP growth has picked up slightly in Nigeria also, driven in part by strong growth in the non-hydrocarbon sectors and rapidly expanding public investment.

Elsewhere, strong growth in construction, manufacturing and services boosted overall economic activity in some of the economies that are still agriculture-dominated, including Burkina Faso, Ethiopia, Kenya and the United Republic of Tanzania. Strong performance of the agricultural sector accompanied the growth impulses from high commodity prices in oil-exporting Angola and mining-dependent Sierra Leone and the Democratic Republic of the Congo. GDP growth has recovered modestly in the Central African Republic, supported by increasing aid flows and domestic investment. In addition, after many years of sluggishness, economic activity has picked up noticeably in Gabon and Seychelles, owing to the strong expansion in construction and services. Similarly, the Ouagadougou peace accord signed in March 2007, if fully implemented, should improve the political and security situation, reduce economic insecurity and induce economic recovery in Côte-d'Ivoire in 2008.

In contrast, GDP has contracted in Chad and Zimbabwe as a result of the strained security and social situation in the former and continued socio-political tensions and unsuitable economic policies in the latter.

Fiscal sustainability is a major concern, especially for some oil-importing countries. Although Africa's overall fiscal position recorded a surplus of 2.4 per cent of GDP in 2007, such an achievement mainly reflects developments in the 13 oil-exporting countries that maintained an average fiscal surplus of 5.2 per cent of GDP in 2007 and 5.4 per cent in 2006. For the oil-importing African economies, the overall budget deficit widened from 0.9 per cent of GDP in 2006 to 1.2 per cent in 2007. The fiscal stance in these countries has been modestly expansionary, as public spending has risen more than government rev-

*Robust growth has been evident in all northern African countries, except Morocco*

*Sub-Saharan Africa has experienced robust but variable growth*

*Fiscal sustainability is a concern for many oil-importing countries*

enue resulting from increased efforts to achieve the Millennium Development Goals and improve public infrastructure.

In most African economies, monetary policy continues to focus on inflation control and has remained restrictive, although the pace and sequence of the tightening have varied across the region. Amidst concerns about inflation, many African oil-producing countries have adopted firm monetary tightening policies to deal with growing excess liquidity fuelled by increased export receipts and capital flows. Under similar conditions, the South African Reserve Bank raised its policy interest rates twice between April and August 2007 when inflation breached the ceiling of the 3-6 per cent target band. The tightening, however, has been more gradual and cautious in Egypt, Morocco and Tunisia, so as not to hinder private investment growth and the strong economic growth needed to reduce high unemployment rates in these economies. With excess liquidity declining and inflationary pressures subsiding, the two central banks of the 15 Communauté financière africaine (CFA) countries have paused, thus diverging slightly from the monetary policies pursued by the ECB, the institutional anchor of the CFA Franc. In contrast, the positive outlook for inflation and exchange-rate stability prompted a continued monetary easing in Mozambique and Ghana.

The recent gains in lowering inflation to relatively low levels have generally been sustained in most countries, despite episodic accelerations in consumer prices in a few. Rising insecurity and/or transport bottlenecks have caused supply shortages, thus generating significant inflationary pressures in the Democratic Republic of the Congo and Eritrea, while rapid increases in public spending or private consumption have moderately pushed up consumer prices (especially those of non-traded goods) in Algeria, Equatorial Guinea, Gabon, Sao Tome and Principe, South Africa and the Sudan. Hyperinflation remains in Zimbabwe owing to food shortages, continued monetization of rising fiscal deficits and steep currency devaluation.

On balance, the inflation outlook appears broadly favourable for most countries. Inflationary pressures will remain a concern in some countries, however. With rising oil prices, subsidies on domestic energy prices may no longer be sustained. Furthermore, some countries will suffer from poor harvests because of inauspicious weather during the planting phases of the 2007/2008 crop cycle, and lower agricultural production and food supplies could add inflationary pressure in some countries.

Despite debt-relief initiatives, Africa's external debt remains high and unchanged, at about $255 billion for 2006 and 2007. While official debt declined considerably with the debt-relief initiatives, debt owed to banks and other private creditors increased in 2007. Meanwhile, domestic resource mobilization remains insufficient for financing the investment needed to achieve the Millennium Development Goals, and African countries will continue to rely on external funding to fill the resource gap in the near future. Reaching the Millennium Development Goals will require that the international community live up to its commitments to scaling-up aid to Africa and that African Governments ensure that external assistance be used to build productive capacity and deliver the necessary public services (see box IV.3).

Africa's economic outlook remains positive in the absence of any major internal or external risks. Growth is expected to strengthen in 2008, driven largely by buoyant domestic demand, booming mining and gas production and a broadly based recovery from a long period of economic decline in a number of countries. There are important downside risks to the outlook. Any sharp slowdown in the global economy will reduce demand for

Monetary policies have remained broadly restrictive

Inflation rates have been kept low, but some risks lie ahead

The outlook is favourable, but both internal and external risks remain

## Box IV.3

# Commitment to scaling up aid to Africa: progress and policy implications

Aid contributes significantly to meeting financing needs in most African countries, covering more than 50 per cent of government investment in some countries and averaging 5.5 per cent of the region's GNI. Yet, because of the significant needs and the lack of domestic resource mobilization capacity, further scaling up of aid is seen as crucial to financing the additional public spending required to achieve the Millennium Development Goals in the region.

After a decline in the 1990s, total net Official Development Assistance (ODA) to sub-Saharan Africa picked up between 2000 and 2005, more than doubling, from $12.6 billion to $32.0 billion. In per capita terms, aid increased from $21 billion in 2001 to $44 billion in 2005. Although these increases seem impressive, the rise in total ODA, especially in 2005, mainly reflects debt relief (see also chapter III). At current trends, the realization of the commitments made by the international community to double aid to Africa by 2010 is increasingly uncertain.

Recently, non-Development Assistance Committee (DAC) donors have increasingly become major players in Africa. As of 2006, existing loans and credit lines from China were estimated to total about $19 billion, and the country has plans to double its aid to Africa by 2009. China's aid is targeted at certain sectors, such as energy, telecommunications and transportation, which have by and large been neglected by the traditional DAC country donors. It should be added, though, that China's financial support is highly concentrated in a small number of oil- and mineral-exporting countries. Furthermore, most of the aid is provided in kind by Chinese companies, using inputs of Chinese origin, including labour.[a] India also offers substantial aid to a number of African countries (for example, in the information technology and health sectors). In general, most of the aid from Asia is tied to purchases from the donor country and little information is available about actual disbursements.

Next to concerns about the sufficiency of the increase in aid volume to the region, greater efforts need to be undertaken to improve the quality of aid, as highlighted by the Paris Declaration on Aid Effectiveness. In a recent survey of government officials from ministries of finance and economic development as well as central banks, conducted by the Economic Commission for Africa (ECA), respondents rated the performance in the area of international financial and technical cooperation mainly as good (40.4 per cent of the respondents) and fair (42.3 per cent) and confirmed that progress has been made in terms of aid efficiency. Respondents also raised important concerns, pointing in particular to gaps with respect to the allocation of aid across countries and transparency and harmonization in the terms of delivery.[b]

There are additional concerns regarding the volatility in aid disbursements. The lack of sufficient predictability of aid inflows limits the scope for Governments to make longer-term investment plans and has been found to have imparted stop-and-go patterns to public investment. Aid volatility also tends to increase nominal and real exchange-rate volatility.[c] In this regard, donors must honor their commitments to increase the quantity of aid and improve its predictability as well as its coordination and alignment with the recipient country's priorities. One way of reducing aid volatility would be for individual donors to align their aid strategies to the medium-term expenditure frameworks of the recipient countries and commit aid disbursements as part of multi-annual agreements.

Proper management of high aid flows will in any case be a challenge to many African countries. Aid flowing to certain sectors may hit on limited absorptive capacity, because of, among other factors, weak institutional strength or human-resource constraints. High aid inflows also tend to enhance pressures on real exchange-rate appreciation. Such pressures have prompted many countries to sterilize a sizeable share of aid flows. Between 1999 and 2005, 37 per cent of the increase in aid to sub-Saharan Africa was not matched by increased spending or absorption in the country but rather led to the build-up of foreign exchange reserves.[d] Although higher reserves help shield countries against external shocks, including aid volatility, reserve accumulation in excess of minimum requirements has opportunity costs as such resources could be made available for investment in growth and poverty reduction. Making increased aid effective for reaching the Millennium Development Goals requires that monetary policies accommodate more expansionary fiscal policies, especially with a view to facilitating higher spending in human capital, infrastructure and other productivity-enhancing activities.[e] The growth effects of such investments will likely only mature gradually over time. Yet short-run inflationary pressures from such expansionary macroeconomic policies are avoidable by ensuring that, among other things, a significant share of the additional spending facilitates the better use of underutilized labour and production capacity.

a Ulrich Jacoby, "Getting together: The new partnership between China and Africa for aid and trade", *Finance & Development*, vol. 44, No. 2, June 2007.

b Economic Commission for Africa, *Economic Report on Africa 2008—Africa and the Monterrey Consensus: Tracking performance and progress*, forthcoming (Addis Ababa, Ethiopia: ECA).

c Economic Commission for Africa, *Economic Report on Africa 2006—Capital flows and development financing in Africa* (Addis Ababa, Ethiopia: ECA); and Economic Commission for Africa policy research report on *Public expenditure and service delivery in Africa: Perspectives on policy and institutional framework* (Addis Ababa, Ethiopia: ECA).

d International Monetary Fund, Independent Evaluation Office, *The IMF and aid to Sub-Saharan Africa: evaluation report* (Washington, D.C.: IMF, March 2007).

e John Weeks and Terry McKinley, *The macroeconomic implications of MDG-based strategies in Sub-Saharan Africa*, International Poverty Centre Policy Research Brief, No. 4 (Brasilia: United Nations Development Programme, IPC).

exports and provoke a steep decline in commodity prices, thus dampening Africa's growth prospects. In addition, sudden private capital flow reversals in some countries, as well as rising oil prices and lower-than-expected aid inflows, might constrain both public and private investment and therefore pose serious risks for the current economic revival. At the domestic level, unpredictable weather changes might cause a decline in agricultural output, weighing heavily in many countries of the region. Finally, the continuation or emergence of civil conflicts constitutes additional risks for the outlook.

## East Asia: robust growth amidst external uncertainties

GDP growth for the East Asian region remained robust at 8.4 per cent in 2007, slightly higher than the growth of 8.3 per cent in 2006. This performance is particularly impressive considering the challenges faced by countries from external factors such as financial market instability, appreciating currencies and muted external demand. In the outlook period, continued uncertainty stemming from the external environment is expected to moderate growth to 7.7 per cent in 2008.

The strong performance of the sub-region was led by China's GDP growth of 11.4 per cent, which was achieved through vigorous investment spending and rapid expansion of exports. Fixed asset investment growth in urban areas in the first ten months of 2007 saw a year-on-year acceleration to 26.9 per cent; property prices surged, with housing prices in 70 cities jumping 9.5 per cent in October from the previous year.[5] China is expected to see a moderation in GDP growth rate in 2008 to 10.1 per cent, as a result of a slowdown in export markets and government measures to cool the economy. Also, domestic demand will increase its weight in aggregate demand growth, especially through increased government spending in rural areas and social sectors.

*China's growth continues to outpace expectations*

Growth in other countries of the sub-region was robust in spite of the more challenging international environment caused by the slowdown of the United States economy and the significant appreciation of national currencies against the dollar. Hong Kong Special Administrative Region (SAR) of China, Indonesia, Malaysia, the Philippines and Taiwan Province of China were able to mitigate the impact of these external factors by adopting various mechanisms to increase domestic consumption and private and public investment. Growth in Viet Nam was also supported by strong domestic demand, while Singapore's economy showed resilience and moved to high value-added exports such as high-tech manufactures, pharmaceuticals and transport engineering.

*Growth in other countries was compounded by the changing external environment*

Thailand exhibited greater vulnerability to the changing international environment. GDP growth declined from 5.0 per cent in 2006 to 4.5 per cent in 2007, as private domestic consumption and investment fell amidst continuing political uncertainty. Following elections at the end of 2007, consumer and business confidence is expected to increase, likely allowing the economy to recover somewhat. GDP is expected to grow at 4.8 per cent in 2008.

*Political uncertainty is clouding growth in Thailand*

Inflation has remained in check across the region. Increasing import costs caused by rising international oil and food prices have been mitigated by currency appreciation in most economies. Inflation in China nonetheless accelerated from 1.5 per cent in 2006 to 4.9 per cent in 2007. From August to October 2007, surging food prices pushed up the consumer price index (CPI) by as much as 6.5 per cent.

*Inflationary pressures are contained*

---

5    National Bureau of Statistics of China, available from http://www.stats.gov.cn/english/statistical data/monthlydata/t20071126_402447429.htm; National Development and Reform Commission, available from http://www.ndrc.gov.cn/jjxsfx/t20071130_176220.htm.

In other countries also, inflationary pressures stem from rising international food prices, as food items have a high weight in the CPI. In the Philippines, for instance, food products make up 50 per cent of the basket for the CPI, while agricultural products and processed food together account for about 42 per cent of Indonesia's CPI.

The currencies of the countries of the region appreciated dramatically against the United States dollar between January 2006 and September 2007, adversely affecting exports (see figure IV.9). Export competitiveness for the countries in the region is also influenced by the position of their currencies vis-à-vis the Chinese renminbi, as China is an important export competitor. The real effective exchange rates of Indonesia, Malaysia, the Philippines and Thailand have all appreciated against the renminbi since 2006. The currency appreciation has had the largest effects on highly price-sensitive exports of labour-intensive, low-tech manufacturing products, such as textiles and apparel, and furniture, as well as agricultural exports. Weakening global demand owing to slow growth in the United States is further affecting export growth in the region.

Some central banks, such as China's, have tried to counter the appreciation of their currency by purchasing more dollars, which has added to their already large foreign-exchange reserves. Since the end of 2006, foreign-exchange reserves of countries in the region have grown by $499 billion. Despite efforts to sterilize, increasing liquidity has led to upward inflationary pressures and a rise in asset prices in some countries. Other countries like the Philippines and Thailand have allowed their currencies to appreciate, but have introduced a host of short-term measures to protect exporters against currency appreciation. For example, the Development Bank of the Philippines (DBP) launched its exporter's hedging programme on 28 June 2007 to protect exporters against currency movements. DBP offers two products for exporters: foreign-exchange insurance, whereby exporters are protected against peso appreciation and have an opportunity to gain in peso

> Currency appreciation and slow external demand are affecting export growth

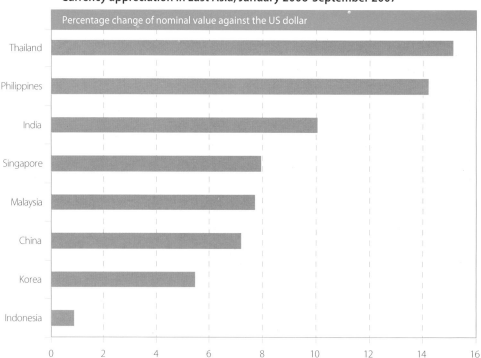

Figure IV.9:
**Currency appreciation in East Asia, January 2006-September 2007**

**Source:** UN/DESA calculations based on IMF, *International Financial Statistics,* November 2007

depreciation; and forward foreign-exchange rate protection, a forward contract between the exporter and DBP whereby only the net difference between the dollar/peso forward rate and the market rate is settled at maturity.

Given the uncertainty in the external environment, many countries in the region have taken measures to reduce their dependence on the external sector by boosting domestic demand. For example, in Indonesia, Malaysia and the Philippines, private consumption and public and private investment led the way in keeping up growth in the second quarter of 2007. There has also been a substantial increase in outward FDI. This is helping reduce upward pressure on national currencies, but is also leading to increased investment income, which is compensating for some of the reduced export earnings. In addition, this year also saw the creation and substantial growth of sovereign wealth funds. The China Investment Corporation and Korea Investment Corporation are examples of State-owned investment companies formed to manage and improve returns on these countries' massive foreign-exchange reserves.

> Measures have been taken to improve domestic consumption

In addition to the challenges related to the depreciating dollar and the slowdown in the economy of the United States, the underlying sub-prime mortgage market crisis could cause problems for credit markets and financial institutions in the region. International financial institutions, primarily hedge funds and banks, have already suffered losses on their holdings of products based on sub-prime mortgages, known as collateralized debt obligations. Another risk that may spill over from losses related to the sub-prime mortgage debacle is related to the difficulty with which banks are able to access finance for their daily operations, as lending financial institutions are worried about banks' exposure to risky mortgage loans, which could lead to contagion effects in the market.

> Problems in financial markets pose downside risks

## South Asia: strong growth in an environment of political unease

Amidst political upheaval and uncertainty, the South Asian region continued its strong growth momentum in 2007, reaching 6.9 per cent in 2007, down from 7.5 per cent in 2006 (see table A.3). Growth was underpinned by the strong performance of industry and services, as well as increased domestic investment. In the outlook, growth is expected to remain high in the region, but will decelerate slightly to 6.7 per cent in 2008.

Regional growth was led by India, which grew by more than 8.5 per cent for the fourth consecutive year. The economies of Bangladesh, Pakistan and Sri Lanka also maintained their growth momentum and are expected to grow at 6.2 per cent or more during 2007 (figure IV.10). Industry and services sectors were major contributors to growth in all these economies; the recovery in agriculture also improved growth performance in Pakistan. Sharp increases in domestic demand, particularly in investment, also supported the strong performance in these countries. In Pakistan, the investment volume grew by more than 20 per cent in 2007. Following a cessation of hostilities among rival political groups, Nepal's economy was expected to recover but growth remained low, at 2.6 per cent, partly owing to continued unrest in some parts of the country, as well as to low investment and poor performance of the agricultural sector. The Islamic Republic of Iran, the only net oil exporter in the subregion is expected to sustain growth at 4.8 per cent owing to high oil prices and despite slow capacity development in the oil sector, a result largely of political interference and subdued foreign investor interest. The Islamic Republic of Iran will continue to rely heavily on imported fuels to compensate for its inadequate refining capacity.

> Industry and services are the major contributors to fast growth

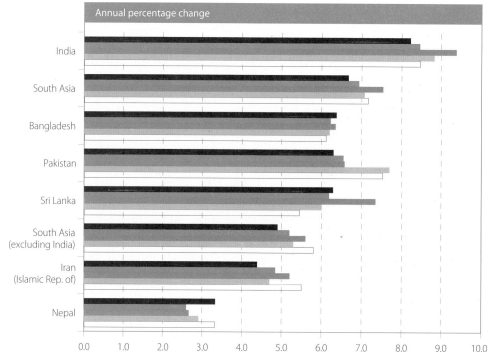

Figure IV.10:
**Rates of growth of real GDP in South Asia, 2004-2008**

Annual percentage change

Legend:
- 2008ᵃ
- 2007ᵇ
- 2006
- 2005
- 2004

**Source:** UN/DESA based on data from Statistics Division and Project LINK.
**a** Forecast.
**b** Partly estimated.

India will continue its strong growth performance

India's economy will remain strong in 2008 and is expected to grow by about 8.2 per cent, maintaining concerns over whether the country has been growing above potential. Although interest rate differentials have attracted further capital inflows in India and the associated currency appreciation has helped to curb inflation, these may have negative implications for exports. The Government's strategy, aiming at high growth with reasonable price stability, now focuses on stimulating investment to enhance production capacity and raise productivity and to reduce shortages in the supply of skilled workers.

Political tensions and volatile oil prices remain a concern

Pakistan may witness a slowing of growth due to political tensions related to general elections in the country. In addition, if the current state of emergency in the country lasts longer than anticipated, economic activity could be affected. In Nepal, with the peace process moving forward, growth prospects have improved and the economy is expected to grow at 3.3 per cent in 2008. Tourism, transportation and services appear to be reviving and the expansion in government spending, particularly on rural infrastructure, could provide greater support for economic activity. In the Islamic Republic of Iran, high oil prices, coupled with expansionary fiscal policy and accommodative monetary policy, are expected to continue to support economic growth. However, volatility of oil prices and international tensions over the nuclear issue create uncertainties for the economic outlook.

Inflationary pressures have been emanating from increasing food and oil prices

Inflation rates remained high in most countries as a result of increasing prices of food, oil and other imported commodities. In Sri Lanka, inflation is expected to reach 15.5 per cent in 2007 as a result of a combination of supply shortages in domestic food crops stemming from unfavourable weather conditions, adjustments to State-mandated fuel prices and a sharp increase in demand. In the Islamic Republic of Iran, inflation is expected to rise to about 17 per cent owing to expansionary fiscal and monetary policies along with a continuous rise in public wages. While inflation was relatively stable in Bangladesh and Pakistan, it remained close to 7 per cent in both countries.

All the countries, except the Islamic Republic of Iran, are following strict monetary policies to contain inflation. Countries have also taken supply-side measures to improve the supply of essential commodities through liberal imports and the lowering of tariffs. Countries will have to remain vigilant about inflationary pressures amidst rising oil prices as these can slow down growth momentum and affect real incomes of the poor in particular.

The Governments in the subregion have maintained an expansionary fiscal stance to ensure higher investment for growth and increase expenditures towards priority sectors such as education, health and physical infrastructure. However, due to failure to raise tax revenues, budget deficits remain high in most countries. In India and Bangladesh, the budget deficit is about 3.7 per cent of GDP, while Pakistan and Sri Lanka run budget deficits of 4.2 per cent and 7.6 per cent, respectively. As a result of accumulated large budget deficits, public debt levels are also high. The share of domestic public debt in total public debt is also on the rise in most countries (see box IV.4).

*Expansionary fiscal policy is generating an increasing public debt burden*

**Box IV.4**

## Public debt dynamics and their implications in South Asia

Despite improvements in recent years, public debt remains a serious problem for most countries in South Asia. The high public debt overhang is putting pressure on interest rates, and inflation is crowding out financial resources available for investment and creating concerns regarding the capacity to service debt in the near future. Reducing the debt overhang is not easy given the pressures to increase public expenditures in these countries to meet the vast needs of poverty-reduction programmes and the delivery of basic services.

Public debt in Sri Lanka reached 93 per cent of GDP in 2006, the highest in the region (see figure). In India, the combined debt of central and state governments increased from about 70 to about 87 per cent of GDP between 1990 and 2002-2004. The public debt ratio has been on the decline in more recent years. Pakistan has reduced its public debt burden from 84 to 57 per cent of GDP between 2000 and 2006. Public debt in Nepal has been decreasing in recent years and stood at 56 per cent of GDP in 2005.

**Domestic and external public debt as a percentage of GDP, 2006**

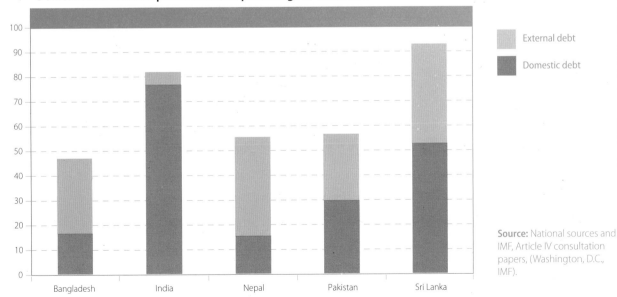

Legend: External debt, Domestic debt

**Source:** National sources and IMF, Article IV consultation papers, (Washington, D.C., IMF).

## Box IV.4 (cont'd)

Despite the recent reductions, South Asia's public indebtedness remains high and of concern to policymakers. Large fiscal deficits have been the source of the increase in public debt. Governments in the region are taking measures, including the introduction of legislation to bring down fiscal deficits to more sustainable levels. Inspired by New Zealand's Fiscal Responsibility Act of 1994, an increasing number of countries have adopted a rule-based fiscal responsibility framework to ensure responsible and accountable fiscal management by present and future Governments and to encourage informed public debate about fiscal policy.[a]

In India, the Fiscal Responsibility and Budget Management Act was passed in August 2003, requiring that the central Government's fiscal deficit not exceed 3 per cent of GDP by 2007/8 (which was subsequently postponed to 2008/9) and that the deficit on the revenue account be eliminated by the same date. The target of lowering the budget deficit to 3 per cent in 2008/9 is likely to be achieved. In Pakistan, the Fiscal Responsibility and Debt Limitation Act was approved in 2005, requiring that total public debt not exceed 60 per cent of the estimated GDP at the end of a period of 10 financial years beginning on 1 July 2003. The Government has already reached this level and is expected to meet the requirement. Sri Lanka passed its Fiscal Management (Responsibility) Act in early 2003, with the aim of containing the overall budget deficit to 5 per cent of GDP and debt to 85 per cent of GDP by the end of 2006. However, for various reasons, these targets could not be achieved and in 2006 the terminal date for achieving the targets was changed to 2008.

These are laudable initiatives pertaining to fiscal planning and transparency. However, the experience of countries in other regions shows that a rule-based fiscal responsibility framework is no guarantee for adequate fiscal consolidation.[b] In addition, there needs to be a strong political will to adhere to the fiscal rules. Raising tax revenues and containing public expenditure can also be used as a tool to reduce budget deficits. While tax revenues have been rising in nominal terms over the years, their share in GDP has not shown much improvement. A simplified tax system, with reduced exemptions, less discretion and improved compliance could help broaden the tax base. The main challenge for Governments, however, may not lie in containing the public deficit in order to reduce the debt burden, but rather in doing so while at the same time changing the composition of public spending towards priority sectors in order not to jeopardize the achievement of social goals.

**a** George Kopits, "Fiscal responsibility framework: international experience and implications for Hungary", Occasional paper, No. 62 (Budapest: Magyar Nemzeti Bank, 2007).

**b** Ibid.

---

*Increasing worker remittances are helping finance a growing import bill*

Import growth is outpacing export growth and causing widening trade deficits in most countries. Worker remittances are substantial and on the rise, providing a cushion to the current-account balance. The value of remittances reached about $6 billion in Bangladesh and Pakistan in 2007. In India, the current-account deficit is expected to remain at about one per cent of GDP in 2007, but at about 5 per cent of GDP in Pakistan. High oil prices are an important factor in Pakistan's rising external deficit. Exporters of clothing and textiles, which have benefited from a quota-free trading environment over the past two years, are likely to face intense competition in 2008 with the removal of restrictions on China's exports to the United States market.

*Strong economic growth is making a bigger impact on unemployment rates*

Unemployment estimates tend to be somewhat unreliable for the countries in the region, in part because of the importance of agriculture and the informal sector in employment generation. Existing data suggest that strong economic growth is helping to reduce unemployment rates. In Sri Lanka, unemployment during the first quarter of 2007 recorded a historic low of 6.2 per cent, continuing its steadily declining trend of the past few years. In Pakistan, the economy has created about 11 million jobs since 2002, thereby reducing the open unemployment rate to 6.2 per cent in 2006.

*Political tensions, uncertain weather conditions and volatility of oil prices are the main sources of uncertainty*

Among the various downside risks, volatility of oil prices remain a major source of uncertainty. Any further increase in the already high oil prices could slow down economic growth, raise inflation and cause problems for macroeconomic balances. Several countries in the subregion have internal conflicts which also add to uncertainty. As in the past, countries are prone to natural disasters. Poor weather conditions, including floods, can adversely affect the agricultural sector. An escalation of political tensions related to elections in Bangladesh and Pakistan could also adversely affect the macroeconomic performance of these countries.

## Western Asia: resurgent oil prices sustain economic growth

With oil prices spiralling upwards and oil production slightly higher in 2007, the Western Asian region has maintained its fifth consecutive year of growth of more than 4.5 per cent. The region is benefiting from the revenue effects of resurgent oil prices, the consequent strength of consumer demand, and increased public and private investment, all of which have propelled growth to 5.7 per cent in 2007. Higher growth is expected in the oil-exporting countries, but the more diversified economies have also obtained growth benefits through various spillover mechanisms. In the outlook, strong regional growth is expected to continue in 2008, at 5.2 per cent, supported by the high global demand and price of oil as well as by robust public and private sector investment expenditures.

Growth in oil revenues has bolstered fiscal and trade-account positions in the Gulf Cooperation Council (GCC) economies.[6] Intraregional FDI and government spending on infrastructure and development projects have increased. The GCC member States recently announced investment plans worth $700 billion between 2006 and 2010 to fund large-scale diversification projects and stimulate broader-based growth. Saudi Arabia is planning several large-scale cities that will expand growth beyond the capital and cover a range of economic sectors. The United Arab Emirates, where oil's share in GDP has been declining steadily, is undertaking reforms to attract FDI to the tourism, real estate and manufacturing sectors.

*Current-account surpluses are driving diversification efforts*

Development of high-tech and high-value-added sectors remains elusive. Although many GCC economies are pursuing diversification strategies, labour productivity growth has not been widespread across the region (figure IV.11). In fact, productivity growth has actually been negative in some of the fastest-growing countries of the GCC since 2000.

Strong growth in the oil-exporting economies has created positive spillover effects on other economies in the region through increased FDI, worker remittances and tourism receipts. This has stimulated growth in Jordan, the Syrian Arab Republic and, to a lesser extent, Lebanon and Yemen. In Jordan, FDI is expected to reach 13 per cent of GDP in 2007; in Lebanon, 5 per cent. FDI inflows to the Syrian Arab Republic amount to only 1 per cent of GDP, however. Tourism receipts remain important sources of income, notably for Jordan, where they have been growing steadily over the past few years. In Lebanon, normally a major tourist destination, receipts from tourism declined 35 per cent during the first half of 2007 as the economy is still suffering from the effects of the conflict with Israel. Worker remittances remain important to several of these countries. They are equivalent to half of the value of exports in Jordan, and to a fifth in Yemen. Recently, the GCC countries have been recruiting more workers from outside the region, leading to slower growth in worker remittances to the other Western Asian countries (see box IV.5).

*Oil-importing economies benefit from spillover effects from oil exporters*

Israel's economy is expected to expand by 5.1 per cent in 2007 and to moderate slightly in 2008 driven by strong export growth, increased investment and robust domestic consumption. Unlike Lebanon, tourism is recovering from the Israeli-Lebanese conflict of 2006. Private consumption rose by 11.8 per cent in the first quarter of 2007, reflecting a

*Israel is sustaining its strong export performance*

---

6    The Gulf Cooperation Council economies comprise Bahrain, Kuwait, Oman, Qatar, Saudi Arabia and the United Arab Emirates.

Figure IV.11:
**Average annual labour productivity growth in Western Asia, 2000-2005**

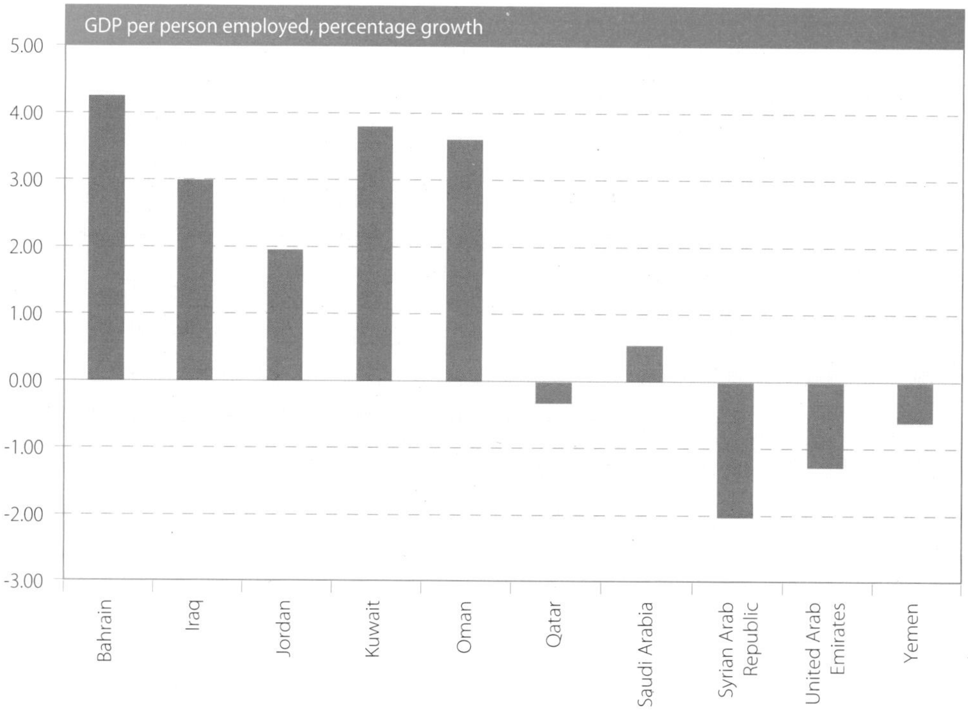

GDP per person employed, percentage growth

**Source:** UN/DESA based on International Labour Organization, *Key Indicators of the Labour Market*, 5th Edition, 2007.

**Box IV.5**

### The impact of the current oil boom on unemployment and inequality in Western Asia

The present economic boom opens a window of opportunity for the countries of the Western Asian region. With continued strong oil prices and steady production, Governments can take advantage of the relative abundance of capital generated by the current oil boom to implement a number of overdue structural changes in their economies, with a view to promoting greater economic diversification as a source for more sustainable growth and employment creation.

Western Asia has the lowest labour participation in the world: only roughly half of Western Asia's working-age population is considered part of the labour force (that is to say, those with or seeking employment) (see figure), even though female participation rates are on the rise. High rates of unemployment and underemployment remain predominant characteristics of labour markets. According to the latest available data, unemployment rates range from 14 to 28 per cent for Jordan, Lebanon, Palestine and Iraq, and hover at about 10 per cent in Yemen and the Syrian Arab Republic.

In some countries, strong economic growth has not translated into significant new job growth. In Jordan, for instance, the unemployment rate has remained virtually unchanged over the past 4 years, while GDP increased at an average annual rate of 6.5 per cent. The degree of job growth varies across the countries of the region, however. Between 2000 and 2005, the oil-rich countries witnessed on average a job growth rate of nearly 5 per cent per year. In the less wealthy countries, employment growth has averaged about 3.5 per cent during the same period.[a] The number of new entrants to the labour markets is increasing at more than 3 per cent per year in Yemen, Iraq, Saudi Arabia and the Syrian Arab Republic, allowing little room for reducing the rate of unemployment. Most new entrants join the ranks of the unemployed owing to the lack of available jobs. In the Syrian Arab Republic about 80 per cent of the unemployed are first-time job seekers; in Jordan they account for about 50 per cent. In addition, many persons resort to the informal sector for employment as for-

a World Bank, "Middle East and North Africa region—2007 Economic Developments and Prospects: Job creation in an era of high growth" (Washington, D.C.: World Bank).

Box IV.5 (cont'd)

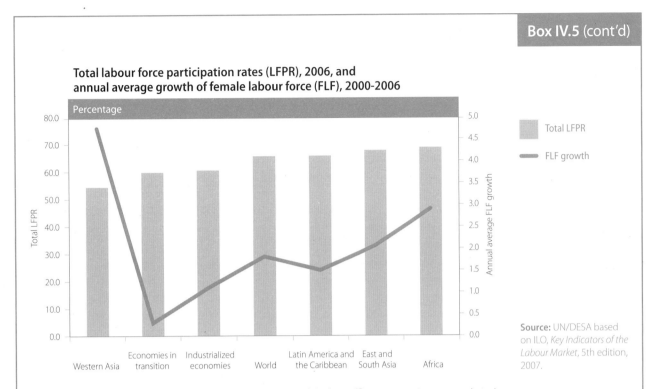

**Total labour force participation rates (LFPR), 2006, and annual average growth of female labour force (FLF), 2000-2006**

Percentage

Total LFPR

FLF growth

**Source:** UN/DESA based on ILO, *Key Indicators of the Labour Market*, 5th edition, 2007.

mal sector jobs are scarce. About one third of the workers of the less affluent countries are employed in the informal sector. Informal sector employment in Yemen and Jordan is estimated at 37 and 33 per cent of the total, respectively.[b] Underemployment is also a common problem, and real wages in some countries have been declining, most notably in public employment.

Labour immigration to the GCC countries from outside Western Asia is having a negative impact on other economies of the region, which rely heavily on remittances for economic growth and are seeing their shares of remittance income displaced. In Jordan and Lebanon, roughly 20–25 per cent of GDP is attributable to remittances, and in the the West Bank and Gaza, remittances make up about 35 per cent of GDP, one of the highest shares in the world. The contrast, however, to the emigration of workers from other countries is the overwhelming presence of expatriate workers in the labour markets of GCC economies, particularly in the private sector. Strong infrastructure growth and diversification efforts in the GCC have increased the demand for workers, but there is a considerable skills mismatch in the national labour force. The newly created private sector jobs are either low-skilled construction jobs or highly skilled more technical employment—for which nationals are either unwilling (in the case of low-skilled employment) or not adequately qualified (in the case of high-skilled employment) to undertake.

As a consequence, throughout the region, nationals have been dependent on the public sector for employment. In the extreme cases of Kuwait and Qatar about 90 per cent of the national labour force works in the public sector—while in other economies of the GCC, the figure lies between 32 and 53 per cent. Although the number of nationals in public sector employment has been declining in recent years, public sector employment outside the GCC, in Jordan and Palestine, has actually grown. Yet the public sector cannot continue to absorb the number of new entrants into the labour markets.

The fast growth of the labour force, by 4.1 per cent on average per year since 1996, presents a challenge for the region with respect to maintaining high rates of employment. Meeting such a challenge will ultimately entail improving private sector employment creation, while at the same time equipping nationals with the necessary skills and training to become more employable. To increase the share of national employment in the private sector requires improved education and skills-training programmes to address market mismatches. Additionally, more broadly based diversification efforts into high-value-added sectors are needed to stimulate better quality job creation.

**b** Ali A.G. Ali and Ibrahim Elbadawi, "Poverty and the labour market in the Arab world: The role of inequality and growth," in *Employment Creation and Social Protection in the Middle East and North Africa*, Heba Handoussa and Zafiris Tzannotos, eds. (The American University in Cairo Press, 2002), pp. 173-194.

sharp increase in spending on durable goods, while export growth was particularly strong for semi and high-tech industrial products. Owing to its strong ties to the United States (which receives 45 per cent of the country's exports), Israel is vulnerable to a slowdown in the United States economy.

The Turkish economy is expected to expand by 5.3 per cent in 2007, subsequently slowing somewhat to 5 per cent in 2008. Slower growth at the beginning of 2007 was brought on by tighter monetary policy in an effort to rein in inflation. With inflation showing signs of receding, the Central Bank of Turkey unexpectedly eased the monetary stance by cutting interest rates in September 2007, lowering the key borrowing rate from 17.50 to 17.25 per cent, and further to 16.75 per cent in October. The cuts reflected the Bank's concern over weak domestic demand and the continuing appreciation of the lira on account of high interest rates attracting strong capital inflows. The recent fall in interest rates coupled with the expectation of a widening of the current-account deficit should lead to a modest depreciation against the dollar in 2008.

Despite the strong growth in the region, employment impacts remain marginal. In the GCC economies, there is widespread unemployment among national workers, and the policies of 'nationalization' have reached their limits in most public sectors, which can no longer absorb new labour-market entrants. The positive economic spillover effects of GCC growth on other countries in the region have not translated into lower unemployment rates. These remain stubbornly high in Iraq, Jordan, Lebanon, the Syrian Arab Republic and Yemen (see box IV.5).

Inflationary pressures are strong throughout the region, caused by a mix of rising import costs, wage pressures, changes in subsidies and taxes, and supply constraints in some economic sectors. Yemen's inflation rate of about 20 per cent is due in part to the elimination of the fuel subsidy and the introduction of a general sales tax. Qatar's 12 per cent inflation is partly driven by rising rents and greater demand for expatriate labour; in the United Arab Emirates, where imports amount to 60 per cent of GDP, imported inflation is prevalent, yet domestically generated inflation is observed in housing.

Furthermore, with most of the region's exchange rates fixed to the dollar, Western Asia is facing higher costs of euro-denominated and other non-dollar imports as the dollar declines. In response, there is pressure to re-examine exchange-rate regimes. In the GCC countries, the combination of accelerating domestic inflation, a continuous weakening of the United States dollar against other major currencies and recent cuts in the Fed's benchmark rates has led to an intense debate on the appropriate exchange-rate policies. This debate is all the more relevant at a time when the Governments of Bahrain, Kuwait, Qatar, Saudi Arabia and the United Arab Emirates must decide whether to proceed with the plans of establishing a monetary union by 2010, or to postpone the target date following Oman's decision in late 2006 to pull out of the single-currency plan. Currently, all GCC countries, except Kuwait, peg their national currencies to the United States dollar.

As a result, monetary authorities face a serious policy challenge: either to follow the Fed's accommodative stance at a time when strong economic growth and increasing inflation rates call for a tightening of monetary policy, or to allow the spread between domestic and foreign interest rates to widen, thereby stimulating capital inflows or further increasing the upward pressure on national currencies. Currently, the central banks are using indirect monetary instruments to mop up excess liquidity. If the dollar continues its slide, discussions regarding revaluation of national currencies will likely take centre stage.

At the same time, the large GCC current-account surpluses and fiscal conservatism are driving high rates of portfolio investments abroad. The oil-exporting countries in the region continue to buy into financial instruments in the United States as well as dollar-based hedge funds outside the United States. The region's gross official reserves are soaring and are expected to reach $400 billion in 2007. Such assets held externally in stabilization funds for future generations are underutilzed with regard to present generations. Foreign reserves are typically held for precautionary motives such as defending floating exchange rates, servicing debt and securing imports. Given the GCC fixed exchange rates, very low debt and immense wealth, the need for such precautionary foreign exchange reserves is questionable and funds may be better suited towards a more strategic range of instruments held by GCC central banks.

*GCC economies remain fiscally conservative*

The medium-term prospects in the region are clouded by the economic slowdown in the United States, which could lower demand for and, subsequently, the price of oil and other non-oil exports from the region. There is also a concern that a continued weakening of the dollar could aggravate the already persistent inflationary pressure in the region. Although there is no immediate impact from the current global financial instability, there is a possibility that the FDI needed to fund projects in the region could be jeopardized in an environment of global credit tightening. Finally, the extent to which geopolitical tensions in the region have an impact on the region's capital flows remains uncertain.

*Downside risks include a global economic slowdown and weaker exports*

## Latin America and the Caribbean: a moderate slowdown in 2008

Growth in the Latin American and Caribbean region will slow moderately in 2008 to 4.7 per cent, down from 5.3 per cent in 2007, in the context of a general slowdown of the world economy. Much of this deceleration will come from the South American countries, which face less favourable terms of trade, as the prices and demand for their export commodities are expected to fall. Central America and Mexico are expected to maintain their relatively slower growth levels. GDP per capita will have risen by more than 20 per cent (over 3 per cent annually, on average) by the time the region completes its sixth consecutive year of growth in 2008.

The present growth phase is characterized by the outpacing of GDP by national income in real terms, as a result of relatively low international interest rates, better terms of trade and large flows of remittances. Since national income is also growing faster than consumption, increased national savings rates are providing financing for more domestic investment. Gross fixed capital formation increased to 21 per cent of GDP in 2007, the highest level in almost two decades, though it is still below the peak levels of the 1970s. The volume of exports of goods and services expanded at a rate similar to GDP growth, slower than in previous years, while the volume of imports of goods and services continued to outstrip the growth of exports for the fourth year in a row. A number of countries in the region are net energy exporters and have benefited from high oil prices. Nonetheless, important supply constraints limit their capacity to provide energy security to the region (see box IV.6).

*Higher national savings spur relatively higher investment levels*

During 2007, external and internal supply shocks (mainly in fuel and food) and strong internal demand caused some inflationary pressures, but core inflation has not risen commensurately. Brazil was able to contain inflationary pressures thanks to its appre-

*Inflationary pressures may increase*

## Box IV.6

# Challenges and opportunities for the energy sector in Latin America and the Caribbean

Although an energy-rich region, Latin America and the Caribbean confront challenges in improving energy supply, efficiency and sustainability, which are afflicted by problems arising from increasing demand, underinvestment and inefficient or unstable relations between energy surplus and deficit countries.

The International Energy Agency's Reference Scenario projects a yearly increase of the region's primary energy demand of 2.3 per cent over the period 2005-2030, half a percentage point above the world's energy-demand growth rate.[a] Whereas, the OECD countries reduced the energy required to produce one unit of output by about 30 per cent between 1980 and 2005, this amount increased by 3 per cent in Latin America and the Caribbean. The region's meagre progress in improving energy efficiency is due mostly to the expansion of energy-intensive transport systems and manufacturing activities, as well as to the expansion of coverage of modern energy supplies to rural sectors. In addition, poor urban air quality in many of the region's major cities has increased the requirements for more sustainable energy generation and use.

The region is a net exporter of energy. In 2005, it exported 168 million tons of oil equivalent (Mtoe), while total production stood at 680 Mtoe. As shown in the table, energy exports are concentrated in only a few countries. The region has important reserves of petroleum (about 115 billion barrels, mostly in the Bolivarian Republic of Venezuela, but also in Mexico and Brazil) and natural gas (more than 7 trillion cubic meters, predominantly in the Bolivarian Republic of Venezuela, Bolivia and Trinidad and Tobago). It also has favourable natural conditions for the generation of hydroelectric power, solar and wind energy, as well as biofuel.

Despite these favourable conditions, several countries (for example, Argentina, Brazil and Chile) recently suffered situations of real or imminent power shortages, while in others (for example, Panama and Peru) the risks of shortages have increased in the context of high economic growth rates. In addition, higher fuel prices have increased the import bill of net fuel importers and imply higher production costs, which may restrict economic growth and is adding to inflationary pressures. Furthermore, being an energy exporter does not exempt a country from supply problems. For example, Paraguay exports electricity but depends on fuel imports, and Argentina has experienced electric power shortages at times of peak demand.

What can be done to improve access to energy, especially in net importing countries? Important measures will need to be taken to shift demand towards more energy saving and the use of more sustainable sources of energy. In this regard, the focus is on a number of actions that could be taken to improve energy supply:

### *Investing in energy infrastructure*

Following the implementation of a series of economic reforms during the nineties, many countries have encountered difficulties in guaranteeing energy supply—mostly due to the lack of investment in transport and distribution infrastructure—and in the generation of electricity and exploration and exploitation of hydrocarbons. It has been estimated that, excluding biofuel, the region will require investments worth $1,374 billion to address energy-supply shortages between 2005 and 2030. About 52 per cent of these would be needed in electricity, 28 per cent in oil and 19 per cent in natural gas. In order to achieve this goal, the participation of public and/or private enterprises, the funding and efficient use of this investment (by the public sector) and the regulation of the energy sector (especially of the private sector) are essential.

Supply should be increased by technological progress that improves access to new reserves and turns new energy resources into economically viable ones. For example, Brazil's Petrobras is a leading player in deep-water oil exploitation. Between the mid-eighties and 2005, the access to deep-water oil tripled Brazil's proven reserves, and recent explorations have also added vast reserves (for instance from the Tupi field), accessible only with the most advanced technology available. If these can be exploited, Brazil would become a net oil exporter. Petrobras is intensifying its cooperation in technological development with the Mexican oil company Pemex, which in recent years

**a** International Energy Agency, *World Energy Outlook 2007: China and India insights* (Paris: Organization for Economic Cooperation and Development, IEA).

Box IV.6 (cont'd)

**Energy production and net energy trade in Latin America and the Caribbean, 2005**

| Million tons of oil equivalent | | |
|---|---|---|
| | Energy production | Net trade balance for energy |
| **Net energy exporters** | | |
| Argentina | 81.05 | 16.49 |
| Bolivia | 13.87 | 8.98 |
| Colombia | 79.46 | 50.16 |
| Ecuador | 28.60 | 17.81 |
| Mexico | 259.20 | 81.27 |
| Paraguay | 6.58 | 2.63 |
| Trinidad and Tobago | 31.40 | 18.29 |
| Venezuela, Bolivarian Republic of | 204.71 | 143.33 |
| **Net energy importers** | | |
| Brazil | 187.83 | -25.14 |
| Chile | 9.12 | -22.01 |
| Costa Rica | 1.84 | -1.99 |
| Cuba | 5.52 | -5.29 |
| Dominican Republic | 1.53 | -5.82 |
| El Salvador | 2.54 | -2.11 |
| Guatemala | 5.41 | -2.86 |
| Haiti | 1.92 | -0.58 |
| Honduras | 1.78 | -2,30 |
| Jamaica | 0.48 | -3.41 |
| Netherlands Antilles | 0.00 | -3.33 |
| Nicaragua | 1.95 | -1.36 |
| Panama | 0.74 | -1.86 |
| Peru | 10.79 | -3.22 |
| Uruguay | 1.02 | -2.23 |

**Source**: International Energy Agency, *Key World Energy Statistics*, 2007.

has been confronted with a fall in proven reserves, putting Mexico's potential as an important oil exporter at risk.

In addition, efficiency and pollution reduction would require the development of user-friendly and technologically advanced transport systems, increased energy saving in private households—through the massive introduction of more efficient energy appliances and building codes—and incentives for energy-saving technologies at the industry level

### Securing the supply of energy importers

The integration of energy systems between energy-rich and energy-poor countries should be developed further. Stable and reliable commercial and political relations are required to facilitate long-term planning in the energy sector that would lead to the integration of energy infrastructure between countries.

### Diversifying the energy matrix

Countries should not rely heavily on one or even a few energy sources and should increase their use of domestic and renewable sources, such as hydroelectric, geothermic, aeolian, solar and biomass

Box IV.6 (cont'd)

energies. The region has a vast potential for hydroelectric power; however, it faces the challenge of designing and constructing dams with minimum negative environmental and social side effects. High energy prices and technological progress could broaden the possibility for the development and utilization of "new" renewable energy sources, such as solar and wind power. Biofuel production has also presented an opportunity for countries with favourable natural endowments. However, countries need to assess the possible risks of displacement of food production, accelerated deforestation, increased land concentration and net effects on rural labour conditions before embarking on the promotion of a biofuel industry. Brazil is the region's main producer of biofuel, especially ethanol, and plans to drastically increase production. Other countries, such as Argentina, Colombia, Peru and Central American countries, are also investing in, or evaluating investment opportunities in, biofuel production. One element to take into consideration is that environmental and social concerns in potential export markets in the developed countries will put pressure on biofuel-producing countries to adopt and enforce production standards to mitigate the related environmental, food-security and social risks of biofuel production. Some countries have shown a renewed interest in nuclear energy, especially countries that already have nuclear power facilities (such as Argentina and Brazil). However, countries with an energy-supply shortage are considering the potential of this source of energy, but are also concerned about related environmental setbacks. In the area of renewable resources, international technological cooperation and investment can contribute to increasing the exploitation of the region's vast potential.

ciated currency. Mexico's inflation has been at the upper end of the Central Bank's target range owing to supply shocks in some food products, but the country's rate of inflation remains below the regional average. Consumer prices in Colombia have been above the inflation target as domestic demand has strengthened. Prices in the Bolivarian Republic of Venezuela have been rising at double digits because of strong domestic demand and shortages in the supply of consumer products. Many countries in Central America are also experiencing rising costs of fuel and other commodities, as they are net importers of such goods. Slightly higher average inflation rates are expected for 2008, especially because of rising prices of fuel and transportation.

**Unemployment is continuing to decrease**

The steady expansion of economic activity has been reflected in an improvement in labour-market indicators. Not only did the average open unemployment rate for the region decreased from 9.1 per cent in 2005 to about 8.0 per cent in 2007, job quality improved also, as reflected in an increase in the share of formal wage employment. Unemployment rates fell visibly in Argentina, Chile, Peru, Venezuela (Bolivarian Republic of) and some Central American and Caribbean countries. However, the impact of stronger labour demand was felt more in the increase in the number of jobs than in higher wage levels. Employment growth (about 3 per cent on average for the region), slightly higher real wages and strong domestic credit growth fuelled a sharp rise in household consumption. During 2008, the region's average unemployment rate is expected to decline modestly, bringing it back to the level of the early 1990s.

**Latin America and the Caribbean's current-account surplus is narrowing**

The current-account balance saw an unprecedented fifth consecutive year of surplus, although it had reached its peak in 2006 and started its descent in 2007. This surplus is largely attributable to an improvement in the region's terms of trade, which have risen by the equivalent of 3.4 per cent of GDP in 2006. A similar increase in the terms of trade was seen in 2007, while lower growth rates of the world economy may lead to a less positive result in 2008. However, most of the regional current-account surplus can be accredited to a small number of countries, namely Argentina, Brazil, Chile, Ecuador, Peru and Venezuela (Bolivarian Republic of), while the rest of the countries have been incurring current-account deficits, especially the Central American countries and Mexico. Export prices of the Central American countries and many Caribbean nations in particular, have not improved, and the trends in their terms of trade and current accounts have therefore been less positive—although some of these countries did receive significant inflows in the form of remittances. In 2007, the growth rate of worker remittances slowed, and a further slowdown is expected in 2008 along with a lower growth of the United States economy. In addition, gross national income and investment have been more sluggish in these countries; they have been registering fiscal deficits, and their external positions are more vulnerable than those of the South American countries in terms of their levels of international reserves and external debt. The region's average real effective exchange rate continued to appreciate in 2007 after a 3 per cent appreciation in 2006. The currencies of Brazil and Colombia appreciated significantly in real terms as they are receiving considerable capital flows. This appreciation has been a contributing factor in the high growth of import volumes.

During 2007, many countries registered an important increase in public spending, which led to a decline of the region's primary surplus (fiscal balance excluding interest payments). The pressure on public spending is expected to persist throughout 2008, while revenues are expected to decrease. Previously, since 2004, the region had experienced increasing primary surpluses and declining overall deficits, especially in countries with improved terms of trade, thanks to increases in export-commodity and tax revenues from greater economic activity.

Primary fiscal surpluses are also declining

The region's external debt burden, whether measured in terms of GDP or with respect to exports, has fallen drastically over the past few years. The reasons for this decrease vary from country to country. Better fiscal management in most countries has reduced the need for external borrowing. Good export performance and current-account surpluses have enabled several countries to pay off debt, while others (such as Bolivia, Honduras and Nicaragua) have benefited from substantial debt relief under the Heavily Indebted Poor Countries (HIPC) Initiative. In addition, central banks throughout the region have expanded their international reserves by more than $50 billion in 2006 to about $80 billion during the first half of 2007. The more buoyant financial conditions generated by the liquidity of international capital markets have also enabled countries to improve their debt profiles with longer maturities and lower rates, while at the same time increasing their share of obligations denominated in local currencies. Their vulnerability to external shocks has also declined since a number of the region's economies, particularly in South America, are less dollarized than they used to be and are therefore less exposed to the recent volatility in the markets.

Most of the monetary authorities in the region gradually applied less expansive monetary policies as the level of economic activity climbed steadily in most countries and expectations of higher inflation rose as a consequence of strong commodity (especially energy) prices. Nonetheless, real interest rates remained fairly low in relation to their historical levels. The Central Bank of Brazil reduced its policy interest rate through most of 2007, but it remains high in real terms. During the second half of 2007, central banks faced an increasingly important dilemma as they tried to curb expected increases of consumer prices and the appreciation of the bilateral real exchange rate versus the United States dollar. Interest rate increases have led to a widening of the spread between rates in Latin America and the United States, stimulating additional financial inflows and further appreciating local currencies. The Central Bank of Mexico became wary of inflationary pressure in the second quarter of 2007 and raised its policy interest rate again in October

Monetary policies have become more restrictive

in order to maintain its targeted objective. Colombia is also attempting to bring inflation back to the target level, while trying to prevent further appreciation of the peso.

Downside risks are both external and domestic

The main risk for the economic growth of Latin America and the Caribbean in 2008 would be a deeper-than-projected fall of global growth rates, which would reduce the region's external demand, worsen its terms of trade and reduce the dynamism of worker remittances. A hard landing of the United States economy and widespread turmoil in the financial markets would also have a deep impact on the growth perspectives of not only the main trade partners but the region as a whole. Internally, the countries of the region will face the challenge of maintaining the positive fiscal results achieved during recent years as pressures aimed at increased spending meet reduced growth rates of revenues. Furthermore, the control of inflation will be a central macroeconomic task for 2008, while some countries will also face an exchange-rate appreciation which might affect future growth—especially through exports—presenting a major policy dilemma.

# Statistical annex

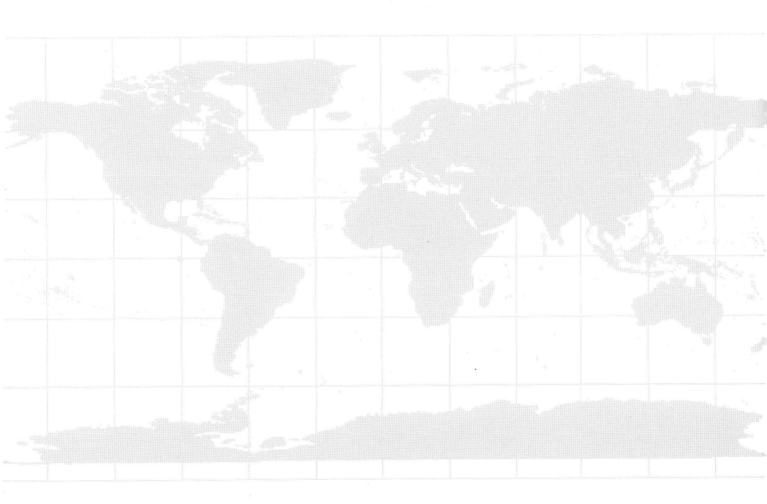

# Annex

## List of tables

Table A.1:
**Developed economies: rates of growth of real GDP, 1998-2008**

| Average annual percentage change[a] | | | | | | | | | | | | |
|---|---|---|---|---|---|---|---|---|---|---|---|---|
| | 1998-2006 | 1998 | 1999 | 2000 | 2001 | 2002 | 2003 | 2004 | 2005 | 2006 | 2007[b] | 2008[c] |
| **Developed economies** | 2.4 | 2.5 | 3.0 | 3.6 | 1.2 | 1.3 | 1.9 | 3.0 | 2.4 | 2.8 | 2.5 | 2.2 |
| United States | 3.0 | 4.2 | 4.4 | 3.7 | 0.8 | 1.6 | 2.5 | 3.6 | 3.1 | 2.9 | 2.2 | 2.0 |
| Canada | 3.4 | 4.1 | 5.5 | 5.2 | 1.8 | 2.9 | 1.9 | 3.1 | 3.1 | 2.8 | 2.4 | 1.9 |
| Japan | 1.0 | -2.0 | -0.1 | 2.9 | 0.2 | 0.3 | 1.4 | 2.7 | 1.9 | 2.2 | 2.0 | 1.7 |
| Australia | 3.6 | 5.2 | 4.3 | 3.5 | 3.8 | 3.2 | 4.1 | 2.7 | 2.8 | 2.7 | 4.2 | 3.6 |
| New Zealand | 3.4 | 0.7 | 4.7 | 3.8 | 3.5 | 4.6 | 3.6 | 5.0 | 2.6 | 1.9 | 3.0 | 2.9 |
| **European Union** | 2.4 | 3.0 | 3.1 | 3.9 | 2.0 | 1.2 | 1.3 | 2.5 | 1.8 | 3.0 | 2.9 | 2.5 |
| *EU-15* | 2.3 | 2.9 | 3.1 | 3.8 | 1.9 | 1.1 | 1.2 | 2.3 | 1.6 | 2.8 | 2.7 | 2.3 |
| Austria | 2.3 | 3.6 | 3.3 | 3.4 | 0.8 | 0.9 | 1.2 | 2.3 | 2.0 | 3.3 | 3.2 | 2.6 |
| Belgium | 2.2 | 1.7 | 3.4 | 3.7 | 0.8 | 1.5 | 1.0 | 3.0 | 1.1 | 3.2 | 2.4 | 2.5 |
| Denmark | 2.1 | 2.2 | 2.6 | 3.5 | 0.7 | 0.5 | 0.4 | 2.1 | 3.1 | 3.5 | 2.2 | 1.1 |
| Finland | 3.5 | 5.2 | 3.9 | 5.0 | 2.6 | 1.6 | 1.8 | 3.7 | 2.9 | 5.0 | 4.4 | 3.1 |
| France | 2.3 | 3.5 | 3.3 | 3.9 | 1.8 | 1.0 | 1.1 | 2.5 | 1.7 | 2.0 | 2.3 | 2.3 |
| Germany | 1.4 | 2.0 | 2.0 | 3.2 | 1.2 | 0.0 | -0.2 | 1.1 | 0.8 | 2.9 | 2.6 | 2.3 |
| Greece | 4.1 | 3.4 | 3.4 | 4.5 | 4.5 | 3.9 | 4.9 | 4.7 | 3.7 | 4.3 | 3.8 | 3.0 |
| Ireland | 6.8 | 8.6 | 10.9 | 9.4 | 5.9 | 6.4 | 4.3 | 4.3 | 5.9 | 5.7 | 4.7 | 3.5 |
| Italy | 1.4 | 1.4 | 1.9 | 3.6 | 1.8 | 0.3 | 0.0 | 1.2 | 0.1 | 1.9 | 1.7 | 1.4 |
| Luxembourg | 5.0 | 6.5 | 8.4 | 8.4 | 2.5 | 3.8 | 1.3 | 3.6 | 4.0 | 6.2 | 5.0 | 3.4 |
| Netherlands | 2.4 | 3.9 | 4.7 | 3.9 | 1.9 | 0.1 | 0.3 | 2.2 | 1.5 | 3.0 | 2.7 | 2.6 |
| Portugal | 2.0 | 4.8 | 3.9 | 3.9 | 2.0 | 0.8 | -0.7 | 1.5 | 0.5 | 1.3 | 1.8 | 2.1 |
| Spain | 3.8 | 4.5 | 4.7 | 5.0 | 3.6 | 2.7 | 3.1 | 3.3 | 3.6 | 3.9 | 3.9 | 2.8 |
| Sweden | 3.2 | 3.7 | 4.5 | 4.3 | 1.1 | 2.0 | 1.7 | 4.1 | 2.9 | 4.2 | 3.6 | 3.8 |
| United Kingdom | 2.8 | 3.4 | 3.0 | 3.8 | 2.4 | 2.1 | 2.8 | 3.3 | 1.8 | 2.8 | 3.0 | 2.3 |
| *New EU member States* | 4.1 | 3.0 | 3.0 | 4.1 | 2.9 | 2.9 | 4.3 | 5.6 | 4.6 | 6.3 | 6.0 | 5.4 |
| Bulgaria | 4.9 | 4.0 | 2.3 | 5.4 | 4.1 | 4.5 | 5.0 | 6.6 | 6.2 | 6.1 | 6.5 | 5.6 |
| Cyprus | 3.8 | 5.0 | 4.9 | 5.0 | 4.0 | 2.0 | 1.8 | 4.2 | 3.9 | 3.8 | 3.8 | 3.2 |
| Czech Republic | 3.3 | -0.8 | 1.3 | 3.6 | 2.6 | 1.9 | 3.7 | 4.6 | 6.5 | 6.4 | 5.5 | 5.0 |
| Estonia | 7.2 | 4.4 | 0.3 | 7.9 | 7.7 | 8.0 | 7.2 | 8.3 | 10.2 | 11.2 | 7.5 | 6.0 |
| Hungary | 4.4 | 4.9 | 4.2 | 5.2 | 4.1 | 4.3 | 4.1 | 4.9 | 4.1 | 3.9 | 2.1 | 3.2 |
| Latvia | 7.6 | 4.7 | 3.3 | 8.4 | 8.0 | 6.5 | 7.2 | 8.7 | 10.3 | 11.9 | 10.0 | 7.0 |
| Lithuania | 6.2 | 7.5 | -1.5 | 4.1 | 6.6 | 6.9 | 10.3 | 7.3 | 7.9 | 7.5 | 8.0 | 6.5 |
| Malta | 2.3 | 3.4 | 4.1 | 6.3 | -1.6 | 2.6 | -0.3 | 0.1 | 3.1 | 3.1 | 3.5 | 3.2 |
| Poland | 3.9 | 5.0 | 4.5 | 4.3 | 1.2 | 1.4 | 3.8 | 5.3 | 3.2 | 6.1 | 6.6 | 5.8 |
| Romania | 3.6 | -4.7 | -1.1 | 2.2 | 5.8 | 5.2 | 5.3 | 8.5 | 4.1 | 7.7 | 6.0 | 5.5 |
| Slovakia | 4.2 | 3.7 | 0.3 | 0.7 | 3.8 | 4.8 | 4.8 | 5.2 | 6.6 | 8.5 | 9.0 | 6.8 |
| Slovenia | 4.0 | 3.9 | 5.4 | 4.1 | 2.7 | 3.5 | 2.6 | 4.4 | 4.0 | 5.7 | 5.3 | 5.1 |
| **Other Europe** | 2.2 | 2.8 | 1.6 | 3.5 | 1.6 | 0.8 | 0.4 | 3.2 | 2.6 | 3.1 | 3.1 | 2.6 |
| Iceland | 4.4 | 6.3 | 4.1 | 4.3 | 3.9 | -0.1 | 2.7 | 7.6 | 7.2 | 4.2 | 1.8 | 2.1 |
| Norway | 2.4 | 2.7 | 2.0 | 3.3 | 2.0 | 1.5 | 1.0 | 3.9 | 2.7 | 2.8 | 3.5 | 3.7 |
| Switzerland | 1.9 | 2.8 | 1.3 | 3.6 | 1.2 | 0.4 | -0.2 | 2.5 | 2.4 | 3.2 | 2.9 | 1.9 |
| *Memorandum items:* | | | | | | | | | | | | |
| Major developed economies | 2.3 | 2.3 | 2.9 | 3.5 | 0.9 | 1.1 | 1.8 | 3.0 | 2.3 | 2.6 | 2.2 | 2.0 |
| North America | 3.0 | 4.2 | 4.5 | 3.8 | 0.8 | 1.7 | 2.5 | 3.6 | 3.1 | 2.9 | 2.1 | 2.0 |
| Western Europe | 2.4 | 2.9 | 3.0 | 3.8 | 1.9 | 1.2 | 1.3 | 2.5 | 1.8 | 3.0 | 2.9 | 2.5 |
| Asia and Oceania | 1.3 | -1.5 | 0.3 | 3.0 | 0.5 | 0.6 | 1.6 | 2.7 | 2.0 | 2.2 | 2.2 | 1.9 |

**Sources**: UN/DESA, based on OECD, *Main Economic Indicators* and individual national sources.

a   Calculated as a weighted average of individual country growth rates of gross domestic product (GDP), where weights are based on GDP in 2000 prices and exchange rates.

b   Partly estimated.

c   Forecasts, based in part on Project LINK.

Table A.2:
**Economies in transition: rates of growth of real GDP, 1998-2008**

Average annual percentage change[a]

| | 1998-2006 | 1998 | 1999 | 2000 | 2001 | 2002 | 2003 | 2004 | 2005 | 2006 | 2007[b] | 2008[c] |
|---|---|---|---|---|---|---|---|---|---|---|---|---|
| **Economies in transition[d]** | 5.6 | -2.9 | 5.2 | 8.5 | 5.8 | 5.0 | 7.2 | 7.7 | 6.6 | 7.5 | 8.0 | 7.1 |
| South-eastern Europe[d] | 4.4 | 5.1 | 2.8 | 4.0 | 3.9 | 4.7 | 4.5 | 5.4 | 4.9 | 5.0 | 6.0 | 5.4 |
| Albania | 7.0 | 9.0 | 13.5 | 6.7 | 7.9 | 4.2 | 5.8 | 5.7 | 5.6 | 5.2 | 5.6 | 6.0 |
| Bosnia and Herzegovina | 6.8 | 16.6 | 9.5 | 5.4 | 4.3 | 5.3 | 4.4 | 5.8 | 5.0 | 5.5 | 6.0 | 6.0 |
| Croatia | 3.7 | 2.5 | -0.9 | 2.9 | 4.4 | 5.6 | 5.3 | 4.3 | 4.3 | 4.8 | 6.0 | 5.0 |
| Montenegro | 3.1 | .. | .. | 3.1 | -0.2 | 1.8 | 2.3 | 4.2 | 4.0 | 6.5 | 6.0 | 5.0 |
| Serbia | 5.2 | .. | .. | 4.5 | 4.8 | 4.2 | 2.5 | 8.4 | 6.2 | 5.7 | 7.0 | 6.0 |
| The former Yugoslav Republic of Macedonia | 2.5 | 3.4 | 4.3 | 4.5 | -4.5 | 0.9 | 2.8 | 4.1 | 4.1 | 3.0 | 4.5 | 4.5 |
| **Commonwealth of Independent States** | 5.7 | -3.6 | 5.4 | 9.1 | 6.0 | 5.2 | 7.6 | 7.9 | 6.8 | 7.8 | 8.2 | 7.3 |
| *Net fuel exporters* | 5.7 | -4.3 | 6.2 | 9.7 | 5.6 | 5.1 | 7.3 | 7.4 | 7.1 | 7.7 | 8.3 | 7.3 |
| Azerbaijan | 14.3 | 10.0 | 7.4 | 11.1 | 9.9 | 10.6 | 11.2 | 10.2 | 26.5 | 34.5 | 29.0 | 25.0 |
| Kazakhstan | 8.0 | -1.9 | 2.7 | 9.8 | 13.5 | 9.8 | 9.3 | 9.6 | 9.7 | 10.6 | 9.0 | 8.3 |
| Russian Federation | 5.3 | -5.3 | 6.4 | 10.0 | 5.1 | 4.7 | 7.3 | 7.2 | 6.4 | 6.7 | 7.5 | 6.5 |
| Turkmenistan | 6.6 | 7.1 | 16.5 | 5.5 | 4.3 | 0.3 | 3.3 | 4.5 | 9.6 | 9.0 | 8.0 | 7.0 |
| Uzbekistan | 5.3 | 4.4 | 4.4 | 4.0 | 4.5 | 4.2 | 4.4 | 7.7 | 7.0 | 7.3 | 8.6 | 7.3 |
| *Net fuel importers* | 6.0 | 0.7 | 1.0 | 5.5 | 7.9 | 5.6 | 9.2 | 11.3 | 5.0 | 7.9 | 7.4 | 7.1 |
| Armenia | 10.3 | 7.3 | 3.3 | 5.9 | 9.6 | 15.1 | 14.0 | 10.5 | 13.9 | 13.3 | 12.0 | 10.0 |
| Belarus | 7.2 | 8.4 | 3.4 | 5.8 | 4.7 | 5.0 | 7.0 | 11.4 | 9.4 | 9.9 | 8.0 | 7.0 |
| Georgia | 5.9 | 3.1 | 2.9 | 1.8 | 4.8 | 5.5 | 11.1 | 5.8 | 9.6 | 9.3 | 11.0 | 9.0 |
| Kyrgyzstan | 3.6 | 2.1 | 3.7 | 5.4 | 5.3 | 0.0 | 7.0 | 7.0 | -0.2 | 2.7 | 7.8 | 7.5 |
| Moldova | 3.4 | -6.5 | -3.4 | 2.1 | 6.1 | 7.8 | 6.6 | 7.4 | 7.5 | 4.0 | 7.0 | 6.0 |
| Tajikistan | 8.1 | 5.3 | 3.7 | 8.3 | 9.6 | 10.8 | 11.1 | 10.3 | 6.7 | 7.0 | 7.4 | 7.0 |
| Ukraine | 5.4 | -1.9 | -0.2 | 5.9 | 9.2 | 5.2 | 9.6 | 12.1 | 2.7 | 7.1 | 6.5 | 6.7 |

**Source**: UN/DESA, based on data of the Economic Commission for Europe.

a    Calculated as a weighted average of individual country growth rates of gross domestic product (GDP), where weights are based on GDP in 2000 prices and exchange rates.
b    Partly estimated.
c    Forecasts, based in part on Project LINK.
d    Excluding Montenegro and Serbia before 2000.

Table A.3:
**Developing economies: rates of growth of real GDP, 1998-2008**

| Average annual percentage change[a] | | | | | | | | | | | |
|---|---|---|---|---|---|---|---|---|---|---|---|
| | 1998-2006 | 1998 | 1999 | 2000 | 2001 | 2002 | 2003 | 2004 | 2005 | 2006 | 2007[b] | 2008[c] |
| **Developing countries[d]** | 4.8 | 2.1 | 3.3 | 5.7 | 2.7 | 3.9 | 5.2 | 7.0 | 6.5 | 7.0 | 6.9 | 6.5 |
| **Africa** | 4.1 | 3.4 | 3.1 | 3.4 | 3.7 | 3.4 | 4.6 | 4.8 | 5.2 | 5.7 | 5.8 | 6.2 |
| North Africa | 4.4 | 5.0 | 3.7 | 3.6 | 3.5 | 3.3 | 5.2 | 4.8 | 4.5 | 5.8 | 5.6 | 6.0 |
| Sub-Saharan Africa (excluding Nigeria and South Africa) | 4.3 | 3.9 | 2.8 | 2.2 | 4.8 | 4.0 | 3.3 | 5.8 | 5.9 | 6.1 | 7.0 | 7.7 |
| Net fuel exporters | 4.4 | 3.9 | 3.5 | 3.8 | 3.0 | 3.5 | 5.8 | 4.7 | 5.9 | 5.9 | 6.6 | 7.4 |
| Net fuel importers | 3.9 | 3.0 | 2.7 | 3.0 | 4.2 | 3.4 | 3.5 | 4.9 | 4.7 | 5.5 | 5.1 | 5.3 |
| **East and South Asia** | 6.1 | 1.3 | 6.0 | 6.9 | 4.5 | 6.5 | 6.8 | 7.8 | 7.5 | 8.1 | 8.1 | 7.5 |
| East Asia | 6.3 | 0.2 | 6.6 | 7.7 | 4.5 | 7.0 | 6.8 | 8.0 | 7.7 | 8.3 | 8.4 | 7.7 |
| South Asia | 5.8 | 4.7 | 4.4 | 4.7 | 4.4 | 5.0 | 7.0 | 7.2 | 7.1 | 7.5 | 6.9 | 6.7 |
| Net fuel exporters | 4.9 | 2.9 | 2.1 | 5.2 | 4.2 | 6.7 | 7.2 | 5.6 | 5.0 | 5.5 | 5.1 | 4.7 |
| Net fuel importers | 6.3 | 1.1 | 6.5 | 7.1 | 4.5 | 6.5 | 6.8 | 8.0 | 7.8 | 8.4 | 8.3 | 7.8 |
| **Western Asia** | 3.8 | 4.1 | -0.7 | 6.2 | -0.4 | 3.1 | 4.7 | 6.9 | 6.5 | 4.6 | 5.7 | 5.2 |
| Net fuel exporters | 4.1 | 4.6 | 0.0 | 5.1 | 2.6 | 2.1 | 5.1 | 6.6 | 6.7 | 4.1 | 6.1 | 5.5 |
| Net fuel importers | 3.5 | 3.5 | -1.6 | 7.5 | -4.2 | 4.4 | 4.2 | 7.2 | 6.2 | 5.3 | 5.1 | 4.7 |
| **Latin America and the Caribbean** | 2.8 | 2.4 | 0.3 | 4.0 | 0.3 | -0.8 | 2.2 | 6.2 | 4.7 | 5.7 | 5.3 | 4.7 |
| South America | 2.4 | 1.3 | -1.7 | 2.7 | 0.3 | -1.9 | 2.4 | 7.4 | 5.4 | 5.8 | 6.2 | 5.2 |
| Mexico and Central America | 3.3 | 5.0 | 4.0 | 6.2 | 0.2 | 1.0 | 1.6 | 4.2 | 3.0 | 4.9 | 3.4 | 3.6 |
| Caribbean | 5.0 | 3.1 | 5.8 | 5.6 | 2.3 | 2.9 | 2.9 | 3.9 | 8.8 | 10.2 | 6.8 | 5.7 |
| Net fuel exporters | 2.7 | 3.7 | -0.1 | 3.9 | -0.5 | -3.0 | 2.5 | 6.8 | 5.4 | 6.6 | 5.4 | 4.6 |
| Net fuel importers | 2.8 | 0.9 | 0.8 | 4.0 | 1.4 | 1.9 | 1.8 | 5.5 | 4.0 | 4.7 | 5.3 | 4.9 |
| *Memorandum items:* | | | | | | | | | | | | |
| Least developed countries | 6.6 | 4.4 | 5.8 | 5.7 | 6.6 | 6.3 | 6.6 | 7.9 | 8.4 | 8.1 | 6.7 | 6.9 |
| East Asia (excluding China) | 4.0 | -4.7 | 5.9 | 7.1 | 1.7 | 5.3 | 4.2 | 6.2 | 5.2 | 5.7 | 5.5 | 5.3 |
| South Asia (excluding India) | 4.9 | 3.0 | 2.7 | 5.0 | 3.7 | 6.0 | 6.8 | 5.8 | 5.3 | 5.6 | 5.2 | 4.9 |
| Western Asia (excluding Israel and Turkey) | 4.0 | 4.5 | 0.2 | 5.0 | 2.7 | 2.2 | 5.0 | 6.5 | 6.3 | 3.9 | 5.9 | 5.4 |
| Landlocked developing economies | 5.2 | 3.1 | 3.3 | 3.6 | 5.5 | 4.6 | 4.5 | 6.9 | 7.1 | 8.5 | 8.4 | 8.1 |
| Small island developing economies | 4.8 | 1.4 | 6.2 | 7.4 | 0.1 | 3.5 | 3.1 | 6.2 | 7.1 | 8.3 | 7.3 | 6.3 |
| **Major developing economies** | | | | | | | | | | | | |
| Argentina | 2.0 | 3.9 | -3.4 | -0.8 | -4.4 | -10.9 | 8.8 | 9.0 | 9.2 | 8.5 | 8.4 | 6.0 |
| Brazil | 2.3 | 0.0 | 0.3 | 4.3 | 1.3 | 1.9 | 1.1 | 5.7 | 2.9 | 3.7 | 4.7 | 4.5 |
| Chile | 3.5 | 3.2 | -0.8 | 4.5 | 3.4 | 2.2 | 3.9 | 6.0 | 5.7 | 4.0 | 5.4 | 5.0 |
| China | 9.2 | 7.8 | 7.6 | 8.4 | 8.3 | 9.1 | 10.0 | 10.1 | 10.4 | 11.1 | 11.4 | 10.1 |
| Colombia | 2.5 | 0.6 | -4.2 | 2.9 | 1.5 | 1.9 | 4.1 | 4.0 | 5.1 | 6.8 | 7.0 | 5.5 |
| Egypt | 5.0 | 7.5 | 6.1 | 5.4 | 3.2 | 4.1 | 3.2 | 4.1 | 4.5 | 6.8 | 7.0 | 7.1 |

**Table A.3** (cont'd)

| | 1998-2006 | 1998 | 1999 | 2000 | 2001 | 2002 | 2003 | 2004 | 2005 | 2006 | 2007[b] | 2008[c] |
|---|---|---|---|---|---|---|---|---|---|---|---|---|
| Hong Kong SAR[e] | 3.5 | -6.0 | 2.6 | 8.0 | 0.5 | 1.8 | 3.0 | 8.5 | 7.1 | 6.8 | 6.1 | 5.7 |
| India | 6.6 | 6.5 | 6.1 | 4.4 | 5.0 | 4.0 | 7.1 | 8.5 | 8.8 | 9.4 | 8.5 | 8.2 |
| Indonesia | 2.3 | -13.1 | 0.8 | 4.9 | 3.6 | 4.5 | 4.8 | 5.1 | 5.6 | 5.6 | 6.2 | 6.0 |
| Iran, Islamic Republic of | 4.8 | 2.7 | 1.9 | 5.1 | 4.0 | 6.7 | 7.2 | 5.5 | 4.7 | 5.2 | 4.8 | 4.4 |
| Israel | 3.4 | 4.2 | 2.9 | 8.9 | -0.6 | -0.9 | 1.5 | 4.8 | 5.2 | 5.1 | 5.1 | 4.3 |
| Korea, Republic of | 4.2 | -6.9 | 9.5 | 8.5 | 3.8 | 7.0 | 3.1 | 4.7 | 4.2 | 5.0 | 4.9 | 5.0 |
| Malaysia | 3.9 | -7.4 | 6.1 | 8.9 | 0.3 | 4.4 | 5.4 | 7.3 | 5.2 | 5.9 | 5.7 | 5.8 |
| Mexico | 3.2 | 4.9 | 3.9 | 6.6 | 0.0 | 0.8 | 1.4 | 4.2 | 2.8 | 4.8 | 3.0 | 3.3 |
| Nigeria | 4.5 | 2.3 | 2.8 | 3.7 | 3.1 | 1.5 | 10.7 | 4.0 | 7.1 | 5.2 | 5.5 | 7.0 |
| Pakistan | 5.1 | 2.6 | 3.7 | 4.3 | 3.1 | 4.6 | 6.1 | 7.5 | 7.7 | 6.6 | 6.5 | 6.3 |
| Peru | 3.5 | -0.7 | 0.9 | 2.9 | 0.2 | 4.9 | 3.8 | 5.2 | 6.4 | 8.0 | 8.0 | 6.5 |
| Philippines | 3.8 | -0.6 | 3.4 | 4.0 | 1.8 | 4.4 | 4.9 | 6.4 | 4.9 | 5.4 | 6.8 | 6.1 |
| Saudi Arabia | 3.5 | 2.8 | -0.7 | 4.9 | 0.5 | 0.1 | 7.7 | 5.3 | 6.6 | 4.3 | 5.0 | 5.2 |
| Singapore | 4.8 | -0.8 | 6.8 | 9.6 | -2.4 | 4.2 | 3.1 | 8.8 | 6.6 | 7.9 | 8.5 | 7.2 |
| South Africa | 3.3 | 0.5 | 2.4 | 4.2 | 2.7 | 3.6 | 2.8 | 3.7 | 5.1 | 5.0 | 4.8 | 4.5 |
| Taiwan Province of China | 4.1 | 4.5 | 5.7 | 5.8 | -2.2 | 4.6 | 3.5 | 6.2 | 4.1 | 4.7 | 4.6 | 4.4 |
| Thailand | 3.1 | -10.5 | 4.4 | 4.8 | 2.2 | 5.3 | 7.1 | 6.3 | 4.5 | 5.0 | 4.5 | 4.8 |
| Turkey | 3.7 | 3.1 | -4.7 | 7.4 | -7.5 | 7.9 | 5.8 | 8.9 | 7.4 | 6.1 | 5.3 | 5.0 |
| Venezuela, Bolivarian Republic of | 2.2 | 0.3 | -6.0 | 3.7 | 3.4 | -8.9 | -7.8 | 18.3 | 9.3 | 10.3 | 8.5 | 6.5 |

**Sources**: UN/DESA, based on data of Statistics Division; IMF, *International Financial Statistics*.

**a** Calculated as a weighted average of individual country growth rates of gross domestic product (GDP), where weights are based on GDP in 2000 prices and exchange rates.

**b** Partly estimated.

**c** Forecasts, based in part on Project LINK.

**d** Covering countries that account for 98 per cent of the population of all developing countries.

**e** Special Administrative Region of China.

Table A.4:
**Developed economies: consumer price inflation, 1998-2008**

| Average annual percentage change[a] | | | | | | | | | | | |
|---|---|---|---|---|---|---|---|---|---|---|---|
| | 1998 | 1999 | 2000 | 2001 | 2002 | 2003 | 2004 | 2005 | 2006 | 2007[b] | 2008[c] |
| **Developed economies** | 1.4 | 1.3 | 2.2 | 2.0 | 1.3 | 1.7 | 1.8 | 2.1 | 2.2 | 1.9 | 1.7 |
| United States | 1.6 | 2.1 | 3.4 | 2.8 | 1.6 | 2.3 | 2.7 | 3.4 | 3.2 | 2.7 | 1.8 |
| Canada | 1.0 | 1.7 | 2.7 | 2.5 | 2.3 | 2.8 | 1.8 | 2.2 | 2.0 | 2.3 | 1.6 |
| Japan | 0.7 | -0.3 | -0.7 | -0.8 | -0.9 | -0.2 | 0.0 | -0.3 | 0.2 | 0.0 | 0.7 |
| Australia | 0.8 | 1.5 | 4.5 | 4.4 | 3.0 | 2.8 | 2.3 | 2.7 | 3.5 | 2.4 | 3.7 |
| New Zealand | 1.3 | -0.1 | 2.6 | 2.6 | 2.7 | 1.8 | 2.3 | 3.0 | 3.4 | 2.5 | 2.6 |
| **European Union** | 2.0 | 1.5 | 2.4 | 2.6 | 2.1 | 1.9 | 1.9 | 2.1 | 2.1 | 2.0 | 2.0 |
| **EU-15** | 1.3 | 1.1 | 1.9 | 2.3 | 2.0 | 1.9 | 1.8 | 2.0 | 2.0 | 2.0 | 2.0 |
| Austria | 0.9 | 0.6 | 2.3 | 2.7 | 1.8 | 1.4 | 2.1 | 2.3 | 1.4 | 1.8 | 1.6 |
| Belgium | 1.0 | 1.1 | 2.5 | 2.5 | 1.6 | 1.6 | 2.1 | 2.8 | 1.8 | 1.6 | 1.5 |
| Denmark | 1.8 | 2.5 | 2.9 | 2.4 | 2.4 | 2.1 | 1.2 | 1.8 | 1.9 | 1.8 | 2.3 |
| Finland | 1.4 | 1.2 | 3.0 | 2.6 | 1.6 | 0.9 | 0.2 | 0.6 | 1.6 | 2.6 | 2.7 |
| France | 0.6 | 0.5 | 1.7 | 1.6 | 1.9 | 2.1 | 2.1 | 1.7 | 1.7 | 1.5 | 2.0 |
| Germany | 0.9 | 0.6 | 1.5 | 2.0 | 1.4 | 1.0 | 1.7 | 2.0 | 1.7 | 1.6 | 1.6 |
| Greece | 4.8 | 2.6 | 3.1 | 3.4 | 3.6 | 3.6 | 2.9 | 3.6 | 3.2 | 2.6 | 2.5 |
| Ireland | 2.4 | 1.6 | 5.6 | 4.9 | 4.6 | 3.5 | 2.2 | 2.4 | 3.9 | 4.9 | 3.0 |
| Italy | 2.0 | 1.7 | 2.5 | 2.8 | 2.5 | 2.7 | 2.2 | 2.0 | 2.1 | 1.8 | 2.0 |
| Luxembourg | 1.0 | 1.0 | 3.1 | 2.7 | 2.1 | 2.1 | 2.2 | 2.5 | 2.7 | 2.1 | 2.0 |
| Netherlands | 2.0 | 2.2 | 2.4 | 4.2 | 3.3 | 2.1 | 1.2 | 1.7 | 1.2 | 1.8 | 2.1 |
| Portugal | 2.8 | 2.3 | 2.9 | 4.4 | 3.6 | 3.3 | 2.4 | 2.3 | 3.1 | 2.4 | 2.0 |
| Spain | 1.8 | 2.3 | 3.4 | 3.6 | 3.1 | 3.0 | 3.0 | 3.4 | 3.5 | 2.7 | 2.6 |
| Sweden | -1.9 | -1.1 | 2.1 | 2.7 | 2.3 | 1.5 | 0.1 | 0.1 | 1.1 | 2.2 | 2.5 |
| United Kingdom | 1.6 | 1.3 | 0.8 | 1.2 | 1.3 | 1.4 | 1.3 | 2.1 | 2.3 | 2.4 | 1.9 |
| **New EU member States** | 15.3 | 9.8 | 11.8 | 8.5 | 4.7 | 3.2 | 4.8 | 3.2 | 2.8 | 3.8 | 3.7 |
| Bulgaria | 18.7 | 2.5 | 10.4 | 7.4 | 5.8 | 2.1 | 6.4 | 5.0 | 7.3 | 8.3 | 7.5 |
| Cyprus | 10.7 | 2.1 | 3.9 | 4.8 | 2.0 | 0.1 | 2.8 | 1.9 | 2.1 | 2.5 | 3.6 |
| Czech Republic | 2.3 | 1.6 | 4.2 | 2.0 | 2.7 | 4.2 | 2.3 | 2.5 | 2.5 | 1.9 | 3.0 |
| Estonia | 8.3 | 3.2 | 4.1 | 5.7 | 3.6 | 1.4 | 3.1 | 4.0 | 4.5 | 6.0 | 7.0 |
| Hungary | 14.2 | 10.0 | 9.8 | 9.1 | 5.3 | 4.6 | 6.7 | 3.5 | 4.0 | 8.0 | 4.2 |
| Latvia | 4.7 | 2.3 | 2.7 | 2.5 | 2.0 | 2.9 | 6.2 | 6.7 | 6.6 | 9.5 | 8.0 |
| Lithuania | 5.1 | 0.7 | 1.0 | 1.3 | 0.3 | -1.2 | 1.2 | 2.7 | 3.8 | 5.5 | 4.8 |
| Malta | 2.4 | 2.2 | 2.4 | 2.9 | 3.0 | 0.6 | 2.7 | 3.0 | 2.8 | 1.0 | 2.0 |
| Poland | 11.6 | 7.1 | 9.9 | 5.4 | 1.9 | 0.7 | 3.4 | 2.1 | 1.1 | 2.5 | 2.9 |
| Romania | 59.1 | 45.6 | 45.8 | 34.5 | 22.5 | 15.2 | 11.9 | 9.0 | 6.6 | 5.0 | 5.8 |
| Slovakia | 6.6 | 10.7 | 12.0 | 7.3 | 3.2 | 8.6 | 7.5 | 2.7 | 4.5 | 2.5 | 2.1 |
| Slovenia | 7.9 | 6.1 | 8.9 | 8.4 | 7.5 | 5.6 | 3.6 | 2.5 | 2.5 | 3.0 | 2.5 |
| **Other Europe** | 0.9 | 1.5 | 2.2 | 1.9 | 1.0 | 1.4 | 0.7 | 1.4 | 1.7 | 1.0 | 2.0 |
| Iceland | 1.7 | 3.2 | 5.1 | 6.4 | 5.2 | 2.1 | 3.2 | 4.0 | 6.7 | 4.9 | 4.0 |
| Norway | 2.3 | 2.3 | 3.1 | 3.0 | 1.3 | 2.5 | 0.5 | 1.5 | 2.3 | 0.8 | 2.7 |
| Switzerland | 0.0 | 0.8 | 1.6 | 1.0 | 0.6 | 0.6 | 0.8 | 1.2 | 1.1 | 1.0 | 1.4 |
| *Memorandum items:* | | | | | | | | | | | |
| Major developed economies | 1.3 | 1.2 | 2.0 | 1.7 | 1.1 | 1.6 | 1.8 | 2.1 | 2.1 | 1.8 | 1.6 |
| Euro area | 1.4 | 1.2 | 2.2 | 2.5 | 2.1 | 2.0 | 2.0 | 2.1 | 2.0 | 1.8 | 1.9 |

**Sources**: UN/DESA, based on OECD, *Main Economic Indicators* and individual national sources.

**a**  Data for country groups are weighted averages, where weights for each year are based on GDP in 2000, in United States dollars.
**b**  Partly estimated.
**c**  Forecasts, based in part on Project LINK.

Table A.5:
**Economies in transition: consumer price inflation, 1998-2008**

| Average annual percentage change[a] | 1998 | 1999 | 2000 | 2001 | 2002 | 2003 | 2004 | 2005 | 2006 | 2007[b] | 2008[c] |
|---|---|---|---|---|---|---|---|---|---|---|---|
| **Economies in transition** | 23.8 | 69.8 | 24.2 | 20.7 | 13.6 | 11.9 | 10.0 | 11.6 | 9.0 | 9.1 | 8.5 |
| **South-eastern Europe** | 11.5 | 9.8 | 17.2 | 21.6 | 5.8 | 3.1 | 3.2 | 5.2 | 5.1 | 3.2 | 3.7 |
| Albania | 20.7 | 0.4 | 0.0 | 3.1 | 5.5 | 2.7 | 2.2 | 2.4 | 2.4 | 2.5 | 2.8 |
| Bosnia and Herzegovina | 5.0 | -0.6 | 1.7 | 1.8 | 0.9 | 0.3 | -0.5 | 2.4 | 6.5 | 2.0 | 2.3 |
| Croatia | 6.4 | 3.7 | 5.5 | 4.6 | 1.7 | 1.5 | 2.0 | 3.4 | 3.1 | 2.5 | 2.8 |
| Montenegro | .. | .. | .. | 22.6 | 18.3 | 6.8 | 2.2 | 2.6 | 2.9 | 3.0 | 3.0 |
| Serbia | 30.2 | 42.4 | 71.2 | 95.0 | 19.5 | 9.9 | 11.1 | 16.1 | 11.7 | 6.8 | 8.0 |
| The former Yugoslav Republic of Macedonia | -1.5 | -1.3 | 6.6 | 5.2 | 2.4 | 1.1 | -0.6 | -0.6 | 3.3 | 2.3 | 2.5 |
| **Commonwealth of Independent States** | 25.2 | 76.3 | 24.9 | 20.6 | 14.4 | 12.9 | 10.7 | 12.3 | 9.5 | 9.8 | 9.1 |
| ***Net fuel exporters*** | 25.4 | 75.8 | 20.0 | 20.4 | 15.1 | 13.3 | 10.7 | 12.4 | 9.6 | 9.6 | 8.8 |
| Azerbaijan | -0.7 | -8.6 | 1.7 | 1.6 | 2.7 | 2.1 | 6.8 | 9.5 | 8.3 | 17.5 | 16.5 |
| Kazakhstan | 7.2 | 8.3 | 13.1 | 8.4 | 5.8 | 6.5 | 6.9 | 7.6 | 8.5 | 8.5 | 7.5 |
| Russian Federation | 27.8 | 85.7 | 20.8 | 21.5 | 15.7 | 13.7 | 10.9 | 12.7 | 9.7 | 9.4 | 8.7 |
| Turkmenistan | 16.7 | 23.5 | 7.0 | 8.2 | 15.0 | 15.3 | 10.0 | 12.0 | 9.0 | 7.0 | 8.5 |
| Uzbekistan | 17.6 | 29.0 | 25.0 | 26.6 | 21.6 | 19.0 | 14.2 | 15.0 | 10.5 | 12.2 | 10.0 |
| ***Net fuel importers*** | 23.7 | 79.3 | 54.8 | 21.7 | 10.1 | 10.3 | 10.6 | 11.6 | 8.4 | 11.1 | 10.5 |
| Armenia | 8.7 | 0.7 | -0.8 | 3.2 | 1.0 | 4.7 | 6.9 | 0.6 | 2.9 | 5.0 | 4.5 |
| Belarus | 74.1 | 295.7 | 168.8 | 61.4 | 42.8 | 28.5 | 18.3 | 10.3 | 7.0 | 8.5 | 10.0 |
| Georgia | 3.5 | 19.3 | 4.2 | 4.6 | 5.7 | 4.9 | 5.7 | 8.2 | 9.1 | 9.5 | 8.5 |
| Kyrgyzstan | 10.4 | 35.9 | 19.6 | 6.9 | 2.2 | 2.9 | 4.2 | 4.4 | 5.6 | 6.5 | 7.0 |
| Moldova | 6.7 | 46.0 | 31.2 | 9.8 | 5.3 | 11.8 | 12.5 | 12.0 | 12.8 | 12.0 | 10.0 |
| Tajikistan | 43.1 | 27.4 | 32.8 | 38.6 | 12.3 | 16.3 | 7.2 | 7.2 | 10.0 | 18.5 | 15.0 |
| Ukraine | 10.6 | 22.6 | 28.2 | 12.0 | 0.7 | 5.2 | 9.0 | 13.5 | 9.1 | 12.5 | 11.2 |

**Source**: UN/DESA, based on data of Economic Commission for Europe.

**a** Data for country groups are weighted averages, where weights for each year are based on GDP in 2000, in United States dollars.

**b** Partly estimated.

**c** Forecasts, based in part on Project LINK.

Table A.6:
Developing economies: consumer price inflation, 1998-2008

| Average annual percentage change[a] | | | | | | | | | | | |
|---|---|---|---|---|---|---|---|---|---|---|---|
| | 1998 | 1999 | 2000 | 2001 | 2002 | 2003 | 2004 | 2005 | 2006 | 2007[b] | 2008[c] |
| **Developing countries by region:** | 10.2 | 7.1 | 5.9 | 5.7 | 6.5 | 6.3 | 5.2 | 5.1 | 5.0 | 5.6 | 5.4 |
| **Africa** | 6.3 | 7.2 | 9.6 | 8.7 | 6.2 | 5.8 | 5.8 | 5.8 | 6.0 | 6.2 | 5.4 |
| North Africa | 3.9 | 2.5 | 2.0 | 2.5 | 2.4 | 3.3 | 6.9 | 3.1 | 5.3 | 5.7 | 4.5 |
| Sub-Saharan Africa (excluding Nigeria and South Africa) | 8.4 | 17.3 | 27.4 | 17.9 | 7.0 | 7.0 | 5.2 | 8.2 | 7.9 | 7.1 | 5.9 |
| Net fuel exporters | 5.5 | 3.6 | 2.9 | 6.5 | 4.6 | 5.9 | 9.3 | 6.7 | 6.3 | 6.5 | 5.5 |
| Net fuel importers | 7.1 | 10.0 | 14.7 | 10.4 | 7.5 | 5.9 | 3.3 | 5.3 | 5.9 | 6.0 | 5.4 |
| **East and South Asia** | 8.2 | 3.3 | 2.6 | 3.2 | 3.1 | 3.6 | 4.6 | 4.2 | 4.3 | 5.5 | 4.9 |
| East Asia | 6.2 | 1.1 | 0.9 | 2.1 | 1.5 | 2.0 | 3.3 | 2.9 | 2.9 | 4.1 | 3.6 |
| South Asia | 14.1 | 10.1 | 7.7 | 6.4 | 7.8 | 8.4 | 8.3 | 8.2 | 8.4 | 9.9 | 8.8 |
| Net fuel exporters | 16.7 | 18.5 | 13.0 | 10.2 | 13.2 | 15.2 | 14.0 | 12.8 | 11.5 | 16.0 | 14.7 |
| Net fuel importers | 7.3 | 1.7 | 1.5 | 2.4 | 2.0 | 2.4 | 3.6 | 3.3 | 3.5 | 4.4 | 3.8 |
| **Western Asia** | 25.0 | 22.3 | 16.1 | 16.8 | 14.8 | 7.8 | 3.6 | 4.5 | 6.0 | 5.1 | 5.8 |
| Net fuel exporters | -2.8 | 3.7 | -1.2 | 0.3 | 0.2 | 2.0 | 1.8 | 3.2 | 4.7 | 5.0 | 4.3 |
| Net fuel importers | 52.8 | 40.9 | 33.4 | 33.3 | 29.3 | 13.5 | 5.4 | 5.8 | 7.3 | 5.3 | 7.3 |
| **Latin America and the Caribbean** | 10.0 | 9.2 | 7.7 | 5.9 | 10.2 | 11.1 | 6.8 | 6.6 | 5.7 | 5.6 | 6.3 |
| South America | 7.6 | 6.1 | 7.0 | 5.6 | 12.9 | 14.1 | 7.0 | 7.7 | 6.5 | 6.3 | 7.4 |
| Mexico and Central America | 15.0 | 15.4 | 9.2 | 6.4 | 5.1 | 4.6 | 4.9 | 4.4 | 3.9 | 4.3 | 4.2 |
| Caribbean | 5.8 | 5.7 | 7.2 | 7.9 | 5.4 | 18.9 | 29.1 | 7.9 | 8.4 | 7.1 | 6.9 |
| Net fuel exporters | 19.3 | 17.4 | 12.0 | 8.0 | 7.8 | 8.7 | 7.2 | 5.8 | 5.2 | 6.2 | 6.5 |
| Net fuel importers | 3.5 | 3.3 | 4.7 | 4.4 | 11.9 | 12.7 | 6.5 | 7.1 | 6.1 | 5.2 | 6.2 |
| *Memorandum items:* | | | | | | | | | | | |
| Least developed countries | 19.6 | 20.3 | 21.7 | 17.7 | 17.4 | 13.8 | 6.7 | 9.2 | 11.9 | 16.4 | 12.5 |
| East Asia (excluding China) | 11.5 | 2.9 | 1.4 | 3.3 | 3.2 | 2.7 | 3.0 | 3.8 | 4.0 | 3.5 | 3.4 |
| South Asia (excluding India) | 14.8 | 15.6 | 11.3 | 9.2 | 11.3 | 12.9 | 12.7 | 12.0 | 10.9 | 14.5 | 13.0 |
| Western Asia (excluding Israel and Turkey) | -2.5 | 3.8 | -1.0 | 0.6 | 0.6 | 2.2 | 2.2 | 3.4 | 5.2 | 5.2 | 4.5 |
| Major developing economies | | | | | | | | | | | |
| Argentina | 0.9 | -1.2 | -0.9 | -1.1 | 25.9 | 13.4 | 4.4 | 9.6 | 10.9 | 8.9 | 11.7 |
| Brazil | 3.2 | 4.8 | 7.1 | 6.8 | 8.5 | 14.7 | 6.6 | 6.8 | 4.2 | 3.6 | 4.0 |
| Chile | 5.1 | 3.3 | 3.8 | 3.6 | 2.5 | 2.8 | 1.1 | 3.1 | 3.4 | 3.9 | 4.1 |
| China | -0.8 | -1.4 | 0.3 | 0.5 | -0.8 | 1.2 | 3.9 | 1.8 | 1.5 | 4.9 | 3.8 |
| Colombia | 18.7 | 10.9 | 9.2 | 8.0 | 6.3 | 7.1 | 5.9 | 5.0 | 4.3 | 5.5 | 4.6 |
| Egypt | 3.9 | 3.1 | 2.7 | 2.3 | 2.7 | 4.5 | 11.3 | 4.9 | 7.6 | 8.4 | 5.7 |
| Hong Kong SAR[d] | 2.8 | -4.0 | -3.8 | -1.6 | -3.1 | -2.5 | -0.4 | 0.9 | 2.1 | 1.4 | 1.4 |
| India | 13.3 | 4.6 | 4.0 | 3.7 | 4.4 | 3.8 | 3.8 | 4.3 | 6.0 | 5.2 | 4.7 |
| Indonesia | 58.4 | 20.5 | 3.7 | 11.5 | 11.9 | 6.8 | 6.1 | 10.5 | 13.1 | 6.5 | 5.8 |
| Iran, Islamic Republic of | 17.9 | 20.1 | 14.5 | 11.3 | 14.3 | 16.5 | 14.8 | 13.4 | 12.0 | 17.0 | 15.5 |
| Israel | 5.4 | 5.2 | 1.1 | 1.1 | 5.6 | 0.7 | -0.4 | 1.3 | 2.1 | 0.5 | 4.4 |
| Korea, Republic of | 7.5 | 0.8 | 2.3 | 4.1 | 2.8 | 3.5 | 3.6 | 2.8 | 2.2 | 2.4 | 2.8 |
| Malaysia | 5.3 | 2.7 | 1.5 | 1.4 | 1.8 | 1.0 | 1.5 | 3.0 | 3.6 | 2.1 | 2.6 |
| Mexico | 15.9 | 16.6 | 9.5 | 6.4 | 5.0 | 4.5 | 4.7 | 4.0 | 3.6 | 4.0 | 4.0 |

**Table A.6** (cont'd)

| | 1998 | 1999 | 2000 | 2001 | 2002 | 2003 | 2004 | 2005 | 2006 | 2007[b] | 2008[c] |
|---|---|---|---|---|---|---|---|---|---|---|---|
| Nigeria | 10.0 | 6.6 | 6.9 | 18.9 | 12.9 | 14.0 | 15.0 | 17.9 | 8.2 | 6.5 | 7.6 |
| Pakistan | 6.2 | 4.1 | 4.4 | 3.2 | 3.3 | 2.9 | 7.4 | 9.1 | 7.9 | 6.9 | 6.2 |
| Peru | 7.2 | 3.5 | 3.8 | 2.0 | 0.2 | 2.3 | 3.7 | 1.6 | 2.0 | 1.5 | 2.5 |
| Philippines | 9.3 | 5.9 | 4.0 | 6.8 | 3.0 | 3.5 | 6.0 | 7.6 | 6.2 | 2.8 | 3.5 |
| Saudi Arabia | -0.4 | -1.3 | -1.1 | -1.1 | 0.2 | 0.6 | 0.3 | 0.7 | 2.2 | 3.2 | 3.0 |
| Singapore | -0.3 | 0.0 | 1.3 | 1.0 | -0.4 | 0.5 | 1.7 | 0.5 | 1.0 | 1.6 | 1.8 |
| South Africa | 7.0 | 5.1 | 5.3 | 5.7 | 9.2 | 5.8 | 1.4 | 3.5 | 4.6 | 6.0 | 5.7 |
| Taiwan Province of China | 1.7 | 0.2 | 1.3 | 0.0 | -0.2 | -0.3 | 1.6 | 2.3 | 0.6 | 1.4 | 2.0 |
| Thailand | 8.1 | 0.3 | 1.6 | 1.6 | 0.6 | 1.8 | 2.8 | 4.5 | 4.6 | 2.2 | 2.4 |
| Turkey | 84.6 | 64.9 | 54.9 | 54.4 | 45.0 | 21.6 | 8.6 | 8.2 | 9.6 | 7.7 | 8.8 |
| Venezuela, Bolivarian Republic of | 35.8 | 23.6 | 16.2 | 12.5 | 22.4 | 31.1 | 21.8 | 16.0 | 13.7 | 17.6 | 20.8 |

**Source**: UN/DESA, based on IMF, *International Financial Statistics*.

a    Data for country groups are weighted averages, where weights are based on GDP in 2000 prices and exchange rates.
b    Partly estimated.
c    Forecasts, based in part on Project LINK.
d    Special Administrative Region of China.

Table A.7:
**Developed economies: unemployment rates,[a, b] 1998-2008**

| Percentage of labour force | 1998 | 1999 | 2000 | 2001 | 2002 | 2003 | 2004 | 2005 | 2006 | 2007[c] | 2008[d] |
|---|---|---|---|---|---|---|---|---|---|---|---|
| **Developed economies** | .. | .. | 6.5 | 6.6 | 7.3 | 7.4 | 7.1 | 6.9 | 6.3 | 5.7 | 5.7 |
| United States | 4.5 | 4.2 | 4.0 | 4.7 | 5.8 | 6.0 | 5.5 | 5.1 | 4.6 | 4.6 | 5.0 |
| Canada | 8.3 | 7.6 | 6.8 | 7.2 | 7.7 | 7.6 | 7.2 | 6.8 | 6.3 | 6.1 | 6.3 |
| Japan | 4.1 | 4.7 | 4.7 | 5.0 | 5.4 | 5.3 | 4.7 | 4.4 | 4.1 | 4.0 | 4.0 |
| Australia | 7.7 | 6.9 | 6.3 | 6.8 | 6.4 | 6.1 | 5.5 | 5.1 | 4.9 | 4.3 | 4.1 |
| New Zealand | 7.4 | 6.8 | 6.0 | 5.3 | 5.2 | 4.6 | 3.9 | 3.7 | 3.8 | 3.5 | 3.6 |
| **European Union** | .. | .. | 8.7 | 8.5 | 8.9 | 9.0 | 9.1 | 8.9 | 8.2 | 7.1 | 6.8 |
| *EU-15* | 9.3 | 8.5 | 7.7 | 7.2 | 7.6 | 8.0 | 8.1 | 8.2 | 7.7 | 6.8 | 6.6 |
| Austria | 4.5 | 3.9 | 3.6 | 3.6 | 4.2 | 4.3 | 4.8 | 5.2 | 4.7 | 4.2 | 4.0 |
| Belgium | 9.3 | 8.5 | 6.9 | 6.6 | 7.5 | 8.2 | 8.4 | 8.4 | 8.2 | 7.4 | 7.1 |
| Denmark | 4.9 | 5.1 | 4.3 | 4.5 | 4.6 | 5.4 | 5.5 | 4.8 | 3.9 | 3.3 | 3.4 |
| Finland | 11.4 | 10.3 | 9.6 | 9.1 | 9.1 | 9.1 | 8.8 | 8.3 | 7.7 | 6.6 | 6.4 |
| France | 11.1 | 10.5 | 9.1 | 8.4 | 8.7 | 9.5 | 9.6 | 9.7 | 9.5 | 7.9 | 7.4 |
| Germany | 9.1 | 8.2 | 7.5 | 7.6 | 8.4 | 9.3 | 9.7 | 10.7 | 9.8 | 8.1 | 7.5 |
| Greece | 10.8 | 12.0 | 11.2 | 10.7 | 10.3 | 9.7 | 10.5 | 9.8 | 8.9 | 8.4 | 8.1 |
| Ireland | 7.5 | 5.7 | 4.3 | 4.0 | 4.5 | 4.7 | 4.5 | 4.3 | 4.4 | 4.6 | 4.2 |
| Italy | 11.4 | 10.9 | 10.1 | 9.1 | 8.6 | 8.4 | 8.0 | 7.7 | 6.8 | 6.1 | 5.9 |
| Luxembourg | 2.7 | 2.4 | 2.3 | 2.0 | 2.7 | 3.7 | 5.1 | 4.5 | 4.7 | 3.3 | 3.0 |
| Netherlands | 3.8 | 3.2 | 2.8 | 2.2 | 2.8 | 3.7 | 4.6 | 4.7 | 3.9 | 2.9 | 2.5 |
| Portugal | 5.1 | 4.5 | 4.0 | 4.0 | 5.0 | 6.3 | 6.7 | 7.6 | 7.7 | 8.0 | 7.8 |
| Spain | 15.0 | 12.5 | 11.1 | 10.4 | 11.1 | 11.1 | 10.6 | 9.2 | 8.5 | 8.2 | 8.6 |
| Sweden | 8.2 | 6.7 | 5.6 | 4.9 | 4.9 | 5.6 | 6.3 | 7.8 | 7.1 | 6.1 | 5.7 |
| United Kingdom | 6.1 | 5.9 | 5.3 | 5.0 | 5.1 | 4.9 | 4.7 | 4.8 | 5.3 | 5.1 | 5.2 |
| *New EU member States* | .. | .. | 12.2 | 12.9 | 13.7 | 12.9 | 12.9 | 11.9 | 9.9 | 8.0 | 7.5 |
| Bulgaria | 12.2 | 16.0 | 16.4 | 19.5 | 18.1 | 13.7 | 12.0 | 10.1 | 9.0 | 8.0 | 7.5 |
| Cyprus | .. | .. | 4.9 | 3.8 | 3.6 | 4.1 | 4.6 | 5.2 | 4.6 | 4.2 | 4.0 |
| Czech Republic | 6.4 | 8.6 | 8.7 | 8.0 | 7.3 | 7.8 | 8.3 | 7.9 | 7.1 | 6.0 | 5.5 |
| Estonia[e] | 9.2 | 11.3 | 12.8 | 12.4 | 10.3 | 10.0 | 9.7 | 7.9 | 5.9 | 4.8 | 4.8 |
| Hungary | 8.4 | 6.9 | 6.4 | 5.7 | 5.8 | 5.9 | 6.1 | 7.2 | 7.5 | 7.6 | 7.8 |
| Latvia[e] | 14.3 | 14.0 | 13.7 | 12.9 | 12.2 | 10.5 | 10.4 | 8.9 | 6.8 | 5.9 | 5.6 |
| Lithuania[e] | 13.2 | 13.7 | 16.4 | 16.5 | 13.5 | 12.4 | 11.4 | 8.3 | 5.6 | 4.4 | 4.2 |
| Malta | .. | .. | 6.7 | 7.6 | 7.5 | 7.6 | 7.4 | 7.3 | 7.3 | 6.7 | 6.5 |
| Poland | 10.2 | 13.4 | 16.1 | 18.2 | 19.9 | 19.6 | 19.0 | 17.7 | 13.8 | 9.8 | 7.4 |
| Romania | 5.4 | 6.6 | 7.2 | 6.6 | 8.4 | 7.0 | 8.1 | 7.2 | 7.3 | 7.0 | 7.0 |
| Slovakia | 12.6 | 16.4 | 18.8 | 19.3 | 18.7 | 17.6 | 18.2 | 16.3 | 13.4 | 11.4 | 10.9 |
| Slovenia[e] | 7.4 | 7.3 | 6.7 | 6.2 | 6.3 | 6.7 | 6.3 | 6.5 | 6.0 | 5.2 | 5.0 |
| **Other Europe** | 3.4 | 3.0 | 2.9 | 2.9 | 3.4 | 4.3 | 4.4 | 4.5 | 3.8 | 2.6 | 2.9 |
| Iceland[e] | 2.8 | 1.9 | 1.3 | 1.4 | 2.5 | 3.4 | 3.1 | 2.1 | 1.3 | 0.9 | 1.3 |
| Norway | 3.2 | 3.2 | 3.4 | 3.6 | 3.9 | 4.5 | 4.4 | 4.6 | 3.5 | 2.7 | 2.6 |
| Switzerland | 3.6 | 3.0 | 2.7 | 2.6 | 3.2 | 4.2 | 4.4 | 4.5 | 4.0 | 3.3 | 3.1 |
| *Memorandum items:* | | | | | | | | | | | |
| Major developed economies | 6.2 | 6.0 | 5.6 | 5.8 | 6.5 | 6.7 | 6.3 | 6.2 | 5.8 | 5.4 | 5.4 |
| Euro area | 10.1 | 9.2 | 8.3 | 7.8 | 8.2 | 8.7 | 8.8 | 8.9 | 8.3 | 7.2 | 6.9 |

**Source**: UN/DESA, based on data of OECD and Economic Commission for Europe.

**a** Unemployment data are standardized by OECD for comparability among countries and over time, in conformity with the definitions of the International Labour Organization (see OECD, *Standardized Unemployment Rates: Sources and Methods* (Paris, 1985)).

**b** Data for country groups are weighted averages, where labour force is used for weights.

**c** Partly estimated.

**d** Forecasts, based in part on Project LINK.

**e** Not standardized.

Table A.8:
**Economies in transition and developing economies: unemployment rates, [a] 1998-2007**

| | 1998 | 1999 | 2000 | 2001 | 2002 | 2003 | 2004 | 2005 | 2006 | 2007[b] |
|---|---|---|---|---|---|---|---|---|---|---|
| **South-eastern Europe** | | | | | | | | | | |
| Albania[c] | 17.7 | 18.4 | 16.8 | 16.4 | 15.8 | 15.0 | 14.4 | 14.2 | 13.9 | 13.6 |
| Bosnia and Herzegovina[c] | 38.7 | 39.0 | 39.4 | 39.9 | 42.7 | 44.0 | 44.9 | 46.6 | 47.7 | .. |
| Croatia | 11.4 | 13.6 | 16.1 | 15.8 | 14.8 | 14.3 | 13.8 | 12.7 | 11.1 | 11.2 |
| Montenegro | .. | .. | .. | .. | .. | .. | 27.7 | 30.3 | .. | .. |
| Serbia | .. | .. | 12.1 | 12.2 | 13.3 | 14.6 | 18.5 | 20.8 | 20.9 | .. |
| The former Yugoslav Republic of Macedonia | .. | 32.4 | 32.2 | 30.5 | 31.9 | 36.7 | 37.2 | 37.3 | 36.0 | 35.6 |
| **Commonwealth of Independent States** | | | | | | | | | | |
| **Net fuel exporters** | | | | | | | | | | |
| Azerbaijan[c] | 1.4 | 1.2 | 1.2 | 1.3 | 1.3 | 1.4 | 1.4 | 1.4 | 1.3 | .. |
| Kazakhstan | .. | .. | 12.8 | 10.4 | 9.3 | 8.8 | 8.4 | 8.1 | .. | .. |
| Russian Federation | 13.2 | 12.6 | 10.5 | 9.0 | 8.0 | 8.6 | 8.2 | 7.6 | 7.2 | 6.1 |
| Turkmenistan[c] | .. | .. | .. | .. | .. | .. | .. | .. | .. | .. |
| Uzbekistan[c] | 0.4 | 0.4 | 0.4 | 0.4 | 0.4 | 0.3 | .. | .. | .. | .. |
| **Net fuel importers** | | | | | | | | | | |
| Armenia[c] | 8.9 | 11.5 | 10.9 | 9.8 | 10.5 | 10.2 | 9.4 | 7.6 | 7.2 | .. |
| Belarus[c] | 2.3 | 2.1 | 2.1 | 2.3 | 3.0 | 3.1 | 1.9 | 1.5 | 1.2 | 1.0 |
| Georgia | 14.5 | 13.8 | 10.3 | 11.1 | 12.6 | 11.5 | 12.6 | 13.8 | .. | .. |
| Kyrgyzstan[c] | 3.1 | 3.0 | 3.1 | 3.2 | 3.1 | 2.9 | 2.9 | 3.3 | .. | .. |
| Moldova[c] | .. | .. | 8.5 | 7.3 | 6.8 | 7.9 | 8.1 | 7.3 | .. | .. |
| Tajikistan[c] | 3.2 | 3.0 | 2.7 | 2.3 | 2.6 | 2.3 | 2.0 | 2.1 | .. | .. |
| Ukraine | .. | 11.6 | 11.6 | 10.9 | 9.6 | 9.1 | 8.6 | 7.2 | 6.8 | 7.0 |
| **Africa** | | | | | | | | | | |
| Algeria | .. | .. | .. | 27.3 | 25.9 | 23.7 | 17.7 | 15.3 | 12.3 | .. |
| Botswana | 20.8 | .. | 15.8 | 19.6 | .. | 23.8 | .. | .. | 17.6 | |
| Egypt | 8.2 | 8.1 | 9.0 | 9.2 | 10.2 | 10.4 | 10.8 | 11.0 | 10.7 | .. |
| Mauritius | 6.9 | 7.7 | 8.8 | 9.1 | 9.7 | 10.2 | 8.5 | 9.6 | 9.1 | .. |
| Morocco | .. | 13.9 | 13.6 | 12.5 | 11.6 | 11.9 | 10.8 | 11.0 | 9.7 | .. |
| South Africa | .. | .. | 25.4 | 29.4 | 30.4 | 28.0 | 26.2 | 26.7 | 25.5 | .. |
| Tunisia | .. | 16.0 | 15.7 | 15.1 | 15.3 | 14.5 | 14.2 | 14.2 | 14.3 | .. |
| **Developing America** | | | | | | | | | | |
| Argentina [d, e] | 12.1 | 13.5 | 14.7 | 18.1 | 17.5 | 16.8 | 13.6 | 11.6 | 10.2 | 9.2 |
| Barbados | 12.3 | 10.4 | 9.2 | 9.9 | 10.3 | 11.0 | 9.8 | 9.1 | 8.7 | .. |
| Bolivia[d] | 6.1 | 7.2 | 7.5 | 8.5 | 8.7 | 9.2 | 6.2 | 8.2 | .. | .. |
| Brazil[f, g] | 7.6 | 7.6 | 7.1 | 6.2 | 11.7 | 12.3 | 11.5 | 9.8 | 10.0 | 9.8 |
| Chile | 6.4 | 10.1 | 9.7 | 9.9 | 9.8 | 9.5 | 10.0 | 9.2 | 7.7 | 6.9 |
| Colombia[h] | 15.3 | 19.4 | 17.3 | 18.2 | 17.6 | 16.7 | 15.4 | 13.9 | 13.0 | 10.4 |
| Costa Rica | 5.4 | 6.2 | 5.3 | 5.8 | 6.8 | 6.7 | 6.7 | 6.9 | 6.0 | .. |
| Dominican Republic | 14.4 | 13.8 | 13.9 | 15.6 | 16.1 | 16.7 | 18.4 | 18.0 | 16.2 | .. |
| Ecuador[i] | 11.5 | 14.4 | 14.4 | 10.4 | 8.6 | 9.8 | 11.0 | 10.7 | 10.1 | .. |
| El Salvador | 7.6 | 6.9 | 6.5 | 7.0 | 6.2 | 6.2 | 6.5 | 7.3 | 5.7 | .. |

## Table A.8 (cont'd)

| | 1998 | 1999 | 2000 | 2001 | 2002 | 2003 | 2004 | 2005 | 2006 | 2007[b] |
|---|---|---|---|---|---|---|---|---|---|---|
| Guatemala | .. | .. | .. | .. | 5.4 | 5.2 | 4.4 | .. | .. | .. |
| Honduras | 5.2 | 5.3 | .. | 5.9 | 6.1 | 7.6 | 8.0 | 6.5 | 4.9 | .. |
| Jamaica | 15.5 | 15.7 | 15.5 | 15.0 | 14.2 | 11.4 | 11.7 | 11.3 | 10.3 | .. |
| Mexico | 2.3 | 1.8 | 1.6 | 1.8 | 2.0 | 2.4 | 2.7 | 3.6 | 3.6 | 3.8 |
| Nicaragua | 13.2 | 10.7 | 7.8 | 11.3 | 11.6 | 10.2 | 9.3 | 7.0 | 7.0 | .. |
| Panama | 13.6 | 11.8 | 13.5 | 14.7 | 14.1 | 13.6 | 12.4 | 10.3 | 9.1 | 7.1 |
| Paraguay[d] | 6.6 | 9.4 | 10.0 | 10.8 | 14.7 | 11.2 | 10.0 | 7.6 | 8.3 | .. |
| Peru[d, j] | 8.5 | 9.2 | 8.5 | 9.3 | 9.4 | 9.4 | 9.4 | 9.6 | 8.5 | .. |
| Trinidad and Tobago | 14.2 | 13.1 | 12.2 | 10.8 | 10.4 | 10.5 | 8.4 | 8.0 | 6.2 | .. |
| Uruguay[d] | 10.1 | 11.3 | 13.6 | 15.3 | 17.0 | 16.9 | 13.1 | 12.2 | 11.4 | 9.5 |
| Venezuela, Bolivarian Republic of | 11.3 | 15.0 | 13.9 | 13.3 | 15.8 | 18.0 | 15.3 | 12.4 | 10.0 | 9.1 |
| **Developing Asia** | | | | | | | | | | |
| China | 3.1 | 3.1 | 3.1 | 3.6 | 4.0 | 4.3 | 4.2 | 4.2 | 4.1 | 4.1 |
| Hong Kong SAR[k] | 4.7 | 6.2 | 4.9 | 5.1 | 7.3 | 7.9 | 6.8 | 5.6 | 4.8 | 4.2 |
| India | 3.6 | .. | 4.3 | .. | .. | .. | 5.0 | .. | .. | .. |
| Indonesia | 5.5 | 6.4 | 6.1 | 8.1 | 9.1 | 9.5 | 9.9 | 10.3 | 10.5 | .. |
| Iran, Islamic Republic of | .. | .. | .. | .. | 12.8 | .. | 10.3 | 11.5 | .. | .. |
| Israel | 8.5 | 8.9 | 8.8 | 9.4 | 10.3 | 10.7 | 10.4 | 9.0 | 8.4 | 7.4 |
| Jordan | .. | .. | 13.7 | 14.7 | 14.4 | 14.8 | 12.5 | 14.8 | 14.4 | .. |
| Korea, Republic of | 6.8 | 6.3 | 4.4 | 4.0 | 3.3 | 3.6 | 3.7 | 3.7 | 3.5 | 3.3 |
| Kuwait | 0.7 | 0.7 | 0.8 | 0.8 | 1.1 | 1.3 | 1.7 | .. | .. | .. |
| Malaysia | 3.2 | 3.5 | 3.1 | 3.5 | 3.5 | 3.6 | 3.6 | 3.6 | 3.3 | 3.4 |
| Occupied Palestinian Territory | 14.4 | 11.8 | 14.1 | 25.2 | 31.2 | 25.4 | 26.7 | 23.5 | .. | .. |
| Pakistan | 5.9 | 5.9 | 7.8 | 7.8 | 8.3 | 8.3 | 7.7 | 7.7 | 6.2 | .. |
| Philippines[l, m] | 9.6 | 9.6 | 10.1 | 9.8 | 10.2 | 10.2 | 10.9 | 7.4 | 7.3 | 7.7 |
| Saudi Arabia | | 4.3 | 4.6 | 4.6 | 5.3 | 5.6 | 5.8 | 61. | 6.3 | |
| Singapore[n] | 2.5 | 2.8 | 2.7 | 2.7 | 3.6 | 4.0 | 3.4 | 3.1 | 2.7 | 2.3 |
| Sri Lanka | 10.6 | 9.1 | 8.0 | 7.7 | 8.7 | 9.2 | 8.5 | 7.2 | 6.6 | .. |
| Taiwan Province of China | 2.7 | 2.9 | 3.0 | 4.6 | 5.2 | 5.0 | 4.4 | 4.1 | 3.9 | 3.9 |
| Thailand | 4.4 | 4.2 | 3.6 | 3.3 | 2.4 | 2.2 | 2.1 | 1.8 | 1.5 | 1.4 |
| Turkey | 6.8 | 7.7 | 6.5 | 8.4 | 10.3 | 10.5 | 10.3 | 10.3 | 9.9 | 9.8 |
| Viet Nam[d] | 6.9 | 6.7 | 6.4 | 6.3 | 6.0 | 5.8 | 5.6 | 5.3 | 4.8 | .. |

**Sources**: UN/DESA, based on data of Economic Commission for Europe; ILO LABORSTAT database and KILM 5th edition; Economic Commission for Latin America and the Caribbean; Asian Development Bank *Asian Development Outlook 2006*; national sources.

a   As a percentage of the labour force.
b   Partly estimated.
c   End-of-period registered unemployment data (as a percentage of the labour force).
d   Urban areas.
e   Break in series:  new methodology starting in 2003.
f   6 main cities.
g   Break in series:  new methodology starting in 2002.
h   13 main cities.
i   Covers Quito, Guayaquil and Cuenca from 2000.
j   Metropolitan Lima.
k   Special Administrative Region of China.
l   Philippines definition: this partly adopts the ILO definition, that is to say, it does not include one ILO criterion which is "currently available for work".
m   Break in series: new methodology starting in 2005.
n   Resident unemployment rate.

Table A.9:
**Major developed economies: quarterly indicators of growth, unemployment and inflation, 2005-2007**

| | 2005 quarters | | | | 2006 quarters | | | | 2007 quarters | | |
|---|---|---|---|---|---|---|---|---|---|---|---|
| | I | II | III | IV | I | II | III | IV | I | II | III |
| | **Growth of gross domestic product[a]** (percentage change in seasonally adjusted data from preceding quarter) | | | | | | | | | | |
| Canada | 1.7 | 3.5 | 4.1 | 3.5 | 3.4 | 1.5 | 1.3 | 1.5 | 3.5 | 3.8 | 2.9 |
| France | 0.8 | 0.8 | 2.3 | 1.9 | 2.9 | 3.8 | -0.2 | 1.9 | 2.3 | 1.4 | 2.9 |
| Germany | 1.4 | 1.6 | 2.3 | 1.1 | 3.4 | 5.4 | 3.0 | 4.0 | 2.2 | 1.0 | 2.8 |
| Italy | -1.0 | 2.6 | 1.6 | -0.4 | 3.1 | 2.5 | 1.2 | 4.6 | 1.3 | 0.3 | 1.5 |
| Japan | 2.9 | 4.0 | 2.7 | 1.7 | 2.2 | 2.1 | -0.2 | 5.5 | 2.6 | -1.6 | 2.6 |
| United Kingdom | 0.9 | 1.8 | 2.1 | 2.6 | 3.3 | 3.3 | 2.7 | 3.3 | 3.2 | 3.3 | 3.0 |
| United States | 3.1 | 2.8 | 4.5 | 1.2 | 4.8 | 2.4 | 1.1 | 2.1 | 0.6 | 3.8 | 4.9 |
| Major developed economies | 2.3 | 2.8 | 3.4 | 1.4 | 3.8 | 2.7 | 1.0 | 3.2 | 1.6 | 2.0 | 3.7 |
| Euro area | 1.1 | 2.3 | 2.5 | 1.6 | 3.6 | 3.9 | 2.4 | 3.2 | 3.1 | 1.3 | 2.8 |
| | **Unemployment rate[b]** (percentage of total labour force) | | | | | | | | | | |
| Canada | 7.0 | 6.9 | 6.7 | 6.5 | 6.4 | 6.2 | 6.4 | 6.2 | 6.1 | 6.1 | 6.0 |
| France | 9.6 | 9.7 | 9.7 | 9.7 | 9.7 | 9.6 | 9.4 | 9.3 | 9.0 | 8.8 | 8.6 |
| Germany | 10.6 | 10.7 | 10.7 | 10.4 | 10.4 | 10.0 | 9.6 | 9.2 | 8.7 | 8.5 | 8.2 |
| Italy | 7.9 | 7.7 | 7.7 | 7.5 | 7.3 | 6.8 | 6.6 | 6.5 | 6.2 | 5.9 | .. |
| Japan | 4.6 | 4.3 | 4.3 | 4.5 | 4.2 | 4.1 | 4.1 | 4.1 | 4.0 | 3.8 | 3.8 |
| United Kingdom | 4.6 | 4.7 | 4.7 | 5.0 | 5.1 | 5.4 | 5.4 | 5.3 | 5.4 | 5.3 | .. |
| United States | 5.3 | 5.1 | 5.0 | 5.0 | 4.7 | 4.7 | 4.7 | 4.5 | 4.5 | 4.5 | 4.7 |
| Major developed economies | 6.3 | 6.2 | 6.1 | 6.1 | 6.0 | 5.8 | 5.8 | 5.6 | 5.5 | 5.4 | .. |
| Euro area | 9.0 | 9.0 | 8.9 | 8.8 | 8.7 | 8.4 | 8.1 | 8.0 | 7.7 | 7.5 | 7.4 |
| | **Change in consumer prices[c]** (percentage change from preceding quarter) | | | | | | | | | | |
| Canada | 1.4 | 3.7 | 3.5 | 0.2 | 2.0 | 4.5 | 0.2 | -1.2 | 3.8 | 6.1 | 0.0 |
| France | 0.6 | 3.6 | 1.4 | 0.9 | 1.2 | 4.2 | 0.5 | -0.4 | 0.5 | 4.2 | 0.8 |
| Germany | 2.2 | 2.5 | 3.3 | 1.1 | 1.0 | 2.7 | 1.5 | 0.1 | 2.7 | 3.3 | 2.2 |
| Italy | 2.0 | 2.8 | 2.4 | 1.4 | 2.0 | 3.1 | 2.2 | 0.0 | 1.7 | 2.5 | 2.3 |
| Japan | -2.7 | 0.5 | -0.7 | 0.0 | -0.4 | 1.7 | 1.1 | -1.1 | -2.1 | 1.9 | 0.8 |
| United Kingdom | 0.8 | 4.1 | 1.9 | 1.8 | 0.1 | 5.3 | 2.6 | 2.9 | 0.6 | 4.2 | -0.5 |
| United States | 2.6 | 5.5 | 4.7 | 2.1 | 2.1 | 7.1 | 2.1 | -3.3 | 4.2 | 8.0 | 1.0 |
| Major developed economies | 1.0 | 3.7 | 2.8 | 1.4 | 1.3 | 4.9 | 1.7 | -1.7 | 2.0 | 5.4 | 1.0 |
| Euro area | 0.4 | 4.8 | 1.8 | 2.5 | 0.0 | 5.8 | 0.4 | 1.1 | 0.7 | 5.3 | 0.3 |

**Sources**: UN/DESA, based on IMF, *International Financial Statistics*; Organization for Economic Cooperation and Development (OECD) and national authorities.

**a**  Expressed as annualized rate. Major developed economies is calculated as a weighted average, where weights are based on annual GDP valued in 2000 prices and exchange rates.
**b**  Seasonally adjusted data as standardized by OECD.
**c**  Expressed as annualized rate. Major developed economies is calculated as a weighted average, where weights are based on 2000 GDP in United States dollars.

Table A.10:
## Selected economies in transition: quarterly indicators of growth and inflation, 2005-2007

| Percentage | 2005 quarters | | | | 2006 quarters | | | | 2007 quarters | | |
|---|---|---|---|---|---|---|---|---|---|---|---|
| | I | II | III | IV | I | II | III | IV | I | II | III |
| | Rates of growth of gross domestic product[a] | | | | | | | | | | |
| Armenia | 8.5 | 11.2 | 12.7 | 18.6 | 8.0 | 14.0 | 13.2 | 14.8 | 11.7 | 10.1 | .. |
| Belarus | 9.9 | 8.5 | 8.6 | 10.7 | 11.1 | 9.6 | 8.5 | 10.8 | 8.2 | 8.7 | .. |
| Croatia | 1.8 | 5.1 | 5.2 | 4.8 | 6.0 | 3.6 | 4.7 | 4.8 | 7.0 | 6.6 | .. |
| Georgia | 8.7 | 10.0 | 12.3 | 7.3 | 8.4 | 7.8 | 9.5 | 11.4 | 11.4 | 13.4 | .. |
| Kazakhstan | 9.0 | 8.8 | 8.9 | 11.2 | 7.7 | 10.8 | 12.7 | 10.6 | 10.5 | 9.9 | .. |
| Kyrgyzstan | 0.5 | -0.1 | -0.6 | -0.1 | 2.2 | 3.5 | 1.9 | 3.4 | 7.3 | 10.8 | 7.8 |
| Moldova | 8.3 | 9.9 | 5.6 | 7.2 | 4.7 | 3.6 | 3.1 | 4.8 | .. | .. | .. |
| Russian Federation | 5.0 | 5.6 | 6.6 | 8.0 | 5.0 | 7.0 | 6.8 | 7.8 | 7.9 | 7.8 | .. |
| Ukraine | 4.8 | 3.3 | 1.0 | 1.8 | 3.2 | 7.1 | 8.1 | 10.3 | 8.0 | 7.9 | .. |
| | Change in consumer prices[a] | | | | | | | | | | |
| Armenia | 4.3 | 0.2 | -1.9 | -0.3 | -2.0 | 1.8 | 6.7 | 5.8 | 4.9 | 4.3 | 2.1 |
| Belarus | 12.4 | 10.6 | 9.9 | 8.6 | 7.8 | 7.1 | 6.3 | 6.6 | 7.5 | 6.9 | 8.1 |
| Croatia | 3.1 | 3.1 | 3.3 | 3.8 | 3.5 | 3.9 | 3.2 | 2.2 | 1.6 | 2.1 | 2.9 |
| Georgia | 9.4 | 9.4 | 6.9 | 7.3 | 5.0 | 9.1 | 13.1 | 9.6 | 10.4 | 7.5 | 7.7 |
| Kazakhstan | 7.0 | 7.7 | 8.0 | 7.6 | 8.5 | 9.0 | 8.7 | 8.3 | 8.0 | 7.8 | 9.8 |
| Kyrgyzstan | 2.6 | 5.0 | 4.5 | 5.2 | 6.2 | 5.7 | 5.3 | 5.0 | 4.8 | 4.8 | .. |
| Moldova | 13.1 | 13.6 | 11.0 | 10.2 | 10.8 | 11.8 | 14.2 | 14.2 | 11.8 | .. | .. |
| Russian Federation | 13.1 | 13.7 | 12.7 | 11.3 | 10.9 | 9.4 | 9.4 | 9.1 | 7.7 | 7.9 | .. |
| Ukraine | 13.6 | 14.6 | 14.5 | 11.6 | 9.7 | 7.2 | 8.0 | 11.4 | 10.2 | 11.4 | 14.0 |

**Sources**: UN/DESA, based on data of Economic Commission for Europe and individual national sources.

**a**    Percentage change from the corresponding period of the previous year.

Table A.11:
**Major developing economies: quarterly indicators of growth, unemployment and inflation, 2005-2007**

| Percentage | 2005 quarters | | | | 2006 quarters | | | | 2007 quarters | | |
|---|---|---|---|---|---|---|---|---|---|---|---|
| | I | II | III | IV | I | II | III | IV | I | II | III |
| | Rates of growth of gross domestic product[a] | | | | | | | | | | |
| Argentina | 8.0 | 10.2 | 9.2 | 9.2 | 8.8 | 7.9 | 8.8 | 8.6 | 7.9 | 8.5 | .. |
| Brazil | 2.8 | 4.0 | 1.0 | 1.4 | 3.9 | 1.1 | 4.4 | 4.4 | 4.4 | 5.4 | 4.0 |
| Chile | 6.6 | 7.2 | 5.2 | 4.2 | 5.0 | 4.0 | 2.6 | 4.3 | 5.9 | 6.2 | 4.1 |
| China | 9.5 | 9.5 | 9.4 | 9.9 | 10.2 | 10.9 | 10.7 | 11.0 | 11.1 | 11.5 | 11.5 |
| Colombia | 5.1 | 6.3 | 5.8 | 1.9 | 5.4 | 6.1 | 7.7 | 8.0 | 8.1 | 6.9 | .. |
| Ecuador | 4.5 | 6.1 | 6.0 | 6.3 | 5.9 | 4.0 | 4.2 | 1.5 | 1.3 | 1.4 | .. |
| Hong Kong SAR[b] | 6.2 | 7.1 | 8.1 | 7.0 | 8.2 | 5.6 | 6.4 | 6.9 | 5.6 | 6.6 | 6.2 |
| India | 8.9 | 8.4 | 8.0 | 9.3 | 10.0 | 9.6 | 10.2 | 8.7 | 9.1 | 9.3 | 8.9 |
| Indonesia | 6.1 | 5.9 | 5.7 | 5.0 | 5.0 | 5.0 | 5.9 | 6.1 | 6.0 | 6.3 | 6.5 |
| Israel | 5.1 | 5.8 | 5.5 | 5.3 | 5.5 | 5.7 | 4.5 | 4.9 | 5.0 | 4.8 | 6.4 |
| Korea, Republic of | 2.9 | 3.4 | 4.8 | 5.5 | 6.3 | 5.1 | 4.8 | 4.0 | 4.0 | 5.0 | 5.2 |
| Malaysia | 5.4 | 3.9 | 5.2 | 5.5 | 6.0 | 6.1 | 6.0 | 5.7 | 5.5 | 5.8 | 6.7 |
| Mexico | 2.4 | 3.2 | 3.1 | 2.5 | 5.5 | 4.9 | 4.5 | 4.3 | 2.6 | 2.8 | 3.7 |
| Philippines | 4.4 | 5.0 | 4.6 | 5.4 | 5.7 | 5.5 | 5.1 | 5.5 | 7.1 | 7.5 | 6.6 |
| Singapore | 4.2 | 6.4 | 8.3 | 8.4 | 10.1 | 8.0 | 7.0 | 6.6 | 6.5 | 8.7 | 8.9 |
| South Africa | 5.7 | 4.7 | 4.9 | 4.7 | 4.9 | 4.9 | 5.0 | 6.6 | 5.7 | 5.0 | 5.1 |
| Taiwan Province of China | 2.2 | 3.1 | 4.4 | 6.9 | 5.1 | 5.1 | 5.3 | 4.1 | 4.2 | 5.2 | 6.9 |
| Thailand | 3.5 | 4.7 | 5.5 | 4.3 | 6.1 | 5.0 | 4.7 | 4.3 | 4.2 | 4.4 | .. |
| Turkey | 7.5 | 4.7 | 8.0 | 10.2 | 6.4 | 9.3 | 4.3 | 4.6 | 6.9 | 3.9 | .. |
| Venezuela, Bolivarian Republic of | 17.4 | 12.0 | 9.4 | 11.1 | 10.3 | 9.4 | 10.2 | 11.4 | 8.6 | 7.8 | 8.7 |
| | Unemployment rate[c] | | | | | | | | | | |
| Argentina | 13.0 | 12.1 | 11.1 | 10.1 | 11.4 | 10.4 | 10.2 | 8.7 | 9.8 | 8.5 | .. |
| Brazil | 10.5 | 9.7 | 9.4 | 9.7 | 9.9 | 10.3 | 10.4 | 9.2 | 9.8 | 10.0 | 9.5 |
| Chile | 8.8 | 9.7 | 10.0 | 8.7 | 8.0 | 8.8 | 8.4 | 6.7 | 6.4 | 6.8 | 7.4 |
| Colombia | 10.4 | 9.1 | 8.6 | 7.8 | 9.4 | 8.5 | 9.7 | 8.9 | 9.8 | 11.0 | .. |
| Hong Kong SAR[b] | 5.9 | 5.8 | 5.9 | 5.2 | 4.9 | 4.9 | 5.1 | 4.4 | 4.1 | 4.3 | 4.4 |
| Israel | 9.2 | 9.0 | 8.9 | 8.9 | 8.8 | 8.8 | 8.3 | 7.8 | 7.7 | 7.6 | .. |
| Korea, Republic of | 4.2 | 3.7 | 3.6 | 3.5 | 3.9 | 3.4 | 3.3 | 3.2 | 3.6 | 3.2 | 3.1 |
| Malaysia | 3.5 | 3.1 | 3.8 | 3.8 | 3.8 | 3.4 | 3.1 | 3.0 | 3.4 | 3.4 | .. |
| Mexico | 3.8 | 3.8 | 3.5 | 3.3 | 3.6 | 3.2 | 4.0 | 3.7 | 4.0 | 3.4 | 3.9 |
| Philippines | 11.3 | 12.9 | 10.9 | 10.3 | 8.1 | 8.1 | 8.0 | 7.3 | 7.8 | 7.4 | 7.4 |
| Singapore | 3.3 | 3.4 | 3.2 | 2.6 | 2.6 | 2.7 | 2.7 | 2.6 | 2.9 | 2.3 | 1.7 |
| Taiwan Province of China | 4.2 | 4.1 | 4.3 | 4.0 | 3.9 | 3.9 | 4.0 | 3.9 | 3.8 | 3.9 | 4.0 |
| Thailand | 2.6 | 2.1 | 1.4 | 1.6 | 2.0 | 1.8 | 1.2 | 1.3 | 1.6 | 1.6 | 1.2 |
| Turkey | 11.4 | 9.5 | 9.4 | 10.6 | 11.5 | 9.2 | 9.0 | 9.8 | 10.9 | 9.2 | 9.0 |
| Uruguay | 12.1 | 12.3 | 12.3 | 12.1 | 12.6 | 10.8 | 10.7 | 9.6 | 9.9 | 9.5 | 9.0 |
| Venezuela, Bolivarian Republic of | 14.3 | 12.1 | 12.1 | 10.4 | 10.8 | 10.0 | 9.9 | 8.7 | 10.2 | 8.4 | 8.6 |

## Table A.11 (cont'd)

| | 2005 quarters | | | | 2006 quarters | | | | 2007 quarters | | |
|---|---|---|---|---|---|---|---|---|---|---|---|
| | I | II | III | IV | I | II | III | IV | I | II | III |
| | Change in consumer prices[a] | | | | | | | | | | |
| Argentina | 8.2 | 8.8 | 9.8 | 11.7 | 11.6 | 11.4 | 10.6 | 10.1 | 9.5 | 8.8 | 8.5 |
| Brazil | 7.4 | 7.8 | 6.2 | 6.1 | 5.5 | 4.3 | 3.8 | 3.1 | 3.0 | 3.3 | 4.0 |
| Chile | 2.3 | 2.8 | 3.3 | 3.8 | 4.1 | 3.8 | 3.5 | 2.2 | 2.7 | 2.9 | 4.8 |
| China | 2.8 | 1.7 | 1.3 | 1.4 | 1.2 | 1.4 | 1.3 | 2.0 | 2.7 | 3.6 | 6.1 |
| Colombia | 5.2 | 5.0 | 4.9 | 5.1 | 4.3 | 4.0 | 4.5 | 4.3 | 5.2 | 6.2 | 5.3 |
| Ecuador | 1.5 | 1.5 | 2.6 | 4.0 | 3.9 | 3.4 | 2.8 | 2.0 | 2.1 | 1.7 | 2.5 |
| Hong Kong SAR[b] | 0.4 | 0.7 | 1.2 | 1.3 | 1.6 | 2.1 | 2.3 | 2.2 | 1.7 | 1.3 | 1.6 |
| India | 4.2 | 4.0 | 3.7 | 5.0 | 4.5 | 5.9 | 6.2 | 6.5 | 7.0 | 6.3 | 6.7 |
| Indonesia | 7.7 | 7.6 | 8.4 | 17.8 | 16.9 | 15.5 | 14.9 | 6.1 | 6.4 | 6.0 | 6.5 |
| Israel | 0.8 | 0.3 | 1.7 | 2.6 | 3.1 | 3.6 | 2.0 | -0.2 | -0.6 | -1.1 | 0.9 |
| Korea, Republic of | 3.3 | 3.0 | 2.3 | 2.5 | 2.1 | 2.2 | 2.5 | 2.1 | 2.0 | 2.4 | 2.3 |
| Malaysia | 2.4 | 2.9 | 3.4 | 3.2 | 3.8 | 4.1 | 3.6 | 3.0 | 2.6 | 1.5 | 1.7 |
| Mexico | 4.4 | 4.5 | 4.0 | 3.1 | 3.7 | 3.1 | 3.5 | 4.1 | 4.1 | 4.0 | 4.0 |
| Philippines | 8.4 | 8.2 | 7.1 | 6.9 | 7.3 | 6.9 | 6.1 | 4.8 | 2.9 | 2.4 | 2.5 |
| Singapore | 0.2 | 0.0 | 0.5 | 1.1 | 1.4 | 1.2 | 0.7 | 0.6 | 0.5 | 1.0 | 2.8 |
| South Africa | 2.9 | 3.2 | 3.9 | 3.7 | 3.8 | 4.0 | 5.2 | 5.5 | 5.9 | 7.0 | 6.6 |
| Taiwan Province of China | 1.6 | 2.1 | 3.0 | 2.5 | 1.4 | 1.5 | -0.3 | -0.1 | 1.0 | 0.3 | 1.5 |
| Thailand | 2.8 | 3.7 | 5.6 | 6.0 | 5.7 | 6.0 | 3.6 | 3.3 | 2.5 | 1.9 | 1.6 |
| Turkey | 9.1 | 10.0 | 10.7 | 10.7 | 10.4 | 11.1 | 11.2 | 9.4 | 10.3 | 9.5 | 7.1 |
| Venezuela, Bolivarian Republic of | 17.0 | 16.4 | 15.4 | 15.2 | 12.6 | 11.2 | 14.6 | 16.1 | 19.1 | 19.5 | 16.1 |

Source: IMF, *International Financial Statistics,* and national authorities.

a   Percentage change from the corresponding quarter of the previous year.
b   Special Administrative Region of China.
c   Reflects national definitions and coverage. Not comparable across economies.

Table A.12:
**Major developed economies: financial indicators, 1998-2007**

| Percentage | 1998 | 1999 | 2000 | 2001 | 2002 | 2003 | 2004 | 2005 | 2006 | 2007[a] |
|---|---|---|---|---|---|---|---|---|---|---|
| | Short-term interest rates[b] | | | | | | | | | |
| Canada | 5.1 | 4.9 | 5.7 | 4.0 | 2.6 | 3.0 | 2.3 | 2.8 | 4.2 | 4.3 |
| France[c] | 4.0 | 3.0 | 4.4 | 4.3 | 3.3 | 2.3 | 2.1 | 2.2 | 3.1 | 4.1 |
| Germany[c] | 4.0 | 3.0 | 4.4 | 4.3 | 3.3 | 2.3 | 2.1 | 2.2 | 3.1 | 4.1 |
| Italy[c] | 4.0 | 3.0 | 4.4 | 4.3 | 3.3 | 2.3 | 2.1 | 2.2 | 3.1 | 4.1 |
| Japan | 0.7 | 0.2 | 0.2 | 0.1 | 0.1 | 0.0 | 0.0 | 0.0 | 0.2 | 0.6 |
| United Kingdom | 7.3 | 5.4 | 6.1 | 5.0 | 4.0 | 3.7 | 4.6 | 4.7 | 4.8 | 5.8 |
| United States | 5.5 | 5.3 | 6.5 | 3.7 | 1.7 | 1.2 | 1.6 | 3.5 | 5.2 | 5.4 |
| | Long-term interest rates[d] | | | | | | | | | |
| Canada | 5.3 | 5.5 | 5.9 | 5.5 | 5.3 | 4.8 | 4.6 | 4.1 | 4.2 | 4.3 |
| France | 4.6 | 4.6 | 5.4 | 4.9 | 4.9 | 4.1 | 4.1 | 3.4 | 3.8 | 4.3 |
| Germany | 4.6 | 4.5 | 5.3 | 4.8 | 4.8 | 4.1 | 4.0 | 3.3 | 3.8 | 4.2 |
| Italy | 4.9 | 4.7 | 5.6 | 5.2 | 5.0 | 4.3 | 4.3 | 3.6 | 4.1 | 4.5 |
| Japan | 1.5 | 1.7 | 1.7 | 1.3 | 1.3 | 1.0 | 1.5 | 1.4 | 1.7 | 1.7 |
| United Kingdom | 5.6 | 5.1 | 5.3 | 4.9 | 4.9 | 4.5 | 4.9 | 4.4 | 4.5 | 5.1 |
| United States | 5.3 | 5.6 | 6.0 | 5.0 | 4.6 | 4.0 | 4.3 | 4.3 | 4.8 | 4.8 |
| | General government financial balances[e] | | | | | | | | | |
| Canada | 0.1 | 1.6 | 2.9 | 0.7 | -0.1 | -0.4 | 0.5 | 1.4 | 0.8 | 0.8 |
| France | -2.6 | -1.7 | -1.5 | -1.6 | -3.2 | -4.1 | -3.6 | -3.0 | -2.6 | -2.3 |
| Germany | -2.2 | -1.5 | 1.3 | -2.8 | -3.6 | -4.0 | -3.7 | -3.2 | -1.7 | -0.7 |
| Italy | -3.1 | -1.8 | -0.9 | -3.1 | -3.0 | -3.5 | -3.5 | -4.3 | -4.5 | -2.5 |
| Japan[f] | -5.8 | -7.4 | -7.6 | -6.3 | -8.0 | -7.9 | -6.2 | -6.4 | -2.4 | -2.7 |
| United Kingdom | 0.1 | 1.2 | 4.0 | 0.9 | -1.7 | -3.4 | -3.3 | -3.3 | -2.9 | -2.7 |
| United States | 0.4 | 0.9 | 1.6 | -0.4 | -3.8 | -4.8 | -4.6 | -3.7 | -2.3 | -2.7 |

**Sources**: UN/DESA, based on IMF, *International Financial Statistics*; OECD *Economic Outlook*; and EUROPA (EU online), *European Economy*.

**a**   Average for the first nine months.
**b**   Money market rates.
**c**   From January 1999 onwards, represents the three-month Euro Interbank Offered Rate (EURIBOR), which is an interbank deposit bid rate.
**d**   Yield on long-term government bonds.
**e**   Surplus (+) or deficit (-) as a percentage of nominal GNP or GDP.
**f**   The 1998 deficit does not take account of the assumption by the central Government of the debt of the Japan National Railway Settlement Corporation and the National Forest Special Account, which amounts to 5.2 percentage points of GDP. Deferred tax payments on postal savings accounts are included in 2000 and 2001.

Table A.13:
**Selected economies: real effective exchange rates, broad measurement,[a] 1998-2007**

| | 1998 | 1999 | 2000 | 2001 | 2002 | 2003 | 2004 | 2005 | 2006 | 2007[b] |
|---|---|---|---|---|---|---|---|---|---|---|
| **Developed economies** | | | | | | | | | | |
| Australia | 103.3 | 104.1 | 100.0 | 95.5 | 99.3 | 110.7 | 120.4 | 127.2 | 132.2 | 140.0 |
| Bulgaria | 88.7 | 92.4 | 100.0 | 107.9 | 112.0 | 120.4 | 125.2 | 127.6 | 135.3 | 142.3 |
| Canada | 102.4 | 101.1 | 100.0 | 96.4 | 94.5 | 102.3 | 104.6 | 108.1 | 111.6 | 111.3 |
| Czech Republic | 101.7 | 99.6 | 100.0 | 106.5 | 118.1 | 116.9 | 121.3 | 129.1 | 133.2 | 137.1 |
| Denmark | 104.7 | 106.2 | 100.0 | 102.4 | 106.4 | 113.6 | 114.2 | 111.7 | 109.6 | 109.3 |
| Euro area | 112.1 | 108.7 | 100.0 | 101.5 | 105.1 | 117.2 | 121.3 | 120.3 | 121.2 | 124.9 |
| Hungary | 102.5 | 100.6 | 100.0 | 107.0 | 113.2 | 114.9 | 118.9 | 119.1 | 115.5 | 119.5 |
| Japan | 88.0 | 96.5 | 100.0 | 89.6 | 83.8 | 83.0 | 83.2 | 78.7 | 73.1 | 69.1 |
| New Zealand | 115.6 | 111.2 | 100.0 | 99.2 | 111.1 | 130.4 | 140.5 | 147.7 | 135.9 | 145.7 |
| Norway | 98.8 | 100.1 | 100.0 | 102.8 | 108.8 | 108.7 | 110.6 | 116.8 | 121.9 | 130.4 |
| Poland | 98.2 | 95.0 | 100.0 | 110.7 | 107.1 | 99.0 | 101.8 | 111.1 | 113.3 | 116.1 |
| Romania | 103.2 | 86.8 | 100.0 | 107.8 | 112.8 | 116.8 | 126.7 | 153.3 | 170.9 | 191.0 |
| Slovakia | 103.1 | 94.9 | 100.0 | 102.1 | 104.0 | 112.3 | 116.8 | 116.9 | 118.2 | 128.3 |
| Sweden | 108.9 | 105.0 | 100.0 | 91.5 | 93.8 | 97.7 | 97.1 | 94.2 | 95.0 | 99.2 |
| Switzerland | 106.9 | 107.0 | 100.0 | 103.1 | 109.2 | 111.0 | 108.9 | 104.8 | 100.2 | 95.2 |
| United Kingdom | 103.5 | 101.8 | 100.0 | 97.1 | 98.1 | 95.4 | 99.6 | 97.3 | 97.0 | 99.5 |
| United States | 98.7 | 99.0 | 100.0 | 105.8 | 105.9 | 97.9 | 92.0 | 89.5 | 86.8 | 83.3 |
| **Economies in transition** | | | | | | | | | | |
| Croatia | 103.5 | 98.5 | 100.0 | 105.5 | 106.4 | 109.6 | 113.5 | 114.3 | 115.2 | 115.9 |
| Russian Federation | 135.3 | 88.4 | 100.0 | 120.7 | 126.5 | 130.9 | 140.6 | 154.6 | 170.2 | 179.0 |
| **Developing economies** | | | | | | | | | | |
| Argentina | 96.5 | 102.2 | 100.0 | 104.9 | 56.0 | 62.4 | 60.8 | 60.1 | 58.5 | 58.0 |
| Brazil | 112.8 | 84.0 | 100.0 | 90.1 | 89.5 | 98.5 | 105.9 | 129.8 | 140.7 | 151.3 |
| Chile | 98.4 | 95.3 | 100.0 | 94.6 | 92.9 | 91.9 | 99.9 | 108.6 | 116.0 | 114.4 |
| China | 102.6 | 97.3 | 100.0 | 105.2 | 102.6 | 97.7 | 96.2 | 98.5 | 100.9 | 102.7 |
| Colombia | 119.3 | 107.2 | 100.0 | 100.4 | 99.0 | 88.0 | 94.8 | 105.0 | 102.7 | 110.6 |
| Ecuador | 84.3 | 78.0 | 100.0 | 102.4 | 110.9 | 114.3 | 114.7 | 121.3 | 130.6 | 124.2 |
| Egypt | 95.4 | 97.9 | 100.0 | 91.0 | 81.5 | 65.4 | 66.2 | 71.9 | 73.9 | 76.0 |
| Hong Kong SAR[c] | 114.0 | 106.2 | 100.0 | 101.7 | 101.3 | 94.9 | 90.0 | 86.7 | 84.1 | 80.1 |
| India | 97.6 | 98.0 | 100.0 | 102.4 | 98.9 | 98.3 | 99.2 | 102.5 | 99.3 | 106.4 |
| Indonesia | 66.0 | 103.4 | 100.0 | 96.0 | 116.0 | 123.0 | 113.8 | 114.3 | 142.0 | 148.9 |
| Israel | 94.2 | 93.7 | 100.0 | 99.6 | 89.6 | 87.4 | 85.4 | 86.4 | 86.8 | 87.5 |
| Korea, Republic of | 83.3 | 93.5 | 100.0 | 90.3 | 93.1 | 92.7 | 95.2 | 105.2 | 112.0 | 111.3 |
| Kuwait | 99.9 | 97.3 | 100.0 | 107.3 | 109.0 | 102.3 | 95.0 | 96.4 | 95.1 | 92.7 |
| Malaysia | 99.2 | 98.9 | 100.0 | 105.3 | 105.2 | 100.5 | 96.0 | 95.2 | 95.4 | 96.5 |
| Mexico | 81.6 | 89.9 | 100.0 | 107.8 | 109.4 | 100.0 | 98.2 | 103.2 | 106.0 | 105.9 |
| Morocco | 97.4 | 99.6 | 100.0 | 97.7 | 98.4 | 98.7 | 97.2 | 94.6 | 94.5 | 93.3 |
| Nigeria[d] | 196.1 | 98.8 | 100.0 | 111.1 | 111.0 | 104.9 | 107.8 | 124.1 | 133.1 | 129.9 |
| Pakistan | 101.9 | 99.5 | 100.0 | 95.4 | 99.9 | 100.9 | 100.5 | 102.4 | 105.7 | 105.1 |
| Peru | 108.7 | 99.8 | 100.0 | 104.0 | 103.9 | 99.9 | 99.6 | 99.5 | 99.3 | 99.1 |
| Philippines | 96.2 | 102.6 | 100.0 | 107.3 | 112.0 | 107.4 | 101.0 | 107.5 | 129.4 | 137.2 |

## Table A.13 (cont'd)

| | 1998 | 1999 | 2000 | 2001 | 2002 | 2003 | 2004 | 2005 | 2006 | 2007[b] |
|---|---|---|---|---|---|---|---|---|---|---|
| Saudi Arabia | 102.2 | 99.1 | 100.0 | 103.4 | 102.0 | 94.2 | 87.7 | 85.0 | 83.9 | 81.2 |
| Singapore | 108.2 | 99.1 | 100.0 | 97.4 | 95.2 | 95.1 | 102.9 | 108.0 | 113.4 | 121.3 |
| South Africa | 105.5 | 101.4 | 100.0 | 90.6 | 80.9 | 107.9 | 117.9 | 119.3 | 112.9 | 102.8 |
| Taiwan Province of China | 101.5 | 95.9 | 100.0 | 95.9 | 93.2 | 89.2 | 90.8 | 89.3 | 88.8 | 87.7 |
| Thailand | 98.4 | 102.1 | 100.0 | 96.6 | 100.6 | 100.1 | 100.4 | 103.2 | 111.7 | 123.8 |
| Turkey | 92.5 | 90.9 | 100.0 | 87.5 | 100.5 | 110.4 | 116.0 | 124.4 | 120.3 | 127.0 |
| Venezuela, Bolivarian Republic of | 89.0 | 96.3 | 100.0 | 109.3 | 92.5 | 93.5 | 98.8 | 99.3 | 107.8 | 119.0 |

**Sources**: JPMorgan Chase and IMF, *International Financial Statistics*.

**a**   Indices based on a "broad" measure currency basket of 46 currencies (including the euro). The real effective exchange rate, which adjusts the nominal index for relative price changes, gauges the effect on international price competitiveness of the country's manufactures due to currency changes and inflation differentials. A rise in the index implies a fall in competitiveness and vice versa. The relative price changes are based on indices most closely measuring the prices of domestically produced finished manufactured goods, excluding food and energy. The weights for currency indices are derived from 2000 bilateral trade patterns of the corresponding countries.

**b**   Average for the first ten months.

**c**   Special Administrative Region of China.

**d**   Data is from International Financial Statistics (IFS) only.

Table A.14:
**Indices of prices of primary commodities, 1998-2007**

| | | Non-fuel commodities | | | | Combined index | | Manufactured export prices | Real prices of non-fuel commodities[a] | *Memorandum item:* Crude petroleum[b] |
|---|---|---|---|---|---|---|---|---|---|---|
| | Food | Tropical beverages | Vegetable oilseeds and oils | Agricultural raw materials | Minerals and metals | Dollar | SDR | | | |
| 1998 | 118 | 150 | 170 | 108 | 91 | 114 | 112 | 110 | 104 | 44.5 |
| 1999 | 98 | 118 | 125 | 97 | 89 | 98 | 95 | 105 | 94 | 63.3 |
| 2000 | 100 | 100 | 100 | 100 | 100 | 100 | 100 | 100 | 100 | 100.0 |
| 2001 | 103 | 79 | 94 | 96 | 89 | 96 | 100 | 98 | 98 | 83.8 |
| 2002 | 102 | 89 | 117 | 94 | 87 | 97 | 99 | 99 | 98 | 88.3 |
| 2003 | 104 | 94 | 137 | 112 | 98 | 105 | 99 | 108 | 97 | 101.8 |
| 2004 | 119 | 100 | 155 | 123 | 137 | 126 | 112 | 117 | 108 | 130.6 |
| 2005 | 127 | 126 | 141 | 132 | 173 | 141 | 126 | 120 | 118 | 183.5 |
| 2006 | 151 | 134 | 148 | 152 | 278 | 184 | 165 | 123 | 150 | 221.3 |
| 2004 I | 118 | 99 | 175 | 130 | 133 | 126 | 112 | 114 | 111 | 111.4 |
| II | 124 | 95 | 162 | 120 | 134 | 127 | 115 | 114 | 111 | 124.7 |
| III | 116 | 99 | 143 | 119 | 137 | 123 | 111 | 115 | 107 | 141.6 |
| IV | 116 | 107 | 141 | 125 | 145 | 126 | 110 | 119 | 106 | 145.0 |
| 2005 I | 129 | 132 | 139 | 126 | 165 | 139 | 121 | 123 | 113 | 159.7 |
| II | 125 | 132 | 144 | 129 | 167 | 138 | 122 | 120 | 115 | 178.8 |
| III | 125 | 120 | 139 | 137 | 173 | 140 | 126 | 118 | 118 | 204.4 |
| IV | 130 | 120 | 139 | 138 | 188 | 147 | 135 | 117 | 125 | 191.1 |
| 2006 I | 151 | 136 | 137 | 149 | 220 | 167 | 153 | 119 | 141 | 209.0 |
| II | 155 | 129 | 141 | 162 | 285 | 188 | 168 | 123 | 153 | 234.6 |
| III | 148 | 133 | 149 | 155 | 301 | 189 | 168 | 125 | 151 | 238.4 |
| IV | 151 | 139 | 164 | 143 | 304 | 190 | 169 | 127 | 150 | 203.1 |
| 2007 I | 155 | 143 | 179 | 165 | 288 | 192 | 169 | 128 | 150 | 198.0 |
| II | 154 | 143 | 209 | 169 | 336 | 207 | 180 | 131 | 158 | 235.5 |
| III | 165 | 151 | 236 | 164 | 322 | 210 | 181 | … | … | 259.0 |

**Sources**: UNCTAD, *Monthly Commodity Price Bulletin*; United Nations, *Monthly Bulletin of Statistics*; and *Middle East Economic Survey*, available from http://www.mees.com/Energy_Tables/basket.htm.

a  Combined index of non-fuel commodity prices in dollars deflated by manufactured export price index.
b  Effective 16 June 2005, the OPEC basket is composed of 11 crudes.

Table A.15:
**World oil supply and demand, 1999-2008**

| | 1999 | 2000 | 2001 | 2002 | 2003 | 2004 | 2005 | 2006 | 2007[a] | 2008[b] |
|---|---|---|---|---|---|---|---|---|---|---|
| **World oil supply[c, d]** (millions of barrels per day) | 74.1 | 76.9 | 77.1 | 76.9 | 79.8 | 83.3 | 84.3 | 85.0 | 85.9 | 87.3 |
| Developed economies | 18.1 | 18.5 | 18.3 | 18.3 | 17.8 | 17.4 | 16.5 | 16.3 | 16.5 | 17.0 |
| Economies in transition | 7.7 | 8.1 | 8.7 | 9.6 | 10.5 | 11.6 | 12.0 | 12.4 | 12.9 | 13.4 |
| Developing economies | 46.7 | 48.6 | 48.3 | 47.3 | 49.7 | 52.5 | 54.0 | 54.4 | 54.6 | 55.0 |
| OPEC | 29.4 | 30.8 | 30.4 | 28.8 | 30.8 | 33.1 | 34.2 | 34.3 | 35.9 | 35.9 |
| Non-OPEC | 17.3 | 17.8 | 17.9 | 18.5 | 18.9 | 19.4 | 19.8 | 20.1 | 18.7 | 19.1 |
| Processing gains[e] | 1.7 | 1.7 | 1.7 | 1.8 | 1.8 | 1.8 | 1.9 | 1.9 | 1.9 | 2.0 |
| **World total demand[f]** | 75.4 | 76.2 | 77.3 | 77.7 | 79.3 | 82.5 | 83.9 | 84.7 | 85.7 | 87.7 |
| Oil prices (dollars per barrel) | | | | | | | | | | |
| OPEC Basket[g] | 17.5 | 27.6 | 23.1 | 24.4 | 28.1 | 36.1 | 50.6 | 61.1 | 65.6 | … |
| Brent Oil | 17.8 | 28.3 | 24.4 | 25.0 | 28.9 | 38.3 | 54.4 | 65.4 | 73.5 | 76.0 |

**Sources**: United Nations, World Bank, International Energy Agency, U.S. Energy Information Administration, and *Middle East Economic Survey*, available from http://www.mees.com/Energy_Tables/basket.htm (accessed on 23 November 2007).

**a**   Partly estimated.
**b**   Forecasts.
**c**   Including crude oil, condensates, natural gas liquids (NGLs), oil from non-conventional sources and other sources of supply.
**d**   Totals may not add up due to rounding.
**e**   Net volume gains and losses in refining process (excluding net gain/loss in the economies in transition and China) and marine transportation losses.
**f**   Including deliveries from refineries/primary stocks and marine bunkers, and refinery fuel and non-conventional oils.
**g**   Data for 2007 is the January to November 2007 average.  Effective 16 June 2005, the OPEC basket is composed of 11 crudes.

Table A.16:

**World trade: changes in value and volume of exports and imports, by major country group, 1998-2008**

| Annual percentage change | 1998 | 1999 | 2000 | 2001 | 2002 | 2003 | 2004 | 2005 | 2006 | 2007[a] | 2008[b] |
|---|---|---|---|---|---|---|---|---|---|---|---|
| **Dollar value of exports** | | | | | | | | | | | |
| **World** | -1.7 | 3.6 | 13.4 | -3.9 | 4.8 | 16.2 | 21.2 | 14.4 | 15.7 | 15.5 | 12.4 |
| **Developed economies** | 1.1 | 1.8 | 7.3 | -2.8 | 3.6 | 15.1 | 18.0 | 9.2 | 13.1 | 15.4 | 12.8 |
| North America | -0.8 | 4.5 | 13.4 | -6.6 | -4.2 | 5.0 | 12.6 | 12.8 | 14.1 | 13.9 | 11.4 |
| EU plus Other Europe | 3.9 | -0.1 | 3.5 | 1.1 | 6.7 | 19.0 | 19.3 | 8.5 | 13.1 | 15.9 | 13.0 |
| Developed Asia | -8.5 | 7.0 | 14.0 | -13.6 | 3.2 | 12.8 | 20.1 | 7.4 | 11.4 | 14.9 | 14.1 |
| **Economies in transition** | -11.6 | -1.4 | 34.2 | -0.7 | 6.3 | 26.5 | 36.4 | 37.2 | 28.4 | 18.1 | 9.9 |
| South-eastern Europe | 0.2 | -6.5 | 16.6 | 3.1 | 6.4 | 20.3 | 32.0 | 27.3 | 21.0 | 17.6 | 14.9 |
| Commonwealth of Independent States | -13.7 | -0.4 | 37.7 | -1.0 | 6.3 | 26.9 | 36.7 | 37.8 | 28.8 | 18.1 | 9.6 |
| **Developing economies** | -7.8 | 8.7 | 27.3 | -6.3 | 7.2 | 17.6 | 26.0 | 21.8 | 18.6 | 15.4 | 12.0 |
| Latin America and the Caribbean | -3.5 | 5.8 | 19.7 | -3.6 | -0.2 | 10.3 | 23.4 | 21.0 | 18.7 | 12.6 | 6.5 |
| Africa | -17.2 | 12.6 | 26.1 | -8.2 | 3.4 | 23.5 | 30.0 | 34.0 | 18.0 | 15.2 | 10.4 |
| Western Asia | -19.6 | 24.8 | 81.4 | -7.0 | 6.6 | 19.1 | 28.3 | 31.3 | 19.6 | 9.4 | 6.4 |
| East and South Asia | -7.6 | 7.2 | 19.2 | -6.7 | 9.8 | 18.6 | 25.7 | 18.6 | 18.5 | 17.6 | 14.7 |
| China | 0.5 | 6.1 | 27.8 | 6.8 | 22.4 | 34.6 | 35.4 | 28.4 | 27.2 | 25.1 | 19.0 |
| **Dollar value of imports** | | | | | | | | | | | |
| **World** | -0.4 | 3.7 | 12.9 | -3.5 | 3.7 | 16.3 | 22.0 | 13.7 | 15.0 | 15.4 | 13.1 |
| **Developed economies** | 3.1 | 5.0 | 10.3 | -3.6 | 3.0 | 16.0 | 19.3 | 11.7 | 13.6 | 13.7 | 11.8 |
| North America | 4.5 | 11.5 | 17.6 | -6.2 | 1.5 | 7.9 | 16.4 | 14.3 | 10.7 | 7.9 | 7.7 |
| EU plus Other Europe | 5.8 | 1.1 | 5.3 | -1.2 | 4.3 | 20.4 | 20.6 | 10.2 | 14.3 | 15.6 | 12.7 |
| Developed Asia | -14.7 | 10.4 | 17.8 | -8.3 | -0.3 | 15.4 | 19.7 | 13.5 | 17.6 | 18.3 | 16.8 |
| **Economies in transition** | -12.4 | -21.0 | 14.8 | 14.1 | 12.0 | 25.2 | 28.4 | 26.5 | 30.0 | 34.5 | 22.9 |
| South-eastern Europe | -0.6 | -6.8 | 12.9 | 13.9 | 20.2 | 19.1 | 21.9 | 17.5 | 15.2 | 20.0 | 13.4 |
| Commonwealth of Independent States | -16.1 | -26.2 | 15.6 | 14.1 | 10.3 | 26.7 | 29.8 | 28.3 | 32.8 | 36.9 | 24.2 |
| **Developing economies** | -7.7 | 2.7 | 19.7 | -4.4 | 4.8 | 16.2 | 27.7 | 16.9 | 16.9 | 17.1 | 14.7 |
| Latin America and the Caribbean | 5.8 | -2.4 | 15.8 | -2.1 | -8.5 | 2.9 | 22.1 | 18.6 | 19.3 | 17.3 | 12.7 |
| Africa | 1.4 | -6.6 | 1.0 | 3.3 | 3.7 | 19.6 | 27.6 | 19.2 | 17.8 | 13.2 | 9.4 |
| Western Asia | -4.2 | 2.1 | 21.7 | 0.0 | 7.0 | 16.3 | 31.7 | 14.6 | 17.3 | 18.9 | 17.2 |
| East and South Asia | -16.3 | 4.1 | 20.6 | -6.7 | 8.8 | 19.5 | 28.3 | 16.8 | 16.2 | 17.1 | 15.4 |
| China | -1.5 | 18.2 | 35.8 | 8.2 | 21.2 | 39.8 | 36.0 | 17.6 | 19.9 | 20.0 | 18.0 |
| **Volume of exports** | | | | | | | | | | | |
| **World** | 5.2 | 4.3 | 13.2 | -1.1 | 4.4 | 5.8 | 10.7 | 7.0 | 9.9 | 7.2 | 7.1 |
| **Developed economies** | 4.3 | 4.4 | 12.6 | -0.9 | 2.2 | 2.5 | 8.3 | 5.3 | 9.5 | 5.8 | 6.1 |
| North America | 1.9 | 3.5 | 14.0 | -5.5 | -2.4 | 0.5 | 6.8 | 6.9 | 7.8 | 7.0 | 6.7 |
| EU plus Other Europe | 6.6 | 4.8 | 11.9 | 2.3 | 3.1 | 2.1 | 8.0 | 4.8 | 10.2 | 4.7 | 6.0 |
| Developed Asia | -1.4 | 4.7 | 12.7 | -6.6 | 6.8 | 7.9 | 12.1 | 4.8 | 9.2 | 8.4 | 5.8 |
| **Economies in transition** | 3.5 | 5.8 | 15.2 | 3.8 | 7.9 | 13.4 | 15.4 | 3.9 | 6.3 | 6.6 | 5.3 |
| South-eastern Europe | 2.9 | -4.7 | 13.5 | 5.5 | 5.3 | 7.7 | 17.6 | 15.8 | 9.6 | 11.1 | 11.3 |
| Commonwealth of Independent States | 3.6 | 7.8 | 15.4 | 3.6 | 8.0 | 13.7 | 15.3 | 3.3 | 6.1 | 6.3 | 4.9 |

## Table A.16 (cont'd)

| | 1998 | 1999 | 2000 | 2001 | 2002 | 2003 | 2004 | 2005 | 2006 | 2007[a] | 2008[b] |
|---|---|---|---|---|---|---|---|---|---|---|---|
| **Developing economies** | 7.4 | 4.0 | 14.5 | -1.9 | 8.5 | 11.3 | 14.5 | 10.3 | 10.9 | 9.4 | 8.7 |
| Latin America and the Caribbean | 13.7 | 0.5 | 4.6 | -0.1 | 1.0 | 6.1 | 11.8 | 7.8 | 6.9 | 4.7 | 4.4 |
| Africa | 15.3 | 3.1 | -9.2 | -2.0 | 2.3 | 9.3 | 8.7 | 11.3 | 4.6 | 7.9 | 8.8 |
| Western Asia | 1.2 | 7.9 | 37.2 | 3.0 | 6.0 | 5.8 | 5.6 | 3.3 | 6.4 | -0.6 | 1.7 |
| East and South Asia | 4.9 | 3.8 | 15.3 | -3.5 | 11.8 | 14.0 | 17.6 | 12.0 | 13.0 | 12.0 | 10.5 |
| China | 6.9 | 17.6 | 35.8 | 9.6 | 28.0 | 31.0 | 28.3 | 22.2 | 22.0 | 18.9 | 13.3 |
| **Volume of imports** | | | | | | | | | | | |
| **World** | 3.0 | 6.1 | 13.8 | -0.5 | 4.1 | 6.6 | 11.0 | 7.3 | 9.3 | 7.0 | 7.3 |
| **Developed economies** | 8.7 | 7.6 | 11.0 | -0.6 | 2.5 | 4.6 | 9.3 | 6.3 | 7.8 | 4.7 | 5.7 |
| North America | 11.4 | 11.1 | 12.3 | -3.6 | 3.2 | 4.7 | 10.8 | 7.2 | 5.2 | 3.3 | 4.0 |
| EU plus Other Europe | 9.8 | 5.9 | 10.7 | 1.0 | 2.0 | 4.0 | 8.8 | 6.4 | 8.6 | 4.3 | 5.8 |
| Developed Asia | -3.7 | 6.6 | 9.0 | 0.3 | 3.2 | 7.0 | 8.0 | 3.4 | 11.4 | 10.7 | 9.7 |
| **Economies in transition** | -7.5 | -18.4 | 21.8 | 14.0 | 11.7 | 15.9 | 19.6 | 8.2 | 20.4 | 21.9 | 15.1 |
| South-eastern Europe | -5.1 | -6.8 | 17.4 | 15.3 | 16.6 | 3.3 | 9.1 | 10.3 | 10.0 | 8.9 | 7.0 |
| Commonwealth of Independent States | -8.5 | -22.9 | 23.9 | 13.8 | 10.7 | 18.8 | 21.7 | 7.8 | 22.3 | 24.1 | 16.3 |
| **Developing economies** | -8.7 | 4.0 | 20.8 | -0.9 | 7.5 | 10.6 | 14.1 | 9.3 | 11.5 | 10.4 | 9.5 |
| Latin America and the Caribbean | 4.7 | -0.9 | 17.5 | -0.4 | -5.4 | 6.2 | 7.9 | 10.0 | 11.7 | 9.2 | 7.2 |
| Africa | -0.8 | -1.3 | 1.8 | 6.3 | 4.2 | 8.6 | 12.1 | 8.8 | 13.6 | 9.0 | 7.7 |
| Western Asia | -5.5 | 4.0 | 22.9 | 2.4 | 7.0 | 7.0 | 18.9 | 7.1 | 12.6 | 7.1 | 9.8 |
| East and South Asia | -16.2 | 4.6 | 20.3 | -2.4 | 12.1 | 12.6 | 15.0 | 9.5 | 11.1 | 11.4 | 10.2 |
| China | 3.2 | 25.2 | 38.4 | 9.9 | 27.3 | 28.0 | 13.8 | 10.9 | 16.4 | 13.2 | 12.4 |

**Sources**: UN/DESA Statistics Division, ECA, ECE, ECLAC, ESCAP, ESCWA and IMF.

**a**    Partly estimated.

**b**    Forecasts, based in part on Project LINK.

Table A.17:
**Balance of payments on current account, by country or country group, summary table, 1998-2006**

Billions of dollars

| | 1998 | 1999 | 2000 | 2001 | 2002 | 2003 | 2004 | 2005 | 2006 |
|---|---|---|---|---|---|---|---|---|---|
| **Developed economies** | -61.9 | -185.7 | -324.2 | -269.5 | -285.7 | -317.1 | -348.1 | -551.4 | -655.8 |
| Japan | 119.1 | 114.5 | 119.6 | 87.8 | 112.6 | 136.2 | 172.1 | 165.7 | 170.4 |
| United States | -213.5 | -299.8 | -417.4 | -384.7 | -459.6 | -522.1 | -640.2 | -754.9 | -811.5 |
| Europe[a] | 60.2 | 22.8 | -28.5 | 19.8 | 66.6 | 90.1 | 142.5 | 65.3 | 15.1 |
| EU-15 | 54.2 | 8.2 | -61.8 | -8.7 | 39.1 | 48.5 | 106.2 | 7.9 | -41.0 |
| New EU member States | -19.1 | -23.2 | -21.8 | -18.6 | -20.2 | -27.4 | -42.4 | -37.2 | -53.4 |
| **Economies in transition** | -10.0 | 21.5 | 47.1 | 31.1 | 25.3 | 30.7 | 56.2 | 80.8 | 89.3 |
| South-eastern Europe | -2.7 | -2.4 | -1.2 | -2.1 | -5.0 | -5.3 | -7.2 | -7.5 | -8.9 |
| Commonwealth of Independent States | -7.4 | 23.9 | 48.3 | 33.2 | 30.3 | 36.0 | 63.4 | 88.3 | 98.2 |
| **Developing economies** | -16.7 | 39.9 | 102.4 | 78.6 | 129.4 | 226.1 | 284.7 | 482.5 | 659.9 |
| Net fuel exporters | -80.3 | -14.8 | 72.0 | 25.1 | 27.0 | 74.3 | 125.8 | 262.1 | 324.3 |
| Net fuel importers | 63.6 | 54.6 | 30.4 | 53.4 | 102.4 | 151.8 | 158.9 | 220.4 | 335.6 |
| ***Latin America and the Caribbean*** | -88.9 | -55.6 | -47.0 | -52.4 | -14.8 | 9.1 | 21.9 | 36.8 | 47.3 |
| Net fuel exporters | -53.4 | -29.8 | -21.2 | -28.7 | -5.5 | 5.8 | 7.9 | 18.6 | 24.9 |
| Net fuel importers | -35.5 | -25.8 | -25.7 | -23.7 | -9.3 | 3.3 | 14.0 | 18.1 | 22.4 |
| ***Africa*** | -21.4 | -11.1 | 18.6 | 5.3 | -5.4 | 5.1 | 11.7 | 36.8 | 54.0 |
| Net fuel exporters | -9.8 | -2.1 | 26.9 | 12.0 | -0.1 | 14.0 | 26.7 | 57.6 | 81.9 |
| Net fuel importers | -11.6 | -9.0 | -8.3 | -6.7 | -5.3 | -8.9 | -15.0 | -20.8 | -27.9 |
| ***Western Asia*** | -20.4 | 2.6 | 37.9 | 31.8 | 23.0 | 44.4 | 71.7 | 141.7 | 165.3 |
| Net fuel exporters | -15.8 | 7.7 | 50.2 | 32.4 | 27.2 | 52.3 | 87.5 | 164.4 | 192.0 |
| Net fuel importers | -4.6 | -5.1 | -12.3 | -0.6 | -4.2 | -7.9 | -15.8 | -22.8 | -26.6 |
| ***East and South Asia*** | 114.0 | 103.9 | 92.9 | 93.8 | 126.6 | 167.5 | 179.3 | 267.3 | 393.3 |
| Net fuel exporters | -1.4 | 9.4 | 16.1 | 9.4 | 5.4 | 2.1 | 3.6 | 21.5 | 25.6 |
| Net fuel importers | 115.3 | 94.5 | 76.8 | 84.4 | 121.2 | 165.4 | 175.7 | 245.8 | 367.7 |
| **World residual[b]** | -88.6 | -124.4 | -174.6 | -159.9 | -131.0 | -60.3 | -7.2 | 11.9 | 93.5 |

**Sources**: IMF, *World Economic Outlook*, October 2007; and IMF, *Balance of Payments Statistics*.

**a**   Europe consists of EU-15, new EU member States plus Iceland, Norway and Switzerland.
**b**   Statistical discrepancy.

Table A.18:
**Balance of payments on current account, by country or country group, 1998-2006**

Billions of dollars

| | 1998 | 1999 | 2000 | 2001 | 2002 | 2003 | 2004 | 2005 | 2006 |
|---|---|---|---|---|---|---|---|---|---|
| **Developed economies** | | | | | | | | | |
| Trade balance | -26.3 | -156.8 | -295.2 | -260.5 | -261.9 | -312.1 | -427.7 | -649.2 | -767.4 |
| Services, net | 82.5 | 81.9 | 75.2 | 67.8 | 85.4 | 100.9 | 151.1 | 190.7 | 228.3 |
| Income, net | 12.4 | 21.0 | 32.0 | 46.0 | 28.8 | 62.1 | 124.4 | 125.9 | 111.6 |
| Current transfers, net | -130.4 | -131.9 | -136.2 | -122.9 | -138.0 | -168.0 | -195.9 | -218.7 | -228.2 |
| Current-account balance | -61.9 | -185.7 | -324.2 | -269.5 | -285.7 | -317.1 | -348.1 | -551.4 | -655.8 |
| **Japan** | | | | | | | | | |
| Trade balance | 120.9 | 121.3 | 114.9 | 69.2 | 92.5 | 104.0 | 128.5 | 93.9 | 81.1 |
| Services, net | -47.7 | -52.2 | -45.9 | -42.7 | -40.7 | -31.4 | -34.3 | -24.1 | -18.2 |
| Income, net | 54.7 | 57.4 | 60.4 | 69.2 | 65.8 | 71.2 | 85.7 | 103.5 | 118.2 |
| Current transfers, net | -8.8 | -12.1 | -9.8 | -7.9 | -4.9 | -7.5 | -7.9 | -7.6 | -10.7 |
| Current-account balance | 119.1 | 114.5 | 119.6 | 87.8 | 112.6 | 136.2 | 172.1 | 165.7 | 170.4 |
| **United States** | | | | | | | | | |
| Trade balance | -246.7 | -346.0 | -454.7 | -429.5 | -485.0 | -550.9 | -669.6 | -787.2 | -838.3 |
| Services, net | 82.1 | 82.7 | 74.9 | 64.4 | 61.2 | 54.0 | 57.5 | 72.8 | 79.8 |
| Income, net | 4.3 | 13.9 | 21.1 | 31.7 | 27.7 | 45.4 | 56.4 | 48.1 | 36.6 |
| Current transfers, net | -53.2 | -50.4 | -58.6 | -51.3 | -63.6 | -70.6 | -84.4 | -88.5 | -89.6 |
| Current-account balance | -213.5 | -299.8 | -417.4 | -384.7 | -459.6 | -522.1 | -640.2 | -754.9 | -811.5 |
| **Europe**[a] | | | | | | | | | |
| Trade balance | 87.8 | 49.8 | 3.8 | 50.9 | 99.2 | 110.0 | 82.1 | 8.0 | -43.6 |
| Services, net | 53.9 | 55.9 | 49.2 | 50.4 | 67.6 | 83.7 | 135.6 | 151.1 | 179.0 |
| Income, net | -12.5 | -12.8 | -12.9 | -16.4 | -30.7 | -13.9 | 27.9 | 28.0 | 7.1 |
| Current transfers, net | -68.9 | -70.1 | -68.7 | -64.9 | -69.5 | -89.7 | -103.1 | -121.8 | -127.4 |
| Current-account balance | 60.2 | 22.8 | -28.5 | 19.8 | 66.6 | 90.1 | 142.5 | 65.3 | 15.1 |
| *EU-15* | | | | | | | | | |
| Trade balance | 117.7 | 68.4 | 9.2 | 53.9 | 97.5 | 108.4 | 77.9 | -6.8 | -56.0 |
| Services, net | 28.5 | 32.1 | 21.4 | 24.2 | 41.7 | 55.7 | 103.2 | 113.6 | 134.1 |
| Income, net | -22.9 | -23.9 | -24.2 | -22.6 | -31.1 | -24.6 | 31.5 | 22.9 | 11.1 |
| Current transfers, net | -69.2 | -68.4 | -68.3 | -64.3 | -69.0 | -91.1 | -106.4 | -121.8 | -130.3 |
| Current-account balance | 54.2 | 8.2 | -61.8 | -8.7 | 39.1 | 48.5 | 106.2 | 7.9 | -41.0 |
| *New EU member States* | | | | | | | | | |
| Trade balance | -29.7 | -28.8 | -28.4 | -26.0 | -25.2 | -28.4 | -33.1 | -33.0 | -46.0 |
| Services, net | 10.8 | 7.6 | 8.9 | 9.1 | 8.1 | 7.6 | 9.4 | 12.6 | 14.4 |
| Income, net | -5.7 | -6.9 | -7.4 | -7.9 | -10.7 | -16.3 | -30.9 | -31.7 | -38.3 |
| Current transfers, net | 5.5 | 4.9 | 5.1 | 6.2 | 7.6 | 9.8 | 12.3 | 14.9 | 16.6 |
| Current-account balance | -19.1 | -23.2 | -21.8 | -18.6 | -20.2 | -27.4 | -42.4 | -37.2 | -53.4 |
| **Economies in transition** | | | | | | | | | |
| Trade balance | -1.6 | 24.9 | 53.6 | 37.8 | 34.3 | 43.4 | 71.8 | 107.3 | 129.9 |
| Services, net | -1.4 | -1.9 | -4.3 | -7.2 | -8.3 | -7.1 | -10.8 | -12.4 | -11.5 |
| Income, net | -12.4 | -7.8 | -9.5 | -6.8 | -9.0 | -16.4 | -17.4 | -28.6 | -45.2 |
| Current transfers, net | 5.3 | 6.4 | 7.2 | 7.2 | 8.2 | 10.8 | 12.6 | 14.4 | 16.1 |
| Current-account balance | -10.0 | 21.5 | 47.1 | 31.1 | 25.3 | 30.7 | 56.2 | 80.8 | 89.3 |

| Table A.18 (cont'd) | 1998 | 1999 | 2000 | 2001 | 2002 | 2003 | 2004 | 2005 | 2006 |
|---|---|---|---|---|---|---|---|---|---|
| **South-eastern Europe** | | | | | | | | | |
| Trade balance | -9.7 | -8.9 | -9.1 | -10.9 | -14.1 | -18.3 | -22.1 | -22.5 | -24.4 |
| Services, net | 2.3 | 1.9 | 2.6 | 3.5 | 3.5 | 6.0 | 6.3 | 6.9 | 7.8 |
| Income, net | 0.6 | 0.6 | 0.3 | 0.1 | 0.0 | -0.4 | -0.4 | -0.9 | -1.2 |
| Current transfers, net | 4.0 | 4.1 | 4.9 | 5.2 | 5.6 | 7.3 | 8.9 | 9.1 | 8.9 |
| Current-account balance | -2.7 | -2.4 | -1.2 | -2.1 | -5.0 | -5.3 | -7.2 | -7.5 | -8.9 |
| **Commonwealth of Independent States** | | | | | | | | | |
| Trade balance | 8.1 | 33.8 | 62.7 | 48.7 | 48.5 | 61.7 | 93.9 | 129.8 | 154.3 |
| Services, net | -3.7 | -3.8 | -6.9 | -10.7 | -11.8 | -13.2 | -17.1 | -19.2 | -19.2 |
| Income, net | -13.0 | -8.4 | -9.7 | -6.9 | -9.0 | -16.0 | -17.0 | -27.7 | -44.1 |
| Current transfers, net | 1.3 | 2.3 | 2.3 | 2.0 | 2.5 | 3.5 | 3.7 | 5.3 | 7.2 |
| Current-account balance | -7.4 | 23.9 | 48.3 | 33.2 | 30.3 | 36.0 | 63.4 | 88.3 | 98.2 |
| **Developing economies** | | | | | | | | | |
| Trade balance | 66.7 | 138.0 | 211.3 | 180.3 | 222.7 | 299.3 | 357.8 | 543.6 | 724.5 |
| Services, net | -52.5 | -48.6 | -56.5 | -62.7 | -61.3 | -61.2 | -58.0 | -61.7 | -87.8 |
| Income, net | -78.3 | -105.4 | -112.7 | -106.5 | -111.2 | -112.3 | -130.4 | -139.7 | -137.6 |
| Current transfers, net | 47.5 | 55.9 | 60.2 | 67.4 | 79.1 | 100.3 | 115.3 | 140.4 | 160.7 |
| Current-account balance | -16.7 | 39.9 | 102.4 | 78.6 | 129.4 | 226.1 | 284.7 | 482.5 | 659.9 |
| **Net fuel exporters** | | | | | | | | | |
| Trade balance | -2.2 | 65.0 | 168.7 | 115.9 | 123.6 | 174.3 | 235.8 | 381.9 | 467.4 |
| Services, net | -55.5 | -52.9 | -61.1 | -59.1 | -59.4 | -63.0 | -72.8 | -86.7 | -120.7 |
| Income, net | -16.2 | -22.0 | -30.2 | -27.1 | -35.2 | -40.0 | -44.8 | -46.1 | -35.9 |
| Current transfers, net | -6.3 | -4.8 | -5.5 | -4.6 | -2.0 | 3.0 | 7.7 | 13.0 | 13.5 |
| Current-account balance | -80.3 | -14.8 | 72.0 | 25.1 | 27.0 | 74.3 | 125.8 | 262.1 | 324.3 |
| **Net fuel importers** | | | | | | | | | |
| Trade balance | 68.9 | 73.0 | 42.6 | 64.4 | 99.1 | 125.0 | 122.0 | 161.7 | 257.1 |
| Services, net | 3.0 | 4.3 | 4.6 | -3.6 | -1.9 | 1.8 | 14.9 | 25.0 | 32.9 |
| Income, net | -62.1 | -83.4 | -82.5 | -79.3 | -76.0 | -72.3 | -85.6 | -93.6 | -101.7 |
| Current transfers, net | 53.9 | 60.7 | 65.7 | 72.0 | 81.1 | 97.3 | 107.6 | 127.4 | 147.2 |
| Current-account balance | 63.6 | 54.6 | 30.4 | 53.4 | 102.4 | 151.8 | 158.9 | 220.4 | 335.6 |
| **Latin America and the Caribbean** | | | | | | | | | |
| Trade balance | -38.5 | -9.7 | 1.0 | -6.2 | 20.4 | 42.3 | 57.5 | 80.4 | 96.4 |
| Services, net | -16.6 | -13.1 | -13.8 | -15.9 | -10.7 | -10.3 | -10.7 | -14.6 | -16.9 |
| Income, net | -51.6 | -53.0 | -55.9 | -56.6 | -54.2 | -59.1 | -68.0 | -80.2 | -92.1 |
| Current transfers, net | 17.8 | 20.2 | 21.7 | 26.3 | 29.8 | 36.2 | 43.1 | 51.2 | 59.9 |
| Current-account balance | -88.9 | -55.6 | -47.0 | -52.4 | -14.8 | 9.1 | 21.9 | 36.8 | 47.3 |
| **Africa** | | | | | | | | | |
| Trade balance | -14.3 | -2.4 | 31.9 | 16.5 | 8.3 | 21.2 | 33.7 | 67.3 | 85.1 |
| Services, net | -8.8 | -7.0 | -7.3 | -7.9 | -9.4 | -8.9 | -10.9 | -14.4 | -16.6 |
| Income, net | -13.9 | -16.5 | -21.9 | -19.7 | -22.2 | -27.8 | -35.7 | -46.9 | -48.1 |
| Current transfers, net | 15.7 | 14.9 | 15.9 | 16.4 | 17.9 | 20.5 | 24.6 | 30.8 | 33.6 |
| Current-account balance | -21.4 | -11.1 | 18.6 | 5.3 | -5.4 | 5.1 | 11.7 | 36.8 | 54.0 |

**Table A.18** (cont'd)

| | 1998 | 1999 | 2000 | 2001 | 2002 | 2003 | 2004 | 2005 | 2006 |
|---|---|---|---|---|---|---|---|---|---|
| **Western Asia** | | | | | | | | | |
| Trade balance | -6.9 | 26.7 | 67.9 | 64.4 | 63.3 | 85.8 | 113.6 | 180.2 | 220.9 |
| Services, net | -17.2 | -22.4 | -24.2 | -26.0 | -28.4 | -27.1 | -30.5 | -32.9 | -60.4 |
| Income, net | 11.0 | 5.4 | 2.4 | 3.4 | -1.0 | -3.0 | -0.5 | 10.2 | 23.1 |
| Current transfers, net | -7.3 | -7.0 | -8.2 | -9.9 | -11.0 | -11.4 | -10.8 | -15.8 | -18.3 |
| Current-account balance | -20.4 | 2.6 | 37.9 | 31.8 | 23.0 | 44.4 | 71.7 | 141.7 | 165.3 |
| **East Asia** | | | | | | | | | |
| Trade balance | 148.6 | 135.5 | 119.7 | 117.0 | 138.4 | 165.3 | 182.8 | 253.0 | 370.7 |
| Services, net | -9.8 | -6.0 | -11.9 | -13.6 | -13.6 | -16.9 | -12.5 | -13.0 | -9.0 |
| Income, net | -17.0 | -35.0 | -29.7 | -27.0 | -26.5 | -14.5 | -18.9 | -13.1 | -11.3 |
| Current transfers, net | 3.6 | 8.7 | 8.8 | 10.1 | 14.5 | 19.7 | 24.6 | 33.6 | 38.5 |
| Current-account balance | 125.4 | 103.2 | 86.8 | 86.5 | 112.9 | 153.6 | 176.0 | 260.5 | 388.8 |
| **South Asia** | | | | | | | | | |
| Trade balance | -22.3 | -12.1 | -9.2 | -11.3 | -7.8 | -15.3 | -29.8 | -37.2 | -48.6 |
| Services, net | -0.1 | -0.1 | 0.8 | 0.8 | 0.8 | 1.9 | 6.6 | 13.2 | 15.2 |
| Income, net | -6.8 | -6.2 | -7.6 | -6.6 | -7.3 | -7.9 | -7.3 | -9.8 | -9.2 |
| Current transfers, net | 17.7 | 19.2 | 22.1 | 24.6 | 27.9 | 35.2 | 33.8 | 40.6 | 47.1 |
| Current-account balance | -11.5 | 0.8 | 6.1 | 7.4 | 13.6 | 13.9 | 3.4 | 6.8 | 4.5 |
| **World residual**[b] | | | | | | | | | |
| Trade balance | 38.7 | 6.1 | -30.2 | -42.4 | -4.9 | 30.7 | 1.9 | 1.7 | 87.1 |
| Services, net | 28.6 | 31.4 | 14.4 | -2.0 | 15.9 | 32.6 | 82.3 | 116.6 | 129.0 |
| Income, net | -78.3 | -92.2 | -90.1 | -67.2 | -91.3 | -66.6 | -23.5 | -42.5 | -71.2 |
| Current transfers, net | -77.6 | -69.6 | -68.7 | -48.3 | -50.8 | -57.0 | -68.0 | -63.9 | -51.3 |
| Current-account balance | -88.6 | -124.4 | -174.6 | -159.9 | -131.0 | -60.3 | -7.2 | 11.9 | 93.5 |

**Sources**: IMF, *World Economic Outlook*, October 2007; IMF, *Balance of Payments Statistics*.

**a**   Europe consists of EU-15, new EU member States plus Iceland, Norway and Switzerland.
**b**   Statistical discrepancy.

Table A.19:
**Net ODA from major sources, by type, 1986-2006**

| Donor group or country | Growth rate of ODAa (2004 price and exchange rates) | | ODA as a percentage of GNI | Total ODA (millions of dollars) | Percentage distribution of ODA by type, 2006 | | | | | | |
| | | | | | Bilateral | | | | Multilateral | | |
| | 1986-1995 | 1996-2005 | 2006 | 2006 | Total | Grantsb | Technical cooperation | Loans and other | Total | United Nations | Other |
| **Total DAC countries** | 0.59 | 3.49 | 0.30 | 103 996 | 73.0 | 75.6 | 20.4 | -2.6 | 27.0 | 5.1 | 21.9 |
| **Total EU** | 1.42 | 2.98 | 0.44 | 58 957 | 68.4 | 70.8 | 15.2 | -2.4 | 31.6 | 4.8 | 26.9 |
| Austria | -1.44 | 8.30 | 0.47 | 1 498 | 72.9 | 73.4 | 10.8 | -0.6 | 27.1 | 1.8 | 25.3 |
| Belgium | -2.34 | 5.71 | 0.50 | 1 977 | 68.7 | 69.0 | 29.3 | -0.4 | 31.4 | 2.6 | 28.8 |
| Denmark | 3.87 | 1.12 | 0.80 | 2 236 | 65.5 | 68.2 | 4.9 | -2.7 | 34.5 | 13.9 | 20.6 |
| Finland | -1.12 | 7.27 | 0.39 | 826 | 59.8 | 58.2 | 9.7 | 1.6 | 40.2 | 12.8 | 27.4 |
| Francec | 2.11 | -0.44 | 0.47 | 10 448 | 73.3 | 78.5 | 23.0 | -5.2 | 26.7 | 1.3 | 25.4 |
| Germany | 0.17 | 1.72 | 0.36 | 10 351 | 67.5 | 73.1 | 29.6 | -5.5 | 32.5 | 1.9 | 30.6 |
| Greece | ... | ... | 0.17 | 424 | 44.6 | 44.6 | 21.0 | ... | 55.4 | 3.2 | 52.2 |
| Ireland | 5.99 | 12.88 | 0.53 | 997 | 60.5 | 60.5 | 1.8 | ... | 39.5 | 11.1 | 28.4 |
| Italy | -0.55 | 2.23 | 0.20 | 3 672 | 56.0 | 60.2 | 5.8 | -4.2 | 44.0 | 2.0 | 41.9 |
| Luxembourg | 12.55 | 12.43 | 0.89 | 291 | 77.1 | 77.1 | 1.3 | ... | 22.9 | 4.1 | 18.8 |
| Netherlands | 0.70 | 2.89 | 0.81 | 5 452 | 80.8 | 83.2 | 10.7 | -2.4 | 19.2 | 7.4 | 11.8 |
| Portugal | 26.90 | 6.34 | 0.21 | 396 | 53.3 | 49.9 | 29.6 | 3.4 | 46.7 | 2.6 | 44.1 |
| Spain | 13.75 | 4.15 | 0.32 | 3 814 | 54.9 | 52.7 | 11.1 | 2.1 | 45.1 | 7.5 | 37.6 |
| Sweden | 1.47 | 4.02 | 1.03 | 3 967 | 71.8 | 71.4 | 4.3 | 0.3 | 28.2 | 13.4 | 14.8 |
| United Kingdom | 1.24 | 6.81 | 0.52 | 12 607 | 68.5 | 69.1 | 7.4 | -0.6 | 31.5 | 4.2 | 27.2 |
| | | | | | | | | | | | |
| Australia | 0.39 | 0.55 | 0.30 | 2 128 | 86.4 | 86.4 | 40.2 | ... | 13.6 | 2.3 | 11.2 |
| Canada | 0.22 | 1.03 | 0.30 | 3 713 | 68.9 | 70.1 | 12.5 | -1.1 | 31.1 | 8.6 | 22.5 |
| Japan | 2.09 | -0.23 | 0.25 | 11 608 | 61.7 | 65.6 | 16.7 | -3.9 | 38.3 | 8.5 | 29.8 |
| New Zealand | 0.34 | 4.53 | 0.27 | 257 | 80.6 | 80.6 | 14.4 | ... | 19.4 | 8.4 | 11.0 |
| Norway | 2.61 | 3.38 | 0.89 | 2 946 | 74.7 | 72.0 | 13.6 | 2.7 | 25.3 | 14.8 | 10.5 |
| Switzerland | 3.33 | 4.01 | 0.39 | 1 647 | 76.2 | 75.4 | ... | 0.8 | 23.8 | 7.0 | 16.8 |
| United States | -3.22 | 8.44 | 0.17 | 22 739 | 89.6 | 93.3 | 37.5 | -3.7 | 10.4 | 2.6 | 7.8 |

**Source**: UN/DESA, based on OECD, *The DAC Journal Development Co-operation Report 2006* and DAC online database, available from http://www.oecd.org/dac/stats/idsonline.

a   Average annual rates of growth, calculated from average levels in 1984-1985, 1994-1995 and 2004-2005.
b   Includes technical cooperation.
c   Excluding flows from France to the Overseas Departments, namely Guadeloupe, French Guiana, Martinique and Réunion.

Table A.20:

**Total net ODA flows from OECD Development Assistance Committee (DAC) countries, by type of flow, 1994-2006**

| | 1994-1995 average | 2001 | 2002 | 2003 | 2004 | 2005 | 2006 |
|---|---|---|---|---|---|---|---|
| | Net disbursements at current prices and exchange rates (millions of dollars) | | | | | | |
| **Official Development Assistance** | 58 800 | 52 435 | 58 292 | 69 085 | 79 410 | 106 777 | 103 996 |
| Bilateral grants and grant-like flows | 35 708 | 33 522 | 39 813 | 50 908 | 57 222 | 83 139 | 78 588 |
| *of which:* | | | | | | | |
| Technical co-operation | 13 574 | 13 602 | 15 452 | 18 352 | 18 672 | 20 926 | 21 165 |
| Humanitarian Aid[a] | 2 380 | 1 943 | 2 779 | 4 360 | 5 193 | 7 169 | 7 799 |
| Debt forgiveness | 3 588 | 2 514 | 4 534 | 8 338 | 7 109 | 24 993 | .. |
| Bilateral loans | 5 017 | 1 602 | 939 | -1 153 | -2 940 | -1 006 | -2 681 |
| Contributions to multilateral institutions[b] | 18 075 | 17 311 | 17 540 | 19 330 | 25 127 | 24 644 | 28 089 |
| | Share of total net flows (percentage) | | | | | | |
| **Official Development Assistance** | 36 | 48 | 80 | 55 | 50 | 35 | .. |
| Bilateral grants and grant-like flows | 22 | 31 | 55 | 41 | 36 | 27 | .. |
| *of which:* | | | | | | | |
| Technical co-operation | 8 | 12 | 21 | 15 | 12 | 7 | .. |
| Humanitarian Aid[a] | 1 | 2 | 4 | 3 | 3 | 2 | .. |
| Debt forgiveness | 2 | 2 | 6 | 7 | 4 | 8 | .. |
| Bilateral loans | 3 | 1 | 1 | -1 | -2 | 0 | .. |
| Contributions to multilateral institutions[b] | 11 | 16 | 24 | 15 | 16 | 8 | .. |

**Source**: UN/DESA, based on OECD, *The DAC Journal of Development Co-operation Report 2006* and DAC online database, available from http://www.oecd.org/dac/stats/idsonline (accessed on November 2007).

a   Excludes refugees in donor countries.
b   Grants and capital subscriptions. Does not include concessional lending to multilateral agencies.

Table A.21:

**Commitments and net flows of financial resources, by selected multilateral institutions, 1997-2006**

| Millions of dollars | 1997 | 1998 | 1999 | 2000 | 2001 | 2002 | 2003 | 2004 | 2005 | 2006 |
|---|---|---|---|---|---|---|---|---|---|---|
| **Resource commitments**[a] | 89 713 | 95 118 | 65 568 | 63 085 | 72 177 | 95 292 | 67 593 | 55 895 | 71 712 | 64 738 |
| **Financial institutions excluding IMF** | 45 760 | 57 928 | 42 770 | 36 882 | 41 787 | 38 523 | 43 053 | 45 678 | 51 385 | 55 700 |
| Regional development banks[b] | 20 431 | 21 133 | 19 437 | 16 235 | 19 349 | 16 751 | 20 393 | 21 468 | 23 039 | 23 088 |
| World Bank Group | 24 899 | 36 352 | 22 899 | 20 238 | 22 004 | 21 382 | 22 230 | 23 743 | 27 677 | 31 901[c] |
| International Bank for Reconstruction and Development (IBRD) | 15 098 | 24 687 | 13 789 | 10 699 | 11 709 | 10 176 | 10 572 | 10 792 | 13 611 | 14 195 |
| International Development Association (IDA) | 5 345 | 7 325 | 5 691 | 5 861 | 6 859 | 8 040 | 7 550 | 8 387 | 8 696 | 9 506 |
| International Financial Corporation (IFC) | 4 456 | 4 340 | 3 419 | 3 678 | 3 436 | 3 166 | 4 108 | 4 564 | 5 370 | 8 200 |
| International Fund for Agricultural Development (IFAD) | 430 | 443 | 434 | 409 | 4 34 | 390 | 430 | 467 | 669 | 711 |
| IMF (billions of dollars) | 41 | 33 | 19 | 22 | 26 | 52 | 18 | 3 | 13 | 1 |
| United Nations operational agencies[d] | 3 453 | 4 290 | 4 198 | 3 803 | 4 690 | 4 569 | 6 740 | 7 617 | 7 708 | 8 345 |
| **Net flows** | 21 227 | 28 825 | -7 450 | -10 859 | 14 931 | 2 001 | -11 655 | -20 235 | -39 609 | -25 864 |
| **Financial institutions excluding IMF** | 6 827 | 9 525 | 5 150 | -59 | 1 431 | -11 199 | -14 755 | -10 235 | 835 | 5 208 |
| Regional development banks[b] | 5 334 | 7 971 | 4 229 | 327 | 1 696 | -3 904 | -8 025 | -6 570 | -1 668 | 2 965 |
| World Bank Group | 1 493 | 1 554 | 921 | -386 | -265 | -7 295 | -6 730 | -3 665 | 2 503 | 2 243 |
| International Bank for Reconstruction and Development (IBRD) | -3 265 | -2 723 | -3 019 | -4 079 | -4 570 | -12 126 | -11 241 | -8 930 | -2 898 | -5 087 |
| International Development Association (IDA) | 4 757 | 4 276 | 3 940 | 3 693 | 4 432 | 4 831 | 4 511 | 5 265 | 5 401 | 7 330 |
| IMF (billions of dollars) | 14 | 19 | -13 | -11 | 14 | 13 | 3 | -10 | -40 | -31 |
| *Memorandum item:* (in units of 2000 purchasing power)[e] | | | | | | | | | | |
| Resource commitments | 78 696 | 87 264 | 62 446 | 63 085 | 73 650 | 97 237 | 62 586 | 47 774 | 59 760 | 54 863 |
| Net flows | 18 620 | 26 445 | -7 095 | -10 859 | 15 236 | 2 042 | -10 792 | -17 295 | -33 008 | -21 919 |

**Sources**: Annual reports, various issues of the relevant multilateral institutions.

a Loans, grants, technical assistance and equity participation, as appropriate; all data are on a calendar-year basis.

b African Development Bank (AfDB), Asian Development Bank (ADB), Caribbean Development Bank (CDB), European Bank for Reconstruction and Development (EBRD), Inter-American Development Bank (IaDB) (including Inter-American Investment Corporation (IaIC)).

c Data is for fiscal year 2006.

d United Nations Development Programme (UNDP), United Nations Population Fund (UNFPA), United Nations Children's Fund (UNICEF) and the World Food Programme (WFP).

e Totals deflated by the United Nations index of manufactured export prices (in dollars) of developed economies: 2000=100.

Table A.22:
## Greenhouse gas emissions of Annex 1 Parties to the United Nations Framework Convention on Climate Change

| Teragram CO$_2$ equivalent[a] | | | | | | | | | | | | |
|---|---|---|---|---|---|---|---|---|---|---|---|---|
| | 1990 | 2000 | 2001 | 2002 | 2003 | 2004 | 2005 | 2006[b] | 2007[b] | 2008[b] | 1990-2008 growth rate | Change from 1990 to 2008 |
| Australia | 418 | 498 | 509 | 511 | 515 | 524 | 525 | 524 | 539 | 546 | 1.5 | 30.5 |
| Austria | 79 | 81 | 85 | 87 | 93 | 91 | 93 | 93 | 95 | 96 | 1.1 | 21.3 |
| Belarus | 127 | 70 | 68 | 68 | 70 | 74 | 76 | 76 | 75 | 72 | -3.1 | -43.3 |
| Belgium | 146 | 148 | 147 | 145 | 148 | 148 | 144 | 144 | 140 | 143 | -0.1 | -1.9 |
| Bulgaria | 117 | 67 | 67 | 64 | 70 | 69 | 70 | 72 | 71 | 70 | -2.8 | -39.6 |
| Canada | 596 | 721 | 714 | 720 | 745 | 747 | 747 | 755 | 761 | 761 | 1.4 | 27.7 |
| Croatia | 32 | 26 | 27 | 28 | 30 | 30 | 30 | 32 | 33 | 34 | 0.5 | 8.9 |
| Czech Republic | 196 | 149 | 149 | 144 | 148 | 147 | 146 | 154 | 152 | 152 | -1.4 | -22.7 |
| Denmark | 70 | 70 | 71 | 70 | 76 | 70 | 65 | 65 | 63 | 60 | -0.9 | -14.9 |
| Estonia | 43 | 19 | 20 | 19 | 21 | 21 | 21 | 21 | 20 | 18 | -4.7 | -57.7 |
| Finland | 71 | 70 | 75 | 77 | 85 | 81 | 69 | 65 | 54 | 51 | -1.8 | -27.5 |
| France | 567 | 564 | 566 | 558 | 561 | 561 | 558 | 550 | 545 | 541 | -0.3 | -4.6 |
| Germany | 1 228 | 1 020 | 1 037 | 1 018 | 1 031 | 1 025 | 1 001 | 1 011 | 1 000 | 994 | -1.2 | -19.1 |
| Greece | 109 | 132 | 133 | 133 | 137 | 138 | 138 | 140 | 142 | 144 | 1.6 | 32.1 |
| Hungary | 98 | 77 | 79 | 77 | 80 | 79 | 80 | 79 | 77 | 75 | -1.4 | -23.0 |
| Iceland | 3 | 4 | 4 | 4 | 4 | 4 | 4 | 4 | 4 | 4 | 0.5 | 9.4 |
| Ireland | 55 | 69 | 71 | 69 | 69 | 69 | 70 | 69 | 69 | 66 | 1.0 | 19.2 |
| Italy | 517 | 552 | 558 | 558 | 573 | 578 | 580 | 587 | 594 | 599 | 0.8 | 16.0 |
| Japan | 1 272 | 1 348 | 1 322 | 1 355 | 1 360 | 1 357 | 1 360 | 1 379 | 1 393 | 1 400 | 0.5 | 10.1 |
| Latvia | 26 | 10 | 11 | 11 | 11 | 11 | 11 | 11 | 10 | 10 | -5.5 | -63.9 |
| Liechtenstein | — | — | — | — | — | — | — | — | — | — | 1.1 | 21.2 |
| Lithuania | 49 | 19 | 20 | 21 | 21 | 22 | 23 | 23 | 23 | 22 | -4.3 | -54.5 |
| Luxembourg | 13 | 10 | 10 | 11 | 11 | 13 | 13 | 12 | 12 | 12 | -0.5 | -8.4 |
| Monaco | — | — | — | — | — | — | — | — | — | — | -0.2 | -3.7 |
| Netherlands | 213 | 214 | 216 | 216 | 217 | 218 | 212 | 215 | 212 | 212 | 0.0 | -0.7 |
| New Zealand | 62 | 70 | 73 | 74 | 76 | 75 | 77 | 78 | 78 | 79 | 1.3 | 27.1 |
| Norway | 50 | 54 | 55 | 54 | 54 | 55 | 54 | 55 | 55 | 56 | 0.6 | 12.3 |
| Poland | 485 | 405 | 402 | 387 | 402 | 397 | 399 | 395 | 390 | 380 | -1.4 | -21.8 |
| Portugal | 60 | 82 | 83 | 88 | 83 | 85 | 86 | 87 | 88 | 90 | 2.3 | 50.1 |
| Romania | 249 | 139 | 143 | 151 | 158 | 160 | 154 | 156 | 157 | 156 | -2.5 | -37.1 |
| Russian Federation | 2 990 | 1 987 | 2 003 | 1 996 | 2 063 | 2 086 | 2 133 | 2 121 | 2 201 | 2 260 | -1.5 | -24.4 |
| Slovakia | 72 | 47 | 51 | 49 | 49 | 49 | 48 | 47 | 47 | 46 | -2.4 | -36.0 |
| Slovenia | 19 | 19 | 20 | 20 | 20 | 20 | 20 | 21 | 22 | 23 | 1.1 | 21.5 |
| Spain | 287 | 384 | 385 | 402 | 409 | 425 | 441 | 458 | 475 | 488 | 3.0 | 69.9 |
| Sweden | 72 | 68 | 69 | 70 | 71 | 70 | 67 | 66 | 65 | 64 | -0.7 | -11.6 |
| Switzerland | 53 | 52 | 53 | 52 | 53 | 53 | 54 | 55 | 56 | 56 | 0.3 | 6.3 |
| Turkey | 170 | 280 | 262 | 271 | 286 | 297 | 297 | 309 | 325 | 341 | 3.9 | 100.5 |
| Ukraine | 924 | 395 | 394 | 400 | 415 | 413 | 419 | 451 | 469 | 488 | -3.5 | -47.2 |
| United Kingdom | 771 | 674 | 677 | 657 | 663 | 660 | 657 | 650 | 654 | 667 | -0.8 | -13.5 |
| United States | 6 229 | 7 126 | 7 015 | 7 047 | 7 089 | 7 190 | 7 241 | 7 153 | 7 092 | 7 042 | 0.7 | 13.0 |
| **All Annex 1 Parties** | 17 379 | 17 719 | 17 645 | 17 681 | 17 964 | 18 111 | 18 182 | 18 182 | 18 256 | 18 318 | -0.1 | -1.2 |

**Source**: UN/DESA, based on data of the United Nations Framework Convention on Climate Change (UNFCCC) on line database, available from http://unfccc.int/ghg_emissions_data/ghg_data_from_unfccc/time_series_annex_i/items/3814.php (accessed on 21 November 2007).

**Note**: Based on the historical data provided by the UNFCCC for the GHG emissions of the Annex 1 Parties up to 2005, the Development Policy and Analysis Division of UN/DESA extrapolated the data to 2008. The extrapolation is based on the following procedure: First, GHG/GDP intensity for each country is modelled by time-series techniques to reflect the historical trend of GHG/GDP. While the trend for each individual country would usually be a complex function of such factors as change in the structure of the economy, technology change, emission-mitigation measures, as well as other economic and environmental policies, the time-series modelling could be considered a simplified, closed form of a more complex structural modelling for these relations between economic output and the GHG emission. Second, GHG/GDP intensity for each country is extrapolated for the out-of-sample period, namely, 2006-2008, based on the time-series modelling. Third, if necessary, the extrapolated GHG/GDP intensity for individual countries can be adjusted according to emission control targets announced by specific countries. Finally, projection of the GHG emission is made according to the forecast of GDP contained in the present report and the extrapolated GHG/GDP intensity.

**a**    Excluding  land use, land-use change and forestry.

**b**    Estimates.

Litho in United Nations, New York
07-58808—January 2008—4,860
ISBN 978-92-1-109155-7

United Nations publication
Sales No. E.08.II.C.2